To many the Boxer Uprising of 1900 is now a half-forgotten episode in the history of China's resistance to progress. Yet the Boxers are regarded by many as the founders of Chinese nationalism; for although the Uprising was a failure, it forced the government to realize that it must modernize the country and put it on an equal footing with the West. Dr Purcell has based his study mainly on newly published Chinese sources and he examines with detachment and fairness the origin and development of this important movement in Chinese history.

Dr Purcell first gives a description of nineteenth-century China, studying its government, armed forces and society, its foreign relations and its attempts at reform. He then examines the Uprising itself, analysing especially the origins and beliefs of the Boxers against the background both of Chinese society and of the Western World. He concentrates on showing at what moment the Uprising switched from an anti-dynastic to a pro-dynastic movement, and his account of Chinese secret societies and of the nature of successful rebellions in Chinese history adds greatly to our understanding of that country. By his use of Chinese sources Dr Purcell has shed much new light on the Boxer mentality. This will be a standard work on the birth of the Chinese nation, of importance to historians of the Far East, to other modern historians and to everyone interested in the emergence of China.

'An enthralling story. Dr Purcell tells it magnificently.'
Nicholas Wollaston in the *New Statesman*

THE
BOXER UPRISING

THE
BOXER UPRISING

A BACKGROUND STUDY

BY

VICTOR PURCELL

CAMBRIDGE

AT THE UNIVERSITY PRESS

1963

PUBLISHED BY
THE SYNDICS OF THE CAMBRIDGE UNIVERSITY PRESS

Bentley House, 200 Euston Road, London, N.W. 1
American Branch: 32 East 57th Street, New York 22, N.Y.
West African Office: P.O. Box 33, Ibadan, Nigeria

CAMBRIDGE UNIVERSITY PRESS

1963

First published　January 1963
Reprinted　　　May 1963

Printed in Great Britain at the University Press, Cambridge
(Brooke Crutchley, University Printer)

CONTENTS

PREFACE

To the West in general the Boxer Uprising of 1900 is a half-forgotten episode in the history of China's resistance to progress: to the historians of the People's China it is the heroic resistance of the Chinese peasantry to foreign Imperialism, which failed in its object only because of its lack of dialectical awareness. But neither of these interpretations seems sufficient in itself to explain every aspect of its origin and development.

After the suppression of the Uprising there was a flood of publications by foreigners giving their personal experiences, and there were nearly as many theories as to the origins of the trouble as there were authors. Dr W. A. P. Martin, for example, gave all the blame to the Empress Dowager, who 'allying herself with the powers of darkness, entered into a diabolical conspiracy in order to keep her people in ignorance and to shield her family from the competition of superior light and knowledge'; Dr A. H. Smith (another American missionary) felt that the Roman Catholics deserved a major share of the blame and the Protestants only a minor one; Mr Broomhall (of the China Inland Mission) traced everything back to the Opium War and to foreign political and economic aggression, and considered that 'to place any responsibility for the outbreak on the missionaries was absurd'. The foreign diplomats, for their part, found it highly convenient to label the Uprising a 'rebellion', since this theory (or fiction?) restored the *status quo*, preserved the unilateral treaties, removed all blame from the Empress Dowager, and allowed the Powers to impose large indemnities, through her government, on the Chinese people.

On the basis of these foreign accounts, the foreign-language press of Shanghai and Tientsin, and the diplomatic archives of Europe and America, Mr G. Nye Steiger, in 1927, produced a study of the Boxers, *China and the Occident*, which, in spite of many shortcomings due to incomplete information, is still in many ways an indispensable book. In it the author put forward a theory of his own, namely that the Boxers were not a religious sect or secret society at all but the legally constituted militia, raised in obedience to decrees of the Empress Dowager in 1898.

vii

More recently (1959), Mr Peter Fleming has published a book, *The Siege at Peking*, based on the existing European material, but utilizing in addition the private papers of Sir Claude MacDonald and the diary of Dr G. E. Morrison. It is a graphic and entertaining account of the siege and the foreign personalities involved, but China itself figures in it only vaguely as a barbaric setting for the somewhat dubious exploits of European chivalry.

In the meantime, published accounts of the Boxers in Chinese and Japanese were accumulating, though few of them were communicated to the West, but since the communists assumed power in China the publication of source material on Chinese history in general has been prodigious and already several collections dealing with the Boxers are available for study.

The first Chinese collection to appear was *I Ho T'uan Tzŭ Liao Ts'ung K'an* (*Source Materials of the Boxer War*), Shanghai, 1951, in four volumes, edited by Chien Po-tsan and five others. These four volumes contain over a million characters and comprise fifty-six items. Many of them had appeared in print before, but five of the titles are those of hitherto unpublished manuscripts, including diaries and letters ('more reliable as sources [remarks Fang Chao-ying] than the so-called *Veritable Records*'). The second collection, *I Ho T'uan Tang An Shih Liao* (*Source Material in Despatches relating to the Boxers*), Peking, 1959, in two volumes, is a collection of official despatches and telegrams from 1896 to 1901, and adds another 800,000 characters or so to our information. Yet a third collection of contemporary diaries, etc., appeared in 1959, namely *Kêng Tzŭ Chi Shih* (*Records of 1900*), compiled by the Institute of Historical Research, Peking, containing important evidence of the clash between the Boxers and the White Lotus referred to in chapter x. Altogether there now exists a body of source material on the Boxers that will take years to sift, and it is likely to be added to still further in the future.

Of the first of the above-named collections as well as of a number of other works in Chinese, use has been made by Mr Chester Tan in his book, *The Boxer Catastrophe* (1955), dealing with selected aspects of the movement. This is an important work, filling a number of gaps in the record, especially as regards events at Court and the diplomacy of Russia, and it recounts at length the activities of the southern viceroys, for the first time giving credit to Shêng Hsüan-huai, Director of Railways and Telegraphs, and the role he played in keeping the south out of the war. (Mr Tan incidentally disposes of Steiger's theory of the origins of the movement, showing that it is based on insufficient evidence, a conclusion endorsed in the present book.)

But since so many questions relating to the Uprising remain un-answered, no apology is required for attempting to answer some of them. The thing to decide was what contribution a Western student of the subject could most usefully make.

In the course of my inquiry into the history of the Boxers over some years the question which has interested me above all others is this. At the time of the crisis in 1900, the Boxers were vowed to the support of the throne and to the destruction of foreigners, yet there is reason to believe that their aim had previously been 'anti-dynastic'. At what point, then, did the change-over take place, and for what reasons? After setting out Lao Nai-hsüan's theory of the Boxer origins, Mr Chester Tan writes, 'The Boxers' slogan of "upholding the Ch'ing Dynasty and exterminating the foreigners" caught the imagination of the people'. The question is—*When* and *Why*? (No previous slogan or aim is mentioned by Mr Tan.) The fact that the communist theory of the Uprising is that it was a peasant movement on the traditional pattern of Chinese revolutions, directed against the Manchu govern-ment as well as the foreign imperialists, makes the answer of the first importance. Can we 'pin-point' the appearance of the slogan 'Support the Ch'ing; Destroy the Foreigner'? This is what I have attempted to do, although the evidence has proved to be conflicting in some respects and the answer given cannot therefore be conclusive.

But the results of such research presented without any background of history would be meaningless to the general reader. So with great daring (some might say, 'with reckless bravado') I decided to provide a number of chapters describing the Manchu Government, Chinese Society under the late Ch'ing, the Impact of the West on China, the Battle of the Concessions, etc., in the light of recent research, to form an introduction to the Uprising. These chapters are necessarily im-pressionistic but they are disciplined by contacts with, and study of, China over a period of forty years. This, of course, will not excuse the errors and other imperfections of the study, but it should be some sort of guarantee that the facts in it are chosen for their significance rather than for their picturesque effect.

My own research into the history of the Boxers is concentrated in chapters VII–XI. Chapter XII is merely a summary of events after the

Boxers had definitely become 'pro-dynastic'. Appendix A relates to the mystery of Ching-shan's diary and includes a hitherto unpublished statement by the late Sir Edmund Backhouse: appendix B is a note on the records of certain British missionary bodies.

Professor Pulleyblank very kindly read the first five chapters in draft, and I have amended and amplified them in the light of his comments. The completed manuscript I submitted to the opinion of Dr Jerome Ch'ên, Dr Joseph Needham, Professor Denis Twitchett, and Dr C. L. Wayper, all of whom commented minutely on the text (the first three from a sinological standpoint and the fourth from that of diplomatic history), and I have done my best to profit by their learning. Dr Arthur Waley, to whom I submitted appendix A, made suggestions for additions to it. To all these gentlemen I offer my grateful thanks.

I have also to thank Dr Lu Gwei-djen, Dr M. I. Scott of the Cambridge University Library, and the staffs of the British Museum, the Foreign Office, the Public Records Office, and the Librarian of the War Office for assistance of various kinds, and the London Missionary Society and the Society for the Propagation of the Gospel for allowing me to inspect their records.

CAMBRIDGE   V. PURCELL
1961

NOTE

The romanization of Chinese here adopted is the Wade–Giles system except when departure from long-established usage may cause confusion (thus the character for 'department' may appear both as *chou* and *chow* in the same sentence). My capitalization tends to vary with the caprice of the authority followed.

The translation of Chinese names for documents submitted to and issued from the Emperor gives rise to difficulty. In *Ch'ing Administration* (Harvard, 1960), John K. Fairbank and Ssŭ-yü Têng give thirteen phrases translated 'memorial', four translated 'commands', four 'decrees', and four 'edicts', as well as a score or so translated 'supplementary memorials', 'endorsements', 'instructions', 'rescripts', etc. Nor do the authorities agree as to the correct translations. In consequence, the renderings given in this book are somewhat arbitrary.

As for the maps, no two contemporary ones agree as to the location of a number of towns or villages, and a few places are to be found (if at all) only in sketch-maps in books. In designing the map on p. 8 a main reliance has been placed on the Chinese map in *IHT*, I (frontispiece).

ABBREVIATIONS

BEFEO   *Bulletin de l'École Française d'Extrême Orient.*

BSOAS   *Bulletin of the School of Oriental and African Studies* (London University).

FC   *Further Correspondence respecting the affairs of China,* printed for the use of the Foreign Office.

FEQ   *Far Eastern Quarterly.*

HJAS   *Harvard Journal of Asiatic Studies.*

IHT   *I Ho T'uan Tžŭ Liao Ts'ung K'an (Source Materials of the Boxer War).*

IHTTA   *I Ho T'uan Tang An Shih Liao (Source Material in Despatches relating to the Boxers).*

IRCE   *International Relations of the Chinese Empire,* by H. B. Morse.

JAS   *Journal of Asian Studies.*

JAOS   *Journal of the American Oriental Society.*

K 24/5/12   (as an example) = 12th day of the 5th month of the 24th year of the Kuang Hsü reign-period. INTER = Intercalary month.

P.R.O.   Public Record Office, London.

RASJ   *Royal Asiatic Society Journal.*

SCC   *Science and Civilization in China,* by Joseph Needham, 1954- .

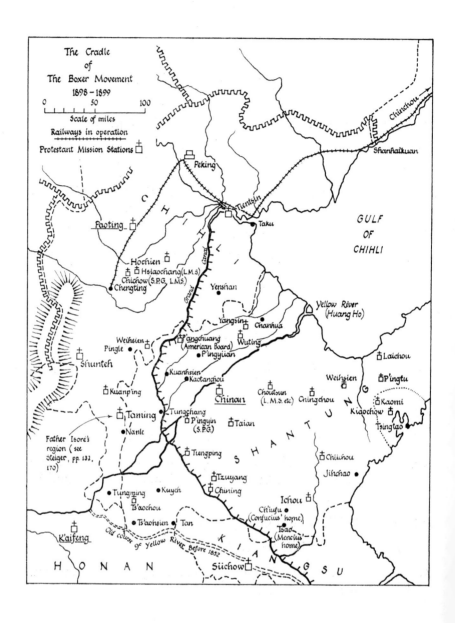

The Cradle
of
The Boxer Movement
1898 – 1899

0   50   100
Scale of miles
Railways in operation
Protestant Mission Stations

C H I H L I

Peking

Tientsin

Taku

GULF
OF
CHIHLI

Shanhaikuan

Chinchou

Paoting

Hochien
Hsiaochang (L.M.S.)
Chichow (S.P.G., L.M.S.)
Chengting

Yenshan

Yangsin
Channua
Wuting

Yellow River
(Huang Ho)

Weihsien
Pingle
Shunteh

P'angchuang
(American Board)
P'ingyüan

Laichou

Kuanhsien
Kaotangchou

Weihsien

P'ingtu

Kuanp'ing

Taming

Nanle

Tungchang

P'ingyin
(S.P.G.)

Taian

Chinan

Choutsun
(L.M.S. etc)

Ch'ingchou

Kaomi

Kiaochow

Tsingtao

S H A N T U N G

Father Isoré's
region (see
Steiger, pp. 131,
170)

Tungping

Chiichou

Jihchao

Tzuyang

Chuning

Tungming

Kuych

T'saochou

Ts'aohsien

Tan

Ichou

Ch'iufu
(Confucius' home)

Tsao
(Mencius'
home)

K'aifeng

Old course of Yellow River before 1852

H O N A N

K I A N G S U

Süchow

Grand Canal

xiv

CHAPTER I

THE MANCHU GOVERNMENT AND ITS ARMED FORCES

If the Boxer Uprising really was a 'rebellion', against what constituted authority did the Boxers rebel? The answer can only be, the Manchu government of China. And since, moreover, this was the same government that the Boxers were ostensibly supporting during the crisis of 1900, it is necessary that we should form some idea of its nature before we consider the history of the Boxers themselves. And, at the same time, some account must be taken of the armed forces of this government, against which the Boxers fought in 1899 and into which they were incorporated in the summer of 1900.

The Chinese governmental system was an organic unity of ruler and people. 'Heaven sees as the people see; Heaven hears as the people hear.' The Emperor's mandate to rule 'all under Heaven' was very unlike the 'divine right' of kings in Europe. There was no dichotomy of body and soul, of Church and State; the Emperor was the high priest of a cosmic *numen*.

It was probably a misfortune for China that in the era in which she was first subjected to the impact of the West an alien dynasty was on the throne, for although the Chinese accepted the Manchu emperor as the *de facto* 'Son of Heaven' who ruled over *t'ien hsia* ('what is below heaven', or the earth in general), they did not think of him as the head of a Chinese 'nation' (*kuo*). One consequence of this was that when Chinese, especially labourers from South China, were hired by the invading foreigner to assist him in attacking the Imperial forces, they had no sense of being guilty of treason against their own country. To enter the international world, China had herself to become a nation, and had there been a native dynasty in power at the time of the onslaught of the foreigner, possessing both physical force and new ideas, the conception of nationhood might well have grown up around the Emperor. If so, the succession of humiliating defeats that China suffered would almost certainly have been avoided, she would probably have taken her place in the modern world much more rapidly than she did, and in consequence she would have had no sense of injury to carry forward into the next century. (Whether this is what actually would have happened, there is, of course, no means of proving—but it is at least a permissible speculation.)

Not that the Ch'ing was an unpopular dynasty. In many respects its reputation is higher with Chinese historians than that of its predecessor, the native Ming. The Chinese were proud to wear the queue, once the badge of servitude to the Manchus. Says E. H. Parker:

The Chinese people, though of course fearing the historical military vengeance of the Manchus, is loyal to the Manchus, not because they are divine rulers, but because the Manchus have from the first been loyal to, and have governed strictly in accordance with, the 'Chinese idea', that intangible fact which has held the Empire together through all vicissitudes, and has swallowed up and assimilated one after another all antagonistic elements.[1]

The Manchus owed their succession to conquest—or, more precisely, to breach of contract, for having come in at the invitation of one of the rival Chinese contenders for the Dragon Throne, they refused to leave. Nevertheless, they claimed to rule by the 'mandate of Heaven', and when finally in 1912 they departed (having forfeited their mandate by misrule) they presumed in their abdication decree to create a 'Republic' to which they bequeathed the government of China.

At the time of the Boxer Uprising the Manchu bannermen were a class of privileged idlers, consuming about a third of the audited revenue. In Peking alone there were about 200,000 Manchu families who had forgotten their own language and were 'in no way distinguishable from the local Chinese',[2] and the same was true of those Manchus who remained in Manchuria. In the provinces, they lived apart as a separate garrison, speaking a dialect of their own, and neither there nor in Peking were they allowed to leave the precincts of the city. They had become useless as soldiers, but were still the ostensible support of the Manchu emperor.

The fate of an ambitious alien is to take colour from his adopted country to the extent of being impregnated with it—he must be more orthodox and more ostentatiously 'patriotic' than the native in order to distract attention from his foreign origins. Thus the Manchus aimed to be more Chinese than the Chinese. Education they used as a prime instrument of policy, insisting upon a neo-Confucian orthodoxy, and by the adoption and extension of such reactionary devices as the 'Eight-legged Essay' (a Ming innovation) in the public examinations, the Manchu emperors froze into hard stone an official culture already tending to petrification.

In face of this parvenu orthodoxy, independent-minded Chinese in the earlier part of the dynasty were all pro-Ming, seeking a return to a comparatively 'golden age'. There was, for example, Huang Tsung-hsi (1610–95), who wrote a political work (1663) underlining Mencius's thesis that the people are more important than the emperor, and that 'the world belongs to the public' (*T'ien-hsia wei kung* from the *Book of Rites*—long afterwards adopted as a slogan by Sun Yat-sen), and there was Ku Yen-wu (1613–82), who advocated the adoption of labour-saving machinery and the opening up of mines, and who also recognized that 'there are some Chinese customs which are inferior to those of foreign countries'. The works of these and other independent-minded scholars were burnt by the thousand copies as 'subversive' during the famous Literary Inquisition of the Ch'ien Lung emperor (1774–81)— to be resuscitated in the late nineteenth century by the reformers to show that 'reform' was really Chinese in origin and not merely an idea adopted from the West.[1]

While eighteenth- and nineteenth-century Europe burgeoned with political change and technological development, Chinese society remained largely static, and the great Ch'ing scholars (such as Tai Chên (1724–77) and Tuan Yü-ts'ai (1735–1815)) applied their talents solely to criticism of the classics like Western Renaissance scholars. Despite the so-called 'T'ung Chih Restoration' (1862–74) and the 'Hundred Days' of 1898 under the Kuang Hsü emperor, it was the alien Manchus even more than the native literati who took refuge in reaction.

It may be questioned, however, whether the Ch'ing was quite so stagnant or sterile a period of Chinese thought as it has been represented. The early Ch'ing scholars reacted against the abstract, metaphysical, and meditative intellectual climate of the Sung and T'ang. Their primary intention was to shift scholarly attention from philosophical discourse to practical action, from the individual to the public. During the middle Ch'ing period there arose a school of empirical research, known as the *K'ao-chêng hsüeh*, which prepared the way for K'ang Yu-wei to use classical learning as a vehicle of political reform. It mirrored also the growth of a proto-scientific spirit in historical research.[2]

On ascending the Dragon Throne, the Manchu monarch assumed

I-2

the sacred character and titles of his office. He was the 'Son of Heaven', the 'Supreme Ruler', the 'August Lofty One', the 'Celestial Ruler', the 'Solitary Man', the 'Buddha of the Present Day', the 'Lord', and he was often addressed in memorials as the 'Lord of Ten Thousand Years'. His alone was the duty and prerogative of worshipping heaven, and this he did with solemn ritual at the winter solstice at the Temple of Heaven in Peking.

On the evening before the solstice the Emperor was borne in a carriage drawn by elephants to the precincts of the temple, where, after offering incense to *Shangti*, the 'Supreme Ruler', and to his own ancestors, he remained until the early morning, and then, dressed in his ceremonial robes, he climbed by stages to the second terrace of the temple and there embarked on the key sequence of ritual and sacrifice. When this was accomplished, by virtue of his worship he had now assumed the additional office of 'Vice-regent of Heaven'.[1]

It was a far cry from the nomad's tent of his not-so-remote ancestors: it was an equally far cry from the gorgeous palaces of Peking to the drab mud hovels which most of his subjects inhabited.

Parker, in his lively and authoritative, if idiosyncratic, account of China,[2] begins his description of the Chinese government, not with the Emperor or even with the central administration, but with the provinces. The Manchu power (he says) 'is a mere absorptive machine, whose very existence (as recent events show)[3] is a matter of comparative unconcern to the provinces, each of which is sufficient unto itself, and exists as an independent unit'.

This was undoubtedly so in a qualified sense, though more recently Chinese writers (as we shall see in a moment) have stressed the effectiveness of the Manchu grip on the villages, and since, in the Boxer Uprising, which took place within the zone of direct Imperial control, the Court exercised an all-important influence on the course of events, I shall first outline the machinery of the central government before mentioning the provinces.[4]

The Ch'ings inherited the autocratic form of government which had been handed down from dynasty to dynasty since the Ch'in and Han (221 B.C. to A.D. 220), but made its organization even more rigid.

Until 1729 the Grand Secretariat (*Nei-Ko*) had been the main organ of government; but then the secret military organization and State affairs began to be managed by a new body called the Grand Council (*Chün-chi-ch'u*, literally, 'Place for Military Strategy').[5]

4

In carrying out its function in advising the Emperor, the Grand Council dealt with almost all governmental matters. It was powerful, but it was nevertheless subordinate to the Emperor. The latter appointed and dismissed the officials of the Council at will, and kept them constantly under surveillance by the censors. Many of them were punished by him from time to time. Moreover, the Emperor could make decisions, if he so desired, without reference to the Council at all. All important information went direct to the Emperor, who imparted as much of it to the Council as he saw fit. In 1802 the Chia Ch'ing emperor issued an edict affirming his sovereign power and laid it down that the Grand Council's main duties were to copy edicts and to expedite their despatch. Only when the Emperor was a minor or in bad health and the Grand Councillors were exceptionally experienced and energetic was the Council able to shape policy on its own. In no real way, therefore, could the Grand Council be regarded as a 'Cabinet' as in a European parliamentary government.

The Imperial College of Inscriptions, *Nan Shu-fang*, advised the Emperor directly on educational and literary matters.

Down to 1901 the central administrative organs of the Ch'ing government were the Six Boards of Ministries, which had been taken over from preceding dynasties. These were the Boards of Civil Office, Revenue, Rites, War, Punishments, and Works. The more important posts in these Boards were, in principle, divided equally between the Manchus and Chinese. At the head of each Board were two ministers (*Shih-lang*) (one Manchu, one Chinese), and below them were a number of junior ministers.

The Six Boards were not subordinate to the Grand Council or the Grand Secretariat, but were directly responsible to the Emperor. While the Grand Council and the Grand Secretariat assisted the Emperor in the over-all management of government affairs, the Boards were each assigned one branch of government.

The functions of these Boards can be briefly indicated. The Board of Civil Office concerned itself with titles, patents, precedence, etc.; the Board of Revenue with the levying and collection of duties and taxes and the payment of salaries and allowances (another of the multifarious duties was taking a census of the population); the Board of Rites concerned itself with the five kinds of ritual observances; to the Board of War was entrusted the duty of 'aiding the sovereign to protect the people' and of directing all military affairs in the metropolis and the provinces; the Board of Punishments had charge of all punishments, 'for the purpose of aiding the sovereign in correcting all people'; and the Board of Works had direction of all public works throughout the empire (which seemingly included the neglect of the Grand Canal so that it had silted up for long stretches of its course, the keeping of roads and bridges in a regular state of disrepair, and the complete failure to control the vagaries of 'China's Sorrow', the Yellow River).[1]

The Board of War (*Ping Pu*) (I speak of it as it was in the eighteenth and nineteenth centuries) had the duty of aiding the sovereign in protecting the people by the direction of all military affairs in the metropolis and the provinces, and of acting as a sort of hinge of the State in collating the reports received from different departments regarding appointment to or deprivation of office, postal and courier arrangements, and some other matters. (A minor bureau of the courier office was called the 'Office for the Announcement of Victories', or *anglicè*, the express-letter department.) The Board of War, however, had no control directly over the household troops, the Peking gendarmerie, the Bannermen, or the twenty-four captains-general of the Banners, and since the land and sea forces were entrusted in a great degree to the local authorities, its duties were really more circumscribed than would at first appear.

Prior to the treaties of 1860, Chinese diplomatic relations had been managed by the provincial authorities. The Office of Colonial Affairs (*Li-fan Yüan*) was the organ of the central government in charge of foreign affairs because all foreign nations were considered to be China's vassal states. Then, on a memorial to the throne by Prince Kung, a new office called the *Tsung-li Ko-Kuo Shih-wu Ya-mên* (Office in General Charge of Affairs Concerning All Foreign Nations), usually called the Tsungli Yamen, was established. (In 1901 it was replaced by a Ministry of Foreign Affairs under the provisions of the Boxer Protocol.)

The general supervisory organ of the Ch'ing dynasty was the Censorate (*Tu-ch'a Yüan*). The title 'censor' recalls to the European mind the Roman censors who were invested with the dreaded *regimen morum* and the superintendence of the State finances, and who, until Sulla's time, could degrade men from, or promote them to, the rank of senator or knight at will; but the Chinese censors had no such powers —they could merely memorialize the Emperor.

6

The Chinese censorate comprised a president, senior and junior vice-presidents, twenty Supervising Censors, and forty-four Inspecting Censors. The Supervising Censors supervised all offices within the capital; the Inspecting Censors divided the nation into districts and inspected the offices of local governments. Censors could in their memorials denounce an official no matter how high his rank. They could pry into, and object to, any matter regardless of its nature. It was their privilege to commend or refute the memorials or reports from officials of all ranks. Even the Emperor's decrees and instructions could be opposed.

However, the authority of censorship was not exercised by the censorate as a body, but by its individual members. Censors enjoyed no privileges of tenure or special protection. It was the Emperor who finally decided their privileges and the licence allowed them. Often the Emperor did not hold a censor responsible for an inaccurate report or a false accusation, but if, no matter how justifiably, an Emperor's favourite were censored, the censor was almost invariably punished. Nevertheless, courageous censors *did* dare to impeach the Empress Dowager for her extravagance and her favouritism of eunuchs (for example, in 1866), and one censor, Wu K'o-tu (1812–79), having submitted a memorial protesting against the illegal succession of the Kuang Hsü emperor, thereupon committed suicide to underline his protest.

Although these Six Boards were the central administrative organs, ministers had no authority to send orders directly to the heads of provincial and other local governments. Commands had to come from the Emperor himself in the form of Imperial instructions and decrees. When two senior members of a Board disagreed, it was customary for them to submit their differences to the Emperor and to ask him to arbitrate. Thus no one member of a Board was ever able to control the entire organization.

The Emperor was obliged to act as a clearing-house for all important matters. . . . The whole Chinese tradition of the personal rule of the Son of Heaven demanded a superman at the head of affairs. The lack of a superman, and the rapid multiplication of state affairs, must be an important factor in the collapse of the Manchu administration during the nineteenth century.[1]

European observers, such as Douglas, Parker, and Giles, insist on the democratic spirit which underlay the whole system of government

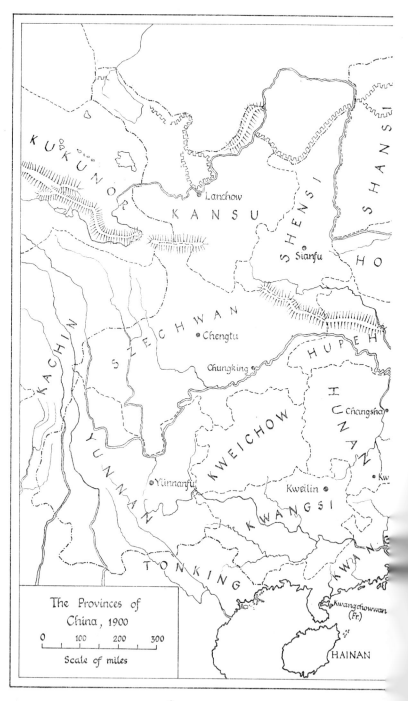

The Provinces of China, 1900

0   100   200   300

Scale of miles

KUKUNOR

KANSU

Lanchow

SHENSI

SHANSI

HO

SZECHWAN

Chengtu

Chungking

HUPEH

Sianfu

KACHIN

YUNNAN

KWEICHOW

Changsha

HUNAN

Yünnanfu

Kweilin

Kw

KWANGSI

TONKING

KWAN

KWA

Kwangchowwan
(Fr.)

HAINAN

8

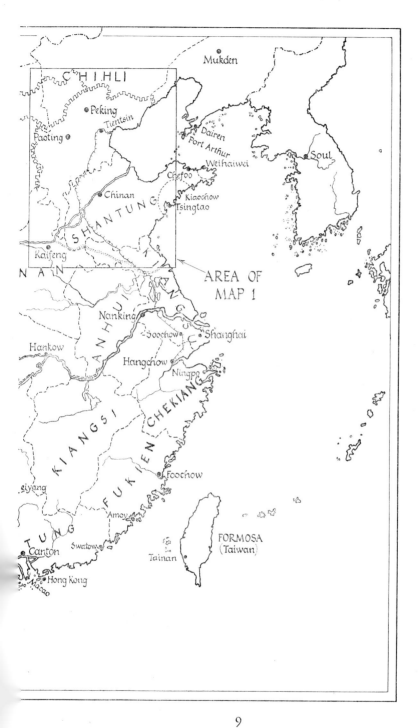

CHIHLI
Mukden
Peking
Tientsin
Paoting
Dairen
Port Arthur
Soul
Weihaiwei
Chefoo
Chinan
Kiaochow
SHANTUNG
Tsingtao
Kaifeng
NAN
AREA OF
MAP 1
Nanking
Soochow
Shanghai
ANHUI
Hankow
Hangchow
Ningpo
CHEKIANG
KIANGSI
FUKIEN
.eiyang
Foochow
Amoy
FORMOSA
(Taiwan)
TUNG
Swatow
Tainan
Canton
Hong Kong
Macao

9

in China.[1] From this assumption it followed that the machinery of government must keep the Emperor in direct touch with the people.

It is not easy to convey to European readers the exact nature of this 'democratic spirit' existing within the structure of such a thorough-going autocracy as Imperial China undoubtedly was, but the truth is that with all the kowtowing, self-abasement, bastinadoing, and placing in cangues, there was still an all-pervading feeling of 'We are all in the same boat'. When governors and ministers erred and were disgraced, they were not merely 'given a bowler-hat' (as used to be said collo-quially of superseded British generals) and allowed to retire to Chelten-ham or Bath to live on their pensions and investments: not only did they forfeit their rank, their honours, and their decorations, but their private fortunes were confiscated as well, and they were lucky to escape with their lives. Even the Emperor's tenure of office was, as we have seen, subject to the 'mandate of Heaven', and no one pitied him too much if he forfeited it. There was a constant and direct relationship between the Emperor and the 'people' and, theoretically at least (according to Mencius), it was the people who were the more important of the two.

Every morning between 7 and 9 (and sometimes earlier) the Grand Councillors met and presented to the Emperor annotated State papers relating to every branch of the administration. With a mark of the 'vermilion pen' the Emperor declared his will, and the papers thus approved were transmitted to the several Boards to be acted upon. To the hands of these authorities also were entrusted the twenty-five seals of government which vouched for the authenticity of the documents to which they were appended.

This picture of an absolute monarch at work must, however, be viewed in the light of the fact that for the greater part of the period 1861–1908 the Emperor was a mere puppet of the Empress Dowager, Tz'ŭ Hsi, and that she in turn was acting on the advice of eunuchs and favourites. The vermilion pen was wielded by the hidden hand. Never-theless, the structure of the government remained unaltered. After the *coup d'état* in 1898 Tz'ŭ Hsi issued decrees in her own name.

It was from the archives of the Grand Council that the *Peking Gazette*, perhaps the oldest 'newspaper' in the world, was compiled. It contained a selection of the Imperial edicts, the memorials, and the official announcements. Special copies were immediately despatched by Imperial couriers to the high provincial authorities. A feature of the

Gazette, strange to those who were familiar with its Western counter-parts, was the candour with which the errors or omissions of everyone concerned, including the Emperor himself, were pointed out for all to see. Its pages presented a complete and graphic picture of the official life of the country from issue to issue.[1]

The Manchus (being parvenus) were great sticklers for etiquette and conventions of language and dress. In 1759, for example, the Emperor standardized the Imperial robes and the Court dress, leaving the robe-makers no latitude of design.[2] And if elaborate protocol is a sign of advanced sophistication, then the Ch'ing was highly sophisticated. For example, an element of Chinese composition, due in part to the struc-ture of the language itself, and in part to the rigorous formality of the written style, was the 'elevation' of characters by different degrees above the columns as a means of indicating respect or reverence in varying gradations of importance. The Chinese devices for this purpose were infinitely more extended than those in vogue in Western countries, either at present or in past times. The rules were laid down with much minuteness in the *K'o Ch'ang T'iao Li,* or Rules for Literary Exami-nations. A single elevation of a character by one space above the general level was employed in referring to abodes of Majesty, the Imperial Court, the attributes of government, proceedings by which the sovereign was addressed, and supernatural powers of beings of a secondary order of importance, together with the places at which their worship was conducted. A double elevation was allotted to characters which referred to the person, attributes, or actions of the reigning sovereign or his consort, and a threefold elevation was due from the sovereign himself towards his ancestors or predecessors of the Imperial line, and their places of sepulture, his guardians during minority, and the powers of nature and other objects of Imperial worship, together with the temples or altars at which this worship was celebrated.

If Imperial China was a 'democracy' (as some claim it was) its hierarchy of government at least was a highly graduated one, in which some were decidedly 'more equal than others'.

The Manchus continued the Chinese Confucian system of govern-ment, but both to maintain it and to keep the upper hand as conquerors meant a careful balancing of Chinese and Manchu personnel in the 'Sino-barbarian dyarchy of the Ch'ing dynasty'.[3]

Since the Manchu conquest, a rough 'fifty-fifty' division of posts at the capital between the two races had been maintained until the Taiping

Rebellion, but to keep their control it was necessary for the Manchus to use the best Chinese talent and to keep it diluted with a proper proportion of Manchus. If the official hierarchy at the capital contained too many Manchu incompetents, the regime might become dangerously inefficient. If the hierarchy in the provinces became all Chinese, Manchu rule might soon collapse. A closer look at the use made of Manchus and Chinese in high office in the 1840's and 1850's (says Fairbank) suggests one of the Ch'ing dynasty's points of breakdown—its use of Manchus in posts beyond their capacity. The evidence suggests that in this period the Manchu component of the 'Sino-barbarian dyarchy' was a source of weakness to the Imperial administration, even though the comparative incompetence of the Manchus had not yet been fully revealed by events.

From the establishment of the Grand Council to the end of the Ch'ing dynasty there were altogether 145 Grand Councillors, of whom seventy-two were Manchus, sixty-four were Chinese, six were Mongols, and three Chinese bannermen. The Mongols and the Chinese bannermen disappeared altogether after the Taiping Rebellion. In the Yung Chêng and Ch'ien Lung periods, from 1723 to 1796, the Manchus on the average accounted for 56 per cent of the personnel, and the Chinese 37 per cent. But in the Chia Ch'ing and Hsien Fêng periods, from 1796 to 1862, the Manchus accounted for 38 per cent and the Chinese 53 per cent. This change was probably due to the full operation of the examination system which gave the Chinese the opportunity to rise in accordance with their abilities. After the Taiping Rebellion, from 1862 to 1908, the Manchus made up 52 per cent of the total and the Chinese 47 per cent. This was due to the fact that the Manchus wanted to increase their power in the central government to counterbalance the increase of power of the Chinese in the provincial governments.[1]

The Manchu government, in fact, was not able to maintain the racial balance in face of the pro-Manchu pressures within the Court. On 17 April 1899 the British Chargé d'Affaires in Peking wrote a despatch to Lord Salisbury saying that the tendency to replace Chinese by Manchus in important political posts of the empire was increasing. He went on: 'So large a proportion of Manchus in the highest positions tends to indicate a retrograde administration as the Manchus are, as a race, very inferior to the Chinese in intelligence and capacity and their appointment to important positions is viewed with disfavour by the Chinese themselves.'[2]

During the Taiping Rebellion and the wars with Britain and France there was a major shift in political power inside China. In the Manchu Court the control of affairs fell more and more into the hands of eunuchs and favourites, while the power of the provinces was gradually increased at the expense of the central government.

The administration of the empire was entirely in the hands of the 'mandarins'—a body of civil servants, divided into nine grades, who owed their appointments (in principle at least) to their success in the official examinations. It is worthy of note that the mandarins (like the gentry as a class, as we shall observe in the following chapter) were distinguished from the general public for all to see by the stone or metal 'buttons' of rank on top of their caps, and by the corresponding bird (crane, pheasant, cock, goose, etc.) embroidered on the breast and back of their official robes, as well as by the graduated clasps of their girdles. Unlike their British counterparts, they never wore an anonymous 'mufti' when on duty (though off duty they might relax in their vests and trousers and scratch their armpits like ordinary subjects). Hence their authority and apartness were made manifest to the people at large in order that they might not be submerged by the democratic spirit around them.

A fact of outstanding importance during the crisis of the summer of 1900 was the great degree of autonomy which the provinces, since the weakening of the Imperial control during the Taiping Rebellion, had enjoyed, for it was this that enabled the southern viceroys and Yüan Shih-k'ai, governor of Shantung, to keep their provinces effectively neutral during the 'war' that ensued in Chihli. Says Parker (who had had long direct experience of such matters):

So long as the provincial government sends its Peking supplies, administers a reasonable sop to its clamorous provincial duns, quells incipient insurrections, gives employment to the army of 'expectants', staves off foreign demands, avoids 'rows' of all kinds, and, in a word, keeps up a decent external surface of respectability, no questions are asked; all reports and promotions are passed; the Viceroy and his colleagues 'enjoy happiness', and everybody makes his 'pile'.[1]

When, in the next chapter, we come to take account of the Imperial control of the examination system, and of the *Pao-chia* and other control devices, we shall conclude that the indifference of Peking to what was happening in the provinces as suggested in this passage is much exaggerated, but we shall yet have to concede that the viceroys and governors still enjoyed considerable freedom of action. Each province had its own army, navy, and system of taxation, besides its own social customs. The dealings with Peking were of an extremely limited kind. The main interest of the central government was in the annual 'appropriation' from the provinces, and Peking knew within a small margin how much each province could raise—or at least how much it could be compelled to disgorge. After the Taiping Rebellion, however, the control by the throne was greatly weakened. Powerful personalities (the degree of their power was decided by the size of their private army) were now the decisive factor. For example, no matter who was governor of Shantung, he was overshadowed either by Tsêng Kuo-fan or by Li Hung-chang as the Chihli viceroy.

The titles 'Viceroy' (or 'Governor-General' which is more correct as a translation), and 'Governor' may occasion some confusion. Each of the eighteen provinces had a governor, who reported on all formal matters to the Boards at Peking and memorialized the Emperor on affairs of a less routine kind, but pairs of provinces usually had a viceroy or governor-general as well. The governor's duties included the supervision of civil servants, the pacification of the people, the transport of grain, and the collection of taxes. In the 'Comprehensive Statutes of the Great Ch'ing' (*Ta-Ch'ing Hui-tien*), compiled during the Ch'ien Lung period, the duties of the two officials were defined thus: 'A Governor-General takes charge of civil and military affairs and vigilantly supervises soldiers and civilians, while a Governor takes charge of educational, financial, judicial, and administrative matters.' In the mid-nineteenth century the duties of governor-general and governors were gradually altered and became almost identical. Both governor-generals and governors had the right to report directly to the throne. Furthermore, they were not subject to direct orders from the Grand Secretariat, Grand Council, or the Six Boards. But although the governor-general's 'button' was a shade higher than the governor's, he was in no way the superior official, and in most cases neither could originate any official action without 'moving' the other. Usually the two memorialized the Emperor jointly. In most routine matters, moreover, they were also bound to act 'on the proposition' of the Provincial Treasurer and the Provincial Judge.

The plum of the service, financially speaking, was the viceroyalty of the Two Kiangs, that is of old Kiang Nan (in 1900, part of Kiang-Su and Anhwei) and Kiang Si, with its seat at Nanking (this was the viceroyalty held by Liu K'un-i in 1900), although the viceroyalty of Chihli (held by Yü-lu in 1900) ranked higher, being responsible for the security of Peking. There was no sub-province in Chihli and consequently no governor, but Shantung, Shansi, and Honan were under the viceroy's wing. Next (in tacit agreement) came the viceroyalty of the Two Kwangs (Kwangtung and Kwangsi) (held by Li Hung-chang in 1900). Each sub-province had its governor, and the viceroy lived at Canton alongside the governor of Kwangtung. The remaining viceroyalties seem to have had no numerical precedence allotted them. They were of Mincheh (Fukien and Chekiang—seat at Foochow) and Hukwang (seat at Wuch'ang, opposite Hankow) (held by Chang Chih-tung in 1900). All the above viceroys, together with their associated governors, were to play an important role in the events of the Boxer Year.

In view of the seeming uncertainty as to the exact division of power between the Emperor and the viceroys and governors, it may be well to quote the summing-up of Li Chien-nung:

Judging from the several key organizations explained above, we reach the following conclusions: (1) All power was in the hands of the Emperor, and (2) within any office all officials counterbalanced one another. The political theories 'divide and rule' and 'balance and check' were fully put into practice by the Manchu rulers. Thus we may say that the monarchical and autocratic organization down to (and including) the Ch'ing dynasty was very strict.[1]

The point of contact between the government and the people was the *hsien*, the 'city district' which was the official unit of Chinese corporate life. There were some 1300 of these altogether[2]—between seventy and one hundred of them on an average per province (Chihli had 140). The area of a *hsien* was about that of an English county. In the purely Chinese regions, it always consisted of a walled city and some 500–1000 square miles round the town. A Chinese was associated through life with the *hsien* of his birth, which was, so to speak, the rallying point of local patriotism.

Since a district magistrate (like the mandarins generally) was not paid enough to live on, it was taken for granted by everybody that he would extract financial profit from everything he touched. He, moreover, only held his appointment for three years (as a safeguard against the accumulation of too much power) and would therefore usually be in a hurry to make hay whilst the sun shone. But no ignominy seems to have attached to him in the public mind for his venality. After all, people received some positive or negative advantages in return for the fee they paid him for performing, or neglecting to perform, a duty. Parker describes him as follows:

His comparatively low 'button' rank places him in easy touch with the people, whilst his position as the lowest of the *yu-sz*, or 'executive', clothes him with an imperial status which even a *Viceroy* must respect. . . . He is so much identified with the soul of 'empire', that the Empire or Government is elegantly styled *hsien-kuan*, 'the district magistrate'. He is the judge in the first instance in all matters whatsoever, civil or criminal, and also governor of the gaol, coroner, sheriff, mayor, head-surveyor, civil service examiner, tax-collector, registrar, lord-lieutenant, aedile, chief bailiff, interceder with the gods; and, in short, what the people always call him—'father and mother officer'.[1]

How oppressive were the mandarins? The 'squeeze' system was a rough and ready method of distribution of wealth, but when the *per capita* income was so tiny, every additional imposition threatened to reduce it below subsistence level. The popular literature and the stage afford positive proof that although the people acquiesced in the system, they were not indifferent to its abuses. Innocent people were arrested, imprisoned, and tortured to shield others who were guilty of the crimes with which they were charged; prisoners were left to languish untried for years in the unspeakable prisons; charges were invented against innocent persons to vent spite or to gratify revenge. The punishments were barbarous (but so were they in eighteenth-century England). In one well-known novel the hero meets a friend in dire distress at the loss of his affianced bride who has been carried off by so exalted an official that he dare not even make a complaint of the wrong done him. In one popular Peking farce an illiterate official figures who has bought his post, and when he takes his place on the bench a woman presents a petition to him which he cannot read. He hands it to his secretary who is no better placed, and finally a poor scholar is sent for to read the document—who furthermore earns the support of the magistrate by marrying the petitioner whom otherwise he would not have known how to dispose of!

The flash-point for a rebellion is not necessarily that of maximum economic distress, as historians of the French Revolution realize when-ever they make a fresh attempt to explain the causes of that great up-heaval. At the same time, economic depression undoubtedly prepares the way for other forces to operate, and such depression existed in China in the last years of the nineteenth century. The blame for this state of affairs has been attributed to a number of causes—inefficient flood control, faulty administration, the failure of the Manchus to maintain some hundreds of thousands of square miles of land appropriated by them at the time of conquest in production, absentee landlordism, and the ruin of China's domestic industries consequent upon the importation of foreign manufactures.

The penetration of foreign economic power into China from 1842 onwards had put increasing pressure on China's domestic industries, and unemployment gradually increased owing to the importation (at privileged tariffs) of foreign manufactures. Furthermore, heavy taxation was required to support the troops employed in fighting domestic and foreign wars and to pay indemnities to foreign nations. After the wars were over, insecurity increased. Defeated troops became vagabonds, and those who were merely disbanded were left without adequate support. Moreover, especially in the northern provinces, for more than twenty years after 1875, no single year was free from natural catastrophe such as great floods and droughts, with which the administrative resources of the Manchu government were inadequate to cope.

The outstanding governmental feature of the period from 1861 until the end of the century was the rise to power of the Empress Dowager, Tz'ŭ Hsi.

When, in 1861, the Hsien Fêng emperor died in Jehol, he had had no son by his wife (who was later known as the Eastern Empress), but by his concubine, Yehonala (later known as the Western Empress or the Empress Dowager Tz'ŭ Hsi), he had one son named Tsai-ch'un. When the latter was five years old he was made heir apparent in accordance with his father's last will. During the child-emperor's minority affairs of State were entrusted to a regency of eight persons with Su-shun at its head, as provided for in the late emperor's will. The will provided, however, that before issuing decrees the eight were to obtain the consent of the two dowager empresses. Later this will was condemned as a forgery (which, says Li Chien-nung, was possibly true as the Hsien Fêng emperor was so swayed by favourites).[1] Adopting the forgery theory, Su-shun and his colleagues ignored the provision regarding reference of decrees to the two dowager empresses and conducted the government on their own authority.

This led to counteraction on the part of the two dowager empresses —no doubt on the instigation of the Western Empress, who was much the more enterprising of the two. A coup was thereupon planned. By a secret decree, Prince Kung was made prince-counsellor, and Su-shun and his colleagues were arrested. Su-shun was decapitated immediately, while two of his senior colleagues were granted the privilege of committing suicide. Henceforth the two empresses listened to State affairs 'from behind the screens', assisted by Prince Kung, who served as prince-counsellor. Prince Kung, however, was kept strictly in his place. When, in 1874, the child-Emperor had just reached the legal age at which he could govern by himself, he died.

It has frequently been explained that *T'ung Chih*, 'Coeval Rule', the reign-title of the Emperor Mu-tsung, signified the coeval rule of the two dowager empresses, but this is apparently not the case. Wên-hsiang, a Grand Councillor and pivotal figure of the new government, explained to Sir Francis Wade that the characters were taken from the *Shu Ching*, and expressed the belief that China's officers and people were alike in desiring '*t'ung* kwei yü *chih*', to return to (or, see restored) *together* a state of order.[1]

The T'ung Chih emperor had left no heir—though his consort was believed to be with child. Nor had he a brother. Immediately after his death, but before it was publicly announced, Tz'ŭ Hsi summoned a meeting of the princes, the grand councillors, and members of the household, and in face of considerable opposition manœuvred the meeting into selecting as the T'ung Chih emperor's successor Tsai-t'ien, the son of Prince I-huan by Tz'ŭ Hsi's youngest sister, then three years of age. Since the boy was the first cousin of the late emperor and therefore of the same generation, he could not be adopted as his son to carry out the filial worship. Had some person qualified for adoption been selected, T'ung Chih would be considered to have an adoptive heir and his widow would have become the dowager empress, thus forcing Tz'ŭ Hsi and the Empress of the East into the background. The title selected for the new reign was 'Kuang Hsü' ('Glorious Succession').

'Glorious' or not, the succession of Tsai-t'ien violated the dynastic laws of succession, and this illegality made the young Emperor the virtual puppet of his aunt, who now became his adoptive mother. The two empresses thereupon resumed their regency. In 1881 the Eastern Empress died, according to Yün Yü-ting's account, poisoned by

Tz'ŭ Hsi,[1] thus removing the latter's nominal colleague and leaving her supreme.

In 1889 the Kuang Hsü emperor was married, and theoretically assumed personal control of governmental affairs, but in practice he still had to report all appointments and administrative matters to Tz'ŭ Hsi for decision. In general, the Court after 1862 was Tz'ŭ Hsi's Court, and the power of the chief eunuch gradually surpassed that of the princes and grand councillors.

In the late spring and early summer of 1898 (as we shall see in chapter v) the Kuang Hsü emperor, now twenty-six years of age, embarked on a programme of radical reform—at first with Tz'ŭ Hsi's approval, but later incurring her enmity. On 21 September the Empress staged a *coup d'état*, the Emperor was imprisoned, and Tz'ŭ Hsi assumed direct control of State affairs. Then ensued a period of reaction, culminating in the Boxer movement of 1900.

The Chinese official system, which allowed no condition of the body politic to remain, in theory at least, unprovided with means for its control, included among its administrative rules a complete scheme of ecclesiastical gradations of rank and authority in connection with the priesthood of both the Buddhist religion and the Taoist order. At the same time, the Imperial institutes refrained from interference with the internal organization of either of these bodies.[2]

In every district, department, and prefecture throughout the empire, two office-bearers called 'Superiors' (*Sêng Lü Ssŭ*) were appointed by the local government authority for the Buddhist religion, by selection from among the leading abbots, subject to the approval of the provincial government. They acted as the medium of communication between the secular authorities and the priesthood, for whose good conduct they were responsible and over whom they exercised certain judicial powers.

For the control of the Taoist priesthood a similar organization was provided, centring in the patriarch or hereditary chief of the order, the Heavenly Master Chang (*Chang T'ien Shih*), in whose person the spirit of one of the earliest of the Taoist mystics was reputed to reside.

While severely punishing heterodoxy when it took a seditious or rebellious form (as we shall see in chapter vii), the emperors were at pains to cultivate the Buddhist and Taoist deities when they manifested dutiful devotion to the throne. An example of this was in 1828, after the repression of the Muslim rebellion under Changkihur, when the

2-2

Tao Kwang emperor issued a decree approving the Taoist God of War, declaring that 'ever since the tripod of our dynasty was firmly established, his majesty Kuan Ti has often gloriously displayed spiritual divine aid', and again, when, in 1855, Kuan Ti again fought on the side of the Imperial troops, the Tao Kwang emperor decreed that the same divine honours should be paid to him as were paid to Confucius.

From this it will be clear that the Emperor was hostile towards heterodoxy only when it was seditious: when it was loyal it was approved.

The Manchus had owed their success to internal disorder and dissension among their enemies as much as to their superior military skill. Their military forces had in Manchuria been an organization of the whole population and when they moved into China they became an inner core of garrison forces, being stationed for the most part in Peking and the key provinces of China proper. The force, which originally numbered about 186,000 men (Parker)[1] was not strong enough either to conquer or to garrison the huge territory of China, and the Manchus had to rely from the beginning, therefore, on the extensive use of Chinese auxiliary forces which went over to their side.

The original Manchu troops were known as the 'Eight Banners' (three of them being of higher caste than the others). Some of the Chinese auxiliaries were, together with many Mongol recruits, incorporated into the Eight Banners which eventually numbered twenty-four though they were generally referred to by their original number. These were divided into three groups—Manchus, Mongols, and Chinese. The Eight Banners constituted a hereditary army; every adult male had a right to be enrolled as a soldier, and by virtue of his enrolment to draw rations (that is, his allowance of tribute rice) whether on active service or not.

In addition there was a much larger force composed partly of the regular Ming garrison forces and partly of the volunteers and local corps that had been organized during the chaotic years of the rebellion in China and the invasion from the north.

Once the victory was won, the main task of the Ch'ing government was to bring these forces under centralized control. A careful system of checks and balances was introduced to make the 'Green Standard' (*Lü Ying*) as these extra-banner troops were called, a part of the central administration.[2] They were subdivided into land and sea forces, and were charged with a large variety of police, conservancy, and other duties rather than purely military ones. Indeed, accustomed as we are in Europe to a purely fighting army, the list of responsibilities imposed upon the Green Standard makes them appear to us rather like a huge constabulary.[1] The appointment of the senior officers and the over-all responsibility was divided between the governor-general, governor, and provincial military commanders, Manchu general, and the *Ping Pu*, or Board of War. In the late nineteenth century the Banners totalled about 200,000–220,000 men while the Green Standard was estimated at between 500,000 and 600,000.[2] But a considerable proportion of these troops existed only on paper, for the officers drew the pay of the missing men. It was a common practice for the officers to keep spare uniforms into which vagabonds and unemployed were inserted whenever there was an inspection by the higher command.[3]

S. Wells Williams (writing about 1847) remarks:

The singular subordination of military to civil power, which has distinguished Chinese policy, makes the study of the army, as at present constituted, a very interesting feature of national history, for while it has often proved inefficient to repress insurrections and defend the people against brigandage, it has never been used to destroy their institutions.[4]

The upshot of the war with Britain was to demonstrate without a shadow of doubt the fact that the Chinese military structure was utterly outmoded. Yet the Manchu government scarcely seemed to realize it— they resorted still to the old devices of delay to avoid the recognition of European power and did nothing for the next twenty years to bring their army and navy up to date. A further defeat, this time at the hands of allied British and French forces, reduced them to diplomatic submission and led to what has become known as the 'T'ung Chih Restoration'—with what effects on the modernization of armed forces will in a moment be discussed.

The military reorganization undertaken by Marquis Tsêng Kuo-fan to meet the Taiping threat constitutes an important chapter in Chinese military history. The original Taiping forces numbered only 30,000 men, but by the time they captured Nanking this total had grown to 3,000,000, organized from many different social groups—secret and religious societies, as well as charcoal-burners, miners, and other economic malcontents. But while the Taipings created several larger integrated armies out of their local corps, they did not succeed in creating one unified military force with interchangeable military commands, nor did they obtain complete control over appointments.

The position of the Heavenly King, Hung Hsiu-ch'üan, as leader of the whole movement, was a sorry one, for he increasingly became a puppet of the military leaders. Nevertheless, for the Manchu government the whole question of the military defence became acute. It was soon shown that the Green Standard was even less capable of defending the government than it had been in previous uprisings, while in some of the early battles the local corps made a good showing. In its plight, the government not only accepted this kind of local defence but began to rely heavily upon it. It was seen that only a new kind of force would be of any avail, and this was the militia which Tsêng Kuo-fan created by transforming the local corps into one large military organization. Officers were drawn from those gentry committed to the reform; the men were recruited, not from the ranks of the unemployed, but from the hardy and loyal peasantry, especially from the mountain villages, and, above all, Tsêng saw to it that they were well paid—four times the pay which soldiers in the regular army were supposed to receive, but did not. As with the Taipings, a severe ideology gave these forces their moral strength, and in their case it was Confucianism. The militia achieved its purpose (aided, to a limited extent, by foreign-led units such as Ward's, and later Gordon's, 'Ever-Victorious Army'), but it was at the cost of the government having to surrender its military and financial authority to the new regional military leaders who became the governors and governors-general of the threatened provinces. 'This [says Franz Michael] meant decisive and lasting shifts in the Chinese structure, resulting in repercussions down to the present day.' Ho Ping-ti remarks:

After a militia was organized in Hunan in 1852, the name pao-chia[1] became almost identical with t'uan-lien, which literally means 'grouping and drill'. It is true that in order to organize t'uan lien there had to be some sort of population registration, but the purpose of registration was mainly the detection of the lawless elements among the local populace and the enlistment of able-bodied adult males for militia service. The shift of emphasis in pao-chia function is nowhere better reflected than in a famous collection of political and economic essays and memorials of the late Ch'ing period in which pao-chia was classified under 'military affairs'.[2]

After the suppression of the Taipings, the Green Standard might have been disposed of with a stroke of the pen and China would not have been any the worse off as regards defence, but the Manchu government nevertheless decided to retain them as being the only troops over which they still had any direct control. Henceforth the local militia and the Green Standard troops existed side by side. Even after the *débâcle* of 1894, when the foreign-trained troops of the militia had, like the rest of the army, fled before the Japanese, it was still decided to retain the Green Standard. To the proposal to dissolve them it was answered that the 'vested rights, even of soldiers, must be considered' (no doubt on the Chinese principle of 'never breaking a man's rice bowl'), and, moreover, if they were not retained, there would be no one to maintain even elementary order in the country towns, to check smugglers, to guard city gates, to escort processions and dignitaries, and to watch passes, fords, and other pivotal points on the lines of communication. But it was decided as a compromise to do away with a quarter or a half of the Green Standard in every province according to the degree of corruption existing in each place. A considerable part of the troops continued to exist only on paper. Apart from the otiose bannermen ('idle, filthy, opium-smoking parasites, who had even neglected to keep up their archery', Parker calls them), the military forces of the empire consisted of (*a*) the ineffective army under military command, and (*b*) the effective army under civilian command. The effective army, such as it was, was under the direct command of the civil authority and was quite outside the official military organization of the empire and the provinces. There was little military force, then, remaining to keep the rickety empire together.

E. H. Parker describes the Chinese army as it was in the last part of the century:

[The Chinese army] was simply a rabble provided with bags of rice, gay flags, umbrellas, fans, rusty guns, gingalls, spears, heavy swords, and (very occasionally) fairly good rifles and cartridges of a date always behind the times. If there was time and money, hired coolies carried the provision bags and the arms, while the soldiers carried the umbrellas, opium-pipes, and fans. If matters were urgent, the soldiers carried all. There was never any medical staff, not even bandages, and (if the warrior did not slink away before shooting began) he hopped off, when wounded, to die or recover in the nearest ditch. His pay was always a doubtful quantity, but he did not mind that much, so long as he was allowed to plunder the people he was marching to defend. When not on the march, entrenching himself, or trying to 'start' the enemy on the run, he spent his time smoking, gambling, or prowling after women. Discipline of any kind there was none; but if the officers were insulted, heads went off in no time; in all other matters officers were disposed to be easy, so long as the men were not too curious about accounts, and were ready to cover the commander's flight when the enemy really 'came on'.[1]

Added to the above absurdities, the Chinese soldier of the nineteenth century had a bull's-eye embroidered on the front of his jacket and the character for 'courage' (*yung*) on the back—suggestive details which the European humorists did not fail to exploit. It is not surprising, therefore, that to the martial West the Chinese soldier was a figure of fun.[1]

But Parker is careful to note that the worthlessness of the army was not due to the men.

I have found my Chinese followers [he says] in all provinces invariably true and staunch to me in times of danger, and I should not hesitate to lead a Chinese force, properly armed and brought into shape under my supervision, against any European troops in existence. The Chinese have not the fighting instinct—that is they do not relish coming to blows just for the fun of the thing—but they are not afraid of death, and they have no little honest pride, gratitude, kindness, and sympathy, with brave and disinterested leaders, such as Gordon.

Andrew Wilson, the historian of Gordon and his 'Ever-Victorious Army' (who had had personal experience in the field) says:

The old notion is pretty well got rid of that they [the Chinese] are a cowardly people when properly paid and efficiently led, while the regularity and order of their habits give place to a daring bordering on recklessness in time of war. Their intelligence and capacity for remembering facts makes them fitted for use in modern warfare, as do also the coolness and calmness of their disposition. . . . Their wants are few; they have no caste prejudice and hardly any appetite for intoxicating liquors. . . . Physically they are on the average not so strong as Europeans, but considerably more than most races of the East: and on a cheap diet of rice, vegetables, salt fish, and pork they can go through a vast amount of fatigue, whether in a temperate climate or a tropical one, where Europeans are ill-fitted for exertion. . . . As sappers, the Chinese are equal to any Europeans.[2]

Regarding the potentiality of the Chinese as officers, Gordon said that his colleague, General Ching, would compare as a leader with any European.

The root of the trouble lay in the rottenness and obtuseness of the higher command—more fundamentally, in the corrupted state of Chinese society.

Owing to the ineffectiveness of the Banners and the Green Standard in national defence and in preserving internal order, the militia more and more assumed their duties. The latter was (as we have said) not responsible to the Board of War, which was not even aware of its strength. The militia now took over from the Green Standard the garrisoning of the larger cities and strategic points. Hence the organized and active section of it became known as the Defence Army (*Fang Chün*), and, in effect, was now the regular army of China.

Faced with this development, it was natural that the central government should seek for some means of counterbalancing the power which the control of the militia placed in the hands of individual subjects of the Emperor. As early as 1865 the Boards of War and Revenue discussed the selection and training of six disciplined Green Standard 'armies' (that is, divisions) in Chihli. The outcome of this discussion was the establishment of what became known as the Disciplined Forces (*Lien Chün*). The organization was copied from the Hunan and Anhwei armies, and their pay was the same. These troops were also used for garrisoning cities and strategic centres. Thus China now possessed two selected corps, the *Fang Chün* and the *Lien Chün*. In 1894 the functions of the militia and the regular troops were delimited in an Imperial edict—the former was to suppress rebellions, and the latter was to put down brigandage and piracy. The more difficult task of protecting the throne was imposed upon the militia, and thus it was that the throne's safety depended on the loyalty and good will of the gentry, and especially of the few 'feudal chiefs'. But the defence of the country from foreign attack was not mentioned. Who was to take care of that?

It must be clear by now that, in default of a fundamental reorganization of Chinese society and at least a measure of industrialization, attempts made at 'modernization' were bound to be piecemeal and superficial. A few scattered units were equipped with foreign-style rifles and artillery, but by 1880 the process had gone no further than this. In the Franco–Chinese War of 1884–5 (notable for the success of a Chinese force against the French at the battle of Longsan) some modern coastal forts were built. At the time of the Sino–Japanese War (1894–5), the Japanese staff estimated that only three-fifths of the Chinese troops mobilized against them were armed with some kind of rifle, the remainder having to make do with a pike, spear, or sword.

But if the modernizing of the Chinese armed forces was neither fundamental nor in any real degree adequate to meet the situation, it nevertheless was continuous, and the seeds of the future expansion of the army were sown in these decades. The most important departure was the employment of foreign personnel to train Chinese troops. Already in 1872 and 1876, Li Hung-chang had sent Chinese officers to

Germany for training, and from time to time French and German officers were employed to train a portion of the armies. But a real start at systematic training did not take place until 1885, when, on General Gordon's advice, Li Hung-chang established a military preparatory school at Tientsin, employing German instructors. Shortly afterwards, Chang Chih-tung founded a military academy near Canton. By 1894, too, there were 'arsenals'—or at least machine-shops—in nine centres. Yet at the same factories where modern arms were, or could be, made the Chinese continued to manufacture gingals and muskets![1]

Nor were the sea forces entirely forgotten. Under the inspiration of the same leaders who were attending to the land forces, an 'Admiralty' was established in 1885, and three years later the Northern, or Peiyang, Squadron was organized. This was a respectable fleet of twenty-eight ships, but its growth was speedily stunted and its maintenance starved by the fact that in 1888 the Empress Dowager diverted a large sum from the naval appropriations to the repair of the summer palace.[2]

Then, in 1894, came the Sino–Japanese War. The disastrous defeat suffered by China can be summarized in a paragraph. War broke out in Korea in July, but it was not until 1 August that it was officially declared. In mid-September the heavily fortified city of Pingyang (Pyongyang) fell to the Japanese. Li Hung-chang's troops retired beyond the Yalu river, pursued by the Japanese, who forced them to retreat across Southern Manchuria. In late October, a second Japanese army effected a landing on the Liaotung peninsula. The great fort of Dairen fell after a one-day attack. This was followed, on 21 November, by the surrender of Port Arthur, the 'Gibraltar of the East'. In Shantung, the Japanese were successful with the same ease—except that Weihaiwei, the haven of the Chinese Northern Squadron, held out until 12 February, being defended by the Chinese fleet. The Treaty of Shimonoseki on 17 April 1895 brought the war to a close.

The one episode that was in any way creditable to the Chinese arms was the way in which, at the naval battle off the Yalu river in September 1894, the Chinese fleet, although short of ammunition, fought on until dark before withdrawing (owing to the peculations of Li Hung-chang's son-in-law, Chang Pei-hua, China's two ironclads had only three heavy shells between them when they went into action). The gallant Chinese Admiral Ting thereupon committed suicide.

The Chinese *débâcle* in the Sino–Japanese War was the event which set in train the scramble of the Powers to gain advantages in the antici-

pated dismemberment of China known as the 'Battle of the Concessions' and which precipitated the Reform Movement in the 'Hundred
Days' of 1898 (see chapter IV), and those in turn prepared the ground
for, if they did not actually bring about, the Boxer Uprising of 1900.

A by-product of the Chinese defeat was the attempt made, at long
last, to create military units which really were modelled faithfully on
Western practice and were not mere adaptations of the Green Standard
or the militia to suit a semi-petrified Confucian society. These were the
Self-strengthening Army of Chang Chih-tung and the Pacification
Army, to be commanded, from December 1895, by Yüan Shih-k'ai.

Chang Chih-tung (1837–1909) was a scholar of the old school, and
a civilian who had entered the service by the 'Front Door' (not
through the militia). Unlike Yuan Shih-k'ai and others, he had held no
military command. His enthusiasm for military reform arose, not from
any admiration for the Western 'way of life', but from a conviction of
its necessity to protect the established order of things. More than most
of his contemporaries, he realized the need for an industrial and
military establishment, but like other educated Chinese (and Manchus,
such as the Empress Dowager) the limitations of Chinese knowledge
of the outside world sometimes gave him the appearance of *naïveté*.
Such was the case when, during the Sino–Japanese War, he commissioned Yung Wing (Jung Hung, 1828–1912) (the first 'returned
student' from America) to secure a foreign loan for the purpose of
hiring a body of mercenaries to launch an attack from the west coast
of the United States to strike Japan in the rear (it was Sir Robert Hart
and Li Hung-chang who blocked this highly unpractical scheme).[1]
But in planning his Self-strengthening Army he demonstrated that he
was both shrewd and unafraid of innovation.

The Self-strengthening Army consisted of eight battalions of
infantry, two squadrons of cavalry, two brigades of artillery, and one
company of engineers—all equipped in the style of European armies.
Thirty-five German officers and N.C.O.'s, headed by Major Baron von
Reitzenstein, were employed to train the new troops. Until Chinese
could be trained, the commanding officers of each unit were to be
Germans. But responsibility for discipline and punishment was to
remain in the hands of the Chinese. Instead of drawing on the gaols and
the professional irregulars (*yung*) for men, the mandarins carefully
selected village youths of good health and character—some of whom
were even said to be able to read and write! The pay was good (the

trained soldiers received fifty *yüan* a month),[1] and free rations and quarters were provided. Like the militia, these new armies were not part of the regularly established forces. Although the throne tried to maintain checks upon them, they were to all intents and purposes 'private armies'.

The German instructors soon made themselves unpopular with the local populace on account of their arrogant behaviour, and when a German corporal was wounded in a fracas, two German gunboats were ordered to Nanking. In the summer of 1896, to avoid further incidents, Liu K'un-i, who had relieved Chang Chih-tung in Nanking, transferred the Self-strengthening Army to Woosung.[2]

The second of these new armies was the Pacification Army (*Ting-wu Chün*), or Newly Created Army (*Hsin-chien Lu-chün*). Yüan Shih-k'ai was (as already mentioned) appointed to command it, and, in mid-December 1895, proceeded to Hsiaochan, near Tientsin, to take over the command. The infantry was divided into two 'wings' of two and three battalions each; the artillery was organized into units consisting of a rapid-fire gun, heavy artillery, and a reserve unit and the cavalry arm consisted of four troops: in addition there were bridging, fortifications, ordnance repair, mine-laying, and telegraph detachments. The organization was not strictly in keeping with that of the German army, but, like the Self-strengthening Army, began closely to resemble the armies of the West. Yüan's brigade even had a brass band (whose purpose, perhaps, was rather to terrify the enemy than to reinforce the morale of the troops). The nominal strength was 7000 men.

The Self-strengthening Army and the Pacification Army were the only troops organized on a strictly Western model that the Chinese possessed at the time of the Boxer Uprising and the allied advance on Peking, but, strangely enough, they were non-combatant during the crisis owing to the masterly inactivity of Yüan Shih-k'ai and Chang Chih-t'ung.

Following the Sino–Japanese War, Jung-lu, as President of the Board of War, sought to improve the defences of Peking. He not only assumed responsibility for the Newly Created Army of Yüan Shih-k'ai, but also sponsored the development of the troops of Sung Ch'ing, the Tenacious Army of Nieh Shih-ch'eng, and the 'Kansu Irregulars' of Tung Fu-hsiang. Of these, only the troops of Yüan and Nieh were a real improvement on the backward militia armies. When Nieh weeded out the Anhwei troops to form his Tenacious Army of thirty battalions, he not only copied the German system but employed German instructors as well. In theory his force consisted of 15,000 men, but the actual strength was probably nearer 10,000.[1] His troops were superior to the average Chinese troops, but never reached the standards achieved by those of Yüan Shih-k'ai.

During the Hundred Days of Reform in 1898, the military decrees issued by the Kuang Hsü emperor were in a large measure a restatement of established policy.

A week after the *coup d'état* of September 1898 (see chapter v), Jung-lu, then Governor-General of Chihli, was appointed to the Grand Council, but the edict announcing the change directed that he was to retain command of the Peiyang military forces. Further edicts appointed him President of the Board of War, and commander-in-chief of the troops under Sung Ch'ing, Yüan Shih-k'ai, Nieh Shih-ch'êng, and Tung Fu-hsiang. Jung-lu then proceeded to reorganize the four armies (now divisions) under his control as an army corps to be known as the Guards Army (*Wu-wei Chün*). A new Centre Division was formed, and the Guards Army now consisted of the Left, Right, Front, Rear, and Centre divisions. In addition to the Guards Army, the other troops in the Peiyang area numbered about 30,000.

The new Centre Division, under Jung-lu's direct command, consisted largely of Manchu bannermen. After formation, the unit was stationed at Nanyüan, south of Peking, and although its authorized strength was 10,000, its actual numbers were probably considerably less. The Front Division, the old Tenacious Army of Nieh Shih-ch'êng, was stationed at Lutai near Tientsin, and late in 1899 it consisted of 10,000 men. The division was well equipped with Mauser rifles, Maxim machine-guns, and various types of artillery, but its discipline was poor. The Left Division, the Resolute Army, under Sung Ch'ing, probably consisted of 10,000 men (nominal strength 20,000). Its weapons were similar to those of the Front Division. The Rear Division, commanded by Tung Fu-hsiang, had formerly been called the 'Kansu Irregulars'. This unit was a disorderly rabble of about 10,000 men, most of whom were Muslims. The Right Division, stationed at Hsiaochun, was Yüan Shih-k'ai's command, now called the Newly Created Army, by far the best unit of the Guards' Army.

In addition to the Guards' Army (total strength about 30,000–40,000 men), the other troops in the Peiyang area numbered about 30,000.[2]

During 1898–9, a widespread, but small-scale, reorganization of the provincial military units also took place under the 'Conservative Reform' edicts of the Empress Dowager—a final attempt to protect the old with the new. But when, in the autumn of 1898, Rear-Admiral Lord Charles Beresford visited China on a mission from the Associated Chambers of Commerce of Great Britain, and inspected all but three of the 'so-called armies', he recorded his opinion that by Western standards Yüan Shih-k'ai's troops were the only completely equipped force in the empire.[1] Otherwise, he found that the Chinese armies were poorly led, badly paid, and deficient in discipline and training.

Beresford gives the strength of Yüan's army as 7400 men, mostly from Shantung. They were armed with Mauser rifles made in Germany. Yüan also had ten six-gun batteries, throwing projectiles from 1 to 6 lb. His cavalry were armed with lances and a Mauser infantry rifle. Beresford thought the men smart and of exceptionally fine physique.

On 1 November 1898 the ancient military examinations, including archery, swordsmanship, and weight-lifting, which had been abolished in the Hundred Days, were re-established by an edict of the Empress Dowager. The excuse she gave in the edict for re-establishing them was that they were only a 'formality'. At the same time, she directed the holders of the two lowest military degrees not serving with the provincial forces to be sent to the foreign-style military academies which were to be established in the provinces. Also, all the military degree-holders were required to learn how to employ firearms as well as bows and swords.

The details of the military promotion examinations are on record. The practical test was in three parts—archery on horseback, on foot, and exercises in gymnastic art, brandishing the cutlass, lifting the weight, etc. The fourth part consisted in writing from memory a paragraph from the classic on the art of war (*Sun Tzŭ Ping Fa*, fourth century B.C.). Father Etienne Zi, the Jesuit author of the *Pratique des Examens Militaires*, wrote in his preface of 1895: 'One may object that physical force and the bow and arrow have lost their preponderating share in battles, and since they are not likely to recover it in the near future, an examination in the use of the rifle and cannon would be more logical.'[2] But no, the age-old formula had to be repeated, and finally the candidate had to write out from memory a passage indicated from the military classic of Sun Tzŭ.

In 1660 the gymnastic exercises were abolished but were restored by the K'ang Hsi emperor; the Chia Ch'ing emperor abolished the cutlass exercises; they were restored by his successor of the Tao Kuang period; in 1807 the Chia Ch'ing emperor decreed that the candidate should write 100 characters from memory instead of having to write an original essay on some military subject. (This was probably the Chia Ch'ing emperor's only military reform.)

On his way home from 'covering' the Boxer affair (as journalists would now say), George Lynch, the war correspondent, went to Canton and saw the Chinese troops there 'practising with bows and arrows at targets when riding on horseback at the full gallop...and taking apparently as much interest in this practice of archery as they did in rifle practice'.[1] This was a month or two after the conclusion of the 'Boxer War'.

CHAPTER II

CHINESE SOCIETY DURING THE LATE CH'ING PERIOD

What was the nature of the society in which the Boxer Uprising took place, and what were the forces operating within it which tended to be favourable or otherwise to rebellion?

Whether the traditional Chinese system should be known, as it is by the founding fathers of Marxism, as the 'Asiatic form of production', or as a 'feudal bureaucratism', or as a 'bureaucratic feudalism', it was certainly very different from anything that Europe ever knew. The *shih*, or scholar-bureaucrats, were peculiar to China and remained the managerial class for two millennia. They were the non-hereditary *élite* in a 'non-acquisitive' society which was inimical to the development of capitalism.

The mandarinate system was so successful that it inhibited the rise of merchants to power in the State, it walled up their guilds in the restricted role of friendly and benefit societies, it nipped capitalist accumulation in the bud... it creamed off for 2000 years the best brains from all levels of society into its own service.[1]

Chinese society has been characterized as 'immobile', but this is incorrect. It has changed very considerably at different epochs, though at periods—certainly in the late nineteenth century—conservatism and the appeal to the past might seem to the uninstructed observer to be due merely to *vis inertiae.*

Among modern students of Chinese society there has been a keen discussion as to the degree of social mobility that existed. Certainly families rose into the estate of the scholar-gentry at all periods, and sank out of it again. On the other hand, the mandarinate appears not to have been quite as 'classless' as has often been stated by nineteenth-century observers, and even in the best and most open periods, boys from learned homes which had good private libraries had a great advantage over the others.

There have not lacked internal critics of Chinese society from Confucius onwards, but up to the end of the nineteenth century these critics as a body attributed the shortcomings of contemporary society to its departure from the standards of China's 'Golden Age', when, under the emperors Yao and Shun, the people enjoyed perfect happiness. They never judged their society by its failure to 'progress'. K'ang Yu-wei was the first 'Utopian' writer. Even the great eighteenth-century novels, *The Dream of the Red Chamber* (*Hung Lou Mêng*) and *The Scholars* (*Ju Lin Wai Shih*), the first a penetrating criticism of the family and marriage system, and the second a satire on the civil service and examinations, inferred that the abuses attacked were in origin due to the neglect of the principles enunciated by the Sage and his disciples—never to the inadequacy of these principles. For this reason, until after the impact of the West, China had never experienced a 'revolution' in the Western sense of the word.

Confucianism was the religion of society *par excellence*; it laid down with minute precision the rules for all social relationships, and since the critics did not dream of questioning its authority there was no room for anything resembling the objective approach of Western social science. Chinese writers generally (and without meaning to) have provided much of the data necessary to social scientists, but it was not until the second and third decades of the present century that Chinese sociologists began to take part in the work of scientific observation and analysis.

The European observers of China, when they came, were not objective or scientific either. They judged Chinese society by the standards of their own, and as many of them were Christian missionaries, they looked only for those things which favoured or impeded their mission. But at least they did look at Chinese society from the *outside*, unconditioned by Confucian assumptions.

A contemporary American sociologist says of these foreign observers:

The main failings of the early works can be summed up, beginning with the lack of objectivity already noted. Most of the writers were missionaries or at least highly self-conscious Christians; in certain areas of behaviour they found it impossible to avoid moralizing. Invariably their attitudes led to faulty reporting and interpretation. Early writers generally failed to specify the sources of their information and we are seldom told to what localities their descriptions apply. Often the writer will blithely include within a single paragraph data drawn from the four corners of the empire.... Also excepting only the most obvious acknowledgement of differences between rich and poor, there is no presentation of the variation in a culture trait that occurs when different classes occupy a common area.... There is no concept of an operating community in the early works; no picture emerges of places that really existed in time and space. Ultimately, the major drawback, which is at the root of other faults, is the absence of a functional approach....[1]

The point, so far as our present inquiry is concerned, is that neither native nor foreign observers were preoccupied with the questions that interest either the modern Western sociologist or the Chinese Marxist seeking to interpret the past in terms of his theories, and when the earlier writers offer information on these questions it is purely incidental and has to be isolated from the remainder of their texts.

Both Marxist and non-Marxist observers have detected in Chinese society of the nineteenth century the existence of class distinctions which were to be the cause of future conflict and rebellion. But to isolate these classes in reading works of the period is not very easy. Indeed, in defence of these nineteenth-century writers from the criticism levelled against them by the modern sociologist quoted above, I would say that in extensive journeys through the Chinese countryside and villages in various parts of China thirty to forty years ago, I did not become aware that 'class' in the economic sense was an important element in the politics of the country, for the poverty was so universal and the share in it seemed so uniform there was apparently no room for friction between 'classes' on the score of the unequal distribution of wealth. This was, of course, a superficial judgment which took no account of the fact that the larger landlords were mostly 'absentee' and enjoyed their real or comparative riches while residing in the towns or the treaty ports. Yet there was some excuse for this impression of equality for, as a modern Chinese historian remarks: 'Because of the general economic backwardness of China, there were no sharply defined castes or classes; there was little struggle of interests between different castes. Political parties were entirely monopolized by the intelligentsia.'[2]

Before turning to the more up-to-date studies of Chinese society, let us glance for a moment at the works of three outstanding foreign observers of the 'pre-scientific' period, keeping as near as we can to the Boxer Uprising—namely those of Sir R. K. Douglas, A. H. Smith, and E. H. Parker.

Douglas, the son of a Church of England clergyman, was a member of the British Consular Service in China from 1858 to 1865, and thereafter was Keeper of the Oriental Books and Manuscripts in the British Museum. His actual experience of China, therefore, belongs to an earlier period, but his book, *Society in China*, was published in 1894 and was intended to be up to date. A. H. Smith, a missionary of the American Board, had been in China for thirty years when his book, *Village Life in China*, was published in 1899.[1] Parker's book, *China: her History, Diplomacy and Commerce*, was published in 1901, after the author had spent over twenty-five years in the China Consular Service of Great Britain and had been retired for only a few years. The first two had missionary sympathies; Parker was very critical of the missionaries, though himself a Christian.

To take Parker first. He considered that China was 'one vast democracy'.[2] The whole social system was one of give-and-take, and every man, be he squeezer, middle-man, or squeezed, had, or hoped to have, a finger in the pie. There was no snobbery in China, though there was plenty of priggishness. Any peasant or greengrocer might buy his way up, and no Chinese was ashamed of his poor relations. There was a sort of live-and-let-live feeling all round. There were no passports, no restraints on liberty, no frontiers, no caste prejudices, no food scruples, no sanitary measures, no laws except popular customs and criminal statutes. China was in many senses one vast republic, in which personal restraints had no existence. The Manchus, as the ruling race, had certainly a few privileges, but, on the other hand, they suffered just as many disabilities. Barbers, play-actors, and policemen were under a mild taboo—more theoretical than real; but aboriginal 'barbarians' might easily become Chinese by reading books and putting on breeches. All men were equal before the Emperor, and all had a fairly equal chance of his smiles and his frowns. The only thing to do was to adhere to custom, and not to overdo things—above all to respect the person of the Emperor as represented by the official uniform (always worn in public) of a mandarin, be he great or small. There was on the whole no jealousy or class feeling in the country: it was simply a question of big fish feeding on little fish, unless and until the little fish could keep out of the way, eat their way up, and become big fish themselves.

Parker allows that there was bribery and corruption at Peking as well as in the provinces, but the solid basis of government was not really bad. From his experience of Chinese officials he would say that the majority of them were no worse than American political 'bosses'— that is, mere 'hacks of a corrupt growth'. Purchase of official rank, and even of office, had been sadly on the increase since China began to get into trouble with rebels and Europeans; even then, though higher office could no longer be bought, the office of *hsien* (district magistrate) might be purchased, and many even higher brevets were on sale. But most magistrates obtained their offices because they had passed high in the examinations, because their parents had served the State well, or because they themselves had earned preferment by special services or efforts of one kind or other.

But once he had obtained his appointment through whatever channel, the magistrate's first care was to repay himself the expense of working for his post and getting it; the next was to feather his nest and to prepare the way for future advancement. His most profitable source of gain was in the collection of the land-tax. The Board at Peking never asked for more than the regulation amount of this, and was uncommonly glad to see even 'eight-tenths' of it paid. By means of juggling with silver rates and copper cash rates (A. H. Smith shows that an official 'hundred' cash ranged between 50 and 80 from province to province), drawing harrowing pictures of local disasters and poverty, by legerdemain in counting and measuring, and charging fees for the receipts, notices, tickets, attendances, and what not, it had come about in course of time that the actual amount of the land-tax collected was anything between twice and four times the legal amount. But the magistrate did not get all the difference for himself since many of his superiors had to be squared in a decorous way.

Then there was the administration of justice. Every magistrate had an entourage of rogues (usually hereditary)—runners, collectors, lictors, and police—for whose maintenance he could rarely afford to pay, and these lived on the 'squeeze' they exacted from witnesses subpoenaed by the Court. Moreover, every *yamen* had hovering in the vicinity a vulture-like multitude of champerty-and-maintenance men who were hand-in-glove with the police. The amount of tyranny and villainy varied in each district with each magistrate.[1]

These are only a tithe of the bribes, douceurs, and produce of blackmail which Parker enumerates as 'indispensable units in the huge structure of corruption (if that be the right term) which was co-extensive with Chinese society'.

A. H. Smith seems at first to confirm Parker's estimate of China as being 'one vast democracy' when in his chapter on 'Village Headmen'[2] he says, 'the management of the village is in the hands of the people themselves', but he qualifies this by adding:

At first this condition of affairs was liable to be mistaken for pure democracy, but very slight enquiry was sufficient to make it evident that while all matters of local concern were theoretically managed by the people, in practice the burden fell, not upon the people as a whole, but upon the shoulders of a few persons, who in different places were called by different titles and whose functions differed as much as their designations.

And earlier he says, 'In China the power is in the hands of the learned and the rich'.[1]

Every Chinese village (says Smith) was a little principality in itself, although it was not uncommon for two or more which were contiguous and perhaps otherwise linked together to manage their affairs in unison, and perhaps using the same set of persons. These headmen were sometimes styled village elders (*hsiang chang*, or *hsiang lao*), and sometimes they were termed merely managers (*shou shih jên*). The theory in regard to these persons was that they were chosen, or rather nominated, by their fellow-townsmen and confirmed in their position by the district magistrate. In some regions this was actually the case, and for the good conduct of the headmen in their office the leading landowners were required to become a security. But in regions where the method of selection was loosest the headmen 'drop into their places—or perhaps climb into them—by a kind of natural selection'. The village elders or managers were not necessarily the oldest men in the village, nor were they necessarily the wealthiest men, though it was probable that every family of property would in some way be represented among them. Nor were they necessarily men of literary attainments, though this might be the case with a few.[2]

Smith points out that the government of China, while in theory more or less despotic, placed no practical restrictions upon the right of free assembly of the people for the consideration of their own affairs. They could meet every day in the year if they wished. There was no government official or censor present, and no restriction upon liberty of debate. The people could say what they liked and the local magistrate neither knew nor cared what was said.

The same writer describes the educational system but does not appear to have anything to say regarding the equality of opportunity (or otherwise) of the people to receive an education or to prepare for the public examinations, and this is true also of Parker. They both seem to assume what has so often been repeated, namely that with the exception of a few proscribed classes all Chinese males were able, without distinc-

tion, to present themselves for the public examinations, and, if successful, were eligible for selection for civil service appointments, and in due
course for the highest offices in the empire. Douglas, for his part,
affirms the equality of opportunity, at least for entry to the examinations, quite specifically:

It is true that the sons of actors, executioners, jailers, and outcasts are prohibited from competing; but, with these exceptions, the lists are open to
everybody, and the veriest booby in the affairs of the world may win the
highest distinction, if only he can write prose and compose verses after the
stereotyped models held up for his admiration.[1]

Douglas begins with the family as the unit of Chinese society. The
head of each household held autocratic sway over all the members of
his family. The very lives of his sons and daughters were in his hands,
and if his conduct, however cruel towards his wife, concubines, and
dependants, was not of a kind to outrage the feelings of his brother
elders (and it took a great deal to do this) it was allowed to pass without
attracting the attention of any public judicial authority. An aggrega-
tion of families formed the village community, every member of which
was compelled to comply with the customs of the group to which he
belonged. The manner of farming his allotted land, the way in which he
conducted his business, and his social relations, all came under the
observation and control of the elders of the community. It often
happened that one family became the possessor of an entire village.
Each group of families had a *Ti-pao*, or headman, who was held responsible for the peace and well-being of the neighbourhood, and who
was commonly assisted in his office by the elders of the village or
district. This office not uncommonly descended from father to son.

The analysis which Douglas gives of the 'classes' of Chinese society
is the traditional Chinese one, and is the one followed by European
writers generally without reference to a class stratification of wealth or
hereditary privilege. First of the four Chinese classes was that of the
literati or scholars. They had certain privileges attaching to their order
and were generally recognized by the mandarins as 'brevet' members
of their own rank. They had, under certain conditions, the right of
entrée into the presence of the local officials, and the law forbade that
they should be punished or tortured until they had been stripped of
their degrees by an Imperial edict. As it would be beneath their dignity
to trade, and as there were many thousands more of them than there
were places for them to fill (it was calculated that there were in 1893

21,168 unemployed provincial graduates), the country was burdened with an idle population who were too proud to work but who were not ashamed to live the life of hangers-on to the skirts of those who were better off than themselves.

The farmers, in common estimation, were the next class below the literati. From the earliest times agriculture had been regarded as an ennobling calling and the Emperor, in the early spring of each year, turned a furrow to inaugurate the farming season; an example which was followed in every province by the viceroy or governor. The Empress, likewise, as soon as the mulberry-tree broke into foliage, picked the leaves for the palace silkworms.

Unfortunately, however, the law as it was administered made the farmer poor and kept him poor. The principal Imperial tax was derived from the land and by the law of succession it was generally necessary, on the decease of the head of the family, to subdivide his possessions, which thus became a diminishing quantity to each generation of his heirs. Low grinding poverty was the result, and a large number of crimes were attributable to disputes arising out of inheritance of the land.

The land all belonged to the Emperor, and was leased out to the farmers. As a rule it was leased by a clan, the members of which cultivated it much on the principle of the village communities. Ten families, as a rule, constituted a village holding, each farming about 10 acres. To each community was allotted a village plot, which was cultivated by each family in turn and from this the tribute grain was collected and paid. The surplus, if any, was divided between the families. The land generally was classified according to its position and productiveness, and paid taxes proportionately. Ten shillings an acre was an average rental for the best land. (It had recently been complained, however, in a memorial to the throne, that through faulty administration the tax frequently amounted to six times its nominal assessment.)[1]

Next below the farmers in popular estimation stood the mechanics, who were even poorer than the farmers and lived perpetually on the verge of destitution. And this in spite of their indefatigable industry. Only the rudest tools were at their disposal, yet it never occurred to them to ask for anything better. The labour market was overcrowded. In many cities, Canton, for example, bricklayers and carpenters stood in the streets for hire and might remain unemployed for days on end. Even when employed their wages were ridiculously small compared with the pay of their colleagues in Europe, whose hours of labour were short compared with theirs. A feature of life in China was the number of itinerant craftsmen—tailors, shoemakers, barbers, blacksmiths—who earned their livelihood on the streets.

Lowest of the four social classes stood the merchant or trader. But (says Douglas), however much in theory the Chinese might despise the merchant princes, their intelligence gained them a position of respect, and their riches assured them consideration at the hands of the mandarins, who were never backward in drawing on their overflowing coffers.[1] It was notable that the Chinese novelists, while satirizing the cupidity of the mandarins, the assumptions of the literati, and the viciousness of the monks, generally left the merchants and traders alone. The latter were, for mutual protection and the promotion of trade, organized into guilds, which were presided over by a president assisted by an elected committee and with a secretary who was generally a graduate.

Allied to the merchant guilds were the trade guilds which were roughly analogous to the trades unions of Europe, but their membership was of masters as well as employees. Douglas did not pretend to any inside knowledge of the workings of these guilds, but so far as he could judge their activities tended to promote fair play and a ready kind of justice. Unjust weights or unfairly loaded goods were unhesitatingly condemned, wages and hours were settled by agreement, and apprenticeship was regulated. Strikes were of frequent occurrence, and the victory was commonly with the workmen, except when their claims were manifestly unjust.

The absence of a hereditary aristocracy (concluded Douglas) deprived the Chinese of a most useful and potent link between the crown and its subjects. There was no body of powerful nobles strong enough to resist the encroachments of the sovereign and to moderate and guide the aspirations of the people, and there were no representative institutions. The result was that there was a constant straining and creaking in the social machine which had many a time ended in fierce outbreaks, and not infrequently in the overthrow of dynasties.

A. H. Smith attributed the 'straining and creaking of the social machine' to social and spiritual rather than political and economic causes. He blamed the monotony and vacuity of village life and the unstable equilibrium of the Chinese family for what he termed the oft-repeated 'social typhoons'. Of each Chinese family, he said, 'a full half has had or will have interests at variance with those of the other half'. Every Chinese wife came by no choice of her own from some other family, 'being suddenly and irrevocably grafted as a wild stock on the tree of her husband'. She was not received with enthusiasm, much less with affection (the very idea of which in such a connection never entered any Chinese mind), but at best with mild toleration, and not infrequently with aggressive criticism. She formed a link with another set of interests from which by disruption she had been severed but where her attachments were created. This is where something more than 'filial piety' stepped in, for the affection of most Chinese children for their mothers was very real and lasting. Thus the wife often sought to profit the family she had left at the expense of the one she had joined.

This was only one of the many causes of family disunity—others were the idea of a daughter as 'a commodity-on-which-money-has-been-lost'; the division of the family land among the sons, which in most cases was accompanied by a domestic tempest followed by a hopeless division between brothers, the liability of a family to pay tax on 'empty grain-tax land', which had to be shared; the widespread selfishness and lack of any sense of responsibility to tell the truth in lawsuits; and other defects of the Chinese character. The hereditary habits of the Chinese (says Smith) in the agglomeration of large numbers of individuals under one head constituted a drift towards disunity and disintegration; the strain upon the temper and the disposition incident to the mechanical collocation of so many human beings in one compound-family was more than human nature could bear.

Smith's cure for this state of affairs was neither a political nor an economic one, but the 'regeneration of the Chinese village through Christianity'. Christianity would dispel the impenetrable ignorance which sacrificed so large a proportion of Chinese infants during the first two years of their life, would prevent a girl from being killed as soon as she was born, and would eventually restore her to her rightful place in the affections of her parents, it would revolutionize the Chinese system of education, providing for the intellectual and spiritual needs of girls as well as boys, would tend to a more rational selection of partners, would make no compromise with polygamy and concubinage, would purify and sweeten the Chinese home, and it would do many more things as well.

I have given specimens of the descriptions of Chinese society by the earlier European observers to indicate their scope and to illustrate some of their shortcomings from a scientific point of view.[1]

The first person, it seems, to stress the importance of a scientific study of Chinese civilization was Pierre Laffitte, a disciple of Auguste Comte, in his *Considérations Générales sur l'ensemble de la civilisation Chinoise* (Paris, 1861), and an attempt at a systematic description of Chinese society was made at the beginning of this century by E. T. C. Werner, a member of the Spencer School of Sociology. For the Manchu period he classified the scholars (*shih*) as the first and leading social group, subdivided into officials and gentry. Werner's classification of Chinese social groups was meant as a case-study of a social structure belonging to what his school called the 'Oriental Stage' in the development of societies. This stage, with its rigidity of social status and absence of any 'true liberty', was believed to have kept the societies which had allowed themselves to be trapped into it from further social advancement.

But this first rather crude and schematic attempt at classification of Chinese society by a sociological school was far outdone by the brilliant sociological studies of the German, Max Weber (1864–1920). Says Franz Michael:

In his broad analysis of the interrelationship between ideological and society development, Weber included China as one of his main typological examples. In contrast to the West, where, as Weber saw it, Protestant ethics were suited to a society based on individual zeal and in which they contributed to the development of capitalism, China's Confucian ideology could not, he thought, contribute to such a development.[2]

China was one of the examples of the bureaucratic State in which Weber had a special interest (Franz Michael continues). For him the tendency of bureaucracy to grow by monopolizing the means of governmental power was a phenomenon of general development. In his discussion of bureaucratic development as well as his general theoretical analysis of society, Weber saw the importance of 'technical economic factors' in general as well as the specific question of the control of the means of production. But Weber saw Marxism as an untenable, monocausal theory which could do no justice to the multiplicity of causal relations recognizable in social history. For him Marx had over-dramatized a 'special case', confusing further 'economic', 'economically determined', and 'economically relevant' factors.

Weber made no direct study of Chinese society, however, and had to rely on the work of the European observers such as those quoted above. At the present day, the application of social and economic theory has been taken much further by specialists who have studied the Chinese sources, and among these is K. A. Wittfogel, who has worked out a theory stressing the part played by the ruling bureaucracy in the control of waterworks in economics depending on irrigated culture. This theory holds that in such economics the large public works necessary for irrigation, flood control, and canalization gave this ruling bureaucracy power over the large mass of peasant labour.[1] Wolfram Eberhard has also elaborated a theory in which the 'gentry' are conceived as families—large families with at least one family centre 'which is often kept for more than a thousand years'. But both these writers have so far confined the detailed application of their theories to remote dynasties and do not agree with one another, so that I can take only passing note of these in a background to the Boxer Uprising.

A study relating to the nineteenth century, however, and one which throws great additional light on our inquiry, is that of Chang Chung-li.[2] This study, in place of the desultory and *ad hoc* observations of nineteenth-century European laymen, is conducted on sociological principles and utilizes Chinese official publications, contemporary Chinese writings, gentry biographies and records, and local gazetteers. It is statistical in treatment and is illustrated by a wealth of tables.

Franz Michael's and Chang's use of 'gentry' to describe this essentially Chinese class is open to objection because of its indissoluble association with the English 'gentry'. To begin with, in contrast to the English gentry, membership of the Chinese 'gentry' was not hereditary—entrance had to be gained by each member, and there was a much greater social mobility in China than in England. The Chinese 'gentry' also were not functionally linked to their land. Moreover, the 'hard-living, hard-riding' style of life of the English gentry was in striking contrast to the Chinese ideal of the scholarly life. In China, landowners were not gentry unless they had an academic degree, while graduates were 'gentry' even if they had no land at all. Thus Squire Allworthy, a landowner who happened also to be an Oxford graduate, would be 'gentry' because of the latter fact; Squire Western, who was semi-literate at most, would not qualify for that title; while Dr Johnson (with no land at all) would still be 'gentry' on the strength of his academic degrees.[3]

But notwithstanding the non-hereditary nature of the Chinese 'gentry', Chang makes it clear that they were much more of a distinct and privileged class than the nineteenth-century European observers were aware, and that the assumption of the existence of 'equality of opportunity' must be greatly modified in view of the privileges that accrued in fact to wealth and family connection.

The status of *shên-shih* or gentry was gained through the acquisition of a title, grade, degree, or official rank which automatically made the holder a member of the group. The educational grades and degrees were generally obtained by passing the government examination (the 'front door' or 'regular' group); they could, however, be obtained through purchase (the 'back door' or 'irregular' group). The higher officials, however, almost invariably entered by the 'front door'. There were also among the gentry those who had obtained admission by means of military degrees or ranks (the holders of the higher military degrees could become military officers, but promotion in the armed forces was usually from the ranks).

The gentry could conveniently be classified in two strata—the higher and the lower. The upper gentry were more privileged than the lower and generally led the latter in the performance of their functions. In the payment of land-tax, for example, the upper gentry were better able to resist excessive charges. They also led in the organization of the local militia. The distinction between the upper and lower gentry was indicated by differences in their garments and hats. For example, the upper gentry wore gold buttons in their hats, while members of the lower gentry had silver ones.

Among the gentry there was a multiplicity of gradations depending on the degrees they held. The lower gentry were not eligible for official posts. The distinction between the upper and lower gentry was an examinational one. Here again corruption was rife. Also on occasions the *chü-jên* (M.A.) degree and peacock's-feathers were awarded for large contributions to a famine relief fund (in 1833 the anger of a censor was aroused by one such case). But although *chü-jên* degrees continued to be gained sometimes through wealth and influence, they were never *legally* obtainable through purchase.

The entrance examination that qualified for entrance into the lower gentry was called *t'ung-shêng*, and those who passed became *Shêng-yüan*, the educated lower gentry. Only males were eligible to apply for admission to the qualifying examination (in three parts). The 'mean people' (slaves—even when freed, members of the families of prostitutes, entertainers, lictors, and the whole boat-dwelling population) were entirely excluded from participation.[1] But although theoretically the pathway to gentry status was open to all others on equal terms, in practice there was discrimination and favouritism. There were malpractices and corruption, and the fact that candidates had to secure a guarantee from gentry members as to their origin and character prevented many from participating in the examinations. Nor did everyone enjoy the economic freedom giving him time to study for the examinations. This was the crux of the matter.

The 'mean people' were excluded from entry to the gentry by the 'back door' as well as by the 'front door'. Purchase was often used to avoid the first stages of entry to the gentry, after which the candidate advanced through the 'front door'.

Other relatively small groups of those admitted to the gentry were by virtue of the Imperial favour (for example, students of the Banner and Imperial Clansmen's schools—as bannermen they were *not* automatically 'gentry'), descendants of early sages, or individuals whose ancestors had rendered service to the throne.

There can be no doubt as to the privileged position of the gentry under the Ch'ing. Respect for them was enjoined in Imperial instructions to magistrates, and in repeated proclamations by the governors. 'The gentry are at the head of the common people [one proclamation ran]; and to them the villagers look up.' The gentry (as has already been remarked) were distinguished by the buttons on their caps, but also by the reservation to them of various luxury articles of apparel— sable, fox, and lynx fur, as well as brocades, fancy embroidery and gold borders for saddles and reins. Commoners who used these were punished. Only gentry members could attend the official ceremonies at the Confucian temples; when clans observed ancestral rites these were performed by clan members who were gentry. All commoners had to address all officials as *Ta-lao-yeh* (Great Excellency) and all gentry without rank as *Lao-yeh* (Excellency).

Furthermore, if a member of the gentry committed a crime, he could not be humiliated. If the offence he committed was so serious as to merit punishment, he was first of all deprived of his honours and positions before he was punished, and since a member of the gentry was the social equal of the local magistrate, the latter could not degrade and punish him. Severe laws protected the gentry against insult—

for example, an under-clerk who insulted a *chü-jên* would receive seventy lashes; if he insulted a commoner he would receive only ten lashes.

Commoners were not allowed to involve gentry in lawsuits as witnesses. Even the lowest of the literary ranks was exempted from chastisement by the bamboo as a kind of 'benefit of clergy'.

The economic privileges of the gentry included special arrangements in their favour regarding tax payment and labour services, and the payment of certain stipends and subsidies was granted for their educational advancement.

It must be allowed, however, that the gentry performed many useful functions. They promoted village welfare and the interest of home areas *vis-à-vis* government officials; they organized the local military corps and collected taxes on behalf of the government in case of need (even if sometimes they usurped this function for their own profit). They undertook cultural leadership, encouraging all the virtues of Confucian society, and presided over village temples, schools, and examination halls. They also promoted public works and supervised irrigation, flood relief, etc.

These items by no means account for the whole of Chang Chung-li's study, and give no idea of the tables in which he analyses a very large number of data regarding the gentry—economic data, gentry participations in functions, the proportion and distribution of 'newcomer' and 'established' gentry, the number of degrees conferred for various examinations during the century, the proportion of gentry in various provinces and its relationship to the size of population before and after the Taiping period, etc. We learn from these, to take one example, that in the post-Taiping period the total number of gentry in China was 1,443,900 (including families, 7,219,500) in a total population of 377,500,000. 'Regular' gentry accounted for 910,597 of the total, and 'irregular' gentry for 533,303 of the family total of 7,219,500. The percentage of gentry (including families) for the whole country was 1·9; for Chihli, 730,910 out of 17,900,000, or 4·1 per cent; for Shantung, 375,015 out of 36,500,000, or 1 per cent; for Shansi, 288,845 out of 10,800,000, or 2·7 per cent (to select the three provinces of special interest to our study).

The conclusion reached is that the 'gentry' were a decidedly privileged and, to a large extent, a self-perpetuating class, and that 'democracy', 'upward mobility', and 'equality of opportunity' were operating only in a very limited way. Nevertheless (as Chang Chung-li concludes):

The examination system did not actually afford equal opportunities to all. Wealth, influence, and family background were powerful factors, operating for the advantage of special groups. Nevertheless, some opportunity did exist for men without these advantages to rise through their own ability and diligence, and many men did indeed rise in this way. If there was not equality in the examination system, there was a general belief in the 'spirit of equality', and this together with the fact that some social mobility did exist helped to stabilize the society and maintain its status quo.[1]

Another conclusion based on detailed research which modifies the above is that of Robert E. Marsh who says:

Statistical and historical data on 572 officials suggest that in the Ch'ing bureaucracy the rule of seniority and other norms operated in such a way as to equalize the chances for advancement of officials from family backgrounds as disparate in privilege as official families and commoner families. Although the vast majority of commoners' sons never became officials, those who did enter officialdom were able to achieve about the same degree of advancement as the sons of official families of the local élite, providing that they had the same amount of seniority.[2]

In the last few decades or so it has become politically expedient for the revolutionaries to emphasize—or even exaggerate—the 'feudal' oppression of the gentry in nineteenth- and twentieth-century China. Perhaps Fei Hsiao-tung's study is an example of this tendency.[3]

The gentry of China fare badly at Mr Fei's hand [says Dr Hummel].[4] Rightly pained at the hardships of the men who till the soil, and keenly conscious of class, he blames the scholar-literati, the merchants, the land-lords, and the active and retired officials for most of the country's political ills. This heterogeneous group he designates, in the jargon of our day, the 'power structure' of traditional Chinese society. One of their failings through the centuries was that they did not bring the emperor under the rule of law as the English did King John under Magna Carta. Instead of restraining his power directly, they supinely attempted by various means to neutralize and soften it. They expected him to rule by a set of ethical principles based on the classics, and reaching back to Confucius and Mencius by a kind of apostolic succession known as *tao-t'ung*. This was the method of persuasion. Another device of this class was the Taoist one of *laissez faire* which is here inexactly termed 'do-nothingism'. Thus an imperial edict that was discovered to be unworkable at the local level was politely ignored or explained away.... The six 'life histories'... which describe certain gentry in the remote province of Yunnan, read much like select biographies of city bosses, unscrupulous politicians, ruthless merchants, or gangsters in one of our [U.S.] great urban centres. Such types certainly existed in China, but it would be wrong to take them, as Mr Fei evidently wants us to do, as typical of China in normal times. . ..

Another study of nineteenth-century Chinese society is that of Hsiao Kung-ch'üan[1] which tends to confirm Chang Chung-li's conclusion that Parker's description of China as 'one vast democracy' was (to say the least of it) an exaggeration.

Mr Hsiao's article opens:

Arthur Henderson Smith, writing near the end of the previous century, characterized the Chinese village organization as 'the self-government of the small communities' and asserted that 'the management of the village was in the hands of the people themselves'. His enthusiasm was shared in varying degrees by other writers, both native and foreign. For good reasons, however, this encouraging view is no longer supported by other writers, native and foreign.

As will be seen from the foregoing pages, A. H. Smith is here quoted out of context, for he modified his statement regarding the management of the village by the people themselves out of existence in his succeeding remarks. Nor can he be accused of entertaining any unduly 'encouraging view' regarding the then state of China. This kind of optimism could more fairly be ascribed to Parker.

However, the notion of Chinese 'democracy' which Chang Chung-li and Hsiao Kung-ch'üan are concerned to dispose of was not merely an illusion of Europeans. Two Chinese observers, Y. K. Leong and L. K. Tao, with some claim to speak, came to a similar conclusion to Parker early in the present century. They wrote:

In its actual working China is a huge republic within which are myriads of petty republics. For the village in China is an autonomous unit. Nominally it is governed by the central government through a hierarchical series of officials. . .but actually, with the exception of paying a nominal land-tax, and in a few other cases, the village is as independent of the central government as any British self-governing colony is independent of the Imperial Government. . . .In China the central government plays but an infinitesimally small part in village life. The village has perfect freedom of industry and trade, of religion, and of everything that concerns the government, and the regulation and protection of the locality. Whatever may be required for its well-being is supplied, not by Imperial Edicts or any other kind of governmental interference, but by voluntary associations. Thus police, education, public health, public repairs of roads and canals, lighting, and innumerable other functions, are managed by the villages themselves.[2]

The notion of village self-government (says Hsiao) ignored the existence of a considerable number of tiny villages, especially in North China, which were too impoverished to afford organization. It failed also to maintain a necessary distinction between two aspects of village organization where it existed, namely between the village as a centre of rural community life and the village as an object of Imperial control, each with its distinct leadership, the one called forth by government action, the other emerging from the rural inhabitants themselves. The failure led to an illusion in which village activities and organization that came as a result of government control appeared as manifestations of local initiative. In reality, a substantial part of the village organization was made up of central government checks and devices that had nothing to do with self-government, and the effect of these was in the long run detrimental to the empire and its inhabitants.

To maintain their hold over the vast Chinese countryside, the Manchus found that the ordinary administrative machinery and the regular military forces were not enough. The *chou* and *hsien* magistracies which formed the base of the administrative pyramid, a total of a little over 1500 posts during the Ch'ing dynasty,[1] were far too few to maintain a direct control over the villages; the troops, stationed in strategic centres, might be expected to cope with revolutionary outbreaks, but they were not numerous enough to police the provinces. Therefore the Manchus devised auxiliary methods for securing their grip on the countryside which developed with the consolidation of their central power and decayed when it decayed.

The complex system thus originated touched practically every aspect of rural life. The most important instrument of this control was the *pao-chia*, a universal system of registration, surveillance, and crime-reporting. It was operated by the people themselves and obviated the necessity of attempting to organize what would have been an impossibly large number of governmental police and spies. Disregarding organic or traditional groupings, every ten households were formed into a *p'ai*, every ten *p'ai* into a *chia*, and every ten *chia* into a *pao*. A headman for each division was nominated from persons residing in the designated area. His duties included the registration of all persons living in, arriving at, or departing from the area, and making reports to the local *yamen* regarding offences such as 'theft, corrupt teaching, gambling, hiding and absconding from justice, kidnapping, coining, establishing a secret society, etc.' At the end of each month the headman of the *pao* submitted to the local magistrate a *kan-chieh* ('willing bond') giving an assurance that all was well in the neighbourhood. All inhabitants were expected to report offensive conduct or suspicious characters to the various headmen and failure to do so was punished as a crime. The villagers were, in short, compelled to police themselves, ostensibly for their own protection, but ultimately in the interests of Imperial authority.

But this was only the beginning. To persuade the landowners to pay their land and *corvée* taxes, the central government installed an elaborate system of agents, known officially as the *li-chia*, in addition to and supplementary to the agents of the local governments. The function of the *li-chia*, however, was not merely admonitory, for it endeavoured to help the peasants to pay their taxes by extending material aid to them, partly through a network of local granaries, officially called the *shê-ch'ang* or *i-ch'ang*, which either made loans to farmers in times of need or gave relief in time of disaster. The *li-chia*, like the *pao-chia*, generally disregarded the natural boundaries of the village. The headmen of the *li* division were selected from the households having the largest number of tax-paying adult males and the largest amount of taxable land among the one hundred and ten households that composed a division; the headman of the *chia* (a subdivision of ten households) was appointed from one of the neighbouring households in the division.[1] Two other scholars remark:

The *pao-chia* was an ingenious mechanism for the execution of central policies at local levels, the maintenance of social stability, and the preservation of order and legality. Ten households formed a *p'ai* under the control of a *p'ai-chang*, ten *p'ai* a *chia* under the control of a *chia-chang*, and ten *chia* a *pao* under the control of a *pao-chang*. The differing levels of *chang* were mutually responsible. The more obvious duties involved reports to the local officials of the Ch'ing on burglary, gambling, the harbouring of criminals, illegal coinage, the sale of salt, gang activities, or the presence of strangers. However, it was the control of the population in a more subtle sense that was the major contribution of the *pao-chia* organization for the operation of the vast Ch'ing empire, the records of the *pao-chia* included all people who belonged to the *pao* in the sense that it was the locus of their permanent domicile and their enduring allegiance. Permanent domicile determined such critical matters as the payment of taxes and the allocation of quotas for the imperial examinations. Furthermore, the social class allocation of the household in the *pao-chia* placards and registers could not be changed casually.[2]

What was the incidence of taxation on the people? Steiger says 'the taxes were ridiculously light'.[3] He estimates that allowing a 100 per cent increase on the 915 million taels (U.S. $74 million) raised by the Imperial government in 1900 to cover extortion, 'squeeze', and cost of transmission, the amount of taxation actually paid by the people was less than 200 million taels (U.S. $16 million), of which less than 23 million taels was spent on the Imperial household, the Imperial clan, and the upkeep of the Manchu garrisons. But in the light of Parker's statement that the actual amount of land-tax collected by the district magistrate was anything between twice and four times the legal amount,[1] and Douglas's that it was six times,[2] this statement of Steiger's requires examination.

Hsia Nai's study of taxation in the Yangtze provinces provides some of the information we require.[3]

During the Taiping Rebellion the Manchu government instituted both temporary exemptions of land-tax and the more permanent reduction of tax-rate in the six Yangtze provinces of Kiangsu, Chekiang, Kiangsi, Hupei, Hunan, and Anhwei. The most important items of the land-tax in these provinces were the 'rice-tribute' and the 'land-poll tax'. The rice-tribute was payable either in kind or in money. For payment in kind the collectors either charged more while measuring, or discounted what was collected. For the payment in money they often fixed the price of rice higher than the market price; in addition, they might set the price of silver in terms of copper coins at a higher rate than the market price and make the taxpayer remit the tax in copper. The 'land-poll' tax was officially payable in silver, but the collectors would only accept copper coins.

Part of the loot had to be handed over by the collectors to their official superiors, another part to the local gentry. Tax-collection was so profitable that a tribe of watchmen and tribute secretaries grew up who bribed the officials with large sums to appoint them to the tax and treasury departments, and it was they who collected the taxes directly.

From the time of the K'ang Hsi emperor (1662–1722) to that of the Chia Ch'ing emperor (1796–1820) the country enjoyed relative peace and stability, so that these exactions could be borne, and the ruthless suppression of any sign of opposition by the Manchu emperors had sufficiently cowed the peasantry into bearing hardships of this sort. But in the reign of the Tao Kuang emperor (1822–50) they could no longer pay the taxes. This was due to loss of agricultural productivity due to neglect of irrigation, the rise in the price of silver, and the increasing corruption in the administration of the tax and rice tribute.

And when the Taipings entered the Yangtze provinces tax reduction could not longer be delayed.

The total amount of tax reduction in the Yangtze provinces amounted to over 1,500,000 taels, more than 6,400,000 strings of cash, and over 10,750,000 *tan* of rice. But over-collection was not an abuse that could be remedied simply by the issue of decrees, and the effectiveness of the official reductions depended on the vigilance of the higher authorities, compelling the local officials to observe the rules.

Soon it became apparent that officials were reverting to their previous practices. Not only did local corruption and over-collection re-emerge at the end of the T'ung Chih period, but owing to financial stringency due to the payment of indemnities, etc., the government even increased the tax quota considerably in the next reign (Kuang Hsü, 1874–1908) in the form of various additional levies.

The most noticeable feature of the tax-reduction movement was that the partial elimination of over-collection and corruption greatly decreased the burdens on the people without appreciably affecting the government revenue.

But what had been gained during the T'ung Chih reign was lost later, and Hsia Nai concludes that

Consequently the taxpayer's burden was greatly increased, and the people became restless. It was not without reason that H. B. Morse attributed the outbreak of the republican revolution to the general discontent of the people against the Ch'ing government. The land-tax was a direct levy, the effect of which was more acutely felt by the people, and the fall of the Ch'ing dynasty was certainly linked to the decline of the tax reduction movement.[1]

The *li-chia* and the granary systems may be regarded as instruments of economic control over the countryside. In addition to this the emperors exercised an ideological control by various means. (How this control was effected, through the educational and examination system, has been described above.) Then there was the *hsiang-yüeh* lecture system, inaugurated in 1652 by the Shun Chih emperor with the promulgation of the *liu-yü* 'the Six Maxims of a Hortatory Edict', in which he exhorted each and all to follow the dictates of social duty and to lead an orderly life.[2] A *hsiang-yüeh*, nominated locally and approved by the magistrate, was to expound the maxims to his fellow-villagers or townsfolk on appointed days of the month.

Another ideological device was the honouring of aged villagers. Confucianism, as is well known, called for respect for old age, and the emperors had perceived the usefulness of this precept. Elderly men were less likely to be revolutionaries than the younger ones and to honour them was one way of maintaining the existing order.

In addition to harnessing the examination system to its own car, the Manchu government made an attempt to extend its moral influence in the countryside through local schools. A government order of 1652 required that a *shê-hsüeh* (community school) be set up in every rural area and that 'persons of honest and sincere character' be appointed as teachers of these schools. These teachers were paid salaries and exempted from *corvée* duties; they were locally selected, but subject to the supervision of the educational authorities.

Within certain limits this system of Imperial control was through service to the Ch'ing rulers. Its elements came from previous dynasties and constituted parts of the Chinese administrative tradition. By making use of them instead of devising new methods of control the emperors may have allayed for the local inhabitants their natural distaste for a foreign rule. But the fact that the control was imposed from above by an autocratic central government tended to weaken the foundations of the empire. Rural community activities may not have been actually stifled but they were not encouraged, and the habitual passivity of the Chinese peasant was intensified. So long as the villagers could eke out a subsistence they remained vaguely discontented but generally placid. 'All things are pre-arranged by fate; for what shall we pray? Today knows not the affairs of tomorrow; how shall we plan?' But there came a point of no return, for in the end the passivity of the peasants not only rendered them unsuitable for performing services to the government, but incapable of protecting themselves against the malpractices of local officials or local bullies.

Meanwhile, the Manchus strove to nurse the economy, chiefly through irrigation, flood prevention, land reclamation, and famine relief. Their efforts, however, proved ineffectual against recurrent natural disasters, the persistent pressure of population on land, and the widespread corrupt practices of local officialdom which had become general since the closing decades of the eighteenth century.[1] Many villagers sank even lower into poverty. The destitute peasants did not remain for ever imperturbable; they became fertile soil for riots and rebellions.

As a factor tending towards social discontent, Imperial land utilization under the Ch'ing has perhaps not yet been accorded its proper weight. During the dynasty the Chinese encroached steadily on Manchu and Mongol territory, pushed back the aborigines of southern and south-western China, and carved out terraces on every slope. Much of this proved shortsighted—as Arthur P. Chew of the United States Department of Agriculture has pointed out: 'The short life of agriculture in the hillsides ended the long life of agriculture on the plains. Every farm won from the mountainside ruined a dozen in the path of the released torrents.'[1]

Even under such circumstances the peasantry played a relatively subordinate role, often being led by frustrated scholars or 'bad gentry', especially in the movements that attained some magnitude. The compiler of the *Huai-an Fu chih* (1884 edition), made these remarks with reference to the Nien uprising:

When the bandits first rose, they comprised not more than several tens of ignorant and brutish fellows. But when more and more persons were coerced into joining them, they included many individuals of notable courage and ability. And when some shameless gentry and titled scholars were found among them, their forces were brought under rigid discipline and clear regulations, and they moved with speed as well as with plenty of cunning tactics.[2]

In many instances a rebellion was the result of the confluence of diverse elements—desperate peasants hoping to obtain food or throw off tax burdens, scholars desiring to vent their wrath against local officials or simply to release their pent-up feeling of frustration. *'Peasants seldom assumed leadership or became organizers; they supplied the movements with the necessary physical force.'*[3]

Thomas Taylor Meadows, in his *The Chinese and Their Rebellions* (London, 1856, p. 24) wrote: 'The Chinese people have no right of legislation, they have no right of self-taxation, they have not the power of voting out their rulers or limiting or stopping supplies. They have therefore the right of rebellion.'

This 'right of rebellion', however, when exercised, carried with it no certainty of success. Without adequate leadership the rebellions usually proved abortive. Even in the most successful movements, as during the Taiping days, the villagers retained much of their characteristic timidity, once the hue and cry of insurrection had abated. It seemed as if centuries of Imperial control had taken the spirit out of them.

It will be seen that the statistical and other methods of the modern social historian have revealed many facts concerning Chinese society which escaped the notice of the nineteenth-century observers, but it must not be forgotten that the motive and objective of the observer, whether his methods be scientific or otherwise, decide the kind of facts to be elicited. The twentieth-century 'community survey' in China was invariably orientated towards reform and to the elimination of undesirable social institutions; the researches of the contemporary social historian are directed either towards discovering the reasons for historical happenings with a like aim or for ascertaining what line of policy is likely to be successful in the future, or for justifying a line of policy to which the researcher (or his party) is already committed.

Marxist theory has only been applied to Chinese history by Chinese communists for the last two or three decades (though it is now being applied with a vengeance). Mao Tse-tung himself, in the formative years of his political theories, was more interested in the present than in the past and it was only once in a while that he glanced any distance backwards. Yet his analysis of the classes in Chinese society, written in 1926, throws some light on the nature of the Chinese classes as they must have been a generation earlier, namely in 1900. His object in undertaking this analysis was to discover the dividing line between those classes that would be likely to favour the Communist Revolution and those that would be likely to defend the *status quo*. 'Who are our enemies [he asks], and who are our friends?'

Mao states that in 1926 the classes of Chinese society were the landlords and *compradores*, the middle class, the petty bourgeoisie, the semi-proletariat, the proletariat (still numbering no more than two million), and the *lumpenproletariat*, namely peasants who had lost their land, unemployed artisans, etc., who had joined the secret societies (among which he names the Triad in Fukien and Kwangtung, the Brothers in Hunan, Hupeh, Kweichow, and Szechwan, the Society of the Great Swords in Anhwei, Honan, and Shantung, the Blue Band, etc.).[1]

Mao, however, does not disregard the traditional class of 'gentry' altogether. He speaks later of smashing the political prestige and power of the landlord class, 'especially of the local bullies and bad gentry', singling out the latter for condemnation on many subsequent occasions, and urges his fellow communists to overthrow their 'feudal' rule. Other rules which he urges the overthrow of are those of the country magistrate and his bailiffs, the clan authority of the elders and ancestral temples, the theocratic authority of the city gods and local deities, and the masculine authority of the husbands.[2]

The above generalizations refer to China as a whole, but when we come to the Boxers, who were most to the front in Shantung, Chihli and Shansi, we shall have to pay closer attention to the local situation. We can say, however, that conditions generally were favourable for an uprising in 1900, but we have yet to discover why this uprising should have taken the particular form of a Boxer movement and why it should have come to a head in these particular provinces.[1]

CHAPTER III

THE IMPACT OF THE WEST

One feature at least of the Boxer Uprising is beyond dispute, namely that it was 'anti-foreign', and, in particular, 'anti-European'. What then was the nature of the impact of the West upon China which had created the anti-foreign sentiment that the Boxers embodied?

The real nature of the change which China has been undergoing for more than a century, and at a greatly accelerated pace during the last decade or so, is the subject of contemporary debate. Whilst Europe was politically in the ascendant in Asia the process was accepted as being 'Westernization' pure and simple, but it is now regarded both by Chinese and European authorities as rather a 'self-modernization' under Western stimuli.

That 'Westernization' as a description of the change which China was undergoing after 1840 is a gross oversimplification is being made increasingly clear by modern sinology. Benjamin Schwartz, for example, says that 'Those who are at all close to Chinese studies are now fully aware that there is much more life and movement here than has been suspected'. The concept of a 'Changeless China' founded on 'Confucianism' is as false as one of a 'Changeless Europe' founded on 'Christianity'. He continues:

It is, of course, conceivable that even a close and profound study of the intellectual history of China will not reveal the range of possibilities and the diversity of elements which we find in the intellectual history of the West. For one thing, Western intellectual history is fed from such highly diverse streams as Greece, Judaea, Rome, and the barbarian north. Is it conceivable, however, that China was dominated for centuries by a completely un-problematic, unchanging something called Confucianism? Or is it possible the monochromatic appearance of the Chinese intellectual historic landscape is, in part, a function of our distance from it, of our feeble grasp of the language, and of the conceptual categories in terms of which issues are discussed?[1]

Since China is now a communist country, it is natural that the interpretation of Chinese history by contemporary Chinese historians should be in Marxist terms, and although there has been considerable difference of opinion among these historians as to detail, the general lines seem to be sufficiently agreed upon. They are as follows:

Like other countries in the world, China went through primitive, slave, and feudal societies. For a long time after entering feudal society she remained stagnant in her economic and social life. A combination of small-scale farming and home handicrafts constituted the main mode of production. But in spite of the slow development of feudal society there emerged some large industries commanding a nationwide market, as, for example, the manufacture of porcelain and of silk. Chinese production was a type of capitalist mass production based on division of labour, co-operation, and the handicraft technique of wage-workers. It was the transitional stage between handicraft production and large-scale machine production. However, the manufactures that did exist contained in themselves the embryo of capitalism. 'If her independent development had not been interrupted by the penetration of foreign capitalism, China would have grown inevitably, though slowly, into a capitalist society.'[1]

With the penetration of China by foreign capitalism, important changes took place within the 'feudal' structure of Chinese society, impelling it to take the road of 'semi-colonization' and 'semi-feudalism'. Thus its independent development was interrupted.

The process of the penetration of China by foreign capitalism corresponded with the development of foreign capitalism itself. There was first the period of free capitalist competition under the 'unequal treaties', but towards the end of the nineteenth century world capitalism entered the stage of imperialism and monopoly took the place of free competition. This gave rise to a more acute conflict among the imperialist powers themselves. Following the Sino–Japanese War of 1894–5, China was forced to concede to Japan the right to set up factories in China. Thereafter an increasing number of foreigners came to China to run factories, build railways, and establish banks, thereby obtaining control over China's industry and banking. In addition, through a series of political loans, the foreign Powers were able to manipulate China's finance and government.

It is, however, in their periodization of modern Chinese history that there is a difference of opinion among Chinese Marxist–Leninist critics. For example, Tai I gives reasons for dividing the whole period into three: (1) from the Opium War to the overthrow of the Mohammedan rising in 1873, being the period of internal revolutionary peasant risings; (2) from 1873 to the suppression of the Boxers in 1901, being the period of competition among the foreign Powers for the carving-up of China and of the national revolutionary fight of the Chinese people; (3) from 1901 to the eve of the 4 May Movement in 1919, being the period of the anti-imperialist, anti-feudal revolution under the leadership of the ruling class and of the transition from the democratic to the new-democratic revolution.[1] Wang Jên-ch'ên, on the other hand, divides this stage into (1) 1840–64, the period of the Chinese people's struggle against the entry of the capitalist Powers and of internal peasant risings; (2) 1864–1901, the period of the Chinese people's struggle against the semi-colonial, semi-feudal State created by reactionaries at home and abroad, and against the carving-up of China by the Imperial Powers; (3) 1901–19, the period of anti-feudal demo-cratic revolution led by the property-owning class.[2]

A Western, non-Marxist concept, which has been extensively applied, is that of 'China's response to Western contact'—which Fairbank considers has 'a definite, though limited value as one avenue of analytic approach to modern Chinese history'.[3]

The response in question was that of China's leaders of the last two generations of the Ch'ing dynasty. This becomes more difficult to study the longer it continues. In its early stages, however, a rather simple pattern emerges: the Chinese scholar-official confronting the foreigner moves from a recognition that China must acquire Western arms to a recognition that she must industrialize by the use of all sorts of Western technology, and subsequently to the recognition that 'self-strengthening' is not to be achieved by material feats of applied technology and industrialization alone, but must be undertaken by a strong and modernized State. In other words, the trend is from arms, to technology and industry, to political institutions, all in the service of a growing nationalism. All these successive phases can be copied from the West, if only the leaders of the day are able to profit by the foresight and recommendations of the scholar-reformers.

But whatever the absolute rate of development in China might be, it could not keep up with the rate of change in nearby Japan or in other parts of the world. Consequently, whatever China did, to Chinese patriots she seemed to be falling behind. 'The central problem for historical measurement is therefore that of China's comparative slowness in effective, organized response.' All that contact with the West succeeded in doing over a long period was to make the Chinese patriot supremely aware of his country's humiliating position. But the slowness of China's response to Western stimuli had the effect of making it deeper and more intense, and when it eventually reached a climax in our day the outcome was all the more spectacular.

But neither this nor the communist type of approach seems to take sufficient account of the basic nature of Chinese civilization and the extent to which it was working out its own destiny, independent of the West, as is being revealed in Joseph Needham's revolutionary work.[1]

It is clear, for example, from Needham's study to date that the Chinese succeeded in anticipating in many important fields the scientific and technical discoveries of the celebrated 'Greek Miracle', in keeping pace with the Arabs (who had all the treasures of the ancient world at their disposal), and in maintaining, between the third and thirteenth centuries, a level of scientific knowledge unapproached in the West. Yet, until Chinese science gradually fused into the universality of modern science with the coming of the Jesuits to Peking in the early seventeenth century, it remained on a level, broadly speaking, continuously empirical and restricted to theories of a primitive and medieval type.[2]

Needham gives a list of twenty-seven mechanical and other techniques (and it is, he makes clear, by no means an exhaustive one) basic to civilization that were transmitted from China to the West before the arrival of the Jesuits, including deep drilling for mining, efficient harness for draught-animals (postilion breast-strap and collar), cast-iron, the segmental arch and the iron-chain suspension bridges, 'Cardan' suspension, the draw-loom, the edge-runner mill, canal lock-gates, the stern-post rudder, metallurgical blowing-engines (water power), and the escapement for clocks, in addition to the well-known inventions of paper, printing, porcelain, and the magnetic compass.

The mechanical techniques transmitted in the opposite direction, from the West to China, during the same period, were only three in number—namely the screw, the force-pump for liquids, and the crankshaft.[3]

Other techniques, such as water-tight compartments for ship-building, paper money, and the use of coal, which the late medieval West knew were used in China, were not adopted by it since none of them fitted into contemporary European patterns.

Why was it that China, which had obtained such a lead in mechanical invention, missed that 'great leap forward' which took place in

Europe? The answer is not yet entirely clear. Perhaps (Needham surmises) the fact that Galileo and Vesalius and their like were Europeans depended not on any intrinsic superiority of the European peoples but upon factors of environment which did not, and could not, operate in other civilizations with a different geographical setting and the different social evolution which this supplied.

China, while indifferent to the religion that the Jesuits brought with them, was eager to profit from their superior mathematical knowledge which made it possible for them to settle the calendar with greater accuracy than the native astronomers. For an agricultural economy, astronomical knowledge as a regulator of the calendar was of prime importance. But the Chinese showed little interest in the other by-products of Jesuit science or in those of the Industrial Revolution when that took place. It was only when in the fourth decade of the nineteenth century China came into violent impact with a West made powerful by its science and industry and her military weakness was revealed, that she began to experience any sense of shortcoming.

The West, for its part, was eventually impelled into aggression by the structure of its economy (itself an inheritance from the Scientific Renaissance). Britain in particular faced the necessity for finding ever-increasing markets for her surplus production and this necessity was always present in the minds of her statesmen. But although Britain in the early nineteenth century wanted Chinese tea and silk, there was little demand in China for Britain's woollen cloth and other products, and it was only the great increase in the opium exports from British-controlled India to China which stopped the drain on British silver and compelled China to export her own silver to make up the balance of payments.

The economic conquest of China by Europeans passed through three broad stages. In the first, the balance of trade changed in favour of the foreigners, the flow of silver reversing its direction about 1826. In the second phase, British manufactures began to pour into China so that a country that had for centuries been famous for its textiles was, by the 1870's, taking in Lancashire cotton goods to the extent of one-third of its entire imports. In the third phase, the inflow of foreign manu-factures was followed by that of foreign capital, bringing with it railways, cotton mills, and similar undertakings requiring a capital accumulation which China lacked.[1]

The theory of economic pressures suffices to explain the increasingly dependent, semi-colonial status of China at the end of the nineteenth century, but it takes no account of the collision in the two civilizations of elements that had no direct connection with economics. We know, for example, that the introduction of machine-made goods into China had a ruinous effect on Chinese handicrafts, but this does not explain why it was that the decline in the artistic value of Chinese porcelain sets in at the end of the Ch'ien Lung reign (1735–96) and why that made in the Chia Ch'ing and Tao Kuang reigns was purely imitative. It must have been due to something, independent of the West, happening inside China itself.

It is becoming increasingly clear to students that the impact between China and the West was not merely that between two societies at different stages of development, but between two civilizations with different world-views. For example, as has been well said, the Chinese, unlike the West, felt that the harmonious co-operation of all beings arose, not from the orders of a superior authority external to themselves, but from the fact that they were all parts in a hierarchy of wholes forming a cosmic pattern, and what they obeyed were the internal dictates of their own natures.

This world-view decided the Chinese conception of law. As Jean Escarra says:

In the West the law has always been revered as something more or less sacrosanct, the queen of gods and men, imposing itself on everyone like a categorical imperative, defining and regulating, in an abstract way, the effects and conditions of all forms of activity. In the West there have been tribunals the role of which has been not only to apply the law, but often to interpret it in the light of debates where all the contradictory interests are represented and defended. In the West the jurisconsults have built, over the centuries, a structure of analysis and synthesis, a corpus of 'doctrine' that ceaselessly tended to perfect and purify the technical elements of the systems of the positive law. But as one passes to the East, this picture fades away. At the other end of Asia, China has felt able to give to law and jurisprudence but an inferior place in that powerful body of spiritual and moral values which she created and for so long diffused over so many neighbouring cultures, such as those of Korea, Japan, Annam, Siam, and Burma. Though not without judicial institutions, she has been willing to recognize only the natural order, and to exalt only the rules of morality. Essentially purely penal (and very severe), sanctions have been primarily means of intimidation. The State and its delegate the Judge have always seen their power restricted in face of the omnipotence of the heads of clans and guilds, the fathers of families, and the general administrators, who laid down the duties of each individual in his respective domain, and settled all conflicts according to equity, usage, and local custom. Few indeed have been the commentators and theoreticians of law produced by the Chinese nation, though a nation of scholars.[1]

In 1474 in Basel, a cock was sentenced to be burnt alive for the 'heinous and unnatural crime' of laying an egg. Similar cases elsewhere are on record, and there was a Swiss prosecution of the same kind as late as 1730. One of the reasons for the alarm was that *œuf coquatri* was thought to be an ingredient in witches' ointments and that a basilisk or cockatrice, a particularly venomous animal, hatched from it. But the interest of the story lies in the fact that such animal trials as this (and they were fairly common in Europe during the period of witch-mania) would have been absolutely impossible in China.

The Chinese were not so presumptuous as to suppose that they knew the laws laid down for non-human beings so well that they could proceed to indict an animal at law for transgressing them. On the contrary, the Chinese reaction would undoubtedly have been to treat these rare and frightening phenomena as *Ch'ien kao* (reprimands from Heaven), and it was the emperor or the provincial governor whose position would have been endangered, not the cock.[2]

When Europeans and Chinese came into collision over conceptions of morality and law in the eighteenth and nineteenth centuries it was not the different nature of the two laws that caused the trouble, but the differing conceptions of 'responsibility'. The Chinese method was (and still is) to fix responsibility in terms, not of 'who has done something' (for example, the cock), but of 'what has happened' (for example, the egg). Because of this emphasis on 'what has happened', the Chinese idea of 'responsibility' reached much further than it did in Europe. For example, in 1784, in Canton, the gunner of *Lady Hughes*, an East Indiaman, who, in firing a salute, did not observe that the gun was loaded with ball and inadvertently killed a Chinese was held 'responsible' by the Chinese authorities, although there had been no *mens rea*, or intention.

But this idea of responsibility arose from the Chinese conception of the interdependence of society and the universe, not from a legal obligation. In 1839 the Hong Merchants appeared at the Canton factories with chains round their necks to indicate the punishment that would befall *them* if the opium was not handed over by the foreigners, as ordered by Lin Tsê-hsü, for they were 'responsible' for the behaviour of the barbarians whom they had 'guaranteed' (*pao*).

Between English and Chinese penal law at this time there was less difference than was the case later when the English law had been reformed. Both were harsh by modern standards. The stealing of sums exceeding twelve pence was punishable in England by death, and it was also a capital crime to attempt to kill, even without wounding, and it was not until 1861 that attempts to kill resulting in bodily injury were taken out of the list of capital crimes.

The Europeans, however, had a legitimate grievance in the faulty *administration* of the law in China and in the uncertainty and injustice resulting from the corruption of the lower officials and the short-comings of Chinese legal procedure.

So many misconceptions as to the real nature of Chinese legal and administrative principles have arisen that it is only now that some of them are being disposed of. The following is an example of the kind of misconception I mean, and is one that has, I hope, now been disposed of by my researches (but perhaps I am too optimistic?).

It was often stated by nineteenth-century European writers that the Chinese 'ruled barbarians (that is, foreigners) with misrule'. The origin of this statement I have traced to Sir J. F. Davis, *The Chinese* (London, 1840), in which he says (p. 28):

The fundamental maxim of Chinese intercourse with foreigners has been accurately translated by Father Prémare as follows, and it is quite sufficient to explain their conduct. 'Barbari haud secus ac pecora. Antiqui reges istud optime callebant, et ideo barbaros non regendo regebant. Sic autem eos non regendo regere, praeclara eos optime regendi ars est.' That is, 'The barbarians are like wild beasts, and not to be ruled by the same principles as citizens. The ancient kings well understood this, and accordingly ruled barbarians by misrule. Therefore, to rule barbarians by misrule is the true and best means of ruling them.'

'To rule by misrule', however, is an obvious mistranslation of the Latin, which itself correctly renders the Chinese original given by Joseph Henri de Prémare in his *Notitia Linguae Sinicae* (Malacca, 1831, p. 203). The Chinese characters in question are *pu chih chih chih*, namely 'govern by not governing them', the *pu* being a negative and not the active *mis*(govern).[1]

This policy was, in fact, part of the time-honoured Taoist principle of *wu wei*, or 'refraining from activity contrary to nature'. This meant refraining from insisting on going against the grain of things, from exerting force in human affairs when the man of insight could see that it would be doomed to failure, and that subtler methods of persuasion, or simply letting things alone to take their own course would bring about the desired result. A very different thing from 'misgoverning' the barbarian! And yet Davis was one of the best informed European writers on China.

Two expensive embassies (in 1793 and 1816) having failed to obtain diplomatic recognition of Britain by China, it was decided, on the termination of the East India Company's monopoly in 1834, to appoint a Superintendent of Trade—a measure desired also by the Chinese. The difficulties which ensued when Lord Napier, who had been appointed in this capacity by the British government, arrived and attempted to deal directly with the Viceroy were due in a great measure to Lord Palmerston's mismanagement, but this fact should not be allowed to obscure the deeper issues involved—namely whether or not China could be compelled to concede diplomatic equality to other nations, to allow freedom of trade, and to provide legal safeguards for foreigners residing in China.

Unfortunately, when the collision between the two civilizations took place these issues were entirely obscured, since the confiscation of the opium was allowed to become the *casus belli*. The war of 1839–42 has therefore been correctly stigmatized as the 'Opium War'.

When the war was debated in the British Parliament from 7 to 9 April 1840, there was no real difference of opinion between the government and the opposition. The motion was carefully framed by the opposition to raise only the question of Palmerston's competence and not to decide whether or not the war should be continued. Macaulay (Whig) waved the Union Jack ('that dear flag') and acclaimed the war: Gladstone (Tory) declared: 'I am not competent to judge how long the war will last, or how protracted may be its operations, but this I can say, that a war more unjust in origin, a war more calculated in its progress to cover this country with permanent disgrace, I do not know, and have not read of.'[1]

However, in the same debate, he also said: 'I do not mean to say that you ought not to send out an armament against China. Far from it. We have placed ourselves under your [the Government's] auspices in a position so unfavourable that we cannot even demand terms of equity without a display of force.'[2]

By the Treaty of Nanking of 1842, indemnities were imposed on China in respect of the opium seized by Commissioner Lin and of the cost of the war, the island of Hong Kong was ceded to Britain in perpetuity, and the five ports of Canton, Amoy, Foochow, Ningpo, and Shanghai were opened to foreign trade. Tariff rates on British goods were to be fixed by mutual agreement, and consequently, in 1843, China signed with Britain the general regulations under which the trade was to be conducted at the five ports above mentioned, and also the supplementary treaty known as the Treaty of the Bogue, which contained articles concerning extraterritoriality and the 'most-favoured nation treatment'. (The opium trade was not mentioned, and continued as before.)

The 'most-favoured nation' clause in the Bogue Treaty (Article VIII) ran as follows: 'Should the Emperor hereafter, for any cause whatever, be pleased to grant additional privileges or immunities to any of the subjects or citizens of such foreign countries, the same privileges and immunities will be extended to and enjoyed by British subjects.'[1]

The other Powers who imitated Britain (or America) in demanding concessions from China inserted a similar clause in the treaties they obtained (invariably by the use, or threat of force), and this ensured the automatic extension to their subjects of any privilege or immunity obtained by other Powers. The United States was the first Power to obtain a treaty after Britain, namely that of Wanghia (Wanghsia at Macao) in 1844, and France obtained a similar treaty at Whampoa the same year.[2]

No provision was made in the treaties for the establishment of foreign settlements, but the local authorities in Shanghai accepted the demands of Britain, the United States, and France for the cession of land on lease for this purpose.

But the treaties of the 1840's did not prove to be a final solution. For one thing, no direct diplomatic relations had yet been established with Peking, and the foreign Powers had to content themselves with dealing with the officials at Canton, since the Emperor had entrusted the direction of foreign relations to the Viceroy of Kwangtung and Kwangsi. The British, whose trading interests were the greatest of the three Western countries, found that the Viceroy and the Cantonese officials were much less amenable than the Manchus, and a dispute immediately started regarding the right of entry to the Chinese city (which had not been conceded in the treaties) and continued for the next few years. This dispute set the pattern for the succeeding ones both in Canton and elsewhere, and indicated an unwillingness on the part of the Chinese in the provinces to accept the spirit of the treaties which had been extorted from an alien emperor, whom they might revere as their ruler but whose interests were not necessarily the same as their own. For this reason, and because the foreign Powers were not yet satisfied with the extent of the concessions they had so far obtained from China, the struggle was bound to be renewed.

In the meantime, the great Taiping Rebellion broke out early in 1851. Some Protestant missionaries were drawn to the support of the Taipings by reason of their Christian pretensions, but the Roman Catholic Church could not give its blessing to a heretical movement. It has been argued that a great opportunity was thus lost to sponsor a dynasty influenced at least by Christian teaching to replace the orthodox pagan Manchus, but the fact that the European Powers feared that the success of the rebellion would mean that the concessions that they had extracted from the Manchus with such difficulty would be repudiated by a native and popular dynasty was sufficient to ensure that the Taipings would receive no support from the West. The Powers were officially neutral in the struggle, but from 1860 onwards they began to give some military support to the Manchus. But it was the internal weaknesses of the Taipings and the fact that the leading Chinese mandarins rallied to its support which saved the dynasty from disaster.

While the fortunes of the Taipings were still in the ascendant and they had occupied a vast region of southern and central China, hostilities broke out again; this time between the Manchu government and Britain and France. The war which ensued is known to Europeans as the Second China War (1857–60) and to the Chinese as the Second Opium War. The aim of the European allies was to consolidate and extend the political and economic privileges which they had secured by the treaties and to obtain full diplomatic representation at Peking.

The occasion for France's entry into the war was the murder of a French Roman Catholic missionary, and the murder of missionaries was to be the stock excuse for intervention by France in the future, both in China and Indochina, as it was to be for Germany's seizure of Kiaochow in 1898. France, little by little, had replaced Portugal as the protector of the Roman Catholic Church in the Far East, but neither Britain nor Germany conceded her jurisdiction over Roman Catholics who were British or German subjects.

The belligerent Powers exacted treaties from China at Tientsin in

1858, and Russia and the United States hastened to profit by the Anglo–French victories and the preoccupation of China with the Taiping Rebellion to obtain similar advantages for themselves. Shortly before the Tientsin treaties were signed, China had submitted to Russian pressure and had agreed that the territory north of the Amur should be Russian and that that east of the Ussuri should be jointly occupied by Russia and China. The United States also took advantage of the situation to obtain a new treaty which secured the same privileges for America that had been given to the British, French, and Russians.

When, however, the foreign diplomats were on their way to Peking to obtain an exchange of ratifications of their treaties, the Taku forts opened fire and the small Anglo–French force suffered heavy casualties and was compelled to retreat. Britain and France again declared war. In 1860 the Taku forts were reduced by a force adequate to the purpose, and the allies occupied Peking. The result was the Convention of Peking which confirmed the provisions of the Tientsin treaties and imposed further onerous terms on China.

At the time of the allied advance on Peking, the British High Commissioner, Lord Elgin, as a punishment for the violation of a flag of truce, ordered the burning of the summer palace near the capital. This was in pursuance of a maxim that was to become the cherished standby of militant Europeans, namely that 'the only thing the Chinese understand is force'. (The behaviour of the French, however, was scarcely less barbarous, and they had already emptied the summer palace of everything movable.)

The treaties of Tientsin and the Convention of Peking, together with the previous treaties of 1842–4, provided the chief legal basis for the relations between China and the Western Powers until well into the next century. It was not until the 1940's that they were fully superseded, and, on the strength of them and their later amplifications, the Western Powers extended their control far into the interior of China. Diplomatic representatives of the Powers were to be appointed to the Manchu Court and might reside in Peking, and the Chinese, for their part, might appoint diplomatic representatives to the Western capitals if they so desired. A number of new ports were opened to foreign trade and residence, namely Newchwang (Manchuria), Tangchow (Chefoo), Taiwan (Formosa), Chaochow (Swatow), and Kiungchow (Hainan). The Yangtze was to be opened to foreign trade; foreigners were to be accorded the privilege of travelling in the Chinese empire outside the treaty ports; indemnities were exacted (and increased by Britain and France in 1860 at Peking) and a portion of them was later assigned by the respective governments to the use of missions and missionaries.[1]

Each of the four Tientsin treaties contains a guarantee of toleration of Christianity and a promise of protection, in the exercise of their faith, not only to missionaries, but also explicitly or by implication to Chinese Christians. Missionaries were allowed, with their families, to travel and live in the interior of China, and protection was to be afforded to them. The right of any person in China to embrace the Christian faith was conceded and the existing edicts against Christianity were to be abrogated.

It seems likely that the Manchu dynasty would have fallen in a decade or two had it not been that the foreigners themselves, after defeating the Manchus, were concerned in maintaining the dynasty in order to dictate, through the Manchu Court, the kind of government that suited their interests.

How did the leading Chinese react to the misfortunes of China in the first and second 'Opium Wars', and how did they think that their country could be saved from further humiliation, or perhaps ruin?[2]

Commissioner Lin was the first Chinese of any influence to recognize that if China were to *resist* the West she must first of all *know* the West. He availed himself of the aid of interpreters and of every work he could procure to obtain a knowledge of every country in the world beyond China—the *Missionary Tracts*, the *Chinese Monthly Magazine*, a *Treatise on Commerce*, a *Description of the United States and of England*, a work on geography, etc.—all more or less abridged or abstracted. The result was the famous geography book, *Hai Kuo T'u Chih*, compiled by Wei Yüan (1794–1856), the well-known scholar and writer on military topics, from Lin's material. Waley, however, points out that Lin's material translated from foreign sources was of limited value owing to the incompetence of his 'linguist' translators.

In the field of diplomacy, Lin and Wei Yüan laid great stress on 'using barbarians to control barbarians'—the Chinese counterpart of the balance of power concept in Western Europe—to persuade the Russians to invade India, and to use France and the United States against Britain, etc. The alternative to Commissioner Lin's policy of coercing the barbarians was to conciliate them. This was still within the traditional Chinese pattern of relations with the barbarians, and did not involve any borrowing from the West or reform of Chinese ways. Under the influence of a conciliatory policy, the Treaty of Nanking was signed with the British in 1842, and the treaties with the Americans and French in 1844. The policy of conciliation was carried out mainly by Manchus—it was *they* who had most to gain by appeasing the foreigner—nothing less than the survival of their dynasty. Ch'i-ying's argument (1844) was that 'the various barbarians have come to live in peace and harmony with us. We must give them some sort of entertainment and cordial reception.'

At the end of the first war with Britain, the Tao Kuang emperor himself showed some interest in shipbuilding for defence, but soon gave it up owing to lack of money. P'an Shih-ch'êng, a Hong merchant, actually had a schooner built and presented it to the Emperor. Nevertheless, by 1860 the rulers of China had wasted twenty years in refusing to face the problems created by Western contact. Their excuse was preoccupation with the Taipings and a new war with the West.

Prince Kung now began, however, to evolve a definite plan to deal with the Western Powers, namely by the creation of the Tsungli Yamen, a special board or subcommittee under the Grand Council to concern itself with all aspects of relations with the Western Powers. As head of this new office, Prince Kung succeeded in establishing a working relationship with the British, French, Russian, and American ministers, in starting a Western-trained Manchu army (the Peking Field Force) armed with Russian guns, and in reinvigorating the central government in Peking.

The ensuing period was characterized by the desire for Western technology, and the establishment of institutions for the study of language and science. In the next decades, the training of students abroad was undertaken under the inspiration of Tsêng Kuo-fan, diplomatic missions were sent to foreign countries, and for the first time the possibilities of industrialization were explored.

What became an outstanding instrument for indirect foreign political control of China was the Imperial Maritime Customs. The origins of this date from 1854, when, owing to the occupation of the native city of Shanghai and the Province of Kiangsu by the Taipings, the Manchu officials were unable to administer the customs revenue, and the British, Americans and French appointed representatives to control the Shanghai customs on behalf of the Manchu government. After the Tientsin treaties of 1858, this system was extended and consolidated.

It was Sir Robert Hart, Inspector General of the Imperial Maritime Customs from 1863 to 1909, who devised and put into effect the whole system of foreign control over the customs administration of China. Under this system, the Inspector General was responsible to the central government of China, and at each port there was a foreign commissioner with his staff. The higher offices were all filled by foreigners. It is true that in every port there was a Superintendent of Customs appointed by the Manchu government and, in theory, the Commissioner was subordinated to the Superintendent, but in practice, the foreign commissioner was responsible only to the Inspector General, who was in turn responsible to the Tsungli Yamen, the government department which had been created under the Tientsin treaties to deal with foreign affairs.

The customs revenue was transmitted to the Manchu Treasury, as heretofore, by the new Imperial Maritime Customs, and this system therefore was acceptable to the Manchus—especially as the greatly increased efficiency of the administration resulted in the practical elimination of corruption and a great progressive increase in the customs revenues. By 1898, the latter accounted for about a third of the central government's entire revenue.

The political significance of this development cannot easily be exaggerated. The foreigners were now able to uphold the Manchu regime with the customs revenues, to neutralize provincial movements towards rebellion or partition, and at the same time to lay down trade and tariff regulations favourable to themselves. But unlike land, salt and pawnshops, which were static as sources of revenue, the customs expanded with the trade and provided the funds for the Self-strengthening Movement.

In 1865 the Inspectorate General of Customs was transferred from Shanghai to Peking, and thenceforward Sir Robert Hart was able to maintain direct contact with his superiors, the Tsungli Yamen. Hart contrived, while strictly adhering to the conditions of his post, to obtain in due course the confidence both of the Chinese and the foreigner. As Morse says,

In all international questions, from negotiating a treaty to settling a land dispute, the Tsungli Yamen in those days of inexperience had constant resort to the advice and help of the Inspector General in Peking, and Viceroys, governors and taotais constantly consulted and acted in conformity with the advice of the commissioners at the ports. . . . The foreign envoys had always supported its [the Customs] authority.[1]

Hart's strategic position made him virtually the Tsungli Yamen's chief adviser. Among the numerous diplomatic matters in which he played a hand were the following. When he went on home-leave to Britain in 1866, the Manchu government, acting on his advice, sent an official and a few students with him. This was the first mission the Manchus had ever sent abroad. It was also on Hart's advice that in 1868 the Manchu government appointed an American, Anson Burlingame, as an envoy to visit various foreign countries. At the Chefoo Conference in 1876, at which the Sino–British Convention was signed (giving many additional advantages to Britain), Hart and G. Detring, Commissioner of Customs at Tientsin, served as assistants to Li Hung-chang, the Manchu plenipotentiary, who negotiated with the British. After the Sino–French War in 1884, Hart played an important role in the conclusion of the peace treaty between China and France. These examples are sufficient to indicate his importance.

That many leading Chinese were not unaware of the ambiguous role played by Hart in furthering the Western penetration of China while improving the revenue-collecting machinery of the Manchus is quite certain. In the 1890's, Ch'ên Chih (described by Hu Shêng[1] as 'a representative of the landlord gentry who leaned towards the bourgeoisie'), in his book *Concerning Practical Matters* (in Chinese), wrote of Hart in the following terms (though he dared not mention him by name):

The annual customs revenues and *likin* amounting to 30 million taels of silver are in the hands of this man. He employs hundreds of his followers in the customs and their salaries cost the country two million taels of silver a year. His counsels prevail at the court and he has gradually gained control over the conduct of the country's foreign policy. Woe to those who defy his authority!... He has obstructed the enforcement of customs tariff regulations and has shown partiality to foreign merchants. He looks sincere but in reality is a blackguard.... He has been knighted by the British Crown, and this is an eloquent proof that he is working for the good of his own country.

In 1876 Li Hung-chang reported secretly, 'We know that Robert Hart is malicious at heart, yet driven by lust for money, he is quite willing to serve us.... These people (such as Hart and Burlingame) can be employed to serve as intermediaries in our dealings with foreign powers.'[2]

It must long have been clear to the mandarins that China was threatened by domination by the foreigner, if not with piecemeal absorption, and in the long run with out-and-out partition. But what steps, if any, did they take towards reforming and strengthening their country to resist the foreign onslaught and to retain the indentity of the age-old Middle Kingdom?

It must be borne in mind that the Manchus were committed by the circumstances of their rule over China to ultra-conservatism. Being barbarian in origin, they were forced by expedience not only to assimilate themselves culturally to the country they had conquered, but to be 'more Chinese than the Chinese'. Hence they were indisposed to any kind of change. At the same time, owing to the necessity of coming to terms with the foreign Powers on whose good-will their continued rule largely depended, they felt constrained to adopt in some measure the innovations which the Powers wished, for their own purposes, to impose upon them.

Foremost among these innovations was the Western conception of international obligations. Commissioner Lin, as far back as 1839, had studied a translation of de Vattel's *Law of Nations* (1758), but it was out of date and it is doubtful whether he was much the wiser for his trouble,[1] but in 1864 a competent translation into Chinese by Dr W. A. P. Martin of Wheaton's *International Law* was published under the auspices of the Tsungli Yamen. Present-day Chinese communist writers take the view that the reason that foreigners such as Hart and Freeman-Mitford felt that the appearance of this translation was 'an event of importance in the history of China'[2] was because the foreigners wanted the Manchus and the Chinese officials to observe the letter of the 'unequal treaties'—a course they strove consistently to avoid. Hart (in 1866) followed this up with a memorial to the Tsungli Yamen which was virtually a textbook on the sacredness of treaties (however imposed), and a warning to the Manchus that adherence to the treaties would, if necessary, be enforced by military action. Yet, as late as 1875, the British Minister, Sir Thomas Wade, was still extremely angry with the Manchus for their failure to fulfil the terms of the treaties.

The Chinese conservatives of the nineteenth century held that the foreigners ruthlessly destroyed a civilization which they did not understand, and one that could have formed a solid basis for a modernized China. In the twentieth century, both the Chinese Nationalists and the Chinese Marxists have convicted the Western Powers of destroying a nascent Chinese capitalism which was emerging from within the country in order to prevent China from competing with them as an equal. On the other hand, even admitting the general Western desideratum of a weak and docile China, it appears that the British did at least genuinely try to help the Chinese to stand on their own feet in the modern world. Mary C. Wright observes:

in the critical formative period of the 1860's it can be shown that the British government adopted for itself and held the other powers to a basic policy of non-intervention and moderate co-operation; and that, at the same time, foreign private groups were effectively prevented from unduly exploiting the unstable situation.[1]

Certainly the general willingness of the Manchus at this time to accept the role of 'pupil' to the foreign 'tutor' encouraged the widely held foreign opinion that, in this T'ung Chih reign, China had entered on a period of 'regeneration'. Colour was lent to this theory by the adoption by the Chinese of a number of other innovations. For example, in 1865 Tsêng Kuo-fan caused to be published from his military headquarters in Nanking a translation of the fifteen books of Euclid's *Elements of Geometry*. This translation was a completion of one begun by Matteo Ricci, the Jesuit, 250 years earlier. Another development was the establishment by the government of a school in Peking for the training of interpreters, called the T'ung Wên Kuan. The Imperial Maritime Customs, under Sir Robert Hart, financed and indirectly controlled the school.[2] In 1866 it was raised to the rank of a college, and in 1869 Dr W. A. P. Martin (in communist China, an American singled out for condemnation as being outstandingly 'anti-Chinese') became its President and retained this appointment until, in 1898, he became President of the newly-founded University of Peking. Arsenals (a very obvious priority) had already been set up in China, but under the direction of foreign engineers and mechanics, and in 1867, Tsêng Kuo-fan, through the persuasion of Yung Wing, China's first 'returned student' (from the U.S.A.), set up a school attached to the Kiangnan Arsenal at Shanghai to train Chinese in the theory as well as the practice of mechanical engineering. In the same year two naval schools, one French and one English, were established in Foochow. But it was not until 1874 that a Polytechnic College was opened in Shanghai, and until 1879 that the Northern Government Telegraph College was started in Tientsin.

These small moves in the direction of the 'modernization' of China did not, of course, go very deep, and the Chinese to all intents and purposes retained their traditional appearance for several decades after the Treaty of Nanking. But now another development of quite a different kind supervened to make even this moderate 'modernizing' process (suitable for what Sun Yat-Sen later termed a 'semi-colony' (*pan chih min ti*)) difficult to maintain and that was the rise of popular feeling against foreigners and everything that was foreign in origin due largely to the activities of the Christian missionaries.

The Tientsin treaties of 1858 had placed the missionaries in a peculiarly favourable position. They were now free to travel and preach anywhere in the empire. Both in the treaty ports and in the interior they acquired property and established residences. Their numbers were not great compared with the huge population of China. By 1897 the Roman Catholic priests (mostly from France) numbered a little over 750, and Protestant missionaries increased from about 189 in 1864 to nearly 1300 in 1889 (mostly from Britain and the United States, the former leading at this time). The converts, however, increased slowly, and by the end of the century the Roman Catholics numbered slightly more than half a million, while the Protestant communicants rose from 5700 in 1860 to about 55,000 in 1893.[1]

But while the numbers of the missionaries were small, the repercussions of their ministry were great. Unlike the Jesuits of the seventeenth century, they aimed no longer at assimilating their religion, as far as was logically feasible, with the native religion of China, but at replacing the latter entirely by the doctrines and observances of their own particular church or sect. Acceptance by the convert of Christianity therefore involved him in complete severance from his native community and compelled him to follow an entirely new code of behaviour. Since, moreover, the missionaries were powerful and enjoyed the support of the consuls of their several countries, their protection of their converts meant that the latter now enjoyed a special status both before the law and in society. In lawsuits they were often represented by the missionaries, and the influence of the latter often procured them immunity from taxation. Added to this, the disregard by the missionaries of the requirements of *fêng-shui*, or geomancy, in siting their churches and missionary stations, was often the occasion of hostility towards themselves.

Incidents involving missionaries occurred in the Kiangs, Kweichow, and Hunan as early as 1862. After that they occurred in quick succession in Yangchow in Kiangsu, Taming and Kuangp'ing in Chihli (now Hopeh), and in various places in Szechwan and Kweichow. And in every instance the Treaty Powers used these as pretexts for obtaining further concessions and brought pressure on the Manchu authorities to suppress the agitation among the people.

The most serious incident of this period became known as the 'Massacre of Tientsin' and took place in 1870. The immediate cause of the outbreak on the part of the inhabitants was the rumour that Chinese children were kidnapped by Roman Catholic priests and nuns in order to use their eyes and their hearts to manufacture medicines. There ensued a mass demonstration against the French missionaries during which French troops were ordered by their consul to open fire. In the ensuing riots the consul was killed and a French church was burned. France threatened war, but being at the time involved in war with Prussia had no troops to spare to send to the Far East. Tsêng Kuo-fan was ordered to Tientsin to arrange a settlement; a number of officials were exiled and sixteen civilians sentenced to death, and the Manchu government paid the French an indemnity of 460,000 taels and sent a special envoy to France to apologize.

While handling the incident Tsêng Kuo-fan expressed the opinion that the various incidents involving foreign missionaries were 'the result of the pent-up grievances of the common people',[1] but the French explanation was that: 'every attempt at reform was considered as sacrilege; even the efforts made to ameliorate the backward Chinese educational system and to introduce the nation to some of the scientific ideas which they completely lacked, were denounced as dangerous innovations'.[2]

But, whatever the true explanation, the Prussian Minister to China, Brandt, reported to his government that the feeling throughout China at this time was so intense that a general rising against the foreigners was anticipated.[3]

The toleration clauses in the Tientsin treaties had been included in consequence of the pressures both of the churches and of contemporary opinion in the Western countries concerned, but a belief in the desirability of missionary endeavour in China was by no means universally held, even among the supporters of the churches in their own countries. In Britain, for example, on 9 March 1869, Lord Clarendon said in the House of Lords: 'Missionaries require to be protected against themselves, and they are a constant menace to British interests.'[4] The Duke of Somerset, recently First Lord of the Admiralty, asked 'What right have we to be trying to convert the Chinese in the middle of their country?'[1] Grey, observing that force could not help any religion, supported Clarendon's reduction in the number of British gunboats in service in Chinese waters.[2] British officials generally did not look with any great favour on the missionaries. Sir Rutherford Alcock, British Minister to China from 1865 to 1871, advised them that the cause of Christianity would be bettered if it did not have the support of foreign governments and if the missionaries would have more patience and moderation in pursuing their enterprise they would be viewed by the Chinese less as political instruments and agents of revolutionary propaganda and more as teachers of religion.[3]

At a time when the Boxer movement was well under way, the Roman Catholic Church succeeded in obtaining recognition from the Manchu government of rights which put its bishops and priests on an equality with the Chinese mandarins within Chinese territory. By a decree of 15 March 1899 Roman Catholic bishops were declared in rank and dignity to be equal to viceroys and governors, and they were authorized to demand to see viceroys and governors; vicars-general and arch-deacons were authorized to demand to see *their* equals, namely prefects of the first and second class; while ordinary priests were to rank with magistrates.

Bishop Favier, however, stated that this extraordinary concession was not extorted from the Chinese government but was accorded by the latter on its own initiative. A similar privilege was offered at the same time to the various Protestant missionary bodies—an offer that was ultimately rejected in spite of arguments in favour of acceptance from some of them. Actually, the rights now conferred legally had been exercised illegally both by Protestants and Roman Catholics for many years, and the present concession was an attempt by the Chinese government to regain control over its Christian subjects by incorporating their spiritual leaders into the official system of the empire, a policy which had been successfully adopted with Buddhism throughout the country, and with Mohammedanism in Yunnan, Shensi, Kansu, and Chinese Turkestan.[4]

The decree, none the less, was widely regarded as an act of desperation on the part of a regime which was about to disintegrate.

Since the Manchu government were hostile to Western ideas and techniques which they regarded as a threat to the conservatism to which they were committed, and with the common people associating every innovation with foreign penetration and interference with their cherished 'way of life', the outlook was not propitious for the speedy 'modernization' of China. The Western Powers, for their part, were not over anxious to introduce China to reforms that would raise her effectiveness in arms or organization to their own level. Nevertheless, the modernization of the country in certain limited respects was very desirable in the interests of their commerce.

The European Powers regarded China primarily in terms of markets. Yet the volume of foreign imports grew slowly, the increase between 1865 and 1885 being only 25 per cent.[1] To speed up the development of China as a market, the introduction of railways and telegraphs seemed an obvious prerequisite. But what were the chances of inducing either the Manchus or the Chinese to look with a favourable eye on such threats to the old order of things, to which, for rather different reasons, they were both attached? In 1876, when some British merchants took it upon themselves to build a railway between Shanghai and Wusung, the Manchu government acquired it—only in order to tear it up!

The attitude of the Manchus and the Chinese mandarins, however, was not consistent or united. For example, a group of 'new officials' arose during the T'ung Chih reign, who were persuaded that the means to power must be secured by a selective copying of the West, and it was they who induced their government to introduce railways and telegraphs from about 1880 onwards, and at the same time a start was made with buying foreign warships wherewith to found a navy.

Opposed to the 'new officials' was the ultra-conservative party which regarded the West with hostility and argued that even the teaching of astronomy and mathematics at the T'ung Wên College would result in 'the collapse of uprightness and the spread of wickedness'. The irony was that the ultra-conservatives were also the 'war party', urging a resort to arms in every critical situation such as that arising from the 'Tientsin Massacre', the conflict with France over Indochina, the dispute with Russia over Ili, and the controversy with Japan on the questions of the Ryukyu Islands, Formosa, and Korea—the very line of action that was bound to fail unless the conservatives abandoned their conservatism and copied at least from the West its superiority in arms! But this 'war party' actually did not want war at all, and relapsed into silence when the conflict appeared imminent. What they sought was the prestige of *words*.

The policy of the group of 'new officials' is not quite so simple to describe. Men like Tsêng Kuo-fan, Tso Tsung-t'ang, and Li Hung-chang, who led them, were far from being revolutionaries. They merely aimed to adopt methods tending to material strength from the West in order to preserve the essence of the existing order.[1]

The achievements of the 'new officials' can be indicated by a few examples. In 1866 Tso Tsung-t'ang established a shipbuilding yard in Fukien under French management; he bought Krupp and other foreign guns which helped him to subdue the 'Nien' uprising; he also established a textile mill in Lanchow. Li Hung-chang's efforts covered a longer period of time, were more considerable than Tso's, and included learning foreign methods as well as utilizing the manufactures and services of foreigners. For example, he utilized the advice of such men as Gordon in military affairs and Hart in foreign negotiations. He bought foreign machinery with which to set up the Kiangnan Machine Building Works in Shanghai in 1865 and the Tientsin Machinery Works in 1867. It was he also who made a real attempt to create a Chinese navy from 1875 onwards with ships bought from Britain and Germany, and invited foreign officers to China to train his sea and land forces. It was Li Hung-chang, too, who finally initiated the building of railways and telegraph lines in China, and these are only a few of his innovations.

Nevertheless, even Li Hung-chang contented himself with the purchase of foreign arms and the employment of foreign instructors and stopped short of radical reorganization of China's armed forces on modern lines. He has been criticized, too (by communist historians), for his policy of planning privately-owned concerns under government supervision, for 'this worked poorly from the start, as the new enterprises were completely controlled by bureaucratic capital, hindering the free development of private capital'.[2] He incidentally managed to build up an enormous private fortune in the process of laying the foundation of China's industry.[3]

The success or otherwise of the 'new' group in modernizing China so that she could successfully resist further encroachment on her sovereignty by foreigners must be judged on the facts. Certainly the continued concessions to foreign demands did not suggest that the process of encroachment had been arrested, or even appreciably slowed down. In 1875 occurred the Margary Incident which gave Britain an excuse for further demands on China which were conceded at the Chefoo Conference in 1876, whereby new treaty ports were opened on the Yangtze and that river was opened to foreign trade. In 1879

Japan (taking a leaf out of the book of the Western Powers) occupied
the Ryukyu (Loochoo) Islands and later formally annexed them; in the
same year the Russians occupied Ili, which the Manchu government
redeemed by raising a loan; in 1884 the Sino–French War broke out
in which the French were victorious on the sea but seriously defeated
on the land (at Langson) yet managed by diplomatic pressure to secure
advantageous terms entailing further loss to Chinese sovereignty; and
similar concessions to the British over Burma were made by China in
1886. In the meantime Japan's ambition to annex Korea (which paid
tribute to China) was becoming clearer every day. When the final
reckoning came in 1894–5 with the war with Japan over Korea, the
Chinese defence system collapsed like a house of cards, the Japanese
gained an easy victory, and the 'modernization' of China was exposed
as a sham.

Let us contrast for a moment China's failure under the Manchus to
adapt herself to meeting the coercive West on an equal footing with
Japan's successful response to the same pressures.

Feeling herself threatened by the expansionism of the West, notably
of Spain, Japan had early in the seventeenth century decided to withdraw behind what we might, in present-day colloquial language, call
a 'bamboo curtain'. No sea-going ships were to be built, no Japanese
might go abroad on pain of death, and no foreigners were to be allowed
on Japanese soil. But mainly through the little peep-hole of Deshima,
a tiny artificial island in the Bay of Nagasaki on which the Dutch were
allowed to remain and trade, Japan kept an eye on happenings in the
outer world. She heard, for example, of the easy military successes of
Britain over China in the Opium War, and when in 1853 Commodore
Perry of the United States Navy arrived with a squadron to demand that
Japan open her doors to foreign trade, she was under no illusions as to
the strength of the West whose challenge she now had to meet. There
ensued a period of reluctance to enter the modern world and of hostility
to the foreigners and their demands, but eventually Japan decided that
she had no alternative but to comply. However, in opening her doors to
the West, the Japanese simultaneously determined that they would copy
from the West the techniques which gave it its military strength but at
the same time they would preserve as intact as possible their own
institutions and way of life. In what is known as the Meiji Restoration
(1868–1912) they did this with a surprising measure of success.

However (as Sir George Sansom points out), 'the achievement was indeed remarkable, but the change (from a feudal regime into a national monarchical government and the founding of a modern industrial State) was not sudden and had been for a long time in gradual preparation'.[1]

Now that the Emperor of Japan was so in fact and not only theory, local autonomy was abolished by decree, and the social system known for convenience as 'feudal' was to be a thing of the past. The pensions of the *Samurai* were commuted and swords were forbidden to be worn. The Japanese now embarked with fervour on the task of modernizing and industrializing their country. Foreigners were brought in to teach and advise. The Japanese navy was reorganized on the model of the British navy; the army was remodelled—first on the pattern of the French army, but when France was defeated by Prussia in the war of 1870, on that of the German army. A measure of representative government was introduced and the laws were so reformed by French and other advice, that before the end of the century the foreigners had no longer any excuse for retaining extraterritorial powers and relinquished them.

But with all this outburst of radical innovation, the Japanese did their utmost to adapt existing national institutions to suit the new needs, and: 'There is not evidence enough to show that because she adapted Western machines and commercial practices to her own uses Japan became Western in the essence of her national character by the close of the nineteenth century.'[2]

But there was a great deal of the 'mushroom' in this almost overnight growth, and the emphasis on national defence caused unbalance and distortion. Nor did Japan, in remodelling herself on the West, avoid copying some of the worst faults of the Western system. Foremost among these was the urge to expansion resulting in imperialistic adventures abroad, in search of markets created by the industrialization of the country. (The Japanese themselves were divided as to the need, but the military party had their way.)

There were many reasons why China did not succeed in following the example of her smaller and younger neighbour, who owed to her the basis of its own civilization—namely the vast size of the country, its provincial divisions, its heterogeneous racial elements, and the fact that an alien dynasty of barbarian origin, now degenerate and clinging desperately to power, occupied the throne. Nor can the Powers be acquitted of using their influence to retard the entry of China into the modern world as an equal and competitor. They had no desire to see capitalism in China developed to the extent of making her independent of their manufactories, and they did not intend that she should build up a military power great enough to challenge their own. What they feared in the last decades of the nineteenth century was that unless they adopted modern methods in sufficient degree the Manchus would be too weak to retain their hold on China, and in the ensuing *débâcle* all that had been gained from them would be lost. Japan, for her part, profited from the fact that during the crucial period of modernization she was saved from the dangers of political and economic domination by foreign Powers through their preoccupations elsewhere. Britain, while supporting the party of reform in Japan, was concentrating her efforts upon gaining trade and influence in China; France was involved with Russia and entangled in Mexico; Russia, though taking an aggressive line (her warships had been hard on the heels of Commodore Perry in 1853), and going so far as to occupy the island of Tsushima in 1861, was compelled by pressure from Britain to withdraw from it; America was occupied with her civil war. There was also the consideration that Japan might be used as a sort of policeman to prevent China getting out of hand.

Apart from China's own inadequacies, the political and economic pressure of the foreign Powers was much greater on China than on Japan. This, Feuerwerker considers,[1] was in large part 'a function of the myth of the Chinese market'. Japan's economic development owed a great debt to the existence of opportunities for the profitable export of Japanese manufactured goods, but China would have to depend entirely on the demand of its domestic market to take up the products of its infant industries. Strenuous efforts by foreigners to promote the sale of their manufactures in the interior of China (in response to the lure of '400 million customers'), combined with the right to undertake manufacturing in the treaty ports, made deep inroads into the limited Chinese domestic markets. The gap left by the breakdown of handicraft production was in a large measure filled by the products of European factories. Moreover, the *Kuan-tu Shang-pan* ('Official Supervision and Merchant Management') system, which initiated such undertakings as the China Merchants' Steam Navigation Company, the Telegraph Administration, the Hua-sheng Mill, Han-Yeh-P'ing Ironworks, and the Imperial Bank of China, failed to turn China into an industrial civilization because they were limited in potential growth by the nature of their organization, were unable to break out of the framework of the old order, and led to the 'bureaucratic capitalism' of the Kuomintang period which stood in the way of efforts to modernize China within a democratic framework.[1]

During all these years the traditional economy of China had been subjected to undermining by foreign capitalist enterprise and was by the 1890's completely dislocated, and since the concentration of the trade and the economic power in the treaty ports brought no compensating advantage to the people of the vast continental hinterland, this fact alone was enough to create a state of widespread discontent which prepared the way for civil commotion. As Ho Ping-ti says:

The absence of a major technological revolution in modern times has made it impossible for China to broaden the scope of her land economy to any appreciable extent. It is true that, after the opening of China in the 1840's, the moderately expanding international commerce, the beginnings in modern money and banking, the coming of steamers and railways, the establishment by both Chinese and foreigners of a number of light and extractive industries have made the Chinese economy more variegated, but these new influences have been so far confined to the eastern seaboard and a few treaty ports. There has been no significant change in the basic character of the national economy. In fact for a century after the Opium War the influence of the West on the Chinese economy was as disruptive as it was constructive.[2]

China's swift defeat at the hands of her pupil, Japan, in 1894, completely upset the calculations of the Western Powers. By the Treaty of Shimonoseki, Japan had not only seized Formosa and demanded a huge indemnity, but was now an Imperial Power on her own account, and able to claim an equality of opportunity with the other Powers. What was more, the Manchu government had been weakened in prestige by the defeat to the extent of being at the mercy, it seemed, of another rebellion like the Taiping, should one arise, and quite unable to resist Japan if she set out to conquer China. In face of the probability of China's break-up, the jealousies and antagonisms of the Powers became acute. There was still repeated talk, in international circles, of 'maintaining the integrity' of China but if, after all, she could not hold together as a unity there would be a terrific scramble among the Powers for possession of the pieces. The scene was thus set for the 'Battle of the Concessions' in which the Powers sought to carve up China into 'spheres of influence'—a kind of vivisection of the anticipated corpse.

CHAPTER IV

THE BATTLE OF THE CONCESSIONS

From the Opium War until her defeat by Japan in 1895, China had suffered the encroachment of the Powers, but when it was suddenly made plain that the country was defenceless against modern military organization and weapons, this encroachment turned into a scramble for concessions which seemed to foreshadow its actual territorial partition. This scramble intensified the Chinese hatred of the foreigner and precipitated the desperate twelfth-hour attempt at modernization known as 'The Hundred Days of Reform'.

Up to 1895 the British had supported China as a bulwark against Russia, but the outcome of the Sino–Japanese War demonstrated in a spectacular fashion that China was quite incapable of defending herself. Nor after the peace of Shimonoseki were they able to take a new, constructive line of their own because Europe was divided into two rival groups of Powers—the Dual (France and Russia) and the Triple (Germany, Austria and Italy) Alliances—to neither of which was Britain attached so that in Asia she had liabilities and risks without friends to share them. Some Britons, like Curzon, advocated a more forceful policy for Britain, whereby she would have taken the lead in the reform of China and insisted on her maintenance as a buffer State, if necessary under British dominion. But this solution would have been opposed not only by the Dual Alliance but by Germany also. Another possible solution would have been to abandon the Open Door and join in the race for spheres of influence. Reluctant to adopt such a course, the British government under Lord Salisbury had fallen back on the difficult task of attempting to reconcile the expansion of the European Powers with the maintenance of the Open Door by means of agreements with France and Russia. But although Japan's demands for the opening up of more Chinese ports suited Britain's interests, she did not find herself able to stand by Japan when the pressure of the other Powers made itself felt.[1]

Some British merchants and writers, however, still entertained hopes for China's future. The experiences of the war, they said, would show even the Chinese mandarins the need for reform and modernization.

But most of the British authorities regarded the situation as beyond redemption. 'Of the existing Chinese Government it is impossible to say a good word, or even to entertain a hope', wrote D. C. Boulger; 'The whole administration is rotten to the core', R. K. Douglas confirmed: Henry Norman went even further, declaring that 'every Chinese official, with the possible exception of one in a thousand, is a liar, a thief, and a tyrant'. 'A more hopeless spectacle of imbecility [Valentine Chirol summed up], made up in equal parts of arrogance and helplessness, than the central government of the Chinese Empire presented after the actual pressure of war had been removed, it is impossible to conceive.'[1]

The question that the British government was called upon to answer at this juncture was how the action of the Franco–Russian Alliance could be neutralized in the Far East. The Russian advance in the Pamirs and the French thrust in the direction of Siam were evidence of the plans of this combination at the expense of Britain.

The Treaty of Shimonoseki, concluding the war between China and Japan, was signed on 17 April 1895. Japan had intended to keep possession of the Liaotung peninsula, but Russia, France and Germany immediately intervened to demand its retrocession to China on the ground that the peninsula, in Japanese hands, would constitute a constant menace to the Chinese capital, would render the independence of Korea illusory, and would henceforth be a perpetual obstacle to peace in the Far East. The Japanese military commanders advised their government that the three Powers acting in concert could not be resisted, with the result that on 5 May Japan yielded completely, even consenting to withdraw from Port Arthur, which was at the tip of the peninsula.

The three Powers, however, although they could act in concert to check Japan, were disunited by their rivalries. All three aimed at gaining the gratitude of the Chinese government in order to obtain advantage for themselves. The Russians, for example, aimed to secure the right to run the Trans-Siberian Railway through Manchuria; the Germans wanted a naval station; the French motives were more obscure, but it was clear enough from the negotiations that they also required a *quid pro quo* of a like order in Tongking. The Russians were to the fore in offering to guarantee a loan to China to enable her to pay her indemnity of $150 million to Japan, but the Chinese government, anxious not to fall too much under the influence of its Russian saviour, opened negotiations with financial circles in London and Berlin. Russia and France then joined to counteract the danger to themselves, offering China a Franco–Russian loan of 400 million francs, which she found herself practically forced to accept. This marked the beginnings of Russian preponderance in China, which was resented by Germany with the result that she became cooler in supporting Russian policy during the prolonged negotiations for securing Japan's full withdrawal from the Liaotung peninsula. But, not being able to afford to estrange France, she continued to support Russian policy in the Far East in general.[1]

The first move towards what threatened to become the dismemberment of China came from the south. Both the French and the British were intent on gaining access to the Chinese markets 'from behind', and the rivalries between them during the previous two decades can be summed up in one phrase as 'a race for Yunnan'. While the British were surveying a railway line from Mandalay to Yunnan, the French (in 1893) took over a large part of eastern Siam, despite British protests. The French, moreover, had an advantage in commanding the Red River route which was by far the shortest into Yunnan. In June 1897 they obtained from China the right to extend the Lungchow railway and also the right to priority in the exploitation of the mines in Kwangtung, Kwangsi, and Yunnan. They now extended their plans to include the exploitation of Szechwan. The British were unable to offer effective resistance to the French programme because the whole French policy enjoyed the vigorous support of the Russians.

The French expansion did not compete with the Russian plans which were much more extensive in their scope. If France had a thousand miles of common frontier with China, Russia had three thousand, and the Trans-Siberian Railway was a vastly more ambitious project than the French railway into Yunnan. It was obvious to close observers that Vladivostok, whose harbour was frozen for four or five months in the year, was not a suitable terminus for the Trans-Siberian Railway, and that the Russians would attempt to obtain an ice-free port in Korea. But if such a port were secured as a terminus for the railway, it was to be expected that they would aim to carry it across Northern Manchuria, thus saving 350 miles of line through the barren wastes of eastern Siberia. In the meantime the Japanese had entrenched themselves firmly in Korea from the beginning of their war with China, and the prospect for a Russian port within their sphere of influence seemed somewhat remote.

86

Witte, the Russian Minister of Finance, however, was willing to wait. His policy was one of economic penetration, and as a preliminary he was determined to establish a Russian bank in China so that the Russians would no longer be dependent on British, German, and French banks for the conduct of their now extensive financial relations with China. The capital for establishing the bank, however, could be obtained only in Paris. A good deal of haggling and manipulation ensued, but the fact that the French government threw its weight on the side of Russia resulted in seven French banks (which had already furnished the funds for the loan to China which Russia had guaranteed) producing the further funds for the foundation of the Russo–Chinese Bank. The charter for the foundation of the bank was granted to the Committee of the Trans-Siberian Railway in December 1895.

During the autumn and winter of 1895–6, the Russian Ministry of Communications made a rapid survey of northern Manchuria. When reports that Russia and China had concluded an agreement which would give Russia the right to construct railways from Vladivostok to Port Arthur by way of Tsitsihar and that Russia was to have the right of anchorage at Port Arthur reached London, *The Times* reacted violently, declaring that the enterprise 'would constitute a destruction of the present balance of power almost unparalleled in its audacity'.[1] But the British government was not disturbed. Lord Salisbury made it clear that his interest was at the moment focused on the Near East and only if Russia demanded exclusive rights for her ships at Port Arthur would Britain protest. Salisbury was concerned to secure Russian co-operation over the Armenian question and to obtain, if possible, a general understanding with Russia which seemed so desirable after the episode of the Kaiser's telegram to Kruger. In a speech at the Guildhall he deprecated 'unnecessary disturbance and alarm' and quoted Lord Beaconsfield's dictum that 'in Asia there is room for us all'. Mr Balfour, in a speech at Bristol in February 1896, reiterated the government view. The British attitude, in fact, amounted to no less than an invitation to the Russians to take a Chinese port, provided only they left it free for the commerce of all nations.

Witte meanwhile encountered difficulties at the Chinese Court in proceeding with his plans. Li Hung-chang, through whom the Russians had hoped to secure their ends, was in disgrace and his successors, mostly staunch conservatives, were negotiating for a second loan to pay the indemnity to Japan with a syndicate of British and

German banks. It was only by the distribution of $5 million in bribes that the Russians were able eventually to get their way. It happened that Li Hung-chang, despite his removal from power at the capital, did become the agency through which the negotiations were concluded, for in 1896, under the influence of Tz'ŭ Hsi, the Chinese government had decided to send him to Russia to represent the Emperor at the coronation of the Tsar.

For his services in negotiating the Russo–Chinese Treaty of 1896, Li Hung-chang probably received a bribe from the Russians equal to $1½ million (U.S.).[1] But he nevertheless pared down the Russian programme almost to the bone. Instead of a concession to the Russian government there was to be one to the Russo–Chinese Bank, the time limit being 80 years, with China retaining the right to buy the concession back from the Bank at the end of 36 years. There was disagreement about the gauge—whether it should be the standard European or the wider Russian one—and the matter was left open. In return for this concession, Li obtained a defensive alliance for 15 years which provided that in the event of any aggression by Japan against Russian territory in Eastern Asia, or that of China or Korea, Russia and China should support one another by force of arms and neither should make a separate peace.

(Li Hung-chang may have accepted the Russian bribe, but it cannot be said that he regarded it as payment for altogether disregarding Chinese interests as he saw them in the existing situation.)

Until the Trans-Siberian Railway was finished, the Russians could not hope to compete with the Japanese forces in the Far East, so that some sort of temporary agreement with Japan was expedient. The outcome of the negotiations, the Lobanov–Yamagata Agreement of 9 June 1896, established something like a condominium over Korea. One Russian historian at least, B. A. Romanov, is of the opinion that the agreement was concluded by the Russians in bad faith, and Langer remarks that the evidence adduced by him 'would seem to leave little doubt on this point'.[2]

But Witte was much more interested in the Manchurian problem. The treaty signed by Li Hung-chang had indeed been approved by the Chinese government, but when it came to details the Chinese temporized. Prince Kung, President of the Tsungli Yamen, is reported to have been in favour of the repudiation of the treaty, and the Empress Dowager refused to receive Li until he had handed over £800 thousand of his ill-gotten gains.[1] Finally, in September 1896, a contract was made between the Chinese government and the Russo–Chinese Bank whereby the latter was to organize a Chinese Eastern Railway Company with a Chinese as President, the line was to be on the Russian wide gauge, the company was to have the absolute and exclusive right of administration of its lands, the railway was to be free from all taxes and imposts, and the goods carried were to pay the Chinese customs duties less a third. The provisions for the retention of the railway for an 80 years maximum period, with the right of redemption after 36 years, were retained. The Russian government held all the shares. The Chinese Eastern Railway had now only to be built.

After the war with Japan, China herself decided to embark on the construction of railways. Of first priority was a line from Peking to Hankow and then on to Canton. The first intention was that only Chinese capital should be employed, but when the Chinese capitalists showed no inclination to entrust their government with such large funds, the latter opened up negotiations with American and Belgian interests (on the supposition that only the United States and Belgium were without ulterior political aims), but, in the event, a Franco–Belgian syndicate was formed, with which, however, the Russo–Chinese Bank was later allowed to join. In May 1897 the Peking–Hankow section was awarded to this financial combination, while the Hankow–Canton section was handed over to the American Development Company with a proviso that if it failed to meet the terms, the Franco–Belgian combination was to take over.

But the contemplated network of railways would not be complete until a junction between the Russian line in Manchuria and the Peking–Hankow trunk line was effected. Here Li Hung-chang proved to be the obstacle, and in spite of a present of a million roubles (the first instalment of an agreed bribe and, as it proved, the last), he opposed the junction of the lines. All he would do was to give a promise that no concession for joining the Russian and Chinese lines would be given to any other Power. At the same time the Russians failed to secure permission to run their line across Manchuria through Kirin—a line further south than the one finally decided on.

It will be seen that it was France and Russia who were taking the initiative in profiting from China's weakness after her defeat by Japan. Their policy was undisguisedly one of 'peaceful penetration'— 'peaceful' being subject to a special interpretation. As Langer points out, however, France and Russia were the Powers least in need of territorial expansion, and in order to obtain any advantage from their acquisitions they had to make them practically national preserves through the application of high tariffs. The British and the Germans, on the other hand, were almost more anxious to preserve open markets than to annex territory. It was only the action of France and Russia that drove them into a policy that was in some ways decidedly contrary to their own interests.

Since the intervention of the three Powers against Japan in 1895, the policy of Germany in the Far East had been dominated by the desire to engage the Russians in Asia and thus weaken the Franco–Russian Alliance as regards Europe. The Kaiser's obsession with the 'Yellow Peril' was an additional inspiration to him in encouraging the Tsar to occupy himself with Far Eastern ambitions. He assured him that even if he had to send all his troops to the Far East he would not only not attack France but would guarantee Russia's rear. In 1895 he commissioned the German artist, H. Knackfuss, to carry out an allegorical picture designed by himself showing (as he described it) 'the Powers of Europe represented by their respective Genii called together by the Archangel Michael, sent from Heaven, to *unite* in resisting the inroads of Buddhism, heathenism, and barbarism, for the defence of the Cross', and he presented the first copy to the Tsar. The Kaiser, in the same description, went on to say, 'Stress is especially laid on the *united* resistance of all European Powers, which is just as necessary also against our internal foes—anarchism, republicanism, and nihilism'.[1]

Germany's own immediate aim, however, was to find naval stations and coaling bases in various parts of the world to support her challenge to the overseas empires of Britain and France. Although German commerce in China was second only to the British, she had no commercial base like Hong Kong, no coaling station, no docking and repair facilities, no fortified naval base. Being almost entirely dependent on Hong Kong, she was thus dependent on British good-will.

In choosing a suitable location for a base on the China coast the Germans tried to avoid collision with British or Russian interests. Kiaochow seemed a possibility, but it was suspected that Russia might have established a lien on this place and have secured an agreement with the Chinese. This did not prove to be the case, for not only had the Chinese refused the Russians a lease of it, but the Russian admiralty had turned it down as unsuitable for their purposes. Kaiser Wilhelm, during his visit to St Petersburg in August 1897, took up the question with the Tsar who answered that although Russia was interested mainly in assuring herself access to the Bay of Kiaochow until she secured Pingyang (Pyongyang) in Korea, she had no objection to the Germans anchoring at Kiaochow in case of need, after securing the consent of the Russian naval authorities. This the Germans interpreted as Russian approval of their desire to make use of the port. When, however, the Russians were officially notified of Germany's intention to acquire it, citing Russian approval for the move, they were displeased and pointed out that the Germans had failed to obtain the prior consent of the Russian naval authorities on the spot. But Germany, in any case, was intent on pursuing the project.

The first German intention had apparently been to send their Far Eastern squadron to winter in Kiaochow, as a preliminary to obtaining a concession of the port from China, but on 1 November 1897 two German Catholic missionaries were killed in Shantung by a Chinese gang in the course of an attempted robbery.[1] The incident came most conveniently. The Kaiser wanted to send the squadron immediately to Kiaochow and declared: 'I am firmly determined to give up our over-cautious policy which is regarded as weak throughout Eastern Asia, and to demonstrate through our use of sternness and, if necessary, of the most brutal ruthlessness towards the Chinese, that the German Emperor cannot be trifled with.'[2]

The Chancellor, Prince Hohenlohe, however, warned his sovereign that he was bound to obtain the prior consent of the Russian government. Wilhelm accordingly telegraphed to the Tsar saying that he was under obligations to the Catholic party in Germany to protect their missions and proposed therefore to establish Kiaochow as a base to operate against the Chinese marauders. To this Nicholas replied promptly, 'Cannot approve, or disapprove your sending German squadron to Kiaochow, as I have lately learned that this harbour had only been temporarily ours in 1895–96'. This the Kaiser, naturally enough in his existing mood, interpreted as meaning, 'Approve'. The German admiral was ordered to Kiaochow forthwith. Wilhelm wrote to von Bülow (who happened to be in Rome):

Thousands of German Christians will breathe more easily when they know that the German Emperor's ships are near; hundreds of German traders will revel in the knowledge that the German Empire has at last secured a firm footing in Asia; hundreds of thousands of Chinese will quiver when they feel the iron fist of Germany heavy on their necks; and the whole German nation will be delighted that its Government has done a manly act.[1]

Quite apart from their fear of German intervention in their sphere of influence, the Russians were constrained by their policy of friendship for China to support the Chinese in their resistance to Germany's new move. For a while they did so and gave the Tsungli Yamen detailed advice, but gradually they withdrew their support from the Chinese and made their peace with the Germans, and the last weeks of 1897 saw the end of the German–Russian dispute.

The Russian motives in this *volte-face* are not difficult to understand. Muraviev, the Russian Foreign Minister, had objected strenuously to the German occupation of Kiaochow because the Russians sincerely feared that the German move would result in a scramble for Chinese territory. They wanted China to remain intact, not from altruistic motives, but because the whole Russian plan of campaign as worked out by Witte envisaged an extension of Russian power by 'peaceful penetration' which would result in the undisputed control of Peking and eventually something like a Russian protectorate over the whole of China. Germany's inflexible attitude over Kiaochow threatened the success of the plan, and to compensate themselves for their disappointment they had resolved to participate themselves in the overt scramble for territory by occupying Port Arthur. The Russians had indeed been intent on securing an ice-free port in Chinese waters for themselves and they had evidently occupied Kiaochow in 1895–6 to see if it would suit their requirements, but had given it up, not only out of consideration for China but also on the advice of the naval authorities who, for technical reasons, decided that it would not suit them.

Early in the summer of 1898 the Tsungli Yamen felt obliged to yield to the Germans, and on 6 March an agreement was formally signed. Germany secured the lease of Kiaochow for ninety-nine years, with a neutral zone 50 kilometres wide surrounding the concession. Two railways, Kiaochow–Weihsien–Chinanfu, and Kiaochow–Ichow–Chinanfu, were to be constructed by a Chinese–German company, and in a zone 50 kilometres wide on either side of these lines German subjects were to be allowed to hold and develop mining properties. And there were other concessions besides. 'The Battle of the Concessions' had been formally inaugurated.

But why did the Russians not seize a port in Korea, of which there were numerous suitable ones, and thus solve the problem of satisfying the demands of their navy without compromising their policy in China? The extended answers are a matter for the diplomatic historian, but the short one is that the new Russian Minister to Japan was convinced that a new arrangement with Japan regarding Korea was both possible and necessary. In his opinion the immense armament of the Japanese was directed against Russia, and when she was ready in 1902 or 1904, the conflict would unquestionably break out over the Korean question. Japanese statesmen, however, desired a *détente* with Russia and it would, therefore, be impolitic for her to establish an unofficial protectorate over Korea.

The Russian statesmen were not agreed on occupying Port Arthur as a *pis aller* for a Korean port. Muraviev put forward the scheme and Witte vigorously opposed it, gaining the support of all the other Ministers. But Muraviev bided his time. He knew that the Tsar was on his side. On 14 December 1897 the German government was informed that, with the consent of the Chinese government, a detachment of the Russian Far Eastern squadron would temporarily anchor at Port Arthur. The Kaiser was overjoyed. He summoned the Russian ambassador and assured him that 'Your enemies, whether they be called Japanese or English, now become my enemies, and every trouble maker, whoever he may be, who wishes to hinder our intentions by force, will meet the German side by side with your warships'. And when two days later his brother, Prince Henry, was just about to leave for the East with additional ships and troops, he made a speech at a farewell dinner to him in the castle of Kiel in which he admonished Henry that 'if anyone should undertake to insult us in our rights or wish to harm us, then drive in with the mailed fist (*fahre darein mit gepanzerter Faust*) and, as God wills it, bind about your brows the laurels which no one in this entire German Empire will begrudge you'. To which Henry replied that his sole purpose was 'to declare abroad the gospel of your Majesty's anointed person'. With such religious bombast was the dismemberment of China inaugurated.[1]

When the negotiations between Russia and China opened in March 1898, the two negotiators on the Chinese side were Li Hung-chang and Chang Yin-huan (1837–1900).[2] On instructions from St Petersburg, the Russian Chargé d'Affaires, Pavlov, and the Russian financial agent, Pokotilov, offered them a bribe of 500 thousand taels each. They protested—but not too much. On 27 March the agreement was signed by which the Russians got all they wanted.

But what were China and the other Powers doing all this time? Why should the other Powers have allowed China to succumb to Russian pressure in this way? The answer lies in their ineluctable rivalry. The British were prepared to recognize the Russian sphere in China if only they could extort a recognition of treaty rights and of the Open Door over the vast territory of China and if the arrangement could be extended to the Near East. The Russians discounted this move as a maladroit attempt to divert them from their ambitions. The British Cabinet then decided on 25 March that Port Arthur was not worth a war. As for the Japanese, though outraged by the seizure of an area by one of the Powers which had forced her to relinquish it only a year or two before, they were not yet ready to challenge Russia in the field. There was, moreover, the chance that they would have to take on France and Germany as well. In addition to this, Muraviev decided to buy them off by making concessions in Korea. By the Nishi–Rosen Agreement of 25 April 1898 the two governments recognized the full independence of Korea and undertook to abstain from all interference in the domestic affairs of that country. In short, the agreement put the two Powers on an equal footing as regards abstention from action, but Japan was given a free hand economically in Korea.

From these transactions the British had been altogether excluded, and could only be mortified by their failure to 'square' the Russians. Chamberlain in particular was not willing to accept Salisbury's *laissez faire* policy without a struggle. Early in February he had written to Balfour warning him that the government would meet with disaster if it did not follow a stronger line in China. Balfour's reply is not on record, but on 8 March the British Ambassador in Washington submitted an unofficial memorandum to the State Department asking if the British government could depend on the co-operation of the United States in opposing action by foreign Powers which might tend to restrict the freedom of commerce of all nations in China, but the American government returned an evasive reply. Chamberlain then sounded the Japanese and after them the Germans, but with similar results.

In this humiliating situation the British government decided that the only thing to do was to meet the public clamour for action by Britain by leasing Weihaiwei, although they knew that its harbour was not deep enough for large ships, was expensive to fortify, and was cut off from the hinterland by a range of high hills. It was not the occupation of the commercial port of Talienwan by the Russians (included in the agreement) which disturbed the British, but of Port Arthur which could never be made into a commercial port but was purely a naval base, commanding the approaches to Peking from the sea. The Tsungli Yamen was perfectly willing to lease Weihaiwei to Britain as a counterbalance to Russia's occupation of Port Arthur, and the Japanese, who were still occupying it pending the payment of their war indemnity, were quite willing to withdraw. The British government had hesitated to join in the scramble for territory in China, especially since (on 1 March) Parliament had passed a resolution 'that it is of vital importance for British commerce and influence that the independence of Chinese territory should be maintained'.

Langer describes the contention of Joseph[1] and others that the Germans started the scramble for Chinese territory as an exaggeration, but admits that their occupation of Kiaochow unquestionably precipitated the Russian action at Talienwan and Port Arthur, the special contribution of Muraviev and the Tsar to the Far Eastern situation. Had Russia pursued the peaceful penetration policy of Witte, making a show of helping the Chinese against the German demands (which she had started to do), her position would have been stronger than ever. As it was, Muraviev wrecked the good understanding with China, placed himself in a position where he had to make concessions to Japan in Korea, and aroused bitter opposition from Britain. Britain, for her part, had erred in her policy over the Chinese loan, but the taking of Weihaiwei was perhaps an even greater blunder. Not only did it involve committing Britain to supporting German aspirations and to giving them assurances that they would never develop the port into a worthwhile base, but (much worse) the occupation was an abandonment of Britain's policy (maintained since 1860) of respecting the integrity of the Chinese empire.[2]

In the meantime the struggle between Britain and France in southwest China had been going on apace. When, in June 1897, the British secured the opening up of the West River to commerce, the French regarded it as a direct blow to their interests. They therefore compelled the Chinese to agree to the eventual extension of their railway in the direction of Nanning and other concessions regarding the employment of French mining engineers in the provinces of Kwangtung, Kwangsi, and Yunnan. They then hinted at their intention of securing a coaling and naval station on the southern Chinese coast, and eventually decided on Kwangchowwan. The Chinese government, having already leased Port Arthur and Talienwan to Russia, thereupon leased Kwangchowwan to France for 99 years and the French flag was hoisted there on 22 April.

Now that the scramble had really started, the British government, constantly prodded by the China Association, the London Chamber of Commerce, and other organizations, began to take a stronger line with China. To counterbalance the French advance in the south, it obtained in June a 99-year lease of territories on the mainland opposite Hong Kong amounting to 355 square miles.[1]

British policy, moreover, aimed at the recognition by China and the Powers of the Yangtze valley as a British sphere of influence—but the Russians were not content to leave them in undisputed possession of it.

The Far Eastern crisis of 1897–8 had left the two chief rivals, Britain and Russia, at daggers drawn. Not only had the Russians planted themselves firmly in Manchuria; they were also invading central China, using Belgian and French financial corporations as spearheads. On 27 July 1898 the Franco–Belgian Syndicate, backed by the Russo–Chinese Bank, secured the definitive concession for the all-important Peking–Hankow line, which, when completed, would bring Russian influence to the banks of the Yangtze. The British protested vigorously against the concession on the grounds that 'a concession of this nature is no longer a commercial or industrial enterprise, and becomes a political movement against British interests in the neighbourhood of the Yangtze'. But the Chinese insisted that the Russians had nothing to do with it, and ratified the grant in August.

A long wrangle between the two Powers ensued, but the Russian Ministers of Foreign Affairs and of War felt the need of some agreement with Britain. They eventually overcame the opposition of their ministerial colleagues, and in April 1899 notes were exchanged whereby Russia undertook not to seek any railway concessions in the Yangtze valley and not to obstruct any application for concessions in that region supported by the British government. Britain, for her part, accepted similar obligations with regard to the area north of the Great Wall. There was also an arrangement in the exchange of notes regarding the Shanhaikwan–Sinminting Railway, which permitted the Russians to obtain concessions for building railways extending the Manchurian line in a south-westerly direction, and traversing the region in which the Chinese line terminating at Sinminting and Newchang was to be constructed.

Although this agreement secured Russian recognition for the Yangtze region as a British railway sphere, it was of limited value because no other Power officially recognized it as such. Moreover, the British had obtained no guarantee of equal trade opportunities in the Russian sphere.

It was at this juncture that the Chinese government (after the Hundred Days of Reform described in the next chapter) set its face against yielding further to foreign demands. In December 1898 it announced that it would grant no further railway concessions, and when the Russo–Chinese Bank applied for the right to build a line into Peking itself, it refused the application and the British supported it in its refusal.

But a much greater rebuff was reserved for the Italians, who had just put forward a request for the lease of Sanmen Bay and the recognition of a large part of Chekiang as a sphere of influence. In March 1899 they learned, to their disappointment, that their request had been flatly rejected by the Tsungli Yamen and in spite of the fact that it was supported by the British government.

No particular notice was paid by the other Powers to Italy's failure to obtain a foothold in China, and in 1899 and the first half of 1900 there was a widespread belief in informed European circles that the definitive partition of China was just round the corner. Lord Charles Beresford, who made an extensive tour of China in the autumn of 1898 as the representative of the Associated Chambers of Commerce of Great Britain, was immensely impressed by the dominant position of Russia. There was no real hope, he felt, of saving the situation unless Britain, Germany, the United States, and Japan could arrange to undertake the reform of China, especially the reform of the Chinese army. But since this was unlikely to happen, Britain might at least salvage something from the wreck if she could secure for herself the Yangtze valley as a sphere of influence.

The British Press echoed Lord Charles Beresford's dismay at the weakness and uncertainty of British policy. In spite of the fact that the Battle of the Concessions was in full fury (partly as a consequence of Britain's own default) the British government still hoped to retain the Open Door in China and was therefore reluctant to stake a claim.

Mr Brodrick, speaking for the government, said in the House of Commons on 9 June: 'We cannot make the Yangtse Valley a province like Shantung or Manchuria, first, because it is infinitely larger, and secondly, because we are not prepared to undertake the immense responsibility of governing what is practically a third of China'.[1]

At this point, however, the British found that their efforts to maintain the Open Door were supported from a somewhat unexpected quarter, for on 6 September 1899 the American Secretary of State, John Hay, circulated his famous Open Door note to Britain, Germany, and Russia. In this note the Powers claiming spheres of influence in China were asked to declare that they would

in no way interfere with any treaty port or vested interest within any so-called 'sphere of interest' or leased territory they might have in China: second, that the Chinese treaty tariff of the time shall apply to all merchandise landed or shipped to all such ports as are within the said 'sphere of interest' (unless they are 'free ports'), and no matter to what nationality they belong, and that duties so leviable shall be collected by the Chinese Government; and third, that it will levy no higher harbour dues on vessels of another nationality frequenting any port in such 'sphere of interest' than shall be levied on vessels of its own nationality [and there were similar provisions for railways inside the 'sphere of interest'].

In other words (says Langer), the American position was exactly that of Britain.

The British and German governments accepted Hay's note, and so did the Italian, French, and Japanese governments when it was presented to them somewhat later. But the crux of the problem lay in Russian policy. Russia's reply, when it eventually came, was a masterpiece of equivocation. The Imperial government (it said) had already demonstrated its firm intention of following the policy of the Open Door by making Dalny (Talienwan) a free port, but no mention was made of the Russian sphere of influence in Manchuria nor of the navigation dues or preferential railway rates. In fact Russia rejected Hay's proposals, as she had done those of Lord Salisbury to the same effect made earlier, and since all the other Powers had made their acceptance provisional on the acceptance of the other governments, the whole programme really fell to the ground. Hay, however, chose to regard the Russian reply as an acceptance of his proposals, and his apparent success greatly enhanced his reputation in the United States. A further note on the Open Door policy was sent to the other Powers in early July 1900, maintaining 'the need to preserve Chinese territory and administrative entity', and this principle was incorporated in the Boxer Protocol of 1901.

United States advocacy of the Open Door was claimed by American publicists in later years as proof of the disinterested nature of American policy towards China as contrasted with the self-seeking cynicism of the other Powers, and for this reason we should take passing note of the present state of opinion on this matter. One distinguished American authority on China, John K. Fairbank, remarks:

In 1899 we enunciated the doctrine of the Open Door for trade, which Englishmen had chiefly formulated. Since 1900 we have stood for the territorial integrity of China, usually without any reliance on British diplomacy. The fact remains that our traditional policy began as an inheritance from the British who, as a trading nation at a great distance from China, wished to preserve China as an open market. The contradictory elements in our China policy can be understood only if we remember that until the early 1920's our interests in China were junior to those of Britain, under whose leadership they had grown up. This allowed us the luxury of constantly denouncing British imperialism while steadily participating in its benefits.[1] In its origin the Open Door was an Anglo–American defensive measure in power politics, without much thought for the interests of the Chinese state.[2] In the circumstances of 1899 John Hay's notes take on a significance quite different from the tradition of benevolence towards China which later became associated with them.[3] Viewed cynically, the doctrine of China's integrity has been a device to prevent other powers, for example, Russia, from taking over areas of China and excluding us from them. But the independence of China has also appealed to Americans as a matter of political justice. It fits the doctrine of the self-determination and sovereignty of weaker nations, which constitutes one of our major political sentiments.[4] [In this last extract Fairbank is speaking of the Open Door doctrine as it was developed after Hay's time.]

In the mutually hostile relations between the United States and communist China after 1949, communist historians have placed the most sinister interpretations on American policy at this period and afterwards. Hu Shêng, for example, says:

It was long noised about that the Open Door policy advocated by the United States was the exact opposite of the policy followed by the other Powers; that while others wanted to 'partition' China, it was the United States proposal that had saved China from the danger of 'partition'; that while others were guilty of aggression against China, it was the United States which aimed at preserving the country's integrity. All these assertions were contrary to the facts. Firstly, the Open Door policy, as suggested by the United States, did not mean that the United States was opposed to aggression in China. It only meant that the United States demanded a share of the loot. That is why the United States raised no protest against the 'spheres of influence' established by the European powers, but only put forward the principle of 'equal opportunity' for all. This meant: 'I also want to share the privileges you enjoy in China. You get your share, and I get mine. Let's all get our shares. Let's continue to recognize the present Chinese Government and enjoy in common all the privileges in China.' Such was the gist of the Open Door policy.[1]

The interchange of notes about the Open Door was in progress simultaneously with the Boxer crisis of 1900. The efforts of Hay had no political bearing on the situation as it was at the turn of the century since the Powers were all busy consolidating their past gains. Russia, in particular, was busy with her construction programme, developing the new commercial port of Dalny, refortifying Port Arthur, and building the southern branch of the Manchurian Railway. The only immediate international danger lay in a possible clash between Russia and Japan.

Russia's chances of earning China's gratitude were ended by the occupation of Port Arthur, and the Chinese reformers now looked to Japan as a model and inspiration. After the coup of September 1898 the Empress Dowager adopted the same policy. Prince Ito urged on the Peking government the necessity of reform if China was to be saved from the Europeans. He himself visited Peking and is reported to have offered China an alliance. In the autumn of 1899 a Chinese mission was sent to Tokyo to solicit support, and soon afterwards some forty Japanese officers were sent to China. Meanwhile, the Japanese League of Culture and Education aimed at the spread of Japanese influence in China and opened schools there as part of its propaganda campaign.

The question the Russians had to decide was whether they would leave the Japanese a free hand in Korea and throw all their energies into consolidating their own position in Manchuria. Witte was certainly in favour of doing so, and whilst he was in power Manchuria was the focus of Russian activity. Thus, when the Eastern Asiatic Company was formed by a group of Russian diplomats and speculators to serve as a cloak for the virtual annexation of northern Korea under the pretext of developing a timber concession, Witte refused to support it. Some 20,000 Russian troops were to be smuggled in disguised as woodmen. The Tsar's support had been obtained by the group and he had provided the 250,000 roubles needed for the reconnaissance of the

Yalu area from his private funds, but Witte was not told of the plans. Owing to the failure to obtain Witte's support the project had to be temporarily shelved in November 1899, but later it was revived with far-reaching consequences.

But this was not the only scheme which was dangerous to Witte's designs for peaceful penetration. The Russian naval authorities had for years set their hearts on the acquisition of a base in Korea. Since 1895 they had concentrated their attention on Masampo and the nearby island of Kargodo (Ko-ye-do) at the southern tip of Korea. The Tsar had been completely converted to the idea. But when during 1899 the Russian Ministry of Marine made several attempts to obtain a concession of land at Masampo, they were in every case anticipated by Japan. Feeling between the two countries ran so high over the matter that in the autumn of that year war between them seemed not at all unlikely. Renewed efforts were made by the Russian Naval authorities to get their way, and on 16 March 1900 a Russian squadron anchored at Chemulpo and the admiral went up to Seoul (Soul). His pressure on the king was so strong that two days later the Russians were granted a lease of land at Masampo for a coaling station and a naval hospital, as well as given the promise of the non-alienation of Kargodo. For a short time the situation was very tense. Practically the whole Japanese navy was mobilized and part of the army too. Only when it became known in April that the Russians, in return for the lease, had been compelled to bind themselves never to apply for land on Kargodo, on the opposite mainland, or in the surrounding islands were the Japanese sufficiently mollified to accept the *fait accompli*.

Whilst all these inroads were being made on Chinese sovereignty, a desperate twelfth-hour attempt to bring China into the modern world so that she might resist her enemies had been made within the country. It had failed, but its repercussions were to have an important bearing on the subject of our study so that we must take some account of the origins of the movement and of its development.

CHAPTER V

REFORM AND REACTION

It was obvious from the course of events that the attempts at reform so far made were insufficient to save China from repeated humiliation. Leaders of Chinese thought were therefore turning their minds towards more radical changes. Sun Yat-sen (from abroad) advocated revolution and the removal of the Ch'ing dynasty: K'ang Yu-wei (a Cantonese like Sun) favoured reforms based on the classics within the existing framework of the Manchu regime. But the time was not ripe for Sun's root-and-branch doctrines to receive a sympathetic reception, and it was K'ang's more conservative programme which was to impress the young scholar-reformers and to attract the attention of the Kuang Hsü emperor.

The Reform Movement of 1898 has been described scores of times by Western writers on China, but almost invariably with the underlying assumption that it was simply another move in the inevitable process of 'Westernization'. So in order to clear the way for a more critical examination of the movement, the outline facts must first be repeated as concisely as possible.[1]

K'ang Yu-wei (1858–1927) was born at Nanhai, Kwangtung, of an old and aristocratic family which for generations had been noted for its neo-Confucian scholarship. He received the *chü-jên* degree in 1894 by passing a provincial examination and the following year took the metropolitan examination in Peking. At this time he submitted a petition to the throne signed by himself and some 1300 other examination candidates. This was the famous *Kung-ch'ê shang-shu* (Petition Presented by the Examination Candidates). It was written by K'ang and strongly urged reforms to prevent China perishing as a nation. The petition was, however, rejected.

Up to this moment K'ang had no knowledge of Western learning to speak of, but on his way to Peking via Hong Kong and Shanghai he was impressed by the honest and efficient administration of the Europeans there and suspected that since their colonies and foreign settlements were so well governed their home countries would be even better managed. This led him to investigate the causes for this superi-

ority and he concluded that European society must have a solid foundation of moral principles as well as of political and natural sciences.
He purchased and read all the Western books in translation that
were available, including popular works relating to industry,
military science and medicine, as well as the Bible. On Western
politics and philosophy, however (says Li Chien-nung), little was
available.

Before leaving Canton, K'ang Yu-wei had already been associated
with his fellow Cantonese, Liang Ch'i-ch'ao (1873–1929), who was to
become his principal lieutenant, and who, in many ways, was more
progressive than his master. Liang was academically precocious and
was just sixteen (seventeen by Chinese reckoning) when he received
the *chü-jên* degree, but in 1890 he failed to pass the metropolitan examination at Peking and did not again submit himself as a candidate for a
higher degree. But in the meantime his mental horizons were suddenly
widened by the realization of the existence of a great world beyond
China, and he was no longer willing to compete for high place in what
he now recognized as an obsolete system.

It was K'ang Yu-wei, however, whom the reformers of the 1890's
looked upon as their leader, and it was not until both K'ang and Liang
were in exile that the differences in their outlook became apparent.
Eventually, K'ang's writings were read by the Emperor himself (on the
introduction, it seems, of Hsü Chih-ching) and he was greatly impressed
by them. In June 1898 he appointed K'ang a second-class secretary of
the Board of Works for service in the Tsungli Yamen, and from that
time onwards he received opportunities to approach the Emperor in
person and soon made him his willing instrument.

K'ang Yu-wei obtained the support of many members of the scholar
class, including, for a while, Chang Chih-tung. His method of propaganda was to organize study clubs and start newspapers. In Peking,
in 1896, he had organized the Ch'iang Hsüeh Hui (Society for the
Study of National Rejuvenation), but this was later closed down on the
petition of a censor. Nevertheless, reform societies sprang up throughout the country, Hunan being the province most affected.

In Tientsin, Yen Fu and others issued the *Kuo-wên Tsa-chih*
(Magazine of National News), in which Yen Fu's translation of Huxley's
Evolution and Ethics and other Essays was first published.

Something of the quality of Yen Fu's thinking can be gathered from
his ridicule of the doctrine of the 'new officials', namely, 'Let Chinese

learning be the essence and Western learning provide the material efficiency' (see p. 79, n. 1), which occurred in the course of a review of Chang Chih-tung's *Exhortation to Study* (*Ch'üan Hsüeh P'ien*), which was published early in 1898 and which was adopted by the reformers as their charter. According to this doctrine the traditional Chinese ideas of administration, justice, and ethics were to be the 'body' (*t'i*) of the new Chinese society, and Western technical know-ledge was to be the 'application' (*yung*). Yen Fu observed:

The use of the body of an ox is to carry heavy burdens; the use of the body of a horse is to run fast. I have never known of an ox's body being used to perform the function of a horse's body. Chinese doctrines have their body and their use, just as Western knowledge has *its* body and *its* use. So long as we keep the two strictly apart they will both function effectively and live, but once we arbitrarily combine them and let the body of one do the work of the other, both will become useless and inert.[1]

The 'Hundred Days of Reform' began in June 1898 with the first of a series of startling decrees issued in quick succession. The more important ones had the following aims—to abolish the old examination system together with the 'Eight-legs' essay; to convert the temples and the outmoded institutions of learning into new-type colleges and high schools; to reduce the number of the Green Standard troops and to intensify the training of the army on modern lines; to do away with sinecure offices; to establish a national bank; to grant all subjects the right to memorialize the throne; to provide a general administration for mining, railways, agriculture, industry, and commerce; to found a national Peking university; to promote new publication and trans-lation bureaus.

Although his innovations were novel enough to frighten the ultra-conservative Court, K'ang Yu-wei was essentially a conservative reformer. He found his inspiration in the *Spring and Autumn Annals*, a work that he looked upon as purposely intended to curb the power of the Emperor, to limit the claims of the nobility, to enlarge the rights of the people, to honour equality, remove domestic struggle and bring reunification, and to abolish bad customs and develop respect for the rule of law. Even when he boldly produced a kind of work quite new to China, namely a 'Utopia', he based it on the *Book of Rites*. Neverthe-less, as its translator says of it: 'One cannot point to any precedent for the *Ta T'ung Shu*, it may truly be characterized as a work of original genius.'[2]

The *Ta T'ung Shu*, although first published in 1902, four years after K'ang had fled into exile, was drafted in 1884–5 and can therefore be included among the works whose spirit at least influenced the Hundred Days of Reform. It is an idea of a universal commonwealth. The sufferings of mankind, said K'ang, were due to barriers between nation and nation, race and race, territory and territory, men and women, one species and another, etc. If these barriers could be removed all would be well. He proposed a world government under which all national States and armies should be abolished and a universal language, calendar, and units of measurement should be adopted. In this commonwealth, men and women would be born free, equal and independent. There would be no restrictions of 'the family': men and women who had lived together for one year might renew the relationship or find new partners; children would be cared for and educated by the State, and there would be no class distinctions. All farms, factories, and business enterprises should be owned and developed by the public.[1]

This utopia was to be attained, not by a revolution, but by reforms within the existing framework of the traditional monarchy. In another book, *K'ung-tzŭ Kai-chih K'ao* (Confucius as a Reformer), K'ang showed how Confucius had actually created the theory of the Golden Age in the past in order to persuade contemporary reformers to imitate the fabulous 'Sage Kings' of old. (K'ang himself, perhaps, was adopting the same stratagem?)

The difference between K'ang Yu-wei and Sun Yat-sen was brought out when later they were both exiles from their native country and carrying out propaganda for their ideas among the Chinese of Southeast Asia. In the first place Sun was anti-Manchu: K'ang was pro-Manchu. Secondly, K'ang considered himself a *chün tzŭ* (scholar gentleman) and had, before 1898, received his support chiefly from others who considered themselves as such, while Sun Yat-sen was ready to speak to 'gamblers, ruffians, bandits, thieves, beggars, hooligans, and jailbirds'. In the third place, K'ang was not prepared to associate with the secret societies of South and Central China, while Sun was in contact with almost all of them and was on very friendly terms with the leaders of these societies abroad. Fourthly, K'ang had been (and secretly still was) favoured by the Emperor and the younger literati, and had worked entirely *within* China itself; Sun, on the other hand, had been forced to work at a distance *outside* China and among the overseas Chinese. Most of these differences disappeared when K'ang, like Sun

Yat-sen, became an exile, but the most important one still remained—namely that K'ang continued to support the Emperor and the dynasty while Sun was their deadly enemy. When the Boxers rose in rebellion in North China, K'ang declared that he could raise an army in the south which could crush the weak Manchu army and save the Emperor.[1]

As for Liang Ch'i-ch'ao, his views also diverged from those of K'ang Yu-wei after their flight in 1898, though not so radically as did those of Sun Yat-sen. In his lifetime his thinking passed through three distinct phases. In the first phase, his aim was 'to rethink Chinese tradition so that Confucianism, to which he was predisposed as a product of the history of his own society, should include what he valued from the West'. Following his master, K'ang Yu-wei, he persuaded himself that the original Confucian text had been falsified by the commentators and that the classics in their purity had foretold the eventual triumph of science, democracy, prosperity, and peace. He therefore called upon his people to emulate Western achievements, cloaking his appeal to 'Western modernization' by invoking the authority of the classics. After the failure of the Hundred Days of Reform and his flight to Japan, roughly between 1898 and 1919, 'he dispensed with the Confucian sugar-coating and covered his Westernism with a new non-culturistic Chinese nationalism'. Tradition (he now held) could be flouted to strengthen the 'nation'. The last phase, from 1919 to his death in 1929, was marked by a disillusionment occasioned by the First World War. Previously he had shared the nineteenth-century European optimism, but now the West had, in spite of the advance of science and the conquest of the material, proved itself spiritually bankrupt. Nevertheless, Liang was no Gandhi, and he proclaimed that the fruits of science could still be used by China because she had always known that not everything was material and had kept herself spiritual and alive. But by this time Liang had himself ceased to be a vital force in Chinese thought and politics and was largely ignored by the Chinese youth movements of the period—worse still, he was now in league with Tuan Ch'i-jui and his Anhwei warlords.[2]

Outstanding among the associates of K'ang and Liang was the latter's friend, the poet and philosopher T'an Ssŭ-t'ung, who became a martyr to the reform movement, disdaining to take to flight at the time of the *coup d'état*, and being executed at the age of thirty-three. His ideas were derived from Confucianism, Buddhism, and Western science as well as from K'ang, whom he respected as a teacher. The main tenets of his philosophic thought are contained in his *Jên-hsüeh* (Science of Love), in which he recommends for every person the freedom that would be possible if there were no boundaries between nations. Because of his fundamental tenet, T'an believed that Western trade was beneficial to China—a revolutionary idea which may have reflected the Western view. He considered that Chinese politics during the preceding two thousand years had been a system for bringing the nation to ruin by hypocrites. The best course, he said, was to get rid of traditional political regulations altogether and to adopt a Western system. He was thus in some ways in advance of K'ang Yu-wei, and certainly of Chang Chih-tung.

We have seen that the reformers were agreed in regarding the existing examination system, and particularly the 'Eight-legs' essay, as strangling the national initiative, and this was in spite of their tenderness for the classics on which the examination system was based. But what *was* this system, and what precisely was the 'Eight-legs' essay? To embark upon a study of Chinese education under the Ch'ing would be to venture beyond the scope of this book, but it might help us to understand something of its nature if we were to glance at a single typical example of the 'Eight-legs' essay of the later nineteenth century.

One 'Eight-legs' essay available to us for study is that written by a candidate named Chang Chêng-yu who obtained the first place at the examination for the degree of *chü-jên* held in Peking in September 1879.[1]

The theme set was: 'Tzŭ-kung said to Confucius: Suppose there was a man of such unbounded beneficence and power that he was able to extend help to every one of the people (who needed it) what would you say of him? Might he not be called humane? Confucius answered: Is humane the right word? Must he not be a Holy Man?'

The candidate (as was required of him) divided his essay into Analysis of the Theme, Amplification of the Theme, Explanation, Post Explanation, Argument First Division, Reassertion of Theme, Argument Second Division, and Argument Third Division.

The last six characters were omitted in the Theme, though the candidate, from his verbatim knowledge of the text, could readily supply them. He was not allowed to introduce into his essay the words that immediately followed the Theme in the classical text, in order, in avoiding so doing, to give scope for his literary skill. In the present case the essayist also proved his skill by covert references to Yao and

Shun (the two legendary emperors) without once introducing them by name.

The following extracts do not by themselves exaggerate the jejune effect of the whole:

Analysis of the Theme. The meaning of the above words is that the humane man, as such merely, would not be able to reach the degree of unbounded beneficence and power supposed by Tzŭ-Kung....

Argument First Division. Every man and woman below the sky, to whom Heaven has given body and soul, should have my sympathy in his joy and sorrow. But if you say that one individual must suffer because I have not been able to reach the whole of humanity, I reply that humanity is not so distant as this....

Argument Second Division. But to Confucius' unerring judgment, a state of things in which all men under Heaven should be as one family, and the whole nation of one mind, was sincerely to be hoped for, and therefore he could not restrain himself from looking afar and aloft (to the days of Yao and Shun)...for such great virtue and spiritual power belonging to the first Emperors, whom Heaven specially endowed....

Argument Third Division. Thus it was that Confucius replied without hesitation—How can you expect this from humanity?...Work of unusual difficulty must await the birth of a man whose mind is en rapport with Heaven and Earth or who is able to assist nature in her processes and to form a co-equal Trinity with Heaven and Earth (a reference to *Chung Yung* (Doctrine of the Mean), chapter xii)....But the humane man may have the desire to perform this work, and if he can succeed so far that men look upon him with hope, who can help going back in imagination (to the days of Yao and Shun)?

The connecting argument is, of course, broken in these extracts, but there is no real logical sequence in the whole; only strict adherence to stereotyped categories. As Mr Bourne remarks:

In writing his essay the candidate is not allowed to express his own thoughts in his own way. He must make his sentences conform in great measure to one or two recognized models. The division into cut and dried sections modifies in many cases the meaning. When, for instance, in the essay the theme is restated in the middle of the argument, if no notice were taken of the division, and the translation ran straight on, the author might appear to be begging the question or arguing in a circle.

To find parallels to the 'Eight-legs' essays in our own civilization we should perhaps have to go back to the medieval Schoolmen, but the skill in fabricating Greek and Latin hexameters which opened the doors to successful careers in the eighteenth and nineteenth centuries was not so very far away from this model.

Observing the state into which their society had fallen it was natural that the Chinese reformers should have looked to the coercive and successful West for standards that they might hope to emulate. The question was where was the essence of the West to be found?

The answer was that the West was also undergoing a vast process of change of whose real nature the great mass of Westerners were themselves unaware. Behind the façade of trade, of monarchs and diplomats, and armies and navies, there was a bubbling ferment of inquiry and speculation. Let us remind ourselves of what was happening in terms of a few of the leaders of nineteenth-century thought.

The publication of *Principles of Geology* in 1830–3, by Sir Charles Lyell (1797–1875), had marked a great epoch in modern geological science, and this paved the way for the revolutionary *Origin of Species* (1859), by Charles Darwin (1809–82), the importance of which is being increasingly recognized even in our own time. Huxley's *Man's Place in Nature*, in which Darwin's ideas were expounded, was published in 1863, but only selections from his writings had been translated into Chinese before the Hundred Days of 1898. Gregor Mendel (1822–84) had propounded his theory of genetics in 1866, but it had been forgotten and was not to be rediscovered until early in the following century; Pasteur, Lister, Metchnikov, had advanced existing conceptions of biology and medicine in great strides; Faraday, Kelvin, von Helmholtz, and Clerk Maxwell had done the same for physics; in 1888 Hertz had been the first human being deliberately to send an electromagnetic wave through space; Marx (1818–83) and Engels (1820–95) had lighted their time fuse, though no one seemed to realize it; Nietzsche (1844–1900) had propounded the idea of the 'Superman' which was to have such a great influence on politics in a coming generation; Tolstoy's (1828–1910) renunciation of violence and wealth had a tremendous impact on his time. Auguste Comte, Herbert Spencer, Samuel Butler, G. B. Shaw, H. G. Wells and many others were moulding the future concepts of society. William Morris had made a systematic attempt to restore the sense of beauty that England had lost in the process of industrializing herself.

What did the Chinese reformers know of these or of the parallel developments which were going on elsewhere in the West? The reply must be—virtually nothing. The missionaries were (to use Joseph Needham's phrase) 'prisoners of their limited motive', namely of their aim to convert the Chinese to Christianity, and they conveyed to the

Chinese only so much of Western knowledge as was conducive to this aim (and this, of course, within the limitations of their own education). Instead of transmitting to China the Copernican system (which many of them privately accepted), the Jesuits of the seventeenth century taught their pupils the Ptolemaic system, which, as orthodox Roman Catholics, they were compelled to do. Their dilemma was not a new one and was one which the later Jesuits were again compelled to face:

Down to the very end of their mission the Jesuits were the prisoners of their limited motive and the Chinese sought persistently to emphasize the continuity of the new science with the old. For example, in 1710 Jean-François Foucquet...and others of the Society wished to make use of the new planetary tables of la Hire, but the Father Visitor would not permit it, for fear of 'giving the impression of a censure on what his predecessors had so much trouble to establish, and occasioning new accusations against our religion'. Any acceptance of the Copernican system would have equally raised doubts about Ricci's teachings.[1]

And, as we shall see, in the nineteenth century the Protestant missionaries were in their turn to become 'prisoners of their own limited motive'—though in fairness it must be remembered that they offered themselves solely as evangelists, not as social revolutionaries.

English was taught in a large number of Protestant mission schools of the higher grade, and in some it was the medium of instruction for Western subjects. But missionary opinion was not solidly in favour of teaching English. Those who supported it argued that many Chinese wished to learn English and that if the missionary did not teach it they would get it elsewhere under non-Christian auspices; that English was superior to Chinese in precision and clearness; that its possessor had open to him a vast field of Western literature which was not, and most of which would not be, translated, and that he was in a position to keep abreast of modern thought. Their opponents contended that few pupils remained in school long enough to acquire sufficient English to enable them to read it well, that its use reduced the time spent on Chinese, and that it tended to separate the student from the masses of his fellow-countrymen, etc.[2]

Although (as we shall see in a moment) the Protestant schools failed for several reasons to make Western learning available to China on a scale adequate to afford a pattern for reform, they did at least open the doors to the acquisition of it. The Roman Catholic schools and colleges, on the other hand, were not intended primarily for the purpose of teaching non-Christians, but for providing the children of Catholics with religious as well as secular instruction, and for preparing Chinese leaders for the Church. The propaganda directed that in the collections of Chinese writings used as texts in the mission schools there should not be anything encouraging to superstition or subversive to faith. In a few institutions French was taught, but it was no part of the Roman Catholic system to introduce the Chinese to Western civilization, other than Christian.[1]

We can gather a fairly exact impression of the extent to which Western learning was available to the literate Chinese, and in particular to the reformers (who had little or no knowledge of foreign languages) from a study of the list of translations from Western languages into Chinese up to 1898.[2]

From the end of the sixteenth century, for the next two hundred years, at least eighty Jesuits of various nationalities took part in translating into Chinese more than 400 works covering fields of knowledge new to the Chinese. More than half of the works related to Christianity, about one-third was scientific literature, and the remainder concerned Western institutions and humanities. It was obvious from this that the principal motive of the Jesuits was religious. Chinese scholars with some knowledge of Western science aided the Jesuits in making these translations, and played an important part in the invention of new terms and translation techniques. Ricci translated more than twenty works into Chinese, including Clavius's *Euclidis Elementorum*, which was regarded by the Chinese as 'the crown of Western studies'. But perhaps his most important contribution was his epoch-making map of the world (1584) based on Ortelius's *Theatrum Orbis Terrarum*. Other translations by Jesuits were of Western books on hydraulics, metallurgy, anatomy, etc., but after Verbiest's death in 1688 the translations made by the Roman Catholic missionaries were relatively insignificant. The works produced in the eighteenth century were mostly theological, and the energies of the Jesuits were turned to translating Chinese works into European languages.

When in the nineteenth century the Protestant missionaries took up the work of translation left by the Jesuits, the nature and quality of their labours was of a different order. The Protestant missionaries established contact primarily with traders and relatively uneducated groups, while the Jesuits cultivated the literati and government officials. Consequently, Protestant translations were mostly tracts of an elementary nature, and most of the non-religious works were prepared for mission schools. Though more numerous, their quality in general was not comparable with that of Jesuit translations. Between 1810 and 1867 all the Protestant writings were devoted to Christianity except for some 12 per cent which touched on Western institutions and sciences.

The abundance of religious material, supported only by a few scientific and educational subjects, indicates that the Protestant missionaries of this period paid scant attention to the interests of the Chinese intellectuals and, therefore, made little impression on the group. Although the missionaries called for elimination of religious propaganda from scientific texts, 'so that they may win their way into the interior, and be prized by native scholars...yet every suitable opportunity is to be taken to bring out the great facts of God, sin, and salvation, that the fragrance of our blessed religion may be diffused wherever they penetrate'.[1]

In the fields of mathematics, astronomy, medicine, and the other sciences, important translations by Protestant missionaries appeared only after 1850. Alexander Wylie contributed many translations in the field of mathematics, especially the completion of Books 7–15 of Euclid's *Elements* (1857), begun by Ricci two and a half centuries earlier. Besides other books on algebra, geometry, etc., Wylie began a translation of Newton's *Principia* which, however, he did not complete.

The missionary translations and writings were all published by missionary presses. At least fourteen of the latter were reported by 1895. About the middle of the century, the Chinese government agencies began to participate in the work. Although it was recognized that Western ideas were potentially dangerous to the established order, Western techniques were generally needed by the government for the defence of the country. During the latter half of the nineteenth century there was a great increase in the translations of works on the natural and applied sciences, which accounted for about 70 per cent of the total. More than half were translated from English, but German, French, Russian, and Japanese works were included.

In 1861 the Chinese government decided to establish a language school known as the T'ung Wên Kuan, to train personnel and translators for the government service, whose President from 1869 onwards was Dr W. A. P. Martin, an American missionary. In 1888 the T'ung Wên Kuan had 125 students and a teaching staff of nineteen, including eight of American, French, German, or British nationality. However, the contributions of this establishment to translation were comparatively insignificant in quantity, for in a period of forty years, only about twenty-six works were translated, including some incomplete and unpublished works.[1]

In Shanghai in 1867 the Kiangnan Arsenal, with its new Translation Bureau, merged with the Kuang Fang Yen Kuan, a foreign language school which had opened in Shanghai in 1863. These two institutions, of which one was engaged in teaching and the other in translation, worked successfully and produced more works than any other government agency. According to a report of 1880, 156 works were translated by the Kiangnan Arsenal, of which ninety-eight titles were published, with a total distribution of 31,111 copies. The translation service continued into the early years of this century, with a total of 178 works published from 1871 to 1905.

In addition to the missionary and governmental translation bureaus, a number of privately sponsored societies came into being, including the Scientific Book Depot (Ko Chih Shu Shê) and the Translating Society of Shanghai (I Shu Kung Hui), which was established in 1897 by a number of Chinese scholars.

Many universities and Chinese publishers also participated in translation after 1895, through the encouragement of the Reform Movement. A number of private publishing concerns also came into being at the end of the nineteenth and the beginning of the twentieth century, at least forty being engaged in translating and publishing.

Between 1850 and 1899 some 567 works were translated into Chinese, 40·6 per cent being on the applied sciences, and 29·8 per cent on the natural sciences; 50·5 per cent being from English, 14·5 per cent from American, 2·3 per cent from French, 29 per cent from German, 0·3 per cent from Russian (2/567), and 15·1 per cent from Japanese originals.

It will be seen that in quantity alone the Western works available in translation to the Chinese in 1895 were quite inadequate to form a representative corpus of Western knowledge to draw upon. But as regards quality and selectiveness the books translated were even less able to convey any real knowledge of the tremendous intellectual activity which was reshaping Western civilization. It was not until 1896 (as we have already seen) that Yen Fu began to translate Huxley's *Evolution and Ethics*, through which Darwin's theory of evolution was first introduced to China. After being serialized, this work was first published in book form in 1899 and was widely used as a textbook. Yen Fu afterwards published translations of classics such as Adam Smith's *Wealth of Nations* (1902), John Stuart Mill's *On Liberty* (1903) and *System of Logic* (1905), Herbert Spencer's *Study of Sociology* (1903), Edward Jenks's *A Short History of Politics* (1904), Montesquieu's *Spirit of Laws* (1906), and William Stanley Jevons's *Primer of Logic* (1908)—several decades after they had appeared in Japanese.

It was Liang Ch'i-ch'ao who first introduced Marx (Mo-k'o-shih) to China in *Hsin Min Ts'ung Pao*, no. 18 (1902), but it was not until many years later that his works were translated into Chinese. During the Hundred Days of Reform Marx was not even a name.

Liang had been eloquent for years on the necessity for translating foreign books. He complained that the T'ung Wên Kuan, the Shui-Shih Hsüeh-T'ang (the Naval College at Tientsin), and the Chih Tsao Chü (Kiangnan Arsenal at Shanghai) had been translating for thirty years and had published only 100 books in the time. Only one book outlining the new agricultural techniques was available in Chinese in the late 1890's.[1]

The missionary who had the greatest direct influence on the Reform Movement was undoubtedly Timothy Richard (1845–1919). He reached China in 1870. His unorthodox methods caused a break with his colleagues of the Baptist Missionary Society, and in 1891 he became Secretary of the Christian Literature Society of China. Richard's strategy was to 'seek out the worthy' for conversion. To his mind Christian missions were under obligation to aid in the reconstruction of the country for the benefit of all Chinese. Richard had great influence on Liang Ch'i-ch'ao and through him on the Kuang Hsü emperor. Liang's doctrine of 'all roads lead from the *Kung-yang* of the Three Ages to science, democracy, and peace' was largely derived from Timothy Richard.

Richard singled out for translation the work he considered would best convey the essence of Western achievement. This was *The Nineteenth Century, a History* (1880), by Robert Mackenzie, a Scottish journalist from Dundee (1823–81). Since the book became perhaps the main source of information about Europe for the leaders of the Reform Movement, including the Emperor himself, it is worth while examining its contents in some detail.

Mackenzie's somewhat truncated 'nineteenth century' opens with Europe convulsed by the Napoleonic wars: 'From the North to the shores of the Mediterranean, from the confines of Asia to the Atlantic, men toiled to burn each other's cities, to waste each other's fields, to destroy each other's lives' (p. 7).

Social conditions generally were in keeping with this deplorable state of affairs. By the time the 'nineteenth century' closed (1880), however, there had been a vast transformation:

> The nineteenth century has witnessed progress beyond all precedent, for it has witnessed the overthrow of the barriers which prevented progress.... Never since the stream of human development received into its sluggish currents the mighty impulse of the Christian religion has the condition of man experienced ameliorations so vast...the nineteenth century has witnessed the fall of despotism and the establishment of liberty in the most influential nations of the world. It has vindicated for all succeeding ages the right of man in his own unimpeded development. It has not seen the re-dressing of all wrongs; nor indeed is that to be hoped for, because in the ever-shifting conditions of man's life the right of one century becomes frequently the wrong of the next. But it has seen all that the most ardent reformer can desire—the removal of artificial obstacles placed in the path of human progress by the selfishness and ignorance of the strong, and the growth of man's well-being, rescued from the mischievous tampering of self-willed princes, is left now to the beneficent regulation of great providential laws.[1]

Europe receives the bulk of the attention, but there is a chapter (Book III, chapter XI) on the Indian Empire, the character of which can be divined from its conclusion:

> England has undertaken to rescue from the debasement of ages that enormous multitude of human beings [the Indians]. No enterprise of equal greatness was engaged in by any people.... Posterity will look only upon the majestic picture of a vast and utterly barbaric population, numbering well-nigh one fourth of the human family, subdued, governed, educated and Christianized, and led to the dignity of a free and self-governing nation by a handful of strangers who came from an inconsiderable island fifteen thousand miles away.[2]

Mention of China is extremely sparse and seems to be confined to two short sentences—'Three times we fought with China' (p. 177), and 'A little later, China was entered by Christianity by the door which the English opened in their determination to force the use of opium on that empire' (p. 211).

Next to Christianity, the nineteenth century owed its progress to science and industry. Two chapters (VII and VIII, Book II) are devoted to 'The Victories of Peace'—the progress of the great industries, the steam-ship, the locomotive, the electric telegraph, newspapers, mechanical invention, the lucifer match, photography, the sewing-machine, and improved weapons. Of the great intellectual speculation and controversies of the nineteenth century, however, there is no mention.

It may seem strange that with all the important historians of the nineteenth century to select from—Ranke, Mommsen, Carlyle, Buckle, Froude, etc.—Timothy Richard should have selected for his labours of translation this minor popular work (already 'dated' when he began to translate it about 1893). The translation was published soon after the outbreak of war between China and Japan. In his introduction Richard asked, 'What is the cause of the foreign wars, indemnities, and repeated humiliations suffered by China during the last sixty years?' And he pointed out that 'God was breaking down the barriers between all nations by railways, steamers, and telegraphs, in order that we should all live in peace and happiness as brethren of one family; but the Manchus, by continual obstruction, were determined from the first to prevent this intercourse'. If this attitude were changed, 'China might still become one of the greatest nations on earth'.

Upon the publication of his translation, Viceroy Chang Chih-tung immediately sent for Richard to go to Nanking, and Viceroy Li Hung-chang telegraphed for him to go to Tientsin. He accepted Chang's invitation, although the outcome was not very encouraging, but he was unable to go north until too late, for Li Hung-chang's army was shattered by the first blow of the Japanese and he was degraded.

In Hangchow, no less than six pirated editions of Richard's translation of Mackenzie's history were on sale, and it is estimated that a million copies were in circulation throughout China. On 12 October 1895, when Richard had an interview with Sun Chia-nai, the Emperor's tutor and personal adviser, Sun and the Emperor were daily reading Richard's history together, and it seems that the Emperor's knowledge of contemporary Europe was largely derived from this source.[1]

Meanwhile Meiji Japan had long been reconciled to the idea of drastic reform, and it is relevant to recall what had been happening in this adjacent country, in which, however, the political and social conditions were so different from those in China.

Just when sanguine missionaries were beginning to think that the eventual Christianization of Japan would only be a matter of time and effort, a serious threat to their hopes appeared within the foreign community itself.[1] Professors at Tokyo University who presented the views of scientific rationalism were gaining an eager following among intellectuals. For many Japanese a materialist philosophy seemed to solve the problem of how to become modern without becoming Christian. Anti-Christian Japanese found their first weapons in the rusty armoury of Thomas Paine's *The Age of Reason*, but the doctrine of evolution offered a much more powerful instrument of attack. It was popularized in Japan from 1877 onwards by Edward S. Morse, the distinguished naturalist of Salem, Massachusetts, who became the first Professor of Zoology in Tokyo University. Books on evolution and materialistic philosophy soon became popular reading among Japanese students. In 1880 Kozu Senzaburo published a translation of Darwin's *Descent of Man*, and Tyndall's famous Belfast address on evolution was published in Japanese by Tokyo University. In 1883, the appearance, in English, among the students, of J. W. Draper's *History of the Conflict Between Religion and Science*, and the works of Herbert Spencer and Alexander Bain, caused anxiety to the missionary body. And this was only the beginning. The arrival of the Reverend Arthur May Knapp in 1887 as the first Unitarian missionary in Japan with his tolerant attitude towards Buddhism and Shintoism constituted a renewed threat to the Christian position.

The later history of the Unitarian mission indicates that the ultimate effect of the liberal doctrines was to make former Christian believers into irreligious freethinkers rather than to provide them with a broader religious faith. In 1900 Saji Jitsunen turned the native Unitarian Church into an ethical culture society which recognized neither prayers nor scriptures. Attempts were made to stop the drift towards agnosticism without success, and the mission had to be abandoned altogether in 1922.

Mr Schwantes concludes:

At first the Japanese regarded Western civilization as unitary, monolithic, to be accepted or entirely rejected, its religion along with its sociology. The controversy over evolution revealed to them serious divisions within Occidental thought, free scientific enquiry being opposed by literal faith. The coming of the Unitarians further complicated the picture; here was a group claiming to be Christian which also stood for scientific truth and freedom of enquiry. The problem of cultural borrowing now became both harder and easier: harder because it was difficult to decide what was truly western and modern, easier because Japan could with a clear conscience make a selection of those elements she desired. In general, she chose those parts of Western culture that fitted in best with her own national predilections.

This was the course which the Chinese reformers of 1898 wished to pursue, but, as we have seen, they were woefully handicapped in making their selection by their lack of information as to the real nature of Western civilization and the direction in which it was tending. It was not surprising that Liang Ch'i-ch'ao was completely disillusioned with the West when the war of 1914–18 took place.

The Empress Dowager had at first acquiesced in the reforms, but when their revolutionary nature began to dawn upon her she became angry, and, when she felt her own safety threatened, alarmed. She thereupon decided to act. Jung-lu was sent to Tientsin to secure control of the army, especially of the modern troops stationed there, and Tz'ŭ Hsi plotted to force the Kuang Hsü emperor's abdication. Upon learning of the plot, the Emperor conferred with K'ang Yu-wei who urged him to secure the support of Yüan Shih-k'ai and to order him to arrest Jung-lu and take over command of the army. But Yüan Shih-k'ai betrayed the plot to Jung-lu, the Emperor was placed under palace-arrest, and K'ang and Liang fled abroad. Six of the leading reformers who could not, or who refused to escape, were executed, and, reassuming the government, Tz'ŭ Hsi set about rescinding the reform decrees. When she had finished, Peking University was the only notable creation of the Hundred Days that was not abolished. But the spirit of reform nevertheless remained alive in the country, and Tz'ŭ Hsi herself felt constrained to inaugurate a programme of innovation which was greatly intensified after the Boxer Uprising had been quelled. Among the immediate results of the *coup d'état* of September, however, was that the sinecure offices were restored to their dispossessed holders, the right of memorializing the Throne was once again limited to high officials, and the traditional examination system, together with the famous 'Eight-legs' essay, was resuscitated.[1]

In summarizing these events we have to keep in mind their bearing on the Boxer movement, and it will be seen in due course how the reaction following the *coup d'état* led by stages to an alliance between the reactionaries at Court and the Boxer rebels in Chihli and Shantung. In particular, the determination of Tz'ŭ Hsi to dethrone the Kuang Hsü emperor (and probably to murder him) prompted the intervention of the foreign diplomats, led by Sir Claude MacDonald, the British Minister, who warned the Empress Dowager of the effect on world opinion should anything untoward happen to the Emperor. Tz'ŭ Hsi was enraged at this interference with her plans, but decided to bide her time. Thus it came about that at the moment when Yü-hsien, the Governor of Shantung, was recalled to Peking 'for audience' in December 1899, Tz'ŭ Hsi was in a frame of mind to listen to him and to the anti-foreign extremists at Court who advocated an understanding with the anti-foreign Boxers.

After the reformers were executed or scattered and the Emperor was safely relegated to the Palace Compound, the Empress Dowager resumed her power as ruler, with Tsai-i (Prince Tuan from 1894) as one of her favourites. A plot to have the Emperor Tê-tsung (of the Kuang Hsü reign) murdered or someone else put in his place was under way, and Tsai-i was active in it since his eldest son, P'u-chün, was to be the Emperor's successor. Owing to the intervention of the foreign diplomats he had to be content with seeing him made Heir Apparent in January 1900, but his anger against the foreigner was intense, and he probably more than anyone else was responsible for influencing the Empress Dowager to favour the Boxers and to summon them to Peking. On 10 June 1900 he was appointed chief member of the Tsungli Yamen, indicating a definite trend towards anti-foreignism. The reactionaries stood for resistance to change of any sort, and the preservation of the Manchu regime and their personal power.

S. L. Tikhvinsky, the Russian authority on China, points out that while the Chinese reformers were insisting on reforms with the object of strengthening China and liberating her from Manchu–Chinese feudal rule and foreign domination, the Powers were interested only in such reforms as would make it easier for them to penetrate China.[1] I do not think that the truth of this can be denied, but whether self-interest is peculiar to capitalist States is a matter for argument. The Powers at this period were without doubt insolent and rapacious, and their present-day nationals (Russians included) must accept historical responsibility for the acts of their forbears—whether there has been a social revolution in their countries in the meantime or not.

What connection could there be between the aims of the reformers and those of the illiterate or semi-literate peasants who constituted the majority of the Boxers? If there was one, it is not easy to trace it, except that they were both unmistakably 'Chinese' in character, and that, in spirit, at least, the 'Utopia' of K'ang Yu-wei was not so very far removed from the 'Golden Age' that the heroes of the novels and plays which inspired the Boxers wished to restore. The important thing is that the failure of the reform movement threw Chinese of all classes back on a negative 'anti-foreignism' which was to give the Court reactionaries and the Boxers a common cause. At the same time, the nascent nationalist patriotism of both Boxers and reactionaries was positive and genuine.

CHAPTER VI

'ANTI-FOREIGN' OR 'ANTI-MISSIONARY'?

Missionary enterprise...was the one great agency whose primary function was to bring China into contact with the best in the Occident and to make the expansion of the West a means to the greater welfare of the Chinese people.

K. S. LATOURETTE, *A History of Christian Missions in China* (1929), p. 843.

Four times in history was China offered the possibility of adopting organized Christianity....But [the missions] always failed, and the fact must be faced by Westerners that the Christian religion in its organized forms has been decisively rejected by the Chinese culture. As Antonio Banfi has put it, this necessarily followed from the highly organic structure of Chinese humanistic morality which could not but view with distaste a religion placing so tragic an accent upon transcendence, and which was therefore so dogmatic and ecclesiastical.

JOSEPH NEEDHAM, 'The Past in China's Present', *Centennial Rev.* IV, 3 (1960).

The fault lies largely with Christianity. It has the misfortune in every alien land of running counter to almost all cherished local institutions. It offends everyone: it antagonizes every creed; it mingles with none, because its fundamental tenets deny the co-existence of any other faith or standard of morality.

PAUL H. CLEMENTS, *The Boxer Rebellion; a Political and Diplomatic Review* (New York, 1915), p. 74

That the Boxer uprising was both anti-foreign and anti-Christian is incontestable, but whether it was essentially anti-Christian or whether it became so only because the missionaries were foreigners has been a matter of controversy. Steiger, for one, is at pains to argue from the known tolerance of one another's existence of the Chinese religious sects that the Boxers could not have been a sect (*chiao*), and, from reasons of prudence at the least, they would not have attacked the Christians. But (as will be demonstrated once again in the ensuing chapters) the Boxers were definitely a *hui*, or secret society, of an anti-Christian nature.

Before the arrival of the Christian missionaries the rebellious sects could scarcely claim that the former were the authors of the country's misfortunes, but with their advent and increase in numbers, which co-incided with a deterioration in the political and economic conditions in

China, they were increasingly the target of their resentment. The anti-foreign, and usually anti-Christian, riots which occurred from the 1860's onwards, were the spontaneous expression of popular feeling, but when they became organized it seems likely that the Secret Societies were behind them. The murder of the two Roman Catholic priests, Henle and Nies, in Shantung on 1 November 1897, which precipitated the German occupation of Kiaochow, has been ascribed by many (including Chester Tan and Latourette) to the machinations of the Great Sword Society, while a few (including Yü-hsien and Steiger, from different motives) have denied any connection between the two. But there were numerous other incidents in which it is fairly plain that the sects were involved. For example, in November 1898 Father Stenz of the Society of the Divine Word was imprisoned in Shantung by Secret Society members, and all over the country there were series of anti-Catholic outbreaks—in Kwangtung, Szechwan, Chekiang, Kwangsi, Hupeh—involving many deaths, certainly part of a general anti-foreign and anti-Christian movement in which the secret societies were active.

In the light of the long history of inter-sectarian tolerance in China and of the inextricable intermingling of creeds there is some prima facie justification for Steiger's incredulity regarding the alleged anti-Christian activity of a heterodox sect, but in confronting Christianity they were dealing with a threat to their own collective existence. None of the Christian sects, for their part, neither Catholic nor Protestant (certainly since the days of the Jesuits), would tolerate a simultaneous adherence to Christian and Confucian–Taoist–Buddhist doctrine. Thus it is that the religious element was strong in the Boxer notices. The foreigners in general (*Yang jên*, Oceanic men) were blamed for the drought of 1900, and one Boxer placard said, 'When the foreigners are wiped out, rain will fall and visitations will disappear',[1] but another notice posted up in Taiyüan in July of that year said, 'The Catholic and Protestant Churches deceive our gods, destroy our belief in our saints, and disobey the precepts of the Buddha. Hence the present famine and other disasters.'[2] A 'Sacred Edict, issued by the Lord of Wealth and Happiness', ran:

The Catholic and Protestant religions being insolent to the gods, and extinguishing sanctity, rendering no obedience to Buddha, and enraging Heaven and Earth, the rain-clouds no longer visit us; but eight million Spirit Soldiers will descend from Heaven and sweep the Empire clean of foreigners. Then will the gentle showers once more water our lands: and when the tread of soldiers and the clash of steel are heard heralding woes to all our people, then the Buddhist Patriotic League of Boxers will be able to protect the Empire and bring peace to all its people.[1]

Yet another began:

Attention: all people in markets and villages of all provinces of China—now, owing to the fact that Catholics and Protestants have vilified our gods and sages, have deceived the emperors and ministers above, and oppressed the Chinese people below, both our gods and our people are angry with them....[2]

Most of the voluminous literature published by Christian missionaries after the Boxer outbreak was written with the object of vindicating missionary activity in China. Both Catholics and Protestants agreed in attributing the uprising to the forces of reaction, and, so far as there was any excuse for popular discontent with the foreigner, it was held to be due to the political and economic action of foreign governments and traders. In cases, however, in which at least a certain degree of Christian responsibility was indisputable, the Roman Catholics and the Protestants were disposed to place the blame on each other. But this partisanship was merely an extension of the jealousies and rivalries which had been common between the two branches of Christianity from the moment that they started working side by side. For example, John, in the *Chinese Recorder*, no. 4 (1871), alleged that the Catholics were doing all they could to obstruct his work: and the *Annales de la Propagation de la Foi* (September 1870) declared that the Protestant work in Laoting, Shantung, was a complete failure. A. H. Smith, in his *China in Convulsion*, certainly contrives to give the impression that the anti-missionary sentiment was mainly the fault of the Catholics. He attributes this to Roman Catholic policy and particularly to the policy of France as protector of the Roman Catholic Church, and quotes A. R. Colquhoun in *Overland to China*:

The blood of the martyrs in China waters the seed of French aggrandizement. France uses the missionaries and the native Christians as *agents provocateurs*; and outrages and martyrdoms are her political harvest. What the preponderance of her commerce does for England the Catholic protectorate does for France—but France makes ten times more capital out of her religious material than Great Britain has ever done out of her commercial. Under the fostering care of the French Government the Catholics have become a veritable *imperium in imperio*, disregarding local laws and customs, domineering over their pagan neighbours, and overriding the law of the land.[3]

Smith also remarks that a potent source of animosity towards the Roman Catholics was to be found in the fact that by the treaty of 1860 extensive property belonging to the Roman Catholic Church (a century or two before) was to be restored to it on presentation of evidence of previous possession, even though the property had changed hands several times in the interim and had often been greatly improved. Smith also instances the fact (which is patent to any visitor to China) that the Roman Catholics had made a practice of erecting huge churches and cathedrals (in Gothic style), dominating the Chinese cities like fortresses (and built to withstand a siege), and sited without any regard to the Chinese prejudices respecting *fêng-shui*, or geomancy.

Nevertheless, the fact is that the Chinese people regarded the Christian missionaries, both Catholic and Protestant, as foreigners and therefore as enemies, and they made no great political distinction between the virtues and vices of Catholicism and Protestantism (though they regarded them as distinct religions). That they did so was the consequence of the inextricability of the political and religious policy of the West, for when there was any conflict between religious principle and political expediency it was the latter that prevailed. Thus, for example, 'the Christian European States assisted the pagan Manchus to crush the Christian, if heretical, Taipings'.[1]

The following extracts from a confidential report on a visit to Manchuria made between 31 July and 31 December, 1897, by Colonel Browne, the Military Attaché at the British Legation in Peking, brings out the Chinese attitude clearly:

It is, perhaps, not strange in this country that though the foreigner is despised, the native who follows the creed of the foreigner frequently obtains power and influence to which he could not otherwise attain. The reason for this is that the mass of the upper classes regard the missionaries as political agents and fear them. The poor know this, and look, in many cases, to the missionary—the honest for protection, the dishonest to further their own ends. These ends may be the evasion of recovery of a debt, or some similar dispute, in which they know that their connection with the Church will influence the Magistrate. It *ought not* to do so, for the Presbyterian missionaries lose no opportunity of letting the Magistrates and others know that they will use no influence when a Christian is before the Court, whether as complainant or defendant; but practically, it *does* influence them, for they attach the same value to these statements by the missionaries as they would to a declaration made by themselves in similar circumstances.

[Colonel Browne gives an example of a carter buying a flag with a Christian device for protection.]

The Roman Catholic priests are simple-minded, hard-working men with no ambition beyond the success of the work to which they have devoted their lives, but they are under a Bishop who directs their policy, and the policy is such as to give ground for the opinion held by many Chinese that missionaries are sent to this land in the interests of their own Government.

The Bishop's passport is said to be technically worded so that he appears to be appointed by the French Government: he travels with a retinue, and flies the French flag in Mukden, and in any town in which he is temporarily residing. Every case in which a convert is concerned is taken up as a case against the Church: it is therefore not a matter for surprise that their members are said to be more numerous than those of the Presbyterian Church.[1]

The mass demonstrations on the part of the peasant population, as in the Boxer uprising, were strongly hostile to Christianity, and for the significant reason that Christianity was 'foreign'. The foreign missionaries were, for the Boxers, the 'Primary Devils'; the native Christian converts were the 'Secondary Devils', equally deserving of death. And although the rural Chinese regarded Protestants and Catholics indifferently as foreigners and enemies, they tended (as has above been remarked) to treat them as adherents of two distinct and conflicting religions, the one supported by the power of England; the other supported by the power of France. The fact was that the aims of Catholicism and Protestantism were *not* identical and their methods conflicted.

The Protestant missionary was often a fundamentalist who believed in the doctrine of Armageddon and of 'the Elect'. As such, he was making an exclusive appeal to that small minority of Chinese who might prove to belong to the latter group. He therefore tended to diffuse his activity over as wide an area as could be covered from his mission station, and welfare work was regarded by him as a side issue. Other Protestant missionaries, however, did regard both medical and educational work as of the highest importance, but since their real objective was the saving of souls and the medical and educational undertakings were primarily to obtain a wider audience, the Chinese (quite apart from their prejudice against innovations) were disposed to value them accordingly.

The Protestant missionaries tended to regard Chinese society as an extension of that of their home countries, and therefore to require the same kind of moral aid. Thus the English missionaries who were mindful of the evil effects of drink in Victorian England regarded the prohibition of wine-drinking in China as a Christian duty, and since the stage in Europe was looked upon by them as being licentious, the convert was enjoined to discontinue patronizing the Chinese drama, the greatest of Chinese amusements. Other minor habits, such as smoking, were frowned on, and 'many little foibles of the European Reformed Churches were erected into dogmas of the Christian religion'.[1]

The Catholic missionary approached his field of action in quite a different spirit. He had in mind the method whereby nearly two thousand years before in the Roman Empire his Church had aimed to create small Christian communities like cells which in time would spread and grow, imperceptibly if possible, by adopting as much of Chinese culture as could be accepted by the Christian religion and slowly changing the rest. There was not to be a sharp break with the past, but rather a conservative transformation from within. The building of the Christian family, not the salvation of the individual soul, was the real aim. When the community was Catholic (they reasoned), the children would automatically be of the Catholic faith.

Both Catholics and Protestants, however, were confronted by a common enemy in the shape of the Chinese attitude of mind. The idea of the complete separation of body and spirit, for example, was alien to Chinese thought. The Confucian was indifferent to the other-worldliness of the Christian faith; the Buddhist sought emancipation from rebirth and the identification of the self with the infinite in Nirvana, though the *Mahayana* had an intermediate 'heaven'; the *hsien* Taoist aimed at a kind of material immortality in which his body would be so preserved and rarefied as to take its place among the *hsien* (or genii). But an even more formidable obstacle to Christian missionary success was not the fanatical devotion of the Chinese to a pagan creed, but their *tolerance*. The Chinese people did not completely reject the Christian faith, but they were unwilling to grant it the exclusive title to belief. Christian missionaries, both Protestant and Catholic, were monopolists; the one true faith (however variously defined) could not exist side by side with another faith.

The Boxer religion (as we shall see) was compounded of all three of the Chinese systems, but with more of Taoism in its makeup than Buddhism, and with only an *influence* rather than an *element* of Confucianism. In these systems, the antithesis of salvation and damnation did not occur, and the prime motive for Christian conduct and orthodox belief was thus absent from the Chinese mind. Nor could the Chinese in general believe that to instil in them a belief in the doctrine of salvation and damnation was the real motive of Christian teaching. That the missionaries should have come all this way from their homes to achieve this end seemed quite improbable to the pragmatic Chinese mind: it was much easier to believe that they were the agents of some foreign power.

Thus it was that what success the Christian missionaries had in gaining converts was due mainly to reasons that they themselves would have reprobated. The very poor were attracted by the material advantages that conversion offered; others welcomed the adoption of a new religion because it automatically discharged them from observing the old rules of Chinese society which they had found it burdensome to follow. Association with success, moreover, was always a powerful inducement to the shrewd Chinese, and the rise in the number of converts after the failure of the Boxer uprising can as fairly be ascribed to this factor as can its decline after the Communist Revolution of 1949.

The missionary side of the debate has been exhaustively stated by many writers. Latourette, the historian of Christian missions in China, sums up the missionary case in the observation reproduced at the head of this chapter. The Chinese side of the debate has, however, rarely been given in terms that are likely to have any appeal for the European reader, but it happens that a contemporary Chinese, resident in Singapore but with close acquaintanceship with China, sets out the Chinese case in English and in terms of both English and Chinese values at the time of the Boxer troubles, and his interpretation of the facts is sufficiently cogent and interesting to justify our taking notice of it in some detail. Wên Ch'ing has the merit, moreover, that he does not hold the missionaries exclusively to blame for the anti-foreign feeling.[1]

Relations between Europeans and Chinese (says Wên Ch'ing) had all along been strained by mutual misunderstanding, followed by each side trying to take advantage of the other. In speaking of the interests of the Chinese, one has to understand that 'interests' meant many things—the Imperial rights and immunities, the privileges of the mandarins, the vested interests of the scholars, and the indefinable claims of the governed. The rights and interests of the millions of ordinary people were perhaps the most important to be considered, especially as in the past they had invariably been neglected. They included the mercantile, the communal, and the religious elements of the national life. The real trouble that any foreign Power created for itself in meddling with the affairs of China was not that caused by military opposition but by the intrinsic nature of Chinese civilization itself. The Manchus had overcome China chiefly by submitting themselves to Chinese civilization. Thus we witness the anomaly of a comparatively small nation dominating many millions of a people physically and intellectually equal, if not superior, to them. If, however, in their policy of non-partition (remember that Wên Ch'ing was writing at the time that the Boxer Protocol was being negotiated) the allies simply continued to bolster up the Manchu dynasty, they would be obstructing the natural evolution of an ancient civilization.

The 'Yellow Peril' had for some time been a spectre in the European imagination, but while white men were shutting the doors of their colonies and settlements in America, Australia, and elsewhere against the Chinese, they were simultaneously claiming the implementation of unheard-of privileges already secured to them by treaty between the sovereign representatives of the 'white' and 'yellow' races, in addition to the right to reside in China with extraterritorial status. The Chinese had yet to perceive the superior sense of justice claimed by missionaries for all Christian nations.

From the Imperial point of view the treaties entered into between the Son of Heaven and the foreign Powers were agreements dictated by superior force, and therefore liable at any moment to be set at naught. And although the privileges claimed by foreigners were embodied in the various treaties, it was very questionable whether the high mandarins ever studied these documents, and it was doubtful even whether copies of the treaties were to be found in Peking—except, perhaps, in the Tsungli Yamen. The provincial authorities certainly remained profoundly ignorant of the conditions of the treaties, and no mandarin seemed to have mastered the provisions with a view to carrying them out. Moreover, the treaties had never appeared in the *Peking Gazette*. The ignorance of the mandarins in this regard was perhaps not surprising when it was remembered that even the details of the great Ch'ing Penal Code were not properly studied. The Manchus looked upon the treaties as evidence of the national humiliation and had been very unwilling to force their subjects to study them, while the Chinese considered that they were not parties to any agreement made between the foreigners and the Manchus without their knowledge or acquiescence. In any case, the right of foreign interference in domestic matters had never been conceded in the treaties.

The subjects dealt with in the various documents agreed upon between the Chinese and the foreigners were viewed from different standpoints by the contracting parties. Diplomacy, as understood by European nations, was still almost an unknown quantity in China. The Chinese regarded it as merely the acknowledgement by the conquered of subjection to the victors and imagined that its operation did not extend beyond certain State functions, including the bestowal of honorary titles, the exchange of presents, the payment of tribute, regular attendances at the Imperial Court, and the customary salutations (*kowtow*, etc.). If the foreigners had swept away the Manchus and set up a king of their own to rule the country, the Chinese and the Manchus would have understood the position well enough. But since the dynasty was left intact, and indeed was supported against the people, as in the case of the Taiping Rebellion, there was no excuse for the foreigners to take it on themselves to interfere in the internal affairs of the empire.

The Imperial regulations provided that an official should not engage in trade, yet the people saw that the main occupation of the officials was conducting trade on behalf of the government. Were not offices sold and bargained for and knocked down to the highest bidder? Justice itself was a commodity and mandarins farmed out the collection of revenues to private individuals. Nor was there anything to prevent a merchant from purchasing office. It was the unfortunate common people who suffered by the corruption. Yet if they rose against the mandarins some foreign Power would almost certainly come to the assistance of the government. While the foreign nations exerted their power to compel the government to treat their own subjects and protégés with every consideration, the natives of the soil had no one to whom they could appeal. The Manchu representatives remained obdurate, while the foreigners looked on with indifference.

In all the treaties there was a clause that provided that the foreign text should be the official one. This provision had led to endless confusion, and contributed to the neglect of these documents by the Chinese. They never felt sure what the foreign phrases and idioms might imply, and they had found by experience that foreign diplomats did not hesitate when it suited them to place any interpretation they liked on the wording of the treaties. For example, the clause tolerating the teaching of the Christian religion read simply enough, but its plain meaning did not contemplate all the consequences that flowed from it. Again, the building of churches and mission stations involved many questions touching the land laws as well as the communal interests of the inhabitants. *Fêng-shui* might be pure superstition, but the natives of China believed that it was as indispensable to their well-being as light and air. The disturbance of the *fêng-shui* by a church spire was considered as much a grievance as the erection of a hideous tannery alongside Westminster Abbey would be in England. Was it not a fact that the missionaries were not amenable to the Chinese law regarding immovable property, and that for all practical purposes the properties acquired by them passed from the sovereignty of the Manchus?

The 'most favoured nation' clause was doubtless an ingenious formula conceived by the diplomats who were afraid that their rivals might, by subtle methods, procure from the Chinese what they would refuse to yield to brute force. Yet it was obvious that this same clause had done much harm to the interests of the foreigners themselves and even greater harm to the Chinese. It instigated international jealousies and it acted as a check to progress, since the frightened Chinese would attempt nothing for fear that they might encourage some foreign nation to seek some new privilege which would have to be conceded automatically to all the others.

The most scandalous of all the many dubious manœuvres of which the foreigners were guilty was over the tariff question. Having, by force, dictated to the Chinese the rate of customs duties leviable on foreign goods, thereby practically robbing the country of its independence, the foreign Powers squeezed every possible advantage in order to benefit foreign goods, regardless of the interests and claims of native producers. European wines, spirits, cigars, etc., in fact all articles used by Europeans for domestic purposes, were by treaty imported duty-free. In Shanghai, Canton, and elsewhere foreigners were importing alcohol, not solely for European consumption, yet the Chinese authorities were powerless to control the traffic. On the other hand, tea, on which the tax paid by the native consumer was computed to be about 25 per cent of the cost of production, might be exported by foreigners from China at the minimum rate of export duty fixed by treaty. In other words, native products bought by a foreigner were entitled to exemption from tax as if they were foreign products.

The opium question was of very long standing. Nothing had done so much harm to the cause of the missionary as the forcing of opium on the people of China. Even native Christians felt keenly about the matter. The missionaries, therefore, had consistently attacked the traffic. Yet even now (1900) the opium duty permitted by the Powers was unfair and inadequate. While the opium revenue in Hong Kong and Singapore had increased enormously, the Chinese government was forced by the cupidity of traders to tax opium at the same old rate. Europeans complained that the Chinese were always trying to evade the responsibilities imposed upon them by the treaties, yet the provisions relating to opium contained in the Chefoo Convention (1875) remained unratified by Britain for over ten years. Had China refused to ratify the treaty *in toto*, it is quite likely that (as in 1860) Peking would have been occupied by the foreigners once again.

Ever since the Japanese victory over the Chinese in 1895 the attitude of many foreign Ministers, especially that of the representatives of two or three European Powers, had been very much resented by the Chinese. Patiently, if not servilely, the mandarins had to endure the fierce looks and fiery language of the foreign Ministers who were always threatening them with war. When the Germans began the actual scramble for territory, the state of affairs became worse. Apart from the intrigues at Court which had played into the hands of Prince Tuan, the Manchus now faced a rising of the Chinese *sansculottes* (the Boxers) who were aware of China's humiliation, and many of the more manly princes took the side of the common people.

Wên Ch'ing (Lim Boon-keng) at this point makes a statement the truth of which is of some direct importance to our study: 'We have seen that the movement was at first anti-dynastic, and that on Prince Tuan joining it the plan of campaign was at once altered; the oppressed thought to redress their wrongs by brute force and savage violence.'[1]

By treaty, the representatives of the Powers were placed on the same footing as the higher Chinese officials. A consul, for example, had the status of a Taotai, and communicated with a person of his rank alone. This arrangement, however, had frequently resulted in practical inconvenience, and when there was trouble the Chinese officials were always blamed. The massacre at Tientsin in 1870 was a case in point. The French consul refused to hold any communication with the Chinese magistrate who appealed to him, informing him that the people were in a terrible state of excitement over the alleged killing of infants during a Roman Catholic religious service, on the ground that he was not of the requisite rank.

Foreigners might travel into the interior of China if provided with a passport, and while there were, of course, under the nominal protection of the Imperial government. But the Imperial government had very little power in the districts and villages. There were no regular police, but only irregular companies of night-watchmen, who were the lowest ruffians as a general rule. Under these circumstances an edict or a despatch from the Tsungli Yamen was of no more value than the paper it was written on. Yet, by arrangement, the passports were all signed by foreign consuls, and the local Chinese authorities had to countersign them, even for travel in districts where a disturbance was going on and which it was not considered safe for a Chinese to enter. The Chinese officials could not prevent an enthusiastic missionary from taking up residence in the middle of a disturbed area. Not a few mandarins, forced to countersign passports under such circumstances, had connived at outrages by the populace, feeling that individuals deserved to suffer vicariously for the folly of their governments.

By Article XVII of the Treaty of Tientsin, complaints by foreign subjects against Chinese must be made to the consuls of the respective countries who, if they thought fit, might consult the Chinese authorities over the matter. This provision was calculated to bring the Chinese officials into contempt with the populace who were thus convinced that they had no discretion of their own and were the mere tools of the foreign consuls.

The circumstances of the residence by foreigners in China necessitated the employment by them of large numbers of Chinese. The treaties never contemplated that subjects of China should cease to be amenable to the laws of the land, but, in practice, the clause which enjoined that the mandarins were not to place restrictions on the merchants in employing natives had resulted in frequent abuses. The servants, clerks, and compradores of foreign houses often escaped punishment for offences committed by them in a Chinese city since it was impossible for the Chinese mandarin to arrest them without the consent of the foreign consul, and the latter would not give his consent until he had inquired into the matter. If the affair was a slight one, say a minor case of assault, the matter might be so explained away by an indulgent master that the consul would see no ground to comply with the Taotai's request. In more serious disputes, foreign merchants would often intervene to protect employees who were valuable to them in their business.

Then the Christian converts were a perpetual source of trouble and nuisance. The Roman Catholic converts and most of the Protestant ones openly defied the laws of the land by refusing to *kowtow* to the magistrate or any other official. The *kowtow*, though degrading from the modern European point of view, had always been the oriental mode of obeisance. In China it was a sign of respect for higher authority, with the same significance as uncovering one's head in the presence of a judge in a European Court. In the eyes of the people it would now appear that the Christians need not respect the officials, since they might stand and talk to them face to face while the unconverted heathen must crawl past them like a worm in the dust.

In many cases, too, the missionary intruded himself into the Chinese court and sat beside the magistrate to hear a case between a convert and a non-Christian native. The influence of the missionaries was very great and the official was often pestered and worried by them. They would ignore all the persuasions of the mandarin, and, in spite of his entreaties, would build a house or a church as if on purpose to injure the *fêng-shui* of a village. Had not some of them written triumphantly of how they had scored off the literati and the heathens and how they had planted their dwellings on the head of the 'subterranean dragon' (of *fêng-shui*) and had even overtopped the temple of Confucius?

If there are honest missionaries, there are also sincere believers in the ancient faith of Cathay to resent the encroachment of foreign priests who preach to the heathen the doctrines of self-imposed poverty (Matthew x. 9; Mark vi. 8), and yet themselves live sumptuously enough in comfortable houses, surrounded by a wife and numerous progeny, in the midst of heathen squalor and misery.[1]

What foreigners compelled the Chinese authorities to impose on the Chinese people no British or American government would dare to inflict on its own population. The perpetuation of the objectionable *likin* tax on internal trade, by its taking over by the Imperial Maritime Customs as an extra security for foreign loans, was one example.

Then there was the navigation of China's inland waterways permitted to foreigners by treaty, which invaded a vast number of native vested interests, without any compensation to those who were dispossessed. The land question, too, was the source of much heartburning. The treaties laid it down that natives should be properly paid for land taken from them, but the mandarins, knowing that certain properties were required by the foreigner, often quietly acquired them beforehand by methods of their own, and disposed of them to the foreigner at a great profit to themselves. The removal of graves (occasioned by the building of railways, etc.) was also a matter of concern to Chinese feeling, since nothing on earth was so sacred as the grave of an ancestor.

As regards the missionaries, some were worthy men who were liked by the people, but others lacked the qualifications which should adorn the character of a minister of religion. Not all missionaries were sensible or sober. Yet the native Christians, being very poor, had to put up with anyone sent to them. Moreover, they must subscribe to creeds framed to suit another race and another civilization. Wên Ch'ing says:

The Europeans, for sectarian motives, have not encouraged any independence of thought among the natives and converts, and as far as the religion of the people is concerned, they have scarcely reached the stage of the Christians of the Middle Ages. All the results of modern exegesis and all the labours of scientific Hebraists are *tabu* in the churches of China. Fearing that the inflow of light might reveal too much, Christianity is still taught to this highly intellectual people in the form of fairy tales, and the only thing that will save the nation is rigidly excluded from the curriculum of studies among native Christians. Scientific philosophy is the one talisman which will dissolve national superstitions into nothingness: but scientific philosophy means impartial and fearless enquiry, which breathes too much of the spirit of a Savonarola, of a Colenso, or of a Darwin, to be acceptable to the missionaries.[1]

An even greater evil perhaps was the mutual contempt with which the converts of the different sects regarded one another. There was no real feeling of love or charity between the worshippers of Jesus (Protestants) and the worshippers of the Lord of Heaven (Roman Catholics). The envy between the missionaries themselves was even less edifying. Meanwhile the heathen could make neither head nor tail of the peculiar dissensions which rent these sects asunder.

Often a native Christian would make over real property to a missionary for the use of the Church. In doing so he practically overlooked all the vested and other rights of the Chinese State, and of his own descendants and kinsmen according to Chinese ideas. Sometimes such rights would be provided for at the time, but after changes of missionaries the Church would claim the land absolutely and disputes would at once spring up between the converts and the kinsmen of the convert who had alienated the property. Not infrequently, from such a little family squabble a great whirlwind was raised involving the whole local community.

There were many reasons why the people looked with extreme disfavour on the Christian religion. Personal inconvenience and many hardships often ensued as the consequence of a Chinese becoming a Christian. If a man had a wife and a concubine, for example, and yet wished for salvation he had first to dissolve his union with the latter, however happy it might be, or the foreign missionaries would not receive him. If the convert were already betrothed to a non-Christian girl, the betrothal would probably be terminated at the instigation of the missionary, and, although Chinese law allowed heavy damages for breach of promise, they were never exacted, for the missionary would appeal to his consul.

A case of almost everyday occurrence was one in which (in the missionary version) 'a native who is very devoted to his Church is persecuted because he refuses to give contributions towards expenses connected with idolatrous worship'. Yet it did not require very much acquaintance with the customs of the Chinese to know that 'joining in idolatrous worship' was a pure invention of the native Christians. It was in fact a remarkably successful ruse for evading the payment of one's just liabilities as a member of the village community (for communal entertainment, upkeep of the temple as a village meeting-place, etc.).

Wên Ch'ing is undeniably prejudiced against the missionaries, but since he correctly expresses the point of view of the great majority of ordinary Chinese of the time, which was a mainspring of their sympathy for the Boxers, and because this point of view receives no expression in the voluminous missionary literature which has shaped the attitude of the ordinary Western reader, it is appropriate that he should be summarized at length in this chapter. He concludes:

These social anomalies and continuous petty injustices combine to aggravate the people's indignation against a sect which teaches the selfish salvation of the individual as against the ancient family altruism—the harmony of the family. The Buddhist priests are held in great contempt because they really live and work on the lines which Buddha and Jesus enjoined on their disciples....It may confidently be said that the Christian religion, maintained at such great cost to China, will tumble to pieces the moment that political advantages are dissociated from the Church.[1]

Many foreign merchants of the Treaty Ports, and even a few diplomats placed the entire blame for the anti-foreign feeling of the Chinese on the missionaries. Many missionaries, for their part, placed the entire blame on the foreign merchants and on the policy of 'grab' which had always been that of the European Powers and (more recently) of Japan. Marshall Broomhall, for example, says: 'To regard the present movement as the result of missionary efforts is absurd...the movement is first and foremost an anti-foreign movement.... That opium should have been a *casus belli* (in the First China War) meant that the possibility of winning a happy and cordial relationship with the Chinese was hopelessly lost.'[1]

A *Statement of Protestant Missionary Societies*, published in *The Times* of 24 August 1900, and in other papers about the same time, set out the Protestant case in considered terms.[2] It may be fairly taken as their answer to Wên Ch'ing. Here are some of the more important passages:

There seems to be a disposition to make the labours of Christian Missionaries responsible for the violent hostility expressed by the Chinese against foreigners. They have been seriously cautioned and counselled by H.M. Secretary of State for Foreign Affairs. The newspaper and periodical press have pointed out in varying terms their power for mischief and the perils which constantly threaten all foreigners in consequence of their action....

In regard to the complaint that missionaries by their enterprise and indiscretion involve themselves in difficulty and then appeal to their own Government for protection and vindication, it may with truth be said that the cases in which this has happened, at least in Protestant Missions, have been so rare and exceptional that no general complaint against Missions can fairly be based upon them....It must, however, be remembered that while missionaries are pursuing their lawful calling they have an equal right with all others to claim the protection of their Government....

It is further complained that missionaries have excited against themselves the hostility of the official classes in China by their habit of interfering in the law suits of their converts, the just administration of the law being constantly prevented by the powerful pressure of the foreigner's influence. A distinction ought to be drawn in regard to this complaint between the Roman Catholic and the Protestant Missions. The former appear to act on the principle that it is the duty of the Church to act as the protector of its members, and its priests have become conspicuous by their general action as advocates of the causes of their converts. The Protestant missionaries, on the other hand, have thought that to adopt this course would not only arouse the hostility of the magistrates, but would also be a strong temptation to unworthy persons to profess themselves converts to Christianity for the purpose of obtaining the help of the missionary in law suits. As a rule, therefore, they have steadfastly, and often to their own disadvantage, declined to interfere. Yet the Chinese administration of justice is so venal and corrupt that it is often exceedingly difficult for the missionaries to stand passively by and see their converts suffering from the grossest injustice without making an effort to help them....

There is no evidence that the persecution of the Christians, and the attacks on missionaries have any religious basis such as was so prominent a feature in the Indian Mutiny....The complaint against Christianity has been mainly that it was a foreign superstition. The Christians have been persecuted because they had adopted a faith which came from foreigners. The missionaries have been objects of attack because they were foreigners.

China is a huge anachronism....They [the Chinese] have grown strong and haughty in their isolation, and have looked with supercilious contempt on the foreign barbarians. The gates of their exclusiveness were shattered and forced open by cannon to compel them to receive a commerce they did not want, and to share in an intercourse they despised....[The opium trade is here described and the now successful Chinese competition with the foreigner in the cultivation of the opium poppy.] Under such circumstances it seems scarcely necessary to saddle on the Christian missionary the responsibility of anti-foreign feeling among the Chinese....China cannot shut out the tide of the world's life, however much she may desire to do so....The best thing Europe and America can do for China at the present crisis is to give it the gospel of Jesus Christ more freely.

To come by a defence of Roman Catholic missionary policy in China comparable to the statement of the Protestant missionaries quoted above is no easy matter. The historians of Roman Catholic missions (Launay, Bernard, Brucker, etc.) do not seem to consider that it is necessary to justify them in the terms of the values appealed to by the Protestants; their activities are vindicated by the authority of the Roman Church and sanctioned legally by the Treaties. Thus intervention by a priest in a law case in which a Catholic convert was involved would require no explanation; it would be his plain duty to protect his charge from injustice caused by faulty law or corrupt administration.

Like the Protestants, the Roman Catholics uniformly ascribe the Boxer uprising to the political and military action of the Powers. A typical Catholic explanation is the following: 'The Boxer Rising was no sudden and unexpected occurrence. It was the fatal and almost inevitable result of the pressures put on China by the foreign Powers, standing round her like vultures to devour her at the first signs of collapse.'[1]

The Catholic criticism of Protestant missionary technique, both before the Boxer Uprising and after it, was the same. The Protestant educational activity did not primarily or immediately aim at conversion, but rather at preparing the ground for it. The subjects taught were mostly secular (and, indeed, it was these matters that interested the Chinese most). It is true that the Protestants in the nineteenth century contributed much more to the Chinese reservoir of Western secular knowledge than did the Roman Catholics, but nevertheless (as has been indicated in the account of reform and reaction (chapter v)), this reservoir was quite inadequate to provide the reformers with the information they needed regarding the forces that were reshaping the Western world.[1]

CHAPTER VII

SECTS AND REBELLIONS

It is a commonplace that in matters of religion the Chinese have shown themselves more tolerant than any other great people in the world. S. Wells Williams (a pioneer American missionary who first went to China in 1833) said:

The complete separation of the state religion from the worship of the common people accounts for the remarkable freedom of belief on religious topics. Mohammedanism and Buddhism, Taoist ceremonies and Lama Temples, are all tolerated in a certain way, but none of them have in the least interfered with the state religion, or the autocracy of the monarch as the Son of Heaven.[1]

The Buddhist 'demonology' (Wells Williams continued) allows the incorporation of the deities and spirits of the other religions, and goes even further in permitting its priests to worship the gods of other pantheons. Thus they could engraft all the native and foreign divinities into their calendar as they saw fit. But although the emperors had at various times shown great devotion to the ceremonies and doctrines of Buddhism, building Buddhist temples at great expense, the teachings of Confucius and Mencius were too well understood among the people to be uprooted or overridden. As regards Taoism, however, the Confucians had reservations, and they felt that the worst crime of the Taoist pontiff was his claim to be the Heavenly Teacher. Since in Confucian eyes no one was greater than the Son of Heaven or emperor, this Taoist assertion must have seemed an insolent affront.[2]

But the Imperial tolerance did not extend to what were called the 'heretical sects' (hsieh chiao), the secret associations which had been common among the people from an early time, even though these claimed to adhere to Buddhist or Taoist doctrines, for the simple reason that they were associated in the Imperial mind with turbulence and rebellion.[3]

The reigning dynasty feared these sects. The rebellions which had overthrown each successive dynasty had invariably followed the same pattern—discontent from economic or political causes centring round a secret sect, the rise of a new leader, and the creation of a new dynasty with this leader as its first emperor. The societies and sects were all based on the principle of sworn-brotherhood as typified in the Peach Garden Legend,[1] and there was invariably an appeal to the nostalgia for a departed 'Golden Age', the 'good old days' of a previous dynasty when things were so much better than they were now, the restoration of which promised to bring improvement in the lot of the masses. The new leader always claimed to be the descendant and representative of the previous dynasty. But most of these rebellions came to nothing and the dynasty survived.

Vincent Shih has analysed nine of the rebellions that can be said to have possessed some sort of 'ideology' apart from merely personal motives—namely those of Ch'ên Shêng and Wu Kuang, 209 B.C., of Liu Pang, 209 B.C., of the Ch'ih-mei (the Red Eyebrows), A.D. 18, of Huang-chin (the Yellow Turbans), A.D. 184, of Huang Ch'ao, A.D. 875, uprisings under the Sung (960–1279), those of the Pai-Lien Chiao (White Lotus) and related sects, rebellions at the end of the Yüan dynasty, and the Liu Tsê (Roaming Bandits) at the end of the Ming.[2]

The ruthless and cruel nature of the Ch'in regime was the ostensible cause of all the uprisings of that period. Ch'ên Shêng and Wu Kuang were among 900 conscripts who, failing to take up their stations at Tatsehsiang at a date appointed by the Emperor, were faced with the alternative of death or rebellion. They appealed to their comrades to rise, asking the novel and startling question, 'Are princes, lords, generals, and prime ministers a race apart?' But there is no reason to assume that they believed in equality for all men or that they aimed at the abolition of the social classes. Their rebellion was merely an expression of a desire to be equal with those in power, a personal sentiment rather than an awakening realization of a new principle.

Liu Pang also exploited the general resentment of bad government and cruel laws and he promised the people a life free from too much governmental interference. His originality was his idea of entering into a covenant with the people—something which had never been suggested before his time. But Liu does not seem to have entertained any ideas of a new social order.

Fan Ch'ung and his followers, the Red Eyebrows, who rebelled in A.D. 18, also appealed to the principle of legitimate succession and made Liu P'ên-tzŭ, a direct descendant of the royal family, Emperor. To distinguish themselves from the troops of his opponent, Wang Mang, Fan Ch'ung's troops painted their eyebrows red. The choice of red as a colour was due to the fact that Liu Pang, the first emperor of the Han, was known as 'the Son of the Red Emperor', and this was an additional insistence on the principle of legitimate succession.

The leader of the rebellion of the Yellow Turbans, Chang Chüeh (A.D. 184), was a religious leader who taught the people a new kind of Taoism and impressed them by his magical healing powers. His patients were told to kneel and confess their wrongdoing, and his teaching was known as the *T'ai-p'ing-tao*. Within a period of ten years he collected followers to the number of several hundred thousands in Ch'ing,[1] Hsü,[2] Yu,[3] Chi,[4] Ching,[5] Yang,[6] Yen,[7] and Yü.[8] Chang organized thirty-six *fang*—a great *fang* consisting of 10,000 men and a smaller one of 6000–7000, each under its own chief. The revolt was heralded by a rumour that the Azure Heaven had ceased to exist and the Yellow Heaven was about to take its place (hence the colour of the turbans), and that in the year of *chia-tzŭ* (184) the world would experience great happiness.

The Taoism of the Yellow Turbans was based on a text called the *T'ai-p'ing ch'ing-ling shu*. Although the general spirit of the text was Taoist, it had assimilated some Buddhist teachings, even though it assailed Buddhism vehemently. It maintained that there are three physical forms—*t'ien*, *ti*, and *jên*. *Tao* pertains to *t'ien* (heaven), *tê* pertains to *ti* (earth), and *jên* (the feeling of humanity) pertains to *jên* (man). The text emphasized quietude and non-action (*wu wei*) as the art of ruling, and *jên* as the necessary qualification of a ruler. It stressed the importance of a state of mind free from desire. It held that heaven and earth and the 'ten thousand things' had received their being from the Primordial Spirit (*Yüan-Ch'i*). This was none other than Nature, held to be empty and non-active. Man in action should not run counter to heaven. In everything he should work in accordance with the principles of *yin* and *yang* and the five elements. The text also prophesied that the Spirit of the Great Peace (*T'ai-P'ing-Ch'i*) was about to become manifest, that a great ruler would appear and that the Spirit of the Great Peace would through him descend to the earth.

The text attacked Buddhism on several grounds—for its neglect of filial piety and other family duties, for the practice of its would-be priests of deserting parents, wives, and children, and for its custom of begging. Nevertheless, it had a theory of *Ch'êng-fu* (meaning to inherit and be responsible for) which was very like the Buddhist doctrine of *Karma*.

141

It is to the Three Changs, the brothers who led the Yellow Turbans, that the origin of the greater part of the Taoist festivals, and in particular the ritual of penitence, is attributed. According to their doctrine, sudden death and sickness were the consequence of sin, but the penitent sinner could deliver himself by a public confession whilst being cleansed by the magic water which the chief of the community gave him to drink. At the equinoctial festivals amulets were distributed which protected their wearers against maleficent demons.[1]

The T'ai-p'ing Taoism was opposed to the destruction of female children—not only for humane reasons but because, in order to be assisted on both his sides, the right and the left, a man needed two wives, and female infanticide meant cutting off the supply of wives. War was condemned since it discouraged the production of children, and a man's worth could be measured by the number of children he had. The principle of *Shou-yi* (preserving the one) was to be followed by a faithful adherent of the Tao in order to achieve immortality, to become a loyal minister or a filial son, or to rid himself of sickness.

Such beliefs are interesting because of their resemblance to those of the Boxers some seventeen hundred years later. But there is little in the Chang ideology that may properly be called political, social, or economic.

Pulleyblank is convinced that the rebellion of An Lu-shan (755–6) in the T'ang dynasty was a great turning-point in Chinese history:

An Lu-shan is not a name which is familiar to Western readers. Even to most Chinese it presents hardly more than a figure of romance. Yet the tremendous consequences which his career had for the Far East entitle him to a place among the great makers of human history. Before him China was a vast unified empire, extending its power far beyond its frontiers. After he raised rebellion it was a shattered and bruised remnant, confined to its own borders, pressed by invaders without and harassed within by parasitic and lawless armies over which a eunuch-ridden central government exerted a precarious suzerainty. The T'ang dynasty never recovered from the blow....[2]

The brilliant epoch of Hsüan-tsung was graced by some of the greatest artistic achievements of the Chinese genius—the poetry of Li Po, the painting of Wu Tao-hsüan and Wang Wei, to mention only the most illustrious names. Much of the T'ang material and cultural achievement was undoubtedly based on the political and economic reforms carried out for the Emperor by Li Lin-fu and his predecessors and assistants. But the foundation was too fragile, too much depended on individual men, and the gigantic effort to turn the Chinese empire into a centralized State degenerated into the satisfaction of personal ambitions and desires of grandeur. An Lu-shan was the avenging nemesis, 'a colossal principle of destruction which the dictator's system had nurtured in spite of itself'. It does not seem, however, that any special 'ideology' emerged with the An Lu-shan rebellion—only the same old lust for personal power.

Huang Ch'ao, a salt merchant, rose in rebellion in 875 in response to a call from Wang Hsien-chih, who had revolted the previous year. The rebellion had the usual causes—famine, government corruption, heavy taxation, and failure on the part of the government to give just reward and punishment.[1] But Huang Ch'ao offered no programme of reform beyond replacing the ruling emperor by himself. The first title he gave himself was that of 'Great Heaven-storming General', and, later on, that of 'Great Heaven-appointed General'. The reason for this was that he first of all conceived the notion that Heaven was on the side of the ruling power, and he therefore resolved to storm it, but later, when his army was on the point of taking the eastern capital, Loyang, in 880, he decided that Heaven was now on his side and he changed his title accordingly.

A feature of Huang's rebellion was that many scholars joined it, but the fact that both the rebels, Wang Hsien-chih and Huang Ch'ao, asked for high official preferment as a price for giving up their rebellious conduct shows that they had no new economic or social ideas to offer to replace those of the time.

There were a number of uprisings under the Sung. The first of note was that of Wang Hsiao-po in 993, when the poverty-stricken people of Szechwan rose in revolt against the concentration of wealth in the hands of the few.[2] Wang's slogan was, 'I hate the unequal distribution of wealth: I shall now equalize it for you'. The second was the reappearance of the above-mentioned *T'ai-p'ing-tao*. This was during the reign of Chê-tsung of the Sung (1086–1100). The Taoist healing cult, founded by Chang Chüeh and Chang Yen of the later Han, had been called the 'Five Pecks of Rice Doctrine' because those who contributed this amount of food to the common store would be freed from their diseases. 'Their followers [said Fang Shao] eat vegetables and worship the devil, and they gather at night and scatter in the daytime.' (This was to be another Boxer peculiarity.) 'When worshipping the devil they always face north, because Chang Chüeh arose in the north.' (Compare the Boxer 'Eight Trigrams' observances.)

In spite of their claim that Chang Chüeh was their originator, the ideology of these rebels of the Sung had little in common with his teachings or with the *Ta'i-p'ing ching*, which was supposedly the text on which he based them. Many elements in the doctrine of the Sung rebels may be characterized as Buddhist—namely the use of the Diamond Sutra, the condemnation of knowledge gained from external sources, the belief that since one brings nothing to this world one should take nothing to the next world, and that life is a source of misery, combined with the practice of vegetarianism, the common sharing of property, and the aim of the attainment of Buddhahood. At the same time they attacked Buddhism because it forbade them to kill. There were besides other elements in their creed distinctly opposed to Buddhism. They expressly denounced Buddha himself as an object of worship, along with other spirits, including ancestral spirits—which was definitely an anti-Confucian act. There was also evidence of the assimilation of non-Chinese ideas into their creed. In particular, their worship of the sun and moon was probably Mazdaist or Manichaean. The phrase 'Ch'ih-ts'ai shih-mo' (vegetarian diet and devil worship), identical in meaning and using the same characters as the description of Manichaeism (*Mo-ni chiao*), but in a different order, was applied to them by Fang Shao in his *Ch'ing-hsi K'ou-kuei*. But from the fact that they worshipped the sun and moon it was more probable that the sect was linked with Mazdaism, even though these could be the symbols of the principles of light in Manichaeism.

All this points to a synthesis of ideas from different sources. The members of the sect shared their property to a certain degree, and considered themselves to be of one family. 'All these suggest features [says Vincent Shih] which became characteristic of Secret Societies.'

The third notable rebellion under the Sung was that of Fang La, which took place in 1120. The *Sung-shih* gives a brief account of it in the biography of T'ung Kuan. The reason for the rebellion is stated there to be the insufferable misery imposed upon the people by the efforts of Chu Mien (d. 1126) to obtain rare plants and stones, but a stronger and more personal reason is given in Fang Shao's *Ch'ing-hsi K'ou-kuei*. It is there stated that Fang La's native place (Muchou in present-day Chekiang) was populous and wealthy, particularly as regards trees for lacquer, paper mulberry (whose bark was used for making paper), fir, and other timber. Great merchants used to visit it regularly. Fang La himself owned some lacquer groves and a manufacturing firm, in respect of which, however, he was oppressively taxed. Fang La resented this but as yet dared not reveal his sentiment. But it happened that just at this time Chu Mien's appetite for rare plants and stones enraged the local population. Fang La took advantage of the situation and gathered round him a crowd of poor people and idlers. With the call of ridding the world of Chu Mien, they rose in rebellion.

Fang La made use of legends and heretical teachings to gain support. Fang Shao states, too, that one day Fang La saw his own reflection in a brook, adorned in cap and gown like a king, and this encouraged him to the highest ambitions. But essentially Fan La's rebellion conformed to type. Its cause was (as usual) corrupt government and heavy taxation. There was, however, the added grievance caused by the appeasement by the authorities of foreign States by annual tributes of silver, silk, and tea, which added tax burdens to those borne already by the common people and which were imposed for purposes that they found hard to understand. Fang La's harangue against the Sung government may be compared to that of the Taipings in the nineteenth century against the concessions to foreigners made by the Ch'ing Court.

The next set of rebellions are those of the White Lotus sect, but since there was a close connection between the White Lotus and the Boxers and we must therefore inform ourselves more fully on this subject, I will, before taking extended note of it, describe the rebellion of 'Roaming Bandits' at the end of the Ming dynasty. This rebellion is associated with the rebel leader, Li Tzŭ-ch'êng, who shattered the authority of the Ming dynasty in the north, captured Peking in 1644, and proclaimed himself Emperor of a new dynasty, the Shun; and Chang Hsien-chung, the homicidal maniac who ruled Szechwan in 1649 and butchered a large part of the population of that province.

What did Li and Chang contribute to the development of Chinese rebel ideologies (asks Vincent Shih)? He scouts the suggestion that Li Tzŭ-ch'êng's idea of land distribution was the forerunner of that of the Taipings for, if the Taipings needed any inspiration for their land system, they had many other sources to go to. As for Chang Hsien-chung's policy, 'it had few ideological elements worthy of consideration'. His main mission was *killing*, which he justified as the 'will of heaven'. Yet when heaven displeased him by thwarting his plans, he ordered his artillery to fire their big guns at it. Paradoxically, he had great respect for Wên Ch'ang, the God of Literature—but only because he had the same surname as himself.

Nearly all of these rebellions were inspired by religious beliefs of some sort or other which could be traced either to Buddhism, Taoist sects, or orthodox Confucianism. However, there were some religious beliefs that could not be considered as common to all rebels. Chang Chüeh's idea of confession of wrongdoing and repentance as a pre-requisite for magical healing, and the belief of the vegetarians and devil-worshippers that death is a state of salvation because life is full of misery, are two of the exceptions. But in the major part of their ideologies the rebels exhibited an astonishingly uniform pattern.[1]

In the field of economics, the rebels seemed to concentrate their attention on land-taxes. Although only a few among them explicitly advocated equal distribution of the land, its concentration in the hands of the few has always been one of the main factors in causing China's rebellions. But there is no indication that the rebels had in mind any new land system that would radically alter the relations between land-lords and tenants and which would in consequence change the tradi-tional social stratification.

Finally, the rebels were also uniformly unimaginative. Apart from Ch'ên Shêng's vague suggestion that birth was no longer the mark of aristocracy, none of them had any positively new idea to offer.

The 'national', or rather racial issue, however, was frequently raised. Thus we find Fang La declaiming against the Sung for appeasing the northern barbarians; the rebels at the end of the Yüan condemned the dynasty because, among other things, it was not Chinese, and the secret societies in Ch'ing times as well as the Taipings used the anti-foreign issue against the Manchu regime to their best advantage.

The final conclusion that Vincent Shih reaches after his study of selected rebellions is that prior to China's contact with the West in modern times there had never been any movement which can be con-sidered as a revolution—that is, 'a major shift in the relations between social classes whereby the dominance of the upper class is destroyed and the lower class emancipates itself from economic exploitation but-tressed by political subordination'.

During the late Ming period an urban movement took place which created a new social order in the towns, marked by an increasing division of labour, and caused economic conflict. Liu Yen gives an analysis of twenty-six rebellions in the towns between 1596 and 1626 during this period, all directed against the powerful eunuchs who collected the taxes from mining. 'These movements [he says] were reflected in the ideological struggle against the Sung orthodoxy and were joined by gentry-adherents.'[1] In contrast to what happened in Western Europe, however, the struggle of the townspeople never developed beyond the economic stage.

Some Chinese writers trace the origins of the White Lotus sect to the Manichees. Manichaeism, which borrowed both from Christianity and Zoroastrianism, was founded by the Persian Mani, who was put to death in A.D. 274. It spread east and west after his death—westward as far as France, where the Albigenses were heretics of Manichaean faith, and eastward to China, where it is first mentioned in A.D. 694. In A.D. 732 the Buddhists initiated a persecution, which was not encouraged by the government, on the ground that this religion was that of the Uigurs, the Turkish tribe then dominant among the nomads, whom the Court was anxious to conciliate, and who were almost entirely Manichaean.[2]

The *Chung Hsi Chi Shih* says:

The White Lily Faith is a branch of the Mani religion [Manichaeism], one of the Three Western Churches of the T'ang dynasty, which was introduced into China at the same time as the Ta Ts'in [Nestorian]. When the Muslim faith was introduced, Mani was brought in too, and thus that faith came between the Religion of the Lord of Heaven [Roman Catholicism] and the Religion of the Place of Heaven [Arabia].[3]

And says Fan Wên-lan:

During the Sung, Yüan, Ming and Ch'ing periods Manichaeism was strictly banned. Its followers were severely punished. Thus the religion split up into many sects and went underground. In the south there were the Mo-chiao, the Chai-chiao, and the Ch'ih-ts'ai-chiao; and in the north there were the White Lotus and the T'ien-li-chiao. . . . According to Hsia Hsieh, *Chung-hsi chi-shih*, the White Lotus was a branch of Manichaeism which used *ch'i-ch'i* [Double seven] as its sign and whose main tenets were a belief in common property and a common colour. The faithful should abstain from eating meat, should chant the classics and incantations of his religion, should never walk over a cross, and should never touch pork. . . .Passing from pure Manichaeism to Mo-chiao and then to the doctrines of the White Lotus, the original doctrines of the religion were gradually lost and their place was taken step by step by Taoist teachings. The White Lotus religion became popular in the countryside, for it was a mixture of Mo-chiao, Taoism, and Buddhism, and its adherents, therefore, were allowed to worship all manner of gods and spirits.[4]

Jerome Ch'ên states that Chu Yüan-chang, the first Ming emperor, was a Manichaean: 'Religious rebels of the Ch'ing dynasty gave their allegiance to the Ming dynasty, not only because it was a Han-Chinese dynasty, but also because its founder was Manichaean. Hence the name of the dynasty was *Ming* "bright".'[1]

In studying the history of Chinese sects and secret societies one must be on one's guard against concluding that identity or similarity of name is proof of organic relationship. The White Lotus sect, for example, considered the most dangerous sect of all by the officials, had no close connection with the Buddhist philosophical school of the same name founded by the great monk Hui Yuan at the beginning of the fifth century. Nevertheless, the two were frequently confused in the public mind. While Buddhist conceptions and ritual were used to some extent by the sects, the Taoist element was the dominant one. For example, the slaughter of a white horse and a black bull by White Lotus adherents in the rising of 1349 (on the model of the Peach Garden Sacrifice) was an impiety which no Buddhist would commit. If this revolutionary Taoist cult had any connection with Buddhism at all, it could only be with the Lamaism which was in favour in North China in the twelfth and thirteenth centuries.

The genuine and orthodox Buddhist school of the White Lotus derived its name from the Mahayana scriptures—the *Saddharma-Pundarika*, 'The Lotus of the Good Law', its principal Bodhisattva being Avalokiteshwara (who changed his sex and became Kuan Yin, the Goddess of Mercy, in China). According to this doctrine, 'man lifted himself above his miseries in the same way that the lotus rises out of the mud'.[2] But the White Lotus sect, which was to become such a force for rebellion in Chinese history, seems to have first earned the reprobation, not only of the Confucian authorities, but also of orthodox Buddhism, sometime in the thirteenth century. The first mention of the fact is in the *Fo Tsu T'ung Chi*, by a monk named Chih P'an in 1343 (but compiled from information of a century earlier) in which he refers to the 'heretical associations which observe the cult of demons'. They are those sects consecrated to Mani (or Muni), to the vegetarians of the White Cloud, or to the White Lotus, and they 'borrow falsely the name of Buddhism to deceive the vulgar, just as among the Five Elements there are toxic vapours'.

Pelliot concludes that the heretical sect of the White Lotus was founded a little before 1133 by a monk named Mao Tzŭ-yüan, and that of the White Cloud a little before 1108 by another monk named K'ung Ch'ing-chüeh from Hangchow. Both sects were of Buddhist origin and appear to have been much freer from Taoist elements than they became in the succeeding centuries.

As a secret political association distinct from a Buddhist religious school, the White Lotus sect appears for certain in 1349, in the form of a revolutionary cult connected with the 'Red Turban Rebellion' which overthrew the Mongol Yüan dynasty. It is mentioned in the Yüan books in one breath with the White Cloud School.[1] Previous to the outbreak, a rumour had been in circulation that a great disturbance was imminent, and that the Buddha Maitreya, the Buddhist Messiah, would appear. The source of the rumour was one Han Shan-tung, the leader of the sect which called itself the White Lotus, who claimed to be a descendant of the house of Sung. The insurgents wore red kerchiefs round their heads. Han Shan-tung was captured and executed, but his son, Han Lin-êrh, took his place. Han Lin-êrh had himself proclaimed 'Emperor' in 1355, but died shortly afterwards. His place, in turn, was taken by a fellow-revolutionary, Chu Yüan-chang, who at some time in his previous career had been a mendicant monk (and was also, as we have seen, alleged to be a Manichee). It was he who, in 1368, became the founder of the Ming dynasty. He is known to history as T'ai Tsu (First Ancestor). The reign-title he assumed was Hung Wu (Militant and Universal).

T'ai Tsu's victory remained an inspiration for the people of China for centuries to come—the man of the people, of pure Chinese blood, who had led a successful revolt against foreign rule. The secret society leaders in particular looked to his example, and the Triad Society of later years was to take as its 'family name' the character 'Hung', from the reign title Hung Wu, as a tribute to him.

By one of those ironic twists of fortune, which not infrequently overtake the successful leaders of revolution, T'ai Tsu soon discovered that the very sect by which he had secured his elevation to the Dragon Throne and similar heterodox sects were a threat to established government, and in 1394 a decree was issued declaring that members of the White Lotus sect and other designated religious societies, together with those Taoist and Buddhist clergy who should neglect to conform to the established ancestral customs, should be punished with death.

Having acquainted ourselves with the outlines of the origins of the White Lotus sect, we may pass on to the Ch'ing dynasty and to the

K'ang Hsi emperor's attempts to repress these subversive societies. He made war simultaneously on both Buddhist and Taoist priesthoods. Since we are concerned more with the northern than the southern provinces in our investigation of the Boxers, we shall keep a lookout for the former in particular.

Side by side, and sometimes merged with the White Lotus sect, were the White Yang sect or Pai-Yang Chiao, and the Red Yang sect (Hung-Yang Chiao), existing especially in Shantung, Honan, Chihli, and Sinkiang, while the White Lotus itself spread over a much wider area, if not over the whole of China. In an edict of 1673, the Emperor singled out for proscription the following sects—the Wu Wei,[1] the White Lotus, the Incense Burners, the Incense Smellers, the Origin of Chaos, the Origin of the Dragon, the All-Submerging Yang, the Perfect Intelligence, and the Mahāyāna. All of these, with the exception of the Perfect Intelligence and the Mahāyāna, would seem from their names to have been of Taoist origin.

When the Manchus established their rule over China, they were soon aware of the conditions under which they held their power. They took over from the Ming penalties relating to the secret cults and embodied them in their penal code. One of the articles they adopted from the Ming code ran as follows:

Religious leaders or instructors, and priests, who, pretending thereby to call down heretical gods, write charms or pronounce them over water, or carry round palanquins [containing idols], or invoke saints, calling themselves orthodox leaders; further, all societies calling themselves at random White Lotus communities of the Buddha Maitreya, or the Ming-tsun religions,[2] or the School of the White Cloud, etc.... finally, they who in secret places have prints and images, and offer incense to them, or hold meetings which take place late at night and break up by day, whereby the people are stirred up and misled under the pretext of cultivating virtue,—shall be sentenced, the principal perpetrators to strangulation, and their accomplices to a hundred blows with the long stick, followed by a lifelong banishment to a distance of three thousand miles.[3]

The attitude of the Ch'ing dynasty towards the heterodox sects was also definitely stated in the so-called 'Sacred Edict' (Shêng Yü) of the K'ang Hsi reign promulgated in 1670. The edict consisted of sixteen maxims enjoining filial and fraternal duties, avoidance of litigation, application to agriculture and the cultivation of the mulberry, etc. Each maxim consisted of seven characters—a poetic or incantatory form.

The K'ang Hsi emperor's son and successor, the Yung Chêng

emperor (1722–35), wrote a long 'Amplification' to his father's Sacred Edict, explaining what his father had meant. Since the style of the 'Amplification' was too classical to be understood by the people, Wang Yeh-po, a Superintendent of the Salt Gabelle, wrote a simpler version. The edict was written on slips of wood and placed in government offices, and an order was issued by the Emperor that it should be read aloud and explained to the people on the first and fifteenth of every month.[1]

The Yung Chêng edition of the Sacred Edict, in explaining the Seventh Maxim, which read, 'Degrade Strange Religions in order to Exalt Orthodoxy' (*Ch'u I Tuan I Ch'ung Chêng Hsüeh*), states that from ancient times three sects had been delivered down—that of the literati (Confucianism), *Tao* (Taoism), and *Fo* (Buddhism). The explanation continues:

Chu Hsi says that the Sect of Fo regard not Heaven, earth, or the four quarters, but attend only to the heart; the Sect of Lao [Lao Tzŭ, the founder of Taoism] are interested exclusively in the preservation of the animal spirits. Afterward, however, there arose a class of wanderers, who, devoid of any sense of independence, stole the names of these Sects, but corrupted their principles, in order to make merchandise of their ghostly and unexamined tales. At first they swindle people out of their money in order to feed themselves. By degrees, they proceed to collect assemblies to burn incense, in which males and females promiscuously mingle, and what is still worse, lascivious and villanous persons creep in secretly among them; they form brotherhoods; bind themselves to each other by oath; meet in the night and disperse at dawn; violate the laws, corrupt the age, and impose on the people—and behold! one morning the whole business comes to light. They are seized according to law, their innocent neighbours injured, and the chief of their Cabal punished with extreme vigour. What they thought would be the source of their felicity becomes the spring of their misery. So it is with the Pai-lien [White Lotus] and Wên Hsiang [Incense-smelling] sects, which may serve as a beacon to all others.

Roman Catholicism (the 'Sect of the Western Ocean') also 'ranks among those that are corrupt'.

The homily concludes with an admonition—'Seek not happiness beyond your own sphere; perform no action beyond the bounds of reason; attend solely to your own duty; then you will receive the protection of the gods....'.

One sect which has not so far been mentioned, but which comes into great prominence in the years 1786–8, and which was regarded as identical with the Boxers, is that of the Pa Kua (Eight Trigrams).

De Groot[1] says that the sect was also identical with the Hung Yang, Pai Yang, Ch'ing Yang, and Lung-hua sects, and was also called the T'ien-li Chiao, or religion of the Rules of Heaven and the Patterns of Nature. It was an offshoot of the White Lotus. The symbolic diagrams in the Chou classic, the *I Ching* (Book of Changes), setting out the ancient cosmogony of China—'a universal repository of concepts which included tables of antinomies (*yin* and *yang*) and a cosmic numerology', consisted of eight trigrams and sixty-four hexagrams.[2]

The Eight Trigrams appear in The Book of Changes (*I Ching*), the first of the Five Classics, used as a book of divination from antiquity onwards. From ancient times, the *yin* and the *yang*, the theory of the two great forces of the universe, had been interwoven into the symbolism of The Book of Changes.

The Eight Trigrams were also used to denominate the divisions of the universe according to the eight cardinal points. Such sectors, called *Kung*, or Mansions, were generally arranged around a ninth, representing the centre of the compass, and thus the sect was often called the Religion of the Nine Mansions. It was subdivided into eight main sections distinguished by the names of the trigrams. Each section had its own religious chief, and one of these was the general head of the whole pattern, a kind of *primus inter pares*.

Says de Groot:

Chên, which is the chief *Kua* of the eight, because it corresponds with East, the first and principal cardinal point, identified by the *Yih* [*I*] (*Book of Changes*) with the dragon, the symbol of Imperial dignity. Head of the division was Li Wên-ch'ing, the Emperor of Mankind....Being head of the principal *Kua*, he was also acknowledged as a chief of the sect as a whole. Originally a carpenter's boy, he had through study and industry become a man of no mean literary attainments, particularly proficient in soothsaying. He had been a member of various associations such as the 'Tiger-tail Whips' (*Hu-wei-pien*), the 'Red Brick Society' (*Hung Chuan Hui*), and the Society of the I Ho Ch'üan ('Boxers') until he became headman of the *Chên* diagram.[3]

The difficulty here is that the *Chên* trigram is *not* the 'chief diagram' according to the authorities (Mayers, Needham, etc.), but the *third*. It is associated with 'East' (originally with 'North-east'), but not with the dragon but the galloping horse or '*flying* dragon'. The associated colour of the *Chên* trigram is 'dark yellow'. Li Wên-ch'ing, the namesake of this chief of the rebels in Chia Ch'ing's time (1813), of 1899, was, as we shall see later, chief of the *Ch'ien* trigram, which actually ranked first and which was associated with 'father', 'dragon', 'horse', 'heaven', 'metal', etc.

It is to be expected that in claiming to be the reincarnation of the earlier Li Wên-ch'ing, the later one would have been chief of the same trigram or 'house' as his predecessor.

De Groot also mentions another chief of a trigram associated with Li Wên-ch'ing in 1813, namely Liu Ch'êng-hsiang, headman of the 'Northern Mansion of the Sect', or the *Kung* denoted by the trigram *K'an* (second son, water, etc.).[1] This '*house*' existed in 1899, but that of the *Chên* trigram does not appear.

The Boxers of 1900 were organized according to these *Kung*, but since only three of them are actually known to have been in existence, it will be sufficient to describe these as examples. Some difficulty arises over the *distinctive* colours of the 1900 Boxers, which will be discussed in chapter XI, and the colours given here are the traditional ones.

In the traditional Chinese system of symbolic correlations, the first trigram (*Ch'ien*) was associated with 'father', 'dragon', 'horse', 'metal', 'south' (according to 'more ancient' Hsien T'ien ('prior to Heaven') or *Fu-hsi* system; 'north-west' according to the 'later' *hou-t'ien* ('posterior to Heaven'), or *Wên Wang* system),[2] 'late autumn', 'early night', 'king', '*deep red*', 'head', 'being, strength, force, roundness, expansiveness', and 'Donator'; the second trigram, *K'un*, was associated with 'mother', 'mare', 'ox', 'earth', 'north' (according to earlier system) or 'south-west' (according to later system), 'late summer, early autumn', 'afternoon', 'people', '*black*', 'abdomen', 'docility', and 'Receptor'; the fourth trigram, *K'an*, was associated with 'second son', 'pig', 'moon and fresh water' (lakes), 'water', 'west' (according to the earlier system), 'north' (according to the later system), 'midwinter', 'midnight', 'thieves', '*blood-red*', 'ear', 'danger, precipitousness, curving-things, wheels', etc., and 'Flowing Motion'.

The system of the Book of Changes (*I Ching*) originated from 'what was probably a collection of peasant omen texts, and accumulating a mass of material used in the practices of divination, it ended up as an elaborate system of symbols and their explanations (not without a certain inner consistency and aesthetic force), having no close counterpart to the texts of any other civilisation'.[3] The symbols or *kua* were made up of sets of lines, some full or unbroken, others broken in two pieces with a space between. By using all the possible permutations and combinations of lines, the eight trigrams and the sixty-four hexagrams, all known as *kua*, were formed. The addition of appendices gave the system a further cosmological and ethical significance.

This sect flourished principally in the region north of the Yellow river, in north-east Honan, and the adjacent regions of Chihli and Shantung. In this region, in 1774, a rebellion of the White Lotus sect was suppressed with great slaughter, and it was also to be a centre of disturbance during the rebellion of that sect in 1813 (see below), and again during the Boxer uprising of 1900.

From September 1786 until October 1788, a rebellion of thousands of adherents to the Pa Kua sect took place. A decree of 22 July 1788 directed that the sect should be extirpated, and some eighty captured members of it banished to Ushi, Kashgar, Yarkand, etc., to be given as slaves to the Muslims there. Yet the decree admitted at the same time that the hymns and formulas of the sect had not been found to contain anything of a rebellious nature, 'nor any single character pointing to any illegality'.[1]

At some point which is not certain[2] the Pa Kua was included by name with the White Lotus, etc., among the prohibited societies.

The series of White Lotus rebellions, ending in 1815, followed the standard pattern—the putting forward of a pretender to the throne who based his claim on descent from the Ming dynasty, accompanied by that of being a reincarnation of the Buddha Maitreya, the admission of women to membership (on occasions they became leaders), and the mixed religious creed, consisting of Taoist and Buddhist elements and also of primitive spirit possession which was believed to ensure invulnerability.[3] With this was combined the sorcery of Taoism, the use of amulets which rendered their wearers invisible, and abstention from certain articles of food and drink. Finally, the colours white and black had a definite place in their ritual, and they always held their meetings at night.

The Ch'ien Lung emperor greatly extended the territory ruled over by his dynasty, and regarded himself (as he wrote in his essay *Shih ch'üan chi* (1792)) as 'the most extraordinary Emperor China had had since ancient times'. Yet it seems that he was to a considerable extent the author of the troubles which overtook his successors. The series of rebellions, which began towards the end of his reign and gathered in force after his abdication, were largely in reaction from his conquests, or arose from the economic and financial stress consequent thereon. Under his rule the administration had become hopelessly corrupt, and he appointed, and supported, governors-general and governors who extracted millions of dollars from the people. The greedy Manchu, Ho-shên, who headed the gang of extortioners, managed to accumulate over 800 million taels in the last twenty years of the reign, and even the most courageous censors dared not attack this fountain-head of corruption until his protector, the abdicated Ch'ien Lung emperor, was out of the way.[1]

Another characteristic abuse during the Ch'ien Lung reign was the practice for high officials, who were then nearly all Manchus, to travel with hundreds of armed retainers whose exactions terrorized the countryside; but on the abdicated emperor's death in 1799, steps were taken to put an end to the abuse—at any rate on paper.[2]

The Ch'ien Lung emperor, moreover, engaged in 'thought control' on a big scale—between 1774 and 1781 there were twenty-four occasions on which he ordered subversive books to be destroyed, and in this respect he was second only to the Emperor Shih Huang-ti of the Ch'in, the 'Burner of the Books'.

Already in 1795 rebellions of the Miao tribesmen disturbed Kweichow and Hunan. Then in 1796, the first year of the Chia Ch'ing reign, the revolt of the White Lotus sect started in Hupeh and Szechwan.

Wei Yüan, in the preamble to his work,[3] advances some interesting theories as to the causes of the insurrections which will be useful for us to bear in mind when we come to consider the origins of the Boxer movement of a century later.

He writes that at the moment of this insurrection the dynasty was at the apogee of its glory and nowhere had its peace been disturbed except by the Miao-tzŭ in Kweichow and Hunan. But now a comet appeared in the west with a tail several fathoms in length; the year passed away before it disappeared, and lo! the struggle of the government armies in the five disturbed provinces was to last into the seventh year, and even after that two more years would be needed to clear the countryside of the remaining rebels. 'Over ten thousand times a myriad gold pieces' were spent in victuals for the armies, a larger amount than it had cost for the conquest of Ili and Kinch'uan, major and minor.

The members of the White Lotus sect (says Wei Yüan) professed to bring relief from disease; they abstained from forbidden food, and fabricated sacred writing and incantations. With all this they misled the people. The beginning of the revolt was to be traced back to the fortieth year of Ch'ien Lung (1775) when one Liu Sung from Pingliang in Anhui placed himself at the head of the faction. Its numbers gradually grew, and finally the leaders declared a fellow-sectary, Wang Fu-shêng (of the Wang tribe in Luyi), to be a descendant of the Ming (and consequently a pretender to the throne).

The Imperial decrees describe the progress of the heresy-hunt which ensued. It was conducted with ruthless vigour. Wang Fu-shêng was captured, but exempted from the death penalty because of his youth and exiled to the New Frontier Province, Sinkiang. A prominent leader of the sect, Liu Chi-hsieh, escaped to Honan.

Then followed imperial orders for search for him on a large scale. . . . The authorities executed these in a wrong way; they ransacked every house, and the policemen and lictors availed themselves of the opportunity to commit cruel iniquities. . . . The Prefect of Wuch'ang caught many thousands in his nets. . . . The wealthy who were ruined [by extortion], and the poor who incurred death could not be numbered. At this moment the people in Szechwan, Hunan, Kwangtung and Kwangsi rose, the army being exhausted with fighting against the Miao tribe. The rigorous prohibitions of the manufacture of salt and cast-metal goods having deprived many people of their livelihood, now increased the popular hatred of the mandarins.[1]

Finally, in the first month of 1796 rebellion started on a large scale. The Viceroy of Hukuang, Pai Yüan, sent about ten thousand Manchu and Chinese troops to the affected area, but the rebels retained the upper hand. By the middle of 1797 the battle was at its height, especially in the districts along the Yangtze in north-east Szechwan. The Chief Commander of the insurgents was one Yao Chi-fu and a woman of the surname Wang. The presence of these Chinese Amazons among the sects has already been noted, and the mixing of men and women on an equality offended the Confucian sense of propriety more than anything else. With the subjugation of the Miao in the same year, however, more government troops were available for use against the rebels. By the end of 1803 the back of the rebellion was broken, and all was over except the 'mopping-up'.

When the abdicated emperor, Ch'ien Lung, died on 3 January 1799, Chia Ch'ing issued a decree to his generals, viceroys and governors in the revolting provinces pointing out that when rebellions had arisen, such as those of Wang Lun or the Muslims of Kansu, his father had been wont to crush them with overwhelming military power in a comparatively short time, but now there had been undue delay and he was worried about it. 'Each day (he complained) that passes by without seeing these sectarian rebels pacified, burdens me with self-reproach for unfilial conduct for the whole of the day.' Yet even when the rebellion was at its height, in edicts and essays Chia Ch'ing moralizes on the causes of the troubles, and tries to excuse the Imperial severity which had provoked the rebellion. The White Lotus sect was not itself to blame for the treason of its adherents, he said, 'the sacred writings recited by Liu Chi-hsieh have no other tendency than to admonish humanity to do what is good, and there was not one word in them relating to rebellion or opposition'. The crime of Liu Chi-hsieh, for which he had been cut to pieces at the stake, was that he had instigated a certain Niu Pa[1] secretly to form rebellious conspiracies; his punishment was due to his own sins and had nothing to do with the White Lotus sect. The same would happen to orthodox Confucians if they erred similarly, said Chia Ch'ing. The edict in question ended with an admonition to the authorities to leave the White Lotus sectaries in peace, 'unless they should hold meetings to stir up trouble'. But this did not moderate the severity of the penalties against the rebels. When in the sixth month of 1800 the rebel chief, Liu Chi-hsieh, was captured in Honan, the emperor ordered him to be sent post-haste to Peking, confined in a cage.[2]

In between the two major rebellions the heresy-hunts were continued. The edicts of this period reveal the Chia Ch'ing emperor's anxiety to follow his father's dictates to wean the people from being led astray as regards spirits and deities and wasting their money on prayers, invocations and sacrifices. These activities included pilgrimages to other provinces, involving journeys of up to thousands of miles, often taking no less than three months. What was more, they established *societies* for the worship of the deities. The viceroys and governors were ordered, therefore, *cautiously* to stop these practices and to prevent the people from gathering together for the purpose of making these excursions which were harmful to agriculture, promoted dissipation, and tended to corrupt hearts and customs.

The more or less 'cautious' action of the mandarins provoked new outbreaks, but the decrees against heterodoxy continued (against the Christians in particular in 1805, 1806 and 1811) and culminated in those against sects in general of 21 July 1812 in response to the recommendation of the censor, Yeh Shao-k'uei.

As before, the Emperor is careful to insist on the tolerant attitude of the throne towards religions in general. The 'positive standard of orthodoxy' (*Ching*) was Confucianism, but 'other doctrines, such as the two religions (Buddhism and Taoism), although not esteemed by Confucianists, can be reckoned to belong to what the *Lun Yü* (Analects) has in view in speaking of happiness by following the *Tao* (path of righteousness)...since they profess to encourage what is good and to reprove what is evil', are allowed a place in the Canon of Sacrifices, and it is not forbidden by law to pray or sacrifice to their gods. But when a sect was established and 'clandestinely transmitted from one to another', that was quite a different matter. It gave scoundrels a chance to make converts and to raise money, and disorder and misfortune to the people followed when the authorities took action. The viceroys and governors in those provinces where the sects were active were now enjoined to bring it home to the people that this kind of thing would not be tolerated. Wei Yüan states quite clearly that the molestation of members of the sects by 'yamen runners' and soldiers was the direct cause of the new rebellion.

This time it was not the White Lotus, as such, that was involved, but an associated sect called the *T'ien Li Chiao* ('The Religion of the Pattern of Heaven'), led by Li Wên-ch'ing,[1] Lin Ch'ing, and others, and operating in Chihli and Shantung. The sect, however, was the same as that of the Pa Kua, and was also practically identical with the Hung-yang, Pai-yang, Ch'ing-yang, and Hung-hua sects.[2] The sacred formula, always recited by members, was 'Praise to the unbegotten Father and Mother in the Home of the Immaterial Void'. Lin Ch'ing was often addressed as the 'Immaterial Void' or as 'he, who is merged with the Tao and the Nirvana'.

Lin enjoined his followers to recite the sacred formula solemnly, morning and evening, with reverent genuflexions towards the highest dual power of Nature, so that all danger of arms, fire and water would be warded off.

Having consulted the stars, Lin learned that of the three religions of the Buddha Maitreya—the Blue, the Red, and the White Ocean—this time the cause of the White Ocean would prosper. Since he himself was manifested to be the Whitest Being (the planet Venus assimilated with the element Metal), he was therefore Emperor of the Heavens, while P'ing K'o-shan, head of the sect in the district of Weihui in Honan, was Emperor of the Earth, and Li Wên-ch'ing, Emperor of Mankind. Lin further learnt from the stars that the enterprise should begin either in the middle of autumn or on the fifteenth of the ninth month (8 October 1813). It was resolved, therefore, that on the last-named day Ch'ên

Shuang and Ch'ên Wên-k'uei should attack the Imperial palace in Peking, while Lin Ch'ing, with a division of rebels supplied by the Emperor of Mankind, should surprise the Emperor on his way back from Kansu to the capital.

The attack on the palace by Ch'êng Shuang failed, but that made simultaneously on the Hsi-hua gate was, at first, more successful. Aided by eunuchs inside the palace who were members of the sect, the insurgents penetrated into the outer courts, but were beaten back, largely owing to the gallantry of the Heir Apparent, the Emperor's second son (afterwards the Tao Kuang emperor), who was studying in the Court library at the time and who rushed to the scene of the trouble on hearing the alarm. Meanwhile, troops belonging to the Imperial princes entered the palace by the Shên-wu gate in the northern wall and attacked the invaders. The latter thereupon tried to set fire to the palace buildings, but at midnight there was a thunderstorm, during which the God of War (*Kuan Ti*) suddenly appeared from his temple amid the roar of thunder and the flashes of lightning. Panic-stricken by this apparition, the invaders threw themselves into the canal which flowed past the temple and the T'ai-ho gate. Unable to climb the perpendicular marble sides, many were drowned or killed by the soldiers, and the remainder were taken prisoner.

The insurrection timed to coincide with the attack on the palace took place as arranged in Honan. The plan to waylay the Imperial cortège had to be given up because the mandarinate in the adjacent districts had received the alarm and had mobilized all the available troops to resist the revolutionaries. To begin with the rebellion spread widely, but the back of it was broken by a military force converging on it from several provinces, reinforced by three extra armies of Manchus and picked Chinese infantry and horse. But other rebellions now broke out elsewhere, including one in Shensi, and it was not until 1816 that the countryside in general could be said to be pacified.[1]

During the White Lotus rebellion, one great defect of Manchu power was revealed. Since the standing army, consisting of the Eight Banners and the Army of the Green Standard, was already too corrupt and degenerate to be of any use, the local militias had to be called upon. A contemporary account says that the militiamen were used as a vanguard; the Green Standard, made up of Chinese, followed; while the Eight Banners came last. When a victory was won by the militia, the government forces were given the credit for it. The military funds were usually embezzled or consumed in elaborate banquets for generals and officers, and the discipline was so bad that the rebellions lasted for years. The militia followed a 'scorched-earth' policy in cleaning up the countryside of rebels, leaving them (and the population in general) no food and shelter. This policy was first applied to Hopeh and then extended to Szechwan, Shensi, Honan and other provinces.[1]

A fact of importance to our inquiry is that Li Wên-ch'ing, the so-called Emperor of Mankind, of the 'Religion of the Pattern of Heaven', in the rebellion of 1796, came from Hua District in Honan, and had been a member of various associations, such as the *Hu-wei-pien*, or 'Tiger-tail Whips', the *Hung Chuan Shê*, or 'Red Brick Society', and the Society of the *I-ho-ch'üan*, or 'Righteous United Fists' (the 'Boxers'), until he became headman of the sect of the Chên diagram (the third of the Eight Diagrams).[2]

Now it happens that in the Pingyüan incident of November 1899 the Boxers were led by another Li Wên-ch'ing (his name is written with the same characters as those of his predecessor of 1796), and the Ming Monk (*Pên-Ming Ho-shang*). The Li Wên-ch'ing of 1899 was also known as Chu Hung-têng ('Red Lantern Chu'—Chu being the surname of the founder of the Ming dynasty).[3]

Was this identity of names coincidental? It scarcely seems so.

The earlier Li Wên-ch'ing, the Emperor of the Earth of the Religion of the Pattern of Heaven, had, as we have seen, been a member of the Boxers of his time. He told a fellow-member of the Pattern of Heaven sect that his ancestry was connected with the characters *mao* (mortise) and *chin* (gold)—hence he adopted the family name Liu, in which both those characters occur, and was henceforth known as Liu Lin or Liu Hsing-kuo (Prosperous Country). He was held to be a reincarnation of one Liu Lin from Ts'ao District in Shantung, who had lived in olden times and had been styled Patriarch or Prophet of the Pre-Celestial Period (*Hsien T'ien*).[4] It seems more than possible that the 1900 Li Wên-ch'ing (*alias* Chu Hung-têng) regarded himself as the reincarnation of his predecessor of a century earlier, whose name he had adopted.

The first official mention of the Boxers, as such, appears to be that in the edict of the fifth year of Yung Chêng (1727) in which they are charged with gathering crowds and stirring up the 'stupid people' under the pretext of practising their boxing cult. Why (asks the Emperor), if they wish to encourage self-defence, do they not learn archery and horsemanship? The governor-generals and governors must order the local officials strictly to prohibit their activities.[1]

They next come to notice in an Imperial decree of the 14th of the 7th month (4 September) 1808 in company with the Tiger-tail Whips, the Shun-tao Society or 'Swords of Obedience' and the Eight Symbols. This decree was issued in response to a request from the censor, Chou T'ing-sun, that these sects might be destroyed. According to his statement, they were very numerous in the districts of Yingchow and Po in Kiangsu, in Hsüchow in Honan, in Kueitê in Shantung, and in Ts'aochow, Ichow and Yenchow—in fact (as we shall see in the coming chapters), in the very same region that was to be in a state of insurrection in 1900.

According to the censor, these societies were composed mainly of country people of bad repute who oppressed loyal subjects and gambled on a large scale, for which purpose they pitched large tents, conspired with the 'yamen brood', and engaged in fights. The Emperor, approving the censor's proposal, instructed the viceroys and governors to track down the leaders of these societies and to punish them severely.[2]

To go forward for a moment to Lao Nai-hsüan, whose famous little book, *I Ho Ch'üan Chiao Mên Yüan Liu K'ao* (*Studies of the Origins of the Boxer Sects*) was published in September 1899.[3] Lao found that the I Ho Ch'üan (Boxers) was a branch of the Eight Trigrams sect, whose early leader, Kao Shêng-wên, a native of Honan, had been executed in 1771. Kao Shêng-wên was chief of the Li (7th) Trigram ('Lightning') of the Eight Trigrams sect.[4] His grandson, Kao Tan-chao, was also sentenced to death in 1814 for being a member of the sect and for admitting fellow-sectaries to his house and giving them food. Kao Shêng-wên's disciples and descendants, however, survived, and, together with the members of other secret societies, continued to be active in the provinces of Honan, Shantung and Kiangnan. In 1818 it was reported that the I Ho sect had spread to Chihli and practised I Ho boxing. Many of its members were again executed, but the society maintained an obscure existence in many districts of Chihli and Shantung and ultimately emerged in 1898 as an active anti-Christian organization.

According to Lao Nai-hsüan, the Boxers of the early nineteenth century were a band of brigands who conspired with lower officials in local government and rendered them a kind of police service, and, trading on this, ran gambling-houses and victimized law-abiding citizens. They had almost entirely been cleaned up by 1815, but the superstition of magical boxing (*shên ch'üan*) kept the tradition of the sect alive in obscurity until it was revived in 1898.

Lao based his statements on the edicts of the Chia Ch'ing emperor.[1] He mentioned that the Boxer monk, Wu Hsiu, captured in Chingchow, and another Boxer leader, Ta Kuei, captured in Kucheng, both admitted belonging to the Eight Trigrams sect. Other Boxers in Chihli also declared their allegiance to the same secret society. Furthermore, the rules of the Boxer society were typically those of the secret societies—for example, those who joined the society must strictly obey orders on pain of execution and the extermination of their families. The charms and incantations of the Boxers as well as their practice of boxing clearly indicated their connection with the secret societies.

Secret societies are, by definition, *secret*, and this in itself is sufficient to explain why information regarding their organization and ritual is so sparse.

The edicts, both in the Chia Ch'ing period and in the 1898–1900 risings, describe the Boxers as behaving like ordinary mountebanks at fairs—erecting matshed booths for gambling, giving exhibitions of sword and staff exercises and fisticuffs, swindling people out of their money, and generally creating disorder. The religious gymnastics, however, which they performed behind closed doors for inducting members or for creating invulnerability are not described in the official documents.

Pugilism, often referred to as 'fisting and gripping', was an ancient art, 'more often regarded as a business than as a sport, in the sense that it was once part of military training'.[2] It had its 'professors', and was even reduced to a science in the *Ch'üan Ching*, or Canon of Boxing. Strange to say, the most famous exponents of the art were Buddhist priests who inhabited the well-known Shaolin monastery. It included *savate*, wrestling, quarterstaff, and even spear-play, and Giles thinks that it was probably the archetype of the modern Japanese science of *jiu jitsu* (which was later elevated into *judo* by the addition of a code of honour). It seems that the Boxers included this kind of 'boxing' in their public repertoire.

But the 'boxing' which earned them their name was rather the system of exercises of a purely Taoist origin which was the means of endowing those initiated with supernatural powers. It was known as

'Spirit Boxing' (*Shên Ch'üan*), 'Supreme Ultimate Boxing' (*T'ai Chi Ch'üan*), or 'Righteous Harmony Boxing' (*I Ho Ch'üan*).

Chinese boxing (*Ch'üan po*), an art with rules different from that of the West, and embodying a certain element of ritual dance, probably originated as a department of Taoist physical exercises. . . . A knowledge of Chinese therapeutic gymnastics came to Europe in the 18th century and seems to have played a part of capital importance in the development of modern hygienic and remedial methods. . . . One is tempted to wonder whether the heliotherapeutic ideas of the Taoists, transmitted in similar Jesuit articles and books, did not exert an effect on the growth of modern physiotherapy.[1]

Taoism was a religion of health which proposed to lead the faithful towards Eternal Life. And, in their search for the Eternal—or, at least, the *Long* Life, the Taoist did not conceive of it merely as an immortality of the spirit but an immortality of the body itself. To them, this was not a matter of choice but the sole solution possible.[2] To become an immortal (*hsien*) imposed numerous obligations on the Taoist adept. It was necessary to 'Nourish the Body', to transform it, and to 'Nourish the Spirit', in order to perpetuate it; in fact to apply oneself to the two techniques—the corporeal and the spiritual. The Chinese, like Bertrand Russell, have never been able to conceive Mind and Matter as separable. It was the conservation of the living body which was always the means of acquiring immortality—or rather the replacement of it in the course of its own lifetime by an immortal body by causing to be born and developing in oneself immortal organs— skin, bones, etc.—which substituted themselves progressively for the mortal ones.[3]

The great difference between European and Chinese ideas of 'immortality' is well brought out in the following quotation:

Europe did not have the same conception of *material* immortality as China. In the West there was a rather clear idea of human survival after death which derived from origins both Hebrew and Christian: heaven, hell and even purgatory were real for both Latins and Greeks in Christendom. . . . Far different were the Chinese conceptions. Of an individual 'soul' there was no clear conviction in any of the great Three Doctrines. Confucianism has always declined to discuss personal survival in the explicit interest of high social morality here and now, whilst to Buddhist philosophy the belief in an individual persisting soul was positive heresy. The Taoists . . . recognized a considerable number of spiritual essences, even godlings, in the human soul-body complex, almost as many indeed as the limbs and viscera of the human organism itself, but there was no place other than earth for them to inhabit as a coherent entity, and after death they simply dispersed, some rising to join the pneuma [*ch'i*] of the heavens, some sinking to mingle with that of the earth, and others disappearing altogether.[1]

The Taoist aspirant for *hsien*-ship was obliged to submit himself to a great deal of training—to practise respiratory techniques, helio-therapeutic and gymnastic techniques, sexual techniques, alchemical and pharmaceutical techniques, and dietary techniques.

This Taoist theory was early incorporated into Chinese medicine, and it is in its medical form that it can be most conveniently studied.[2]

The object of *Kung-fu*[3] was to render its votaries immortal, or at least greatly to increase their span of life, to create resistance to disease, to make life happier, and to make muscles and bones insensible to fatigue and to the severest injury from accident, fire, etc. Nor was the benefit to the soul arising from the exercises and the merit accruing to the individual therefrom to be lightly esteemed.

The exercises were minute and complicated. There were three principal basic postures—standing, sitting and lying—and in each posture there was a stretching, folding, raising, lowering, bending, extending, and abducting of the arms and legs. The head, eyes and tongue had each their allotted movements and positions. The tongue was charged to perform inside the mouth such operations as balancing, pulsating, rubbing, shooting, etc., in order to excite salivation; the eyes had in succession to close, open, turn, fix and wink. The Taoists claimed that when they had gazed for a long time, first on one side and then on the other, at the root of the nose, the torrent of thought was suspended and a profound calm enveloped the soul as a preparation for a 'doing-nothing' inertia which was in turn the prelude to communi-cation with spirits. For respiration, there was an equally intricate set of directions, and a corresponding set of spiritual states was thereby induced.

The physical and spiritual exercises together constituted what European observers in a somewhat oversimplified way called 'boxing'. But 'boxing' was by no means the whole of the Boxer cult. Incanta-tions and magical practices, for example, could summon down millions of spirit soldiers to fight against the enemies of the sect.

There were two stages of induction—the first of initiation (*yen fa*), and the second when the initiated member was 'under the spell' (*shang fa*).[4]

What were the other similarities that we can detect from our history between the Boxers and the White Lotus sect? To begin with, they both mixed Buddhism and Taoism. In the placards they posted up[1] and in their incantations[2] the Boxers appealed to Lao Tzŭ, Amida Buddha, to Kuan Kung (Lord Kuan, the God of War), to Kuan Yin (the Goddess of Mercy), the Upper, Middle and Lower Eight Genii, and to other Taoist and Buddhist gods and Lohans. They claimed to be able to attain invulnerability by certain religious exercises; women were accepted by them as equals and often as leaders (there was an associated women's society named the 'Red Lantern' sect) (Hung Têng Chao); they had among their members those who claimed to be descended from the Ming emperors. In these, and a dozen other ways, the Boxers indicated their descent from the White Lotus sect. In one respect only did they differ from them, and that was a vitally important one—in the crucial phases of their activity at least, they were pro- and not anti-dynastic.

Having traced the ancestry of the Boxers to the White Lotus group of secret societies, it remains for us to take note, though much more briefly, of the southern or Triad group.[3]

The Triad Society, it is clear from its ritual and its rules, had a common origin with the White Lotus of north, west and central China, but developed characteristics of its own. A main reason for the separation of the groups was the cultural and linguistic distinctions between the provinces. In the provinces of the north and centre, that is to say in fifteen out of the traditional eighteen of China proper, varieties of 'Mandarin' were generally spoken, but in the remaining three (Kwangtung, Kwangsi and Fukien) there were several distinct dialects. Not only were the speakers of the northern and southern groups mutually unintelligible, but so also were the speakers of the separate southern dialects among themselves. This distinction has been attributed partly to the fact that the territory of China expanded under strong dynasties and contracted under weak ones, leaving the south-eastern provinces isolated upon contraction,[4] and to the influence of the succession of Tartar invaders on the northern group (e.g. in diminishing the number of vocables).

It is remarkable that there is no record of the activities of the secret societies of the south until the Ch'ing dynasty, though they undoubtedly existed before then. When they appear the southern societies are not called 'sects' (*chiao*) but 'societies' (*hui*).

The first of these southern societies to come to notice was the *T'ien*

Ti Hui (*T'in Tei Wui* in Cantonese), or 'Heaven and Earth Society'. The society was also commonly known as the *Sam Tim Wui* (Cantonese), or 'Three Dot Society', a name which may have arisen from its use of esoteric characters in each of which the 'three dot' abbreviation of the character for 'water' is incorporated. Yet another title was *Sam Hop Wui* (Cantonese), or 'Three in Accord Society'—the 'three' being Heaven, Earth and Man. It is from the last-named title that the common name in English for this group of secret societies, 'Triad', is derived. 'Triune' is occasionally substituted for 'Triad'.

The Triad Society was (and still is at least among the Chinese of South-east Asia) a sworn brotherhood, in the tradition of the Peach Garden. The traditional aim was embodied in the slogan 'Overthrow the Ch'ing; Restore the Ming'. From its inception it became a very powerful force among the people of South China.

At the time of its formation, the founders adopted the character 'Hung', 'Flood', or 'Vast', to be the secret or clan name of the brethren, which is the same as in 'Hung Fan', the 'Great Plan' or 'Deluge Plan', the title of a section of the Book of History (*Shu Ching*), and in the reign-title of the first Ming emperor (*Hung Wu*, 1368–98). Because of this, the fraternity was, and still is, widely known as the Hung Brotherhood, but although its name is derived ultimately from one of the Confucian classics, the society had a long traditional association with Taoism.

Triad members give 1674 as the year in which their society originated, and there is no reason why this date should not be accepted.[1] This was the period of the revolts against the Ch'ing intended to restore the Ming dynasty. The rebellion was finally crushed in 1681 with great slaughter, and it is said that some 400,000 people fled into the mountain fastness of Kwangsi, and that the province of Kwangtung was nearly depopulated, some 700,000 people being executed within a month. Many thousands of families left the country, some 100,000 people going to Formosa, where they continued to resist the Manchus until 1683.

Like the White Lotus, the Triad was always associated with revolts. The first of these on a big scale took place in Formosa in 1787,[2] and it was some years before it was overcome. As a result of this revolt, the *T'in Tei Wui* was outlawed, and the novel, *Shui Hu Chuan*, 'Romance of the River Banks', or 'Water Margin',[3] extolling the exploits of Triad heroes, was banned by the Manchus in 1799. From this time onwards, the society comes increasingly to official notice, and its name is included in the 1801 edition of the Penal Code as one of the societies, the leadership of which would entail beheading and membership strangulation.

A series of Triad rebellions took place in 1853. The first of these was the 'Dagger' or 'Small Knife' rebellion at Amoy. The rebels borrowed the name of a society which operated in Anhwei under the title 'Small Knife'—with which, however, it had no connection. In May, Amoy was captured by 2000 men and held for three months. In the second of the rebellions, in 1853, Shanghai was captured. The rising was organized and conducted by men from Fukien and Kwangtung. The Chinese city was sacked and the Triads remained in control for eighteen months. Then the Imperial troops entered the city and in their turn looted and set fire to it.

Both these rebellions occurred during the early years of the Taiping Rebellion (1850–64). The latter, however, was not a Triad revolt, though writers (for example, S. Wells Williams) have frequently regarded it as such. Apart from the Taiping Rebellion, however, the whole of the provinces of Kwangtung and Kwangsi were in a ferment through the risings of authentic Triad groups. Canton itself was invested for a time, and the Pearl River, the artery of trade, was under Triad control. Dissension among Triad leaders, however, led to their piecemeal defeat. The Imperial troops then rounded up the inhabitants (irrespective of their Triad associations), took them off to Canton, and there beheaded them at the rate of seven or eight hundred a day until almost a hundred thousand had been killed. It was estimated that in Kwangtung province alone, during this period of Triad suppression, one million people were executed.

This was not the end of the Triad revolts. In 1892 there was another serious one, this time in the area of Sunning, to the south-west of the mouth of the Pearl River. These revolts had no direct connection with those in the north in 1898–1900, but their existence is evidence of the generally disturbed state of China.

The success of the Triad in capturing Shanghai may have stimulated the appearance of branches north of the Yangtze. These included the Elder Brother Society (*K'o Lao Hui*), the Green Group (*Ch'ing P'ang*), and the Red Group (*Hung P'ang*). Of these, I need take special notice only of the *K'o Lao Hui*.

It seems to be generally agreed that the *K'o Lao Hui* originated during the Taiping Rebellion among soldiers of the Imperial army.

Serious disturbances were attributed to the society in 1870 and 1871, and the *Peking Gazette* of 25 May 1876 contained a report from the Governor of Kweichow in which the society was said to be active all over Hunan, Hupeh, Fukien, Yunnan, Kweichow, Szechwan, Shensi, Anhwei, and Kiangsi. In 1891 the society was plotting a rebellion, which was frustrated by the arrest of the leader, Ch'ên Chin-lung, and of C. W. Mason, a British subject in the Customs Service in Shanghai, who was a member of the society.[1]

The great majority of the Chinese in South-east Asia (numbering about 12 million in the 1960's) originate from the three southern provinces of Kwangtung, Fukien and Kwangsi, and when their for-bears emigrated they took the Triad Society with them, and it became a source of embarrassment both to the colonial governments and to their successors.[2]

Although the Taiping Rebellion was by far the greatest rebellion of the nineteenth century and came within an ace of bringing the Manchu dynasty to an end, it was not of the same order of origin as the Boxers, and our interest in it, therefore, must be confined to recalling its broad outlines.

The rebellion of the Taipings, the 'Society of the Worshippers of God', lasted for fourteen years (1850–64), involved twelve provinces, ruined six hundred cities, and cost some twenty million lives.

Its originator was Hung Hsiu-ch'üan, a Hakka from Kwangtung province, who had repeatedly failed at the literary examinations. In 1847, after one of those failures, he suffered a cataleptic fit in the course of which he saw a vision in which a venerable old man lamented that the people on earth neglected him. From the old man he received a sword and seal to ward off demons and evil spirits (gifts very much in the Taoist tradition, and articles which figure in the traditional history of the Triad). Before long Hung decided that the venerable old man of his vision was God (*Shang-ti*) and that he himself had been chosen as the medium of salvation for the people. A local dispute between the Hakkas and the Punteis (native Cantonese) at this time led to the dis-possession of many Hakkas, who now became vagrants, and those provided the nucleus of Hung's following of malcontents. From this, it was a short step to the traditional anti-dynastic rebellion. Hung Hsiu-ch'üan took the title of 'Heavenly King' (*T'ien Wang*), and declared that he was the younger brother of Christ. A hierarchy of Princes of the Heavenly Kingdom of Universal Peace (*T'ai P'ing T'ien*

Kuo) was then established. The 'Heavenly King' now adopted a code in which Christianity (as understood by Hung from his limited reading and conversations with an American missionary) provided the foundation. Buddhist and Taoist temples were destroyed as the work of unbelievers.

In the Taiping administration the smallest unit was the family. Every twenty-five families formed a larger unit, to each of which belonged a public storehouse and a church. Military, religious, judicial and social affairs, in this larger unit, were managed by an officer who might roughly be called a 'master-sergeant' (*liang-ssŭ-ma*).[1] He seems to have served as a military chaplain, an army officer, a teacher, and a judge. Above the *liang-ssŭ-ma* were several higher officials governing larger groups of families up to the number which composed an army (*chün*). In an army, there were two officers in charge of land, taxes, revenue and expenditure. There was a 'chain of command' running right up to the 'Heavenly King' who was thus able to keep his finger on the pulse of the entire Taiping nation. The system was apparently derived from the *Chou Li* (Institutes of the Chou Dynasty) which was probably compiled in the second century B.C.

The Taiping government was theocratic, the Heavenly King being the spiritual and temporal ruler. Since the original five kings and the hierarchy of officials beneath them had both civil and military duties, civil and military administration were virtually identical. Soldiers were at the same time farmers. *The Land System of the Heavenly Dynasty*[2] assigned responsibility to the master-sergeant in such matters as marriages and all auspicious and inauspicious events within his twenty-five families. For help and guidance it was necessary to pray to God; all traditional superstitions were entirely to be disregarded. Young boys were to go to church every day to study the Old and New Testaments under the instruction of the master-sergeant. Every Sunday men and women were to go to church. The sexes were, however, in spite of the high status of women in the Taiping empire, to be segregated for worship and hymn-singing.

The Taipings aimed at three goals—public ownership of land, equal allotment of surplus money and food, and a self-supporting economy. *The Land System of the Heavenly Dynasty* laid down that land was to be divided into nine grades according to its productivity. It was to be allotted by a simple counting of mouths in each family. Surplus production was to be transported to deficiency areas. All in the empire were expected to enjoy together the good fortune bestowed by the Heavenly Father, Almighty God. Everybody should have land to till, rice to eat, clothes to wear, and money to spend. All men and women of sixteen and over were to receive one share of land, while those who were younger were to receive half a share. At harvest time, the master-sergeant was to retain enough grain to sustain each person in his group until the next harvest, and to send the rest to the national storehouse. Wheat, cloth, chickens, dogs, silver and cash were to be handled in the same manner. The master-sergeant was to render an account of receipts and expenditure to the officials appointed for the purpose. All marriages, month-old birthdays and other celebrations were to be at the expense of the national exchequer, due economy being observed. Throughout the empire mulberry trees were to be planted, and the women were to learn sericulture and to make garments. Every family was to raise five hens and two sows. Pottery-making, smith's work, carpentry, and masonry were to be taken care of by the corporal of the smallest unit and his five soldiers.

The sources of the ideas embodied in the Taiping reforms were the *Institutes of the Chou Dynasty* and the works of *Mencius*, supplemented by and interwoven with the tenets of Christianity. Only part of the programme was implemented, and the public ownership of land remained for the most part untried owing to the fact that the Taiping army chiefly occupied cities and towns and the people in the country districts were uncooperative because of the constant warfare afflicting their lives. Nevertheless, public ownership of money and property was strictly enforced. When the Taiping capital was established at Nanking, a sacred treasury and storehouses were established, and all property and money obtained in the military expeditions was deposited in these.

Unlike the Boxers (at least at the moment of crisis) half a century later, the Taipings were strongly anti-Manchu. 'The empire is God's empire', the Heavenly King declared, 'and not that of the barbarian Manchus.' The Manchus, he said, had changed the national dress, forced the Chinese to wear a queue, employed corrupt officials who robbed the masses, and compelled the Chinese to become demons (*kuei*). 'The waves of the Eastern Sea cannot wash their sins away', he said.

The Taipings failed for a number of reasons. In the sphere of military tactics, they concentrated on forward movement with a total disregard of measures to secure their rear. In contrast, the Hunan army under Tsêng Kuo-fan and Hu Lin-i advanced cautiously, taking every precaution to see that their rear was not infiltrated or their communications cut. The Taipings took no adequate measures to administer their conquest, and created no civil service other than their master-sergeants. Except for Li Hsiu-ch'êng, the 'Loyal Prince', they paid no regard to the feelings of the populace. The other leaders were mediocre and there was dissension among them ending in a series of murders. Everyone in the 'Heavenly Capital' lived in a state of acute apprehension and mutual suspicion. The 'Heavenly King' soon abandoned himself to luxury and debauchery, living surrounded by numerous concubines and shut off from the world with little knowledge of what was happening elsewhere in the Heavenly Kingdom.

As to political philosophy, the Christian elements neutralized those that were national and pro-Chinese. Furthermore, the Christianity of Hung Hsiu-ch'üan was second-hand and insincere, being merely an instrument of his own ambition. The Confucianism of his opponent, Tsêng Kuo-fan, on the other hand, was authentic, and his personal behaviour above reproach. Nevertheless, many of the Taiping ideals of a socialist or communist nature were remembered after their kingdom had been destroyed, and the Taiping Rebellion is now regarded by the communists as an aborted social revolution.

The Taipings attached great importance to art. At their capital, T'ienching, they organized 'Battalions' and 'Boards' of 'Embroidery', 'Weaving', and 'Sculpture' (including carving) respectively to supervise production. In spite of the wholesale destruction which followed after their defeat by the Manchus, many of these works of art have survived. The subjects, however, are all scenery, birds, animals and flowers in the traditional style with no Christian symbolism whatever.[1]

Modern Chinese scholars are very much interested in the Taiping Rebellion, and a large number of studies are being made to elucidate its progress and nature. It has been interpreted, for example, as a 'peasant revolution of the highest form', because of the participation of the newly risen class of 'urban commoners'. These 'forerunners of the proletariat' included the charcoal-burners, miners, handicraft workers, sailors and porters, with the Triad Society as their original political organization.[2] Taxation under the Taipings was apparently lighter than under the Manchus.[3]

The Manchus during the nineteenth century were troubled by a number of other rebellions in addition to the Taiping and those of sectarian origin above described. There were the risings of the 'national minorities',[1] and of the Nien, or 'Torch-Bearer', movement, beginning during the early days of the Taiping Rebellion (1855) in Kiangsu, Anhwei, Shantung, and Honan, and lasting until 1868. The Nien developed into the northern ally of the Taipings, and grew stronger when a detachment of the latter joined them after the fall of Nanking.

Chiang Siang-tseh[2] considers that the Nien were a secret society descended from the White Lotus and therefore connected with the Boxers, and the Boxers certainly regarded themselves as the heirs of the Nien. In exactly the same areas where the Nien were scattered (Ying-chou, Pochou, Hsüchou, Kueitê, Ts'aochou, Ichou and Yenchou) the following secret societies existed side by side—the Shun Tao Hui, the Hu Wei Pien ('Tiger-tail Whips'), the Eight Symbols, and the Boxers.

It is of interest to note that the Nien called their leader 'Great Prince with the Heavenly Mandate' (*Ta Han Ming Ming Wang*), a title which implied that the Nien defied the Manchu emperor not only as a ruler but as a non-Chinese ruler. In 1861 the government forces found two Nien seals among their war booty. On one of them was engraved *Hsing Han Mieh Hu* 'Revive the Chinese and eradicate the Barbarian (Manchu)', and on the other, *Sao Ch'ing Li Ming* ('Sweep away the Manchus and re-establish the Ming'). These slogans must have still been alive in the memory of many Chinese in the region in the time of the Boxer Uprising about forty years later.

The many other revolts that the Manchus had to face, such as those of the Hui, a people who lived in Yunnan and north-west China (in 1855, 1863, 1868–72), and the Muslim risings which took place after the break-up of the Taipings (in Kansu (1864–5), the Salar movement in Shensi (1855–73), in Kansu again (1895), and the rebellion of Yakub Beg in Turkestan) had no direct connection with that of the Boxers.[3]

Sun yat-sen's frustrated rising in Canton in October 1895 was much more in the line of China's subsequent political development than the Boxer uprising was to be. The Hong Kong Hsing Chung Hui, founded by him, had as its objects: to establish newspapers to teach the masses, to establish schools to educate the talented, to develop industry for improving the livelihood of the people—anything that might help China's prosperity was to be promoted. But although the object was to overthrow the Ch'ing, what form of government China should have was not indicated. At this time it seems that Sun did not oppose the monarchical institution if the emperor was Chinese. But his movement, so far, had no definite 'ideology'.[4]

CHAPTER VIII

THE REAPPEARANCE OF THE BOXERS

In the years immediately before and after the Sino–Japanese War, Britain, France, Germany, Japan, Russia, and the United States began to export capital to China and to establish banks there which issued their own notes. This development was as much to provide the machinery for financing foreign loans to China as for meeting the requirements of the expanding import trade and foreign capitalist enterprise. To pay the indemnity imposed on China by the Treaty of Shimonoseki, the Manchu government had to obtain foreign loans, and between 1894 and 1899 loans totalling 370 million taels[1] were obtained in this way. This sum was four and a half times the total annual revenue of the Manchu treasury from domestic sources. To secure the loans, the foreign lenders obtained further liens on the Imperial Maritime Customs and then on the salt gabelle in addition.

During the thirty-five years between 1864 and 1899 the value of China's imports rose from 51 million to 264 million taels. Her foreign trade, which had formerly had a favourable balance of two million taels per annum, now had an unfavourable one of 69 million taels per annum. China's silver reserves were virtually exhausted. The influx of machine-made cloth and yarn had seriously affected the urban and rural handicrafts, especially workshops working on a family basis, and many millions of villagers were thus deprived of a livelihood.

The situation became worse and worse throughout the whole of 1898. The military expenditure of the Sino–Japanese War and the huge indemnity imposed on China led finally to bankruptcy. The pre-war foreign debt amounting to 15 million taels grew to 200 million, and to cover this debt large shipping, mining and railway concessions were made to foreigners. In order to guarantee the repayment of the debts, foreigners were allowed to supervise the government revenue. An attempt to raise a domestic loan of 100 million taels was made in 1898, but only about half of it was subscribed in spite of the fact that the government proposed to bestow mandarin rank on those who did subscribe and to penalize those who refused to do so.

Meanwhile, as the authority of the central government weakened, the remission of revenue from the provincial governments was delayed or stopped entirely, and, even when money was remitted to Peking, it was not in silver but in drafts such as those on the Bankers' Association of Shansi (*Shansi P'iao-hao*), which were often difficult to convert into cash. It was estimated that about 50 per cent of the salt tax and the *likin* were withheld by the local officials. The tax burden on farmers and petty merchants who were within direct reach of the central government was correspondingly increased. The government was now faced with a financial crisis.[1]

Other contributory reasons for this crisis are not hard to isolate. For example, the subsidiary treaty of trade and commerce between China and Japan, signed at Peking on 21 July 1896, had conceded the right of the Japanese to carry on trade, industry, and manufacture at any of the Treaty Ports, and the privilege was at once shared by all nations through the 'most-favoured nation' clause in their own treaties with China. As soon as Kiaochow was occupied and a German sphere of influence was established in Shantung, German capital began to flow into the interior, seeking coal, iron, gold-mining and railway concessions. 'The promoters [says A. H. Smith] entered a land where nobody knows or cares anything about "progress".' They built roads, factories and railways, utterly ignoring Chinese prejudices regarding *fêng-shui*. They acquired farm land by enforced sale and compelled the Chinese government to purchase it on their behalf at low prices, sometimes selling it again at a profit. Hostility against the foreigner was thus aroused anew. Anti-foreign enmity was meanwhile also growing elsewhere, and anti-missionary outbreaks were reported from many places. Missionaries and converts were attacked and murdered and mission property destroyed. This was even more the case in South China than in the north, and it is curious that the outbreak of 1900 should have taken place in Shantung and Chihli, provinces traditionally loyal to the throne, rather than in the traditionally disaffected south.

It is true, of course, that German investment in Shantung and Russian investment in Manchuria brought some good to the peasants of Shantung. Crowds of poor and landless peasants from the interior of the province and from Shanghai and other southern ports collected at Tsingtao to take advantage of the demand for labour. But the scale of the foreign investment was not large enough to settle the problem of poverty among Chinese farmers, and the influx of population from the

174

south, due in part to the famines in Kiangsu in 1897 and 1898, actually stimulated the disturbances in Shantung.

The only railways that had been built in North China before 1899 ran from Peking to Tientsin and thence to Suichung, and from Peking to Chêngting. Inland water navigation, the right of which was conceded to foreigners in 1898, had no appreciable influence on the Boxer Uprising because there was no river in northern China on which foreign steamers were permitted to navigate except the Paiho, connecting Tientsin with the Yellow Sea. But imports of foreign goods, especially of machine-made cotton goods and petroleum, rapidly increased between 1896 and 1899, and this had its effect on the livelihood of the peasants.

In some villages every family has one or more looms, and much of the work is done in underground cellars where the click of the shuttle is heard month in and month out from the middle of the first moon till the closing days of the twelfth. But now the looms are idle and the weaving-cellars are falling into ruins. Multitudes who own no loom are able to spin cotton thread, and thus earn a bare support—a most important auxiliary protection against the wolf always near to the Chinese door. But lately the phenomenal activity of the mills in Bombay and Japan, and even in Shanghai itself, has inundated the cotton districts of China with yarn so much more even, stronger, and withal cheaper than the home-made kind, that the spinning-wheels no longer revolve, and the tiny rill of income for the young, the old, the feeble, and the helpless is permanently dried up. Many of the innumerable sufferers from this steady advance of 'civilisation' into the interior of China have no more appreciation of the causes of their calamity than have the Japanese peasants who find themselves engulfed by a tidal wave caused by an earthquake or gradual subsidence of the coast. Yet there are many others who know perfectly that before foreign trade came in to disturb the ancient order of things, there was in ordinary years enough to eat and to wear, whereas now there is a scarcity in every direction, with a prospect of worse to come. With an experience like this, in many different lines of activity, the Chinese are not to be blamed for feeling a profound dissatisfaction with the new order of things.[1]

Apart from China's economic and administrative weakness, the disturbed state of the country, especially of the north, can in some important measure be ascribed to the reform of the army after the defeat of Japan. Peculation by generals and other officers was rife and took the form of claiming pay in respect of troops who existed only on paper (k'ung-ê), cutting the rations (k'o-k'ou), and levying contributions on towns and villages (t'an-p'ai).

A decree issued in December 1897, immediately after the German occupation of Kiaochow, said:

...The essential part of national defence is the perfection of armament and military preparation. However, the financial unbalance between revenue and expenditure is too great at the present time. So I have repeatedly admonished the Governors, Viceroys, and Generals of the provinces to stop the exploitation of the *likin* tax, to weed out superfluous soldiers...to inspect the nominal rolls of troops and to prohibit fictitious returns.[1]

A further decree of 20 February 1898 announced that: 'It is an urgent necessity to bring about a reduction in the number of the soldiers and a curtailment of military expenditure.... I am troubled and annoyed all day long and breathe a deep sigh at this feeding of useless soldiers and the exercise of authority by decrepit officers.'[2]

On 5 September 1898 an edict was issued ordering the authorities in Kwangtung and Kwangsi to establish militia units in every village within one month and in the other provinces to do the same within three months. On 5 November the provinces were again urged to build up their militia, especially in Chihli, Shantung, and Fukien. Says Muramatsu: 'It was on the basis of this second decree that Steiger mistakenly considered that the Society or *T'uan* of Boxers was organized under the influence and supervision of the central government.'[3]

But in order to raise funds for the modernizing of the army it was necessary to get rid of the aged and redundant personnel. The Governor of Shantung reported in April 1898 that he had reduced the regular and volunteer forces by 30 per cent and that he intended to reduce the remainder by 20 per cent. In the same month Honan province announced a plan for the reduction of its military establishment by no less than 70 per cent, and Chihli reported that 7247 officers and men had been discharged in the spring of 1899.

The consequence of these measures was to stimulate the Boxer movement in two ways—on the one hand by creating bands of unemployed ex-soldiers, and on the other by obliging the Ch'ing government to keep the peace by re-establishing the *Hsiang-t'uan*, or village militia, in the provinces. The effect of the order for the reduction of the forces was that good soldiers who would not readily obey the orders of their corrupt superiors were dismissed, while the generals continued to make false returns of the strength of their armies. The reduction of the troops caused a weakening of the garrisons and of the policing of the provinces, while the countryside became infested with unemployed but able-bodied ex-soldiers who were desperate in their search for a livelihood.

According to a decree of 21 January 1899, after a year of decrees enjoining the reduction in the number of soldiers, it was stated that 'in many places the hungry formed themselves into mobs and brigands caused trouble', and that 'certain officials attribute these disturbances to the insufficiency in the armed forces resulting from too speedy discharges'. Unless the unemployed ex-soldiers were fortunate enough to be taken on by the new Westernized army they joined the secret societies or combined with bands of rascals to live on the local community. Moreover, after the demobilization of 1896, arms and ammunition were often sold secretly and illegally by corrupt officers, and this made the unrest even more dangerous.

During the late spring and summer of 1898 the situation was greatly worsened by the famines caused by the poor harvest of the preceding year. This was especially the case in Kiangsu, Anhwei, Shantung, and Honan in 1897, 1898 and 1899, and there was abnormally dry weather in Chihli in 1899 and 1900. In the spring of 1897 there was a heavy drought in northern Kiangsu, especially in the Hsüchou, Haichou, Fêngyang and Huaiin districts, regions immediately contiguous to Shantung. The germination and growth of wheat and barley was hindered and a very poor harvest followed. In the summer of the same year prolonged rain caused floods at Shawoho and at Huaiho, and the rice crop, too, diminished sharply. Already at the beginning of December 1897 a large number of vagabonds from the north had attempted to enter the southern provinces across the Yangtze from Kuachow and, being refused entry by the local officials, had formed themselves into mobs and attacked the yamens.[1] By the spring of 1898 the number of vagabonds had greatly increased. A hundred thousand hungry people moved about from place to place crying for food. In the summer of this year the river Huai repeatedly flooded eastern Anhwui and northern Kiangsu. More than five million refugees were reported to have left their districts. Therefore, when the existence of Boxers in northern Shantung was reported, the Peking government feared that they might combine with the hungry refugees in Kiangsu.

In 1898 a great flood of the Yellow River occurred. The river had overflowed its banks at Tungwahsiang in Honan in 1855 and had then begun to take its present northern course. After the change of the river's course the repairing of the dykes was left to villagers living along the river since the government was busy suppressing the Taiping Rebellion. As a result, the engineering lacked any co-ordinating plan, and the river at Chinan became too narrow to take the inflow of the swollen waters. Subsequently the Yellow river had overflowed almost yearly and had fully earned its traditional name of 'China's Sorrow' with the farmers of Shantung. In August 1898 it overflowed through four breaches in its banks on either side in the neighbourhood of Tunga, and the flood covered almost the entire Shantung plain. The submerged area to the south amounted to 2600 square miles, while that on the north side was even larger. The collection of land-tax and rice tribute was postponed or cancelled. Relief measures were ordained by Imperial decrees, but the increase in the groups of homeless peasants, noted already at the beginning of October, became more and more serious during the winter. This was still the year 1898, the year of the Hundred Days Reform and the *coup d'état*, and while the struggle for power was in progress at Court, the situation in Kiangsu, Anhwei and Honan went from bad to worse.

The sudden changes in the economic situation consequent upon the opening of Tsingtao as a free port and the influx of foreign capital and merchandise into the interior are analysed by A. H. Smith as follows:

1. The appearance of a new kind of foreigner, the 'promoter', whose interests and behaviour differed from those of the old type foreign residents who had been government officials, merchants, and missionaries. A rapid increase in their influence was accompanied by an inflow of capital.

2. Unemployment caused in the native labour market by imports of machine-made goods such as cotton yarns, matches, and kerosene [paraffin], and by the construction of railways and progress in inland water navigation. The lack of elasticity in the local labour market made the situation still more unbearable.

3. The increasingly evil influence of opium smoking and the opium trade, which penetrated into the interior through the increase in imports of the drug and the beginning of poppy cultivation in Shantung.[1]

Meanwhile the international situation was impinging notably on the provinces of the north and adding to the unrest. The Germans, in particular, engaged in the construction of the port of Tsingtao and surveying the hinterland to investigate the possibilities for mining and railway enterprises, aroused intense antipathy among the farmers, landlords, and gentry of Shantung by their arrogant behaviour. In March 1899 three Germans prospecting near Jihchao in southern Shantung were attacked by a mob and narrowly escaped with their lives.

At once the German authorities took reprisals by sending 250 soldiers to burn down two villages from which the mob had come. They also seized the town of Jihchao in retaliation for the arrest and maltreatment of a German missionary stationed there and, after occupying it for a fortnight, they seized five members of the gentry as hostages for the carrying out of the terms they had imposed on the town.[1]

Then, on 28 February, Italy demanded the lease of Sanmen Bay in eastern Chekiang as a coaling station and the establishment of a 'sphere of influence' in the neighbourhood. The demand was refused by the Chinese government on 4 March, and Italy thereupon sent an ultimatum to Peking and despatched warships to the Yellow Sea to make a demonstration. Although the Chinese government had just made submission to the Germans over the Jihchao incident, they had reached the limit of their endurance and they refused to yield to the Italian threat. In October 1899 the Italian ships withdrew, but their presence off the coast of China had had the effect of alarming the inhabitants of the coastal territories and increasing their hostility towards foreigners.

The factors mentioned by A. H. Smith had an impoverishing effect on the population of North China in 1898-9, but they are not sufficient by themselves to explain why the Boxer movement suddenly increased in violence after the autumn of 1898. Muramatsu considers that the famines of 1897-9, causing the migration of hungry multitudes into Chihli, were probably more important as a direct influence. Nor, incidentally, does Dr Smith allow that dissatisfaction with the missionaries and converts was a *root* cause of anti-foreignism (apart from the coerciveness of the Roman Catholics) and tends to suggest that the missionaries themselves were the innocent victims of foreign political and economic penetration.

That China as a whole was ripe for rebellion must by now be apparent to the reader, and especially so in the north. While the Boxers were as yet comparatively harmless to the government, a rebellion of some dimensions, caused it seems entirely by the hunger of the people, *did* break out. This was the Woyang rising and was staged by local brigands (*T'u-fei*) according to the official accounts. The leader was one Niu Shih-hsiu, the cousin of an army officer who had died and whose ammunition had fallen into the hands of the rebels. In December 1898 Niu rallied the starving people to his flag and rose in rebellion. The rebels established a stronghold at Mount Shihkung and attacked and plundered towns and villages. The Peking government ordered Yü

Chang, the governor of Honan, Tung Hua-hsi, governor of Anhwei, and Liu K'un-i, viceroy of Liangchiang, to co-operate in surrounding the rebels, which they did, and at the end of February 1899 they were suppressed completely.

But meanwhile a more formidable uprising was in the making. An interval of eighty years separates the mention of the Boxers in the decrees of 1818 from their reappearance in those of 1898. Nor do they come to notice in the interval in any records which have so far been adduced as evidence. Reasons have already been given in chapter VII for believing that they nevertheless had a continuous existence, and they certainly regarded themselves as being of the same sect, or sects, which had risen against the Manchus in the Chia Ch'ing reign, and also as the heirs of the Nien rebels. But since such various accounts have been given of their rise in the last years of the nineteenth century, it will be appropriate to describe their resurrection in terms of the existing controversies.

Before this is attempted it must be pointed out that accounts of the rise of the Boxers derived mainly from European sources suffer from the fact that Europeans in general, because of language difficulties and their isolation from the general population, did not become aware of the existence of the Boxers for something like a year after they had forced themselves on the attention of the Chinese officials. Omitting for a moment the evidence of Father Isoré (which will be discussed in due place), the first European reference to the *I Ho Ch'üan* I have so far been able to trace is that of Dr S. MacFarlane, of the London Missionary Society, in a letter written on 28 May 1899.[1] Yet the Boxers were first mentioned by name in Chinese in correspondence between the Grand Council and the Governor of Shantung in May 1898, some twelve months previously.[2]

We have seen that Lao Nai-hsüan regarded the Boxers as a secret society associated with the 'White Lotus', 'Eight Diagrams', and 'Red Fist' sects or societies and similar heretical and revolutionary associations, and all the Chinese authorities seem to agree with him.

Lao had originally been a magistrate at Wuch'iao in south-eastern Chihli for ten years and in June 1898, after serving in another district for two years, he had been transferred back to Wuch'iao. It was about this time that the Boxers began to be active in south-eastern Chihli, and he made a study of their origins. In September 1899 he published his celebrated treatise, *I Ho Ch'üan Chiao Mên Yüan Liu K'ao* (*Historical*

Origins of the Boxers). Two or three months after this work appeared, Yüan Shih-k'ai, as acting governor of Shantung, was endeavouring to check the spread of the I Ho Ch'üan in his province and gave this explanation his official approval, having large numbers of Lao's pamphlet printed and circulated as a warning to the people not to support or to join the organization.

Lao's theory, however, Steiger refuses to accept. Commenting on it he says:

Yet this explanation of the movement is in such complete disaccord with a number of important facts that it must be rejected as absolutely untenable. In the first place it is impossible to believe that a secret society, holding heretical doctrines and known to have revolutionary aims, would deliberately go out of its way to institute a campaign of bitter hostility against Christian missions, and thus stir up against itself the activities of the officials and the complaints of the foreign diplomats. Such procedure would have been contrary to all that is known of the history of the secret societies in China, and is without precedent in the history of the country (p. 129).

There had (said Steiger) been but one recorded instance of a deliberate attack upon Christianity by a *religious* secret society, and, even in this case, the motive for the attack was non-religious. In the summer of 1895 the *Ch'ih-t'sai Ti*, or 'Vegetarians', massacred a number of Protestant missionaries at Kucheng in Fukien. In the trial of the murderers it was proved that the Vegetarians had attacked the missionaries because they considered them responsible for having caused the governor of the province to move troops into the districts where the Vegetarians were practically in control. It was true that the *Ko Lao Hui* (Elder Brother Society) was often implicated in anti-foreign outbreaks, but it was a purely revolutionary organization with no religious significance, and its avowed purpose in attacking foreigners was to involve the Manchu dynasty in difficulties with the foreign Powers.[1]

Some writers have attempted (continues Steiger) to avoid this weak point in Lao's theory by assuming that the I Ho Ch'üan was originally heretical and revolutionary, but that it was later 'captured' by the Empress Dowager and her lieutenants and turned against the hated foreigners. In support of this explanation (which was obviously a rejection of the original account) it had been asserted that the organization had first been called the *I Ho Ch'üan Hui*, and that the *Hui* was later abandoned in return for Imperial sanction. But although the Ch'üan did practically absorb the *Ta Tao Hui* (Great Sword Society),

Steiger holds that there is no contemporary evidence that the I Ho Ch'üan was ever called a *hui*.

There was other evidence (Steiger further argues) for rejecting the assumption that the I Ho Ch'üan was a branch of the 'White Lotus' (or 'White Lily') sect, but the most positive was that of Dr Arthur H. Smith who said that there was no evidence whatever that the 'White Lily' in Shantung and the I Ho Ch'üan had ever any connection with one another.

Dr Porter[1] had identified the Boxers with the Great Sword Society and described them as a 'society something like the German Turners who add a spiritism to their gymnastics'. This was several months (says Steiger) before the name I Ho Ch'üan was used. The first appearance of the English name 'Boxers' in print was in the *North China Herald* of 2 October 1899, but it had been used much earlier, however, by the missionaries in their correspondence. I Ho Ch'üan was the name by which the society was designated in all the diplomatic correspondence in Peking, and even in the translations of decrees which were eventually issued by the government, but the 'official', or correct, name for the organization (again according to Steiger) was *I Ho T'uan*, 'Righteous and United Band' or 'Militia'. 'The substitution of *Ch'üan* for *T'uan*, as the third character in the name of the organization, was simply a pun which was perpetrated by its opponents' (p. 134). Says Steiger: 'So far as it has been possible to discover, the earliest use of the name "I Ho Chuan", by any foreigner in China, was a letter written on October 14, 1899, by Dr H. D. Porter of the American Board mission at Pang-Chuang, in Shantung' (p. 131).

Steiger wishes to establish that *Ch'üan* was a late 'pun' for *T'uan*— but his information here is not correct as the I Ho Ch'üan is referred to as such in a letter of 28 May 1899, from Dr S. MacFarlane of the London Missionary Society to the headquarters of the Society in London,[2] nearly five months before Dr Porter's letter was written.

Let us now examine Steiger's argument in some detail. In the first place, by the laws of Chinese punning, '*Ch'üan*' would not be an acceptable pun for *T'uan*, but apart from this fact, surely the 'correct' name would be the one used in the original Chinese decrees? In the Chia Ch'ing decrees the Boxers are already known as I Ho Ch'üan and this by itself disposes of the suggestion that the term was a late nineteenth-century pun. When we come to examine the documents relating to the re-emergence of the Boxers we shall find that in the earliest

reference to them in a memorial of Chang Ju-mei, governor of Shantung, in May 1898, the Boxers are called *I Ho T'uan* (*T'uan* be it noted,
not *Ch'üan*). This circumstance is consistent with Steiger's theory, but
Lao Nai-hsüan, in his study of September 1899, calls the society by its
traditional name of I Ho Ch'üan.[1] In the edicts of 1, 5, 6, 9, 11 and
19 April, 25 June, 8 and 19 July, and 3, 20 and 21 November 1899,
referring to the disorders in Shantung, there is mention of secret
societies in general (*hui*), rebels (*fei*), and vagabonds (*t'u*), but not of
specific societies, but in that of 28 November the Great Sword Society
(*Ta Tao Hui*) and the Red Fist Society (*Hung Ch'üan Hui*) are referred
to by name.[2] In this edict the Boxers themselves appear as the *Ch'üan
Min* (Boxer People).[3] In the decree of 19 February 1900 they are called
the *I Ho Ch'üan Hui*, and are specifically included among the 'secret
societies' (*ssŭ li hui ming*).[4] In the decree of 12 April they are called
the *I Ho Ch'üan Fei* (Boxer rebels),[5] and in that of 20 April the *I Ho
Ch'üan Hui* again.[6]

The Boxers are referred to as the *I Ho T'uan* in the decree of
23 May 1898, and in that of 1 May 1900.[7] In the decree of 9 May 1900
the two appellations are combined in the portmanteau name of *I Ho
T'uan Ch'üan Hui* (I Ho-Band—Boxers-Society). In a decree of
6 June they are again referred to as *Hui* (*I Ho Ch'üan Hui*).[8] In most
of the remaining decrees they are called the *Ch'üan Fei* (Boxer rebels).
In short, there are scores of references in the official and other documents which contradict flatly Steiger's statement that 'there is no
contemporary evidence that I Ho Ch'üan was ever called a *hui*'.

Steiger's theory of the origins of the Boxers is that they were
'volunteer militia recruited in response to express commands from the
throne' in decrees of the Empress Dowager dated 5 November and
31 December 1898 ordering that the local militia be strengthened and
improved and that it be instructed in the use of modern arms and in the
drill and discipline of the regular army. It did indeed absorb un-
authorized bodies such as the Great Swords, but Lao Nai-hsüan's
statement that the Boxers were 'a secret and heretical body affiliated
with the White Lotus sect' is (says Steiger) to be rejected as contrary
to the prevailing evidence. He sums up by saying:

The traditional account of the origins of the I Ho Ch'üan, either as it was
given by Lao Nai-hsüan or as it has been modified by subsequent writers,
must be rejected. The so-called Boxers were a T'uan, or volunteer militia....
Whatever the Boxer movement may have become—or may have threatened

to become—by the spring of 1900, it was, in the beginning neither a revolutionary nor heretical organization: it was a lawful and loyal volunteer militia, whose existence was fully justified by the reasonable apprehensions of the government and the people (p. 146).

Steiger's main theories have been disposed of in detail by Chester C. Tan. Steiger (says Tan) was handicapped by insufficient information from Chinese sources, as is indicated by his undue reliance on the evidence of missionaries such as H. C. Porter and A. H. Smith. But in view of Muramatsu's belief that the Boxers nevertheless had some sort of understanding with the provincial authorities as early as May 1898, we shall have to examine the now available source material in further detail.

One thing we can be certain of and that is that Steiger's faith in the good-will of the sects towards Christianity is without firm base. The Boxers were an anti-foreign movement, and their hostility was directed primarily against the missionaries and their converts because they were the foreigners who most immediately impinged upon their lives, their liberties and their religion. In the time of Chia Ch'ing the Boxers had not been anti-foreign or anti-Christian because the foreigners and Christians had not yet arrived on the scene. But only a year or two before the re-emergence of the Boxers, the Great Sword, a society related to the Boxers and afterwards absorbed by them, had shown its unmistakable hostility towards the Christian missions in Shantung. 'Indeed, now that the reactionaries were in power and a strong foreign policy was adopted, it might well have been the thought of the secret societies that this was a good time to conciliate the officials and the public by unfurling a popular banner of antiforeignism.'[1]

Dr A. H. Smith's statement that he could discover no connection between the Boxers and a society called the 'Six Times Sect'[2] (a branch of the White Lily or White Lotus) could not (says Tan) be taken to prove that there was no connection between the Boxers and other secret societies in the district, nor could Dr H. C. Porter's failure to mention the sects be accepted as evidence that they were not involved in the Boxer movement. The foreign missionaries had, indeed, very limited means for discovering what was going on among the people, and they had to rely almost exclusively on the information given them by their converts.

The difficulty raised by the fact that the Boxers adopted the ritual and magic formulae associated with the sects and heretical societies and that they used charms and incantations whereby they believed that they could enlist the aid of supernatural powers to render them invulnerable and invincible is explained away by Steiger by an elaborate theory of his own. Since, he says, the arsenals of the empire could hardly produce modern weapons in sufficient quantities to supply the needs of the regular troops, no modern weapons were for the time being available for the militia organizations, which continued to be armed with swords, spears, and a few firearms of a very limited sort. But the militia could at least be trained in accordance with the up-to-date military methods and the T'uan were therefore taught squad and company drill, the 'goose-step', etc., which had been introduced into the training of the Peiyang army by the German and Japanese military instructors. Says Steiger: 'It requires little exercise of the imagination to visualize the metamorphosis by which these physical exercises became, in the mind of the Chinese peasant, magic rites which would confer supernatural strength and invulnerability upon all who religiously performed them' (p. 143).

On the contrary (as Chester Tan comments) it requires, indeed, a great stretch of imagination to suppose that the Chinese peasants would mistake the Western drills for the magic rites. The fact is (as we shall see in a moment) the Boxers from the beginning displayed the characteristics of the secret sects to which they belonged. But did they, none the less, enjoy some measure at least of official approval or sympathy?

As we have seen in chapter 1, the militia (*T'uan-lien*) had been widely used in the mid-nineteenth century against the Taipings and had virtually displaced the regular troops as the standing army of China. Li Ping-hêng, governor of Kwangsi in 1886, had indeed advised against their use because to be effective they must be extensively trained, and having been drilled only twice a month they could not be expected to confront a strong army. Yet in 1898 the militia were viewed with great favour by the Reform party. When the reform movement was well under way, Chang Yin-huan (who had attended Queen Victoria's Diamond Jubilee as China's envoy) had recommended that the militia system, rather than Western conscription, be adopted. This recommendation was promptly accepted, and an Imperial decree was issued on 5 September ordering all the provinces to reorganize the militia in accordance with Chang's suggestions within a period of three months, except for Kwangsi, which was to comply with the order within one month. Two weeks later the *coup d'état* took place and the reformers were swept away. But the idea of general militia training survived the reaction.

The decree issued by the Empress Dowager on 5 November 1898 dealt with the organization of the *Pao-chia* (Constabulary) and the drilling of militia.[1] The *Pao-chia* (the decree said) afforded protection against bandits, while the militia could give the nation military protection. The latter only required regular training in tactics to make them reliable in an emergency. Beginning in Chihli, Mukden and Shantung, the generals, viceroys, and governors of the several provinces must advise the gentry and common people so that measures might be carried out with the utmost energy.

The militia were organized under the supervision of the local governments—thus perpetuating a decentralizing trend unpropitious to Manchu power. Usually a headquarters was set up in the capital of the province with branch offices in the localities. The officers were selected by, or with the approval of, the local governments.

Says Steiger: 'The "Righteous and Harmonious Bands" as *I Ho Tuan* should properly be translated, were, therefore, perfectly legitimate and customary bodies for local defence, and were, after November 5, 1898, expressly authorized and encouraged.'

Certainly the I Ho T'uan was *not* called into being by the edict of 5 November 1898, for it had already been referred to by that name in May of that year, five months earlier, as one of the volunteer organizations active along the border between Shantung and Chihli, declaring hostility against the Christians. The Imperial Court then ordered Wang Wên-shao, viceroy of Chihli, and Chang Ju-mei, governor of Shantung, to investigate and maintain order. In his reply to the Imperial edict Chang Ju-mei reported that it was the intention to embody the members of the Boxers into the local militia.

Chester Tan's comment on Steiger's theory is as follows:

The Boxer societies were not formed in response to the Imperial decrees, for before November 5, 1898, the first decree ordering the organization of the militia, they had already existed and operated. The fact that the local authorities and the Imperial Government repeatedly attempted to place the Boxers within the militia so as to control them more effectively should prove that they were two different entities.[2]

It will be seen that Steiger does not state that the Boxers were 'formed in response to the Imperial decree' of 5 November, but that after that date they were 'expressly authorized and encouraged'. His statement, therefore, is not incompatible with their pre-existence in May of that year, but infers that they had no *locus standi* before November.

Chester Tan accepts the explanation of Lao Nai-hsüan that the I Ho Ch'üan was a branch of the Eight Diagrams sect, whose early leader was Kao Shêng-wên, a native of Honan, who was executed in 1771. His descendants and disciples, however, had survived and, together with other societies, the Boxers continued to operate in the provinces of Honan, Shantung and Kiangnan. But Tan adds that it is difficult to say to what extent the Boxer movement was initiated by the heretical sects, for if they played an important role in organizing the movement, their illegal status made it impossible for them to reveal themselves. There are no records as to exactly how and when the I Ho Ch'üan were first organized, but the evidence is that they began as volunteer associations. But it is beyond doubt that the movement was dominated by the 'heretical' elements.

It is convenient at this point to take account of the views of another authority on the Boxers, namely of Muramatsu, who compares the theories of Steiger and M. N. Roy as to their origins.[1] Mabendra Roy considers that the uprising was the reaction of the peasant farmers to their poverty and misery caused by feudalistic exploitation.[2] He asserts that the connection of the Ch'ing dynasty with the Boxers was just a fortuitous and temporary expedient in the summer of 1900. Chujo Ichiko holds another opinion, he considers the Boxers to be a religious and secret association, a branch sect and remnant of the White Lotus (thus adopting Lao Nai-hsüan's theory, which he expands). Its aims, therefore, were opposed to those of the *T'uan-lien* (militia) which was a semi-governmental police and military system for the suppression of revolutionary activity and the protection of the dynasty, gentry and landlords.[3]

Muramatsu comments:

It is no doubt wrong...when Steiger says that they [the Boxers] were organized for the first time under the decree of 5 November 1898. But, on the other hand, I cannot agree with Roy's opinion when he believes that the Boxer activities were mainly due to economic exploitation and poverty, and Ichiko's when he insists that the Boxers had no connection at all with the government and the militia system. The attitude of the Boxers from the beginning was anti-foreign and anti-Christian, their concern international rather than internal.... It seems quite possible that they might have had some

very intimate relation to the village militia, because the authorities of Shantung province revealed their intention to accept the Boxers into the *Hsing-
t'uan* to control them, and to this the Peking government, too, seems to
have given tacit consent in May 1898.

The sects related to the White Lotus had, as we have seen, many
aliases, and it is a mistake to defer recording the reappearance of the
Boxers until the moment when they are mentioned again *by name*. The
Great Sword Society, for example, which came into prominence during
the events leading to the German occupation of Kiaochow, was undoubtedly of the same family as the Boxers, with the same cult of
invulnerability, and, as we shall see, its members were absorbed in large
numbers both into the Boxers and into the regular forces and the militia.

We have already a hint that the expression 'The Boxers' is in the
nature of an oversimplification. There are, it seems, a number of
elements of diverse kind involved and if we are ever to get to the
bottom of the mystery of the Boxer change of aim we must examine
the sequence of events, starting a few months after the Treaty of
Shimonoseki. To this end the 1959 collection of documents (*IHTTA*)
provides us with invaluable information.

On 2 July 1896 (K 22/5/22), Liu K'un-i, governor-general of the
Two Kiangs, telegraphed Peking to say that disturbances were being
caused by the Great Sword Society in the Ts'ao and Tan districts in
south-west Shantung. They were in conflict with the Christians, and
were robbing shops and salt depots. The militia were engaging them.
An acknowledgement from the Grand Council of the following day
spoke of the 'Sword Rebels' using the extermination of the Christian
converts as a pretext for their robbery and violence, and ordered Li
Ping-hêng, governor of Shantung, to co-operate with Liu K'un-i in
their suppression. Both in Shantung and Kiangnan the people were
forming bands for their own protection.[1]

The German Minister had now begun to complain of attacks on
German missionaries and on 4 July 1896 (K 22/5/24) Li Ping-hêng
reported by telegram that he had sent the newly appointed Provincial
Judge, Yü-hsien, to various districts in Shantung to investigate the
troubles. A telegram from a foreign missionary stationed at Chinan,
the provincial capital, had stated that in the Tan district a church and
converts' dwellings had been burnt. Another telegram from Liu
Kun-i of the following day reported further burnings of Christian
property in the Maliang region.

188

The telegraph now began to be kept very busy with communications between the districts and the provincial capital, and between the provincial capital and Peking. On 5 July (K 22/5/25) Li Ping-hêng reported a series of incidents starting on 28 June (K 22/5/18) in Ts'aochou which were the work, he said, of the Great Sword Society. Yü-hsien had been ordered to proceed to the area with the local officials to restore order and to punish the offenders. Liu K'un-i reappears the same day in a telegram to Peking reporting more burnings by the Great Sword in Hsüchoi and Taofu. The militia had been sent after them, but they had made their escape to Maliang. In a subsequent engagement between them and the militia, 200 of the bandits had been killed or wounded. One of the leaders, Ch'ên Wu-ai, had fled to the Tan district. A further 500 members of the Great Sword had now appeared on the scene and further battles had ensued. The rebels were displaying great boldness and ferocity. Eighty to ninety of them had been killed by the militia and regular troops and thirteen prisoners had been taken, together with hundreds of weapons and a dozen war horses.

A telegram from the Grand Council to Li Ping-hêng of 7 July 1896 (K 22/5/27) referred to the return of a rebel leader, Liu Shih-tuan, to the Tan district where he had gathered over a thousand followers. Li was enjoined to order Yü-hsien and others to exert all their energy to run the rebels to earth and liquidate them lest they should become a running-sore on provincial society. Was Liu Shih-tuan still in Tanchou? If not, where was he? On 8 July (K 22/5/28) Li Ping-hêng wired to say that Liu had been captured by the regular troops of the Tan district and that the Provincial Judge, Yü-hsien, had been ordered to conduct his trial and to administer punishment.

The next document of importance is a memorial from Li Ping-hêng dated 3 August 1896 (K 22/6/24). In this he spoke of the collaboration between the secret society rebels of the Ts'ao and Tan regions of Shantung with those of the T'angshan in Kiangnan. After the arrest of their chief leader, Liu Shih-tuan, peace had been restored among the people, but before this, on 24 June (K 22/5/14), Li had received a telegram from the Tsungli Yamen stating that more churches had been burnt at several places in T'angshan and other districts by persons associated with the Great Sword Society. Liu-K'un-i and Li Ping-hêng were co-operating by sending troops to the scene of the disorders along the common boundaries of their provinces.

The Great Sword (continued Li) was the same as the Golden Bell.

It had a very long history and in spite of the efforts of the local officials to suppress it, it continued to exist. The year before, the coastal districts were in a state of unrest, and the inhabitants, believing the claims of members of the Great Sword to invulnerability against bullets and cannon, had joined it in considerable numbers. Not only did the stupid rely on its magical powers to protect themselves and their families from harm, but rascals took advantage of its cover to engage in rapine. Crowds gathered and riots ensued. Li Ping-hêng, however, uttered a warning against attempting to deal with the trouble by indiscriminate executions since this would tend to create desperadoes who would resort to even greater violence.

The origin of all the trouble created by the secret societies (said Li Ping-hêng) lay in the basic conflict between the people and the Christians. The two could not live side by side in harmony because the native converts, with the support and protection of the foreign missionaries, victimized the ordinary people. When cases were brought before the local magistrates the latter were afraid of incurring foreign hostility and usually gave judgment in favour of the converts. Feeling that the local authorities were unable to redress their grievances, the ordinary people combined for self-defence and the result was that clashes occurred and churches and chapels were burned.

In the course of this long memorial Li Ping-hêng gave the names of a number of the leaders, some of whom had been captured. The Great Sword Society had been guilty of ransacking salt depots, 'Peking' and general stores, and stealing food and horses. On the other hand, the situation in which they operated had been created by abuses on the part of the foreign missionaries and converts which had aroused the temper of the ordinary people to fever pitch.

An addendum to Li Ping-hêng's memorial, giving further details of the Great Sword troubles, is dated 12 August 1896 (K 22/7/4).

For 1897, only three telegrams are reproduced in this series, all from Li Ping-hêng, but they must be only a selection from the scores that were sent, for this was a year of great international tension as well as of civil ferment.

The first is a short one dated 27 July (K 23/6/28) reporting that 400–500 members of the Great Sword Society had surrounded a Christian church in the village of K'uchuang in the T'angshan district of Kiangnan and that soldiers had been sent to the scene of the trouble, but the second, of 15 November (K 23/10/21), is longer and of even graver significance, since it reports the landing in strength of German troops at Kiaochow Bay and other places on the Shantung coast the previous day.

On 1 November 1897 two Roman Catholic priests of the German mission in Shantung, Fathers Nies and Henle, were murdered by armed men who attacked the German mission at the little village of Kia Tchouang (Chiachuang), district of Kiuyé (Kuyeh), Tchao Tcheou (Ts'aochou) Prefecture.[1] A year later, Bishop Anzer, the German Bishop of Shantung (says Steiger), identified the assassins as members of the Great Sword Society, but this has never been conclusively established and was categorically denied by Yü-hsien.

Two days after the receipt of Li Ping-hêng's telegram reporting the landing of the Germans, the Grand Council replied with another ordering him not to move his troops in spite of this aggression, so as not to give the Germans any excuse for extending the sphere of their hostilities. In the same telegram, Li Ping-hêng was informed that he was to be replaced forthwith as governor of Shantung by Chang Ju-mei. (This was in consequence of the pressure brought on the Tsungli Yamen by the German Minister who held Li responsible for the murder of the missionaries.) Chang Ju-mei, said the telegram, was now on his way to take over the appointment.

In the meantime the Germans had continued their pressure on Peking for the acquisition of a permanent base in Shantung. The Chinese government, confronted by the occupation of Kiaochow, first of all offered them an island in place of it, but fortified by an understanding with Britain and Russia, the Germans insisted on remaining where they were. At last China gave in, and (as we have already seen in chapter IV) on 6 March 1898 a convention was signed whereby Kiaochow was leased to Germany for ninety-nine years. A separate agreement provided for German and Chinese co-operation in the building of railways and the working of mines. When things did not go exactly as they wanted them to, the Germans resorted at once to direct and violent action.

The first telegram of 1898 from Chang Ju-mei, the new governor, to be reproduced in this collection, is that of 20 April (K 24/3/30). He referred to the alleged renewed activities of the Great Sword and said that he had sent Yü-hsien to inquire into the matter. Yü-hsien had now submitted his report and in it he stated that the Great Sword was no longer operating and had therefore nothing to do with the present disturbances. The real cause of the renewed trouble, he said, was the German landings. It was a case of 'outside troops interfering in inside affairs'. There was no provision in any treaty for the German action. Yü-hsien (Chang Ju-mei added) had been ordered to soothe the outraged feelings of the populace.

The same matter was again taken up at length in Chang Ju-mei's memorial of 18 May 1898 (K 24/INTER 3/28). According to Yü-hsien's further statements, the Great Sword had not been active in Shantung for the previous two years. When Yü-hsien had arrested the leader of the society, Liu Shih-tuan, and had executed him, his followers had dispersed, and extensive inquiries by the local officials had failed to discover any subsequent trace of the Great Sword Society. However, in Ts'aochou and Tanchou bad characters had repeatedly joined the Christians and had relied on their church membership to victimize the ordinary law-abiding inhabitants. The latter had been groaning under this oppression for a long time, but dared not speak out for fear of the churches. On this occasion the German missionaries had alleged that the Great Sword Society was responsible for the incidents and had demanded that troops should be sent to the region to suppress them, but it was the bad characters inside the churches who had actually created the trouble. It was they who had won the ears of the foreign missionaries and had worked on their fears, and, in their panic, the missionaries had appealed to military might. So long had this sort of thing been going on that the morale of the ordinary people was completely undermined. Nevertheless, the Provincial Judge had strictly enjoined on the local officials to exhort the gentry to obey the Imperial edict of the previous year and to encourage harmonious relations between the people and the converts. But, for their part, the converts must give obedience to the local authorities.

We now come to the document of 22 May 1898 (K 24/4/3), which is a short telegram from Chang Ju-mei reporting to the throne the appearance of a new society, which was to turn out to be the Boxers themselves. The day before (Chang said) he had received information that in the Tungming region on the borders of Chihli and Shantung there existed a recently established *I Min Hui* (Righteous People's Society—a *hui* it will be noticed). It had already taken root in Chihli, Honan and Kiangsu provinces. Its object was to cause trouble with the foreign religion. He (Chang Ju-mei) had immediately communicated with the viceroys and governor of the provinces in question so that they might issue orders forthwith for stamping out this new society.[1]

This telegraphed memorial was replied to next day in a decree to the Grand Councillors instructing them to send a telegram to Wang Wên-shao, viceroy of Chihli, stating that it had come to Imperial notice that on the border of Shantung and Chihli a group of people who called themselves without official sanction the *I Min Hui* were distributing placards in Chihli, Anhui and Kiangsu provinces calling on the people to prepare an assault on foreigners and Christians. There were many people training in Chihli and at Kuantien in Shantung, and the Court had learnt that they were spreading their cause through placards and notices. Taking advantage of the situation, brigands might cause disturbances. Therefore the Grand Councillors were immediately to order Wang Wên-shao, Chang Ju-mei, and Liu Shu-t'ang (viceroy of Honan) to send an adequate force to the affected localities to carry out a detailed investigation and to press the local officials to prohibit the agitation. In Kiangsu province, although it was at a considerable distance from Peking, there were masses of starving people who might be incited to band together to create disorder. Liu K'un-i, too, was to be ordered to instruct his officials to investigate and prevent any further spread of these disturbances.[2]

In response to this decree, Chang Ju-mei carried out extensive inquiries and reported his findings to the throne in a lengthy memorial of 30 June (K 24/5/12). The contents of this memorial we shall consider carefully in the next chapter.

CHAPTER IX

'PRO-DYNASTIC' OR 'ANTI-DYNASTIC'? I

In obedience to the decree of 23 May 1898 (K 24/4/4) Chang Ju-mei carried out investigations lasting over a month and reported back to the throne on 30 June (K 24/5/12).[1] He began by giving a history of the disturbances on the Shantung–Chihli border. Many of the inhabitants of the region were practising 'boxing', he said, and had established village bands (*Hsiang T'uan*). Their object was the protection of their persons and property. The name they originally gave themselves was *I Ho*, which they afterwards changed to *Mei Hua Ch'üan* (Plum Blossom Fists). In recent years they had changed it back to *I Ho*, or *I Min*, but they regarded themselves as a newly established society. Before the building of Christian churches in the region[2] they had already organized to protect their homes and families against bandits and the like, but since the arrival of the missionaries friction had developed between the people and the newcomers in which they became involved. The result was that year by year the 'Boxer People' (*Ch'üan Min*) had grown rapidly in numbers. They formed into private bodies on their own and were not organized or interfered with by the officials. But now the local officials and gentry had been enjoined to transform these private bodies into public ones, to convert 'Boxer Irregulars' (*Ch'üan Yung*) into 'People's Militia' (*Min T'uan*). The Provincial Judge, Yü-hsien, had been instructed to investigate further and report.

As a result of their combined inquiries, Chang Ju-mei had ascertained with certainty that the body referred to as the *I Min Hui* was actually the *I Ho T'uan*. There was no sign at present, however, of any trouble. When the authorities had established *Pao-chia* and *T'uan-fang* (neighbourhood constabulary and village militia) in these areas, they intended to include the Boxers in the *Hsiang T'uan* (village militia units) and to appoint suitable persons to officer them in due course.

It is clear that Chang Ju-mei (prompted, no doubt, by Yü-hsien) wished at this juncture to minimize the danger of the Boxers to good order, although they were already at an early date posting placards declaring their intention to kill the converts.[3]

The next reference to civil commotion is in a telegram of 4 August 1898 (K 24/6/17)[1] from Chang Ju-mei stating that on the borders of Chihli and Shantung a notorious bandit named T'ung Chên-shên had collected some hundreds of men from the Yuch'ing district of Honan and had joined up with other bad characters from Kiangnan. They had been engaged by troops from Tanchou and about a dozen had been killed and the same number captured, including T'ung Chên-shên himself. The rest had fled. The troops had also captured a 'little red flag inscribed with rebellious characters', carried by the insurgents. There is a further reference to the 'little red flag inscribed with re-bellious characters' in Chang's memorial of 14 September 1898 (K 24/7/29),[2] but he does not say what these characters were. There is no suggestion in the telegram that any of the rebels were 'Boxers', but they were undoubtedly secret society members.

About this time there were other serious developments which we must summarize from other sources. In October rebels identified as 'Boxers' gathered their forces round Weihsien and Kuanhsien, between Shantung and Chihli. During the night of 25 October they attacked the house of Chao Lu-chu, a Chinese Christian, in Kuanhsien, and drove him and his family out of the district. Within six days they had assembled as many as a thousand men with forty or fifty horses.[3] Against them, Yü-lu, the governor-general of Chihli, had taken strong action, although he ad-vocated the use of suppression and peaceful persuasion at the same time.

Meanwhile, as the Boxers of Chihli were being disbanded, their brethren in Shantung started rioting again. From Kuanp'ing they moved to Kuanhsien, killed two Christians and wounded a third, and set fire to a chapel and over a hundred houses belonging to the converts. The troops despatched from Chihli at the request of Chang Ju-mei now arrived on the scene and the Boxers were trapped. Their leader, Yao Lo-chi, was captured together with fifteen others, four Boxers were killed, and the rest fled.[4]

One further telegram, of the 24th year of Kuang Hsü, namely that of 21 January 1899 (K 24/12/10), from the Grand Council to Chang Ju-mei, gives an alarming picture of the situation in the border region. It speaks of the assembling of nearly 10,000 'robbers' (tsê) in Chihli and in the Kueitê-Ts'aochou region of Shantung. Chang Ju-mei was ordered to direct his forces, in combination with those of Liu K'un-i and others from Kiangnan and Anhwei, to cut off the retreat of these rebels and exterminate them.

It seems that at the beginning of 1899 large bands, whom the officials were intent on crushing, were in the field in this part of China, openly in rebellion against Manchu authority. These are not identified as the I-ho T'uan, which according to Chang Ju-mei and Yü-hsien was a harmless organization created spontaneously by the people to protect themselves against the depredations of the Christians. The attempt made from June 1898 onwards to absorb the Boxers into the *Pao-chia* and the militia was no doubt with the hope of diverting them from revolutionary aims. During 1899, however, other bands of rebels appeared who were also described as 'Boxers' but who were undisguisedly anti-dynastic.

There can be no doubt that the return of Yü-hsien to Shantung as governor in April 1899 marked a turning-point in the career of the Boxers. Yü-hsien had been transferred to a post in Hunan a few months previously, but was now selected by the Empress Dowager to succeed Chang Ju-mei. Notice of the appointment was conveyed to Chang Ju-mei in a decree of 14 March (K 25/2/3).[1] While Yü-hsien was on his way from Hunan (there was no railway as yet) the Imperial decrees continued to be addressed to Chang Ju-mei. The first to be addressed to Yü-hsien was dated 11 April 1899 (K 25/3/2).[2]

For the first months of 1899, however, the interest both of Peking and the new Governor of Shantung was concentrated rather on the menacing behaviour of the Germans in Kiaochow than on the Boxers, and Yü-hsien's memorials are concerned primarily with this.

In March 1899 (as has already been mentioned) a party of three Germans was attacked by villagers near Jihchou in Shantung. The villagers had already been beaten off, but the German authorities in Kiaochow despatched troops to this area, burned two villages to the ground, and seized the town of Jihchao and held it.[3] Yü-hsien's memorials to Peking of 30 April, 20 May, and 31 May, and the edicts addressed to him on 19 May, 5 June, and 8 July are all concerned with the Germans, but the missionary question was simultaneously to the forefront. The feelings of the people were almost equally disturbed by the coercion to which they felt themselves subjected by the German soldiers and by the German and other missionaries. The areas affected by the German military reprisals were in a different part of Shantung to that in which the Boxers were active, but they nevertheless inter-communicated. Yü-hsien, as was to be expected, did not fail to under-line the grievances of the Chinese against the missionaries and he complained that the foreign Ministers listened only to the missionaries' side of the case.

Yü-hsien's memorials and telegrams of the first six months of his governorship give the impression that the Boxers were not causing any particular anxiety to the officials. This, however, was far from being the case, as we can ascertain by reference to another source, namely the narrative of Chiang K'ai, the Magistrate of P'ingyüan (who was to be dismissed by Yü-hsien after the Boxer riots of October).[1]

Chiang K'ai relates that he was transferred from Chüchou on 23 April 1899 (K 25/3/14). On arrival in P'ingyüan he was informed of the activities of the I Ho Ch'üan in Szüchingchêng, in the neighbouring Ên district. Some said that the Boxers came from Kuanhsien in eighteen bands; others said that they came from Tungch'ang in Ts'aochou, without giving any details as to their formations, and Chiang K'ai could not say which of the accounts was the true one. Early in the fourth month (10 May–7 June 1899) a Roman Catholic priest wrote to tell him that the Boxers were active in the village where he was stationed and were behaving with great violence. The whole neighbourhood was in a state of excitement, and the priest requested him to act at once to repress the sect. This letter was followed up by a personal interview between the priest and the magistrate.

Chiang K'ai at once proceeded to investigate and discovered a number of facts about the Boxers. They operated only at night time, and dispersed during daylight. They were closely connected with the Great Sword Society; they carried charms, recited incantations, and boasted of their invulnerability; they were armed with spears, swords, guns and cannon; their chief god was Yang Chien (apparently from the novel, *Pilgrimage to the West*) and they addressed him as *T'ai Lao Shih* (Great Elder Teacher); they prophesied that the next year of the cycle (*Kêng Tzŭ*, that is, 1900) would be the year of the great (Taoist) *Kalpa* (*Chieh*) in which the Jade emperor would send down to earth his spirit soldiers. On the eighth day of the fourth month (6 May 1900) they would take Peking, they said. Their leader, whom they addressed as Great Teacher Elder Brother (*T'ai Shih Hsiung*) was one Chu Hung-têng ('Red Lantern Chu'). Some said he was a native of Jênp'ing; others said he was from Lichuachuang in Ch'anch'ing. His title (*hao*) was T'ien Lung ('Dragon of Heaven'). Chu's real name, it appeared, was Li Wên-Ch'ing (a name possessed by an earlier rebel leader of the White Lotus fraternity).[2] His surname, Chu, is that of

Chu Yüan-chang, the founder of the Ming dynasty. The characters for his personal name, Hung-têng, usually given (by Chiang K'ai and others) are those meaning 'Red Lamp', referring no doubt to the 'Lamp of 10,000 years' in Taoist symbolism (and as in the name of the women's parallel association to the Boxers). But Chi Pi-hu (*IHT*, IV, 443) gives two different characters, *Hung* meaning 'flood' or 'vast' (as in the title of the famous southern Secret Society, the Hung League) and *têng* meaning 'to ascend' (the character for 'lamp' without the 'fire' radical). Most likely both forms were used by Chu Hung-têng's supporters since this kind of word-play is typical of the secret sects. *Hung* ('flood' or 'vast') occurs in the reign-title of Chu Yüan-chang, namely *Hung Wu* 'vast military'. Chu's associate was one known as the 'Ming Monk'.

When Chu Hung-têng eventually appeared in person (in the P'ingyüan region in October), Chiang K'ai said that he wore a big red 'wind hat' (of the type used in winter) and red trousers; the leading files of his troops carried two red flags, and all their weapons were decorated with red cloth. Red was still (*shang*—as if to signify that it was changed later) their colour, signifying 'south' and 'fire', in order to distinguish them from the other symbols (trigrams).

When they first came out (continues Chiang K'ai), they kowtowed towards the south-east; they used a drum for giving orders; among them were Buddhist monks and Taoist priests; in their formations, four men composed a section; they were skilful in taking cover and retreating and advancing swiftly; all of them came from other parts of the country; among them were many 'prowling ex-soldiers' (*yu yung*) who were good fighting men.[1]

The influence of the Boxers and the Great Sword had penetrated into the provincial army of Shantung. A member of the Boxers who had come to P'ingyüan from Chinan said that half of the two battalions of the Left Wing of the provincial army were members of the Great Sword. (That this was so was no doubt in consequence of Chang Ju-mei's absorption policy of June 1898.)

The provincial authorities, and the Governor in particular, were very partial to the Boxers, and when those in control of affairs (asked Chiang K'ai) 'treated the Boxers like sons and feared the foreigners like tigers', what could a mere district magistrate do? The Boxers themselves said, 'The Governor supports us; how then can the Magistrate be against us?'

Chiang K'ai was alarmed by the situation, but in spite of his tele-grams to headquarters could obtain no help or instructions. The local officials dared not act on their own initiative, and in the neighbourhood of P'ingyüan Chu Hung-têng had assembled 200–300 men.

Under the heading of 25 October 1899 (K 25/9/21) in his narrative, Chiang K'ai relates how a Roman Catholic priest (Martin Ên?) wrote to him saying that the Governor neglected to take into account the interests either of the people or of the throne, and that *when the Boxers erected a great flag at the provincial quarters, inscribed with the characters Pao Ch'ing; Mieh Yang ('Protect the Ch'ing; exterminate the foreigner')* '*Yü-hsien was delighted*'.[1] As we shall see in the next chapter, this is one of the earliest references in Chinese to the celebrated slogan of 'Boxer Year'.

What was Yü-hsien's real attitude towards the Boxers? To the extent that they were anti-dynastic he must, as a Manchu and a mandarin, have regarded them as his enemies and therefore to be suppressed, but to the extent that he regarded them as merely anti-foreign and potential supporters of the Ch'ing he would have looked upon them as his friends. His biographer in the *Draft History of the Ch'ing Dynasty* (*Ch'ing Shih Kao*) definitely states: 'The Boxers called themselves the *I Ho Ch'üan* until Yü-hsien renamed them the *I Ho T'uan*, upon which they adopted a flag inscribed with the character *Yü*' (this being the first character in Yü-hsien's name).[2]

If we are to believe that it was Yü-hsien who renamed the Boxers *I Ho T'uan*, then he must have done so sometime prior to May 1898, for they were already called that at that time. But there is no evidence of any close association between Yü-hsien and the Boxers as early as this, and the adoption of a flag bearing his name (which we have no reason to doubt) must have taken place after he had become governor, probably late in 1899.

Dr A. H. Smith, writing of the period of the P'ingyüan affray (October 1899) says:

Yü Hsien a few months previously had been merely a prefect of Tsao Chou in South-West Shantung where he was generally believed to have originated the Ta Tao Hui or Great Sword Society....He had a band of men drilling with large swords in the courts of his yamen every day. What more natural that his people should look on him as the tutelary deity of the whole I Ho Chuan, as he was supposed to be, and as later it turned out that he actually was.[3]

Whatever Yü-hsien's real attitude towards the Boxers, it is not revealed in his correspondence with Peking, at least up till November. A Manchu, fanatically devoted to the interests of the dynasty, as he saw them, he could be depended on to act vigorously in their defence when he felt them threatened. In July 1899 it came to his notice that two notables in the province had recently organized a corps of volunteers in the native district on their own responsibility, without first asking for the necessary official sanction, and furthermore had made levies in money and kind on the locality for its support. This fact Yü-hsien reported to the Court in a memorial. Private armies of this kind were of necessity a challenge to the central authority, and Tz'ŭ Hsi responded forcibly. The gentry in question were to be deprived of whatever official rank they possessed and they were to be placed under the strict surveillance of the local authorities for their good behaviour in the future.[1]

Yü-hsien's real attitude towards the Boxers did not become obvious in official correspondence until after the P'ingyüan affair of October. At the head of about 300 men, Chu Hung-têng looted the houses of Christians, and when six of them were arrested Chu challenged the district troops. Government reinforcements then came up from Chinan and a battle took place in which twenty-seven Boxers were killed and the rest were dispersed.

When the news of the clash reached Yü-hsien he ordered an investigation, and his anger fell not on the Boxers but upon the local magistrate, Chiang K'ai, whom he blamed for mismanaging the situation and whom he held responsible for the death of innocent villagers. Yü-hsien removed him from his post and imprisoned the chief constable who had arrested the rioters.

Yü-hsien's official account of the P'ingyüan affair is given in his memorial of 8 November 1899 (K 25/10/6).[2] 'Your slave', he wrote (as a Manchu should) 'has conducted an investigation into the matter.' It is to be noticed that in it Chu Hung-têng and his followers are referred to by him as 'highwaymen' or 'robbers' (tao-fei). Chu had escaped, and the fault, said Yü-hsien, lay with the magistrate, Chiang K'ai, who had failed to discriminate between the good and the bad men and who, by calling in the military, had caused the death of innocent people. The commander of the forces, Yüan Shih-tun (who, it turned out, was the younger brother of Yüan Shih-k'ai),[3] also came in for censure and was transferred to another post.

The P'ingyüan troubles (Yü-hsien continued) arose from the lack of harmony between the Christians and the Boxers (*Ch'üan Hui*). The rascally underling, the 'burrowing-worm',[1] Ch'ên Tê-ho, the chief constable, had been inspired by the converts to arrest six law-abiding citizens. The magistrate, Chiang K'ai, had misunderstood the situation and had listened to Ch'ên Tê-ho. This had resulted in injustice to which the public would not submit. The crowd that assembled to protest, ordinary good citizens and Boxers together, amounted to no more than 500–600 all told. They wanted to march to the district capital to demand the release of the six men on bail. This was the moment when Chu Hung-têng had appeared on the scene to take advantage of the situation. A mob numbering several thousands then proceeded under his leadership to break into a dozen houses belonging to the converts. Thereupon the Prefect of Chinan had hastened to P'ingyüan, arrested Ch'ên Tê-ho, the cause of the trouble, and put him in irons. He then released the six men. Thereupon most of the good citizens had returned to their homes. But the Boxers did not yet completely disperse, and the robbers outside the village planned further trouble. The military commander, Yüan Shih-tun, had thereupon ordered his troops to open fire. Twenty or thirty of the bandits were killed while the troops suffered three casualties. Thereupon the remainder of the robbers made off in all directions. Four ordinary citizens, who had no connection at all with the affray, also lost their lives. Two lodging-houses near the village temples were robbed and a number of small articles were stolen. Yüan's soldiers arrested sixteen men, but Lu Ch'ang-i, the Prefect of Chinan, decided that they were innocent citizens and released them.

Such importance did Yü-hsien attach to the affray that he followed up his first report with a second and third describing his investigations in further detail. The whole matter arose originally, he found, from a quarrel between a Christian convert, one Li Chin-p'ang, and an ordinary Chinese, Li Ch'ang-shui, which caused a breach of the peace. The chief constable, the 'burrowing-worm' Ch'ên Tê-ho, was involved in the quarrel, and he was besides guilty of cheating and victimizing the ordinary people to such an extent that they were aroused to a fury of resentment. The ensuing civil commotion Chu Hung-têng and his fellow bandits were able to exploit. When the crisis occurred, the magistrate, Chiang K'ai, had failed to distinguish between the guilty and the innocent and had allowed Ch'ên Tê-ho to make indiscriminate arrests. On arrival in P'ingyüan and upon investigating the matter the

Prefect decided that Ch'ên Tê-ho was the principal culprit and there-fore arrested him and sent him to the provincial capital for trial. As for Yüan Shih-tun, who had given the order to fire, he should have exer-cised more care to prevent the loss of innocent lives. But it must be taken into consideration that he was a high-spirited officer who had behaved with courage, and his case, therefore, ought to be dealt with with discrimination. He should be relieved of his command, but whether or not he should be transferred to Yüan Shih-k'ai's military command for further service was a matter he must leave to the decision of the Court. Ch'ên Tê-ho, however, should be severely punished as a warning to others.

By the time he wrote his third report Yü-hsien made the discovery that Chiang K'ai had previously been a magistrate at Chüchou, but he was a very dull and stupid fellow and had caused such trouble by his blunders that Yü-hsien's predecessor and one-time chief governor, Chang Ju-mei, had transferred him to P'ingyüan. But he had not learned his lesson and mended his ways.

An edict of 20 November (K 25/10/18)[1] approved Yü-hsien's recommendations *in toto*.

Yü-hsien's appointment as governor of Shantung had reflected a stiffening in the policy of the Court towards the foreigners. On 21 November (K 25/10/19) the Grand Council conveyed an edict to Yüan Shih-k'ai and Yü-hsien recalling previous Imperial injunctions to deal severely with the bandits 'who relied on their conflict with the Christians as a pretext' to cause disturbances in Shantung. It recalled also that Yü-hsien had reported having issued strict instructions to his civil and military officers to suppress them. Now on top of this, an international crisis had arisen. Since the previous month, Italian war-ships had been cruising off Chefoo and other ports in Shantung. The edict went on to order Yüan Shih-k'ai to make urgent preparations to consolidate his line of military defence.[2]

That same day the Grand Council conveyed to all the viceroys and governors of provinces the famous decree ordering firm resistance to foreign aggression. The Powers (it said) were thrusting one another aside like ravening tigers in their rush to tear China into pieces. Since China at the moment was so weak both financially and militarily she could scarcely be suspected of wanting war, but nevertheless she must not be goaded beyond endurance. Confiding in the justice of her cause she would face her persecutors. 'Peace', therefore, was not the word that should be on the lips of the higher officials; nor should they nourish the thought of peace in their hearts. With her immense population and boundless natural resources China need fear no invader.[1]

In the meantime the reports of the P'ingyüan affair were agitating the *corps diplomatique* in Peking. P'ingyüan was situated in the religious 'sphere of influence' allotted by agreement among the missionary organizations to the American Board, and its missionaries were in agitated correspondence with Mr Conger, the United States Minister to China. The latter protested to the Tsungli Yamen against Yü-hsien's handling of the riots, and Yü-hsien defended himself by telegraphing that he had taken strong measures to repress the rioters but that the Christian converts had fired on them when they retreated into Chihli through P'angchuang (which happened to be the mission station super-intended by Dr A. H. Smith). In retaliation they had burned a mission-ary chapel there. But Mr Conger persisted, and on 5 December he replied to the Yamen's latest note by demanding Yü-hsien's removal from his governorship. The Court then decided to temporize. On 7 December 1899 Yü-hsien was summoned to Peking 'for an audience' of the Empress Dowager and Yüan Shih-k'ai was ordered to Shantung as acting governor.[2]

On the eve of his departure for Peking, that is to say on 6 December, Yü-hsien submitted a memorial to the Empress Dowager setting out his relations with the Great Sword and the Boxers from the beginning. This he supplemented by another memorial of 26 December.[3] These documents merit our close attention.

Yü-hsien wrote that in 1896 (K 22) he was Intendant of Circuit of Yenyi. In this capacity he had investigated the activities of the Great Sword. Its leaders of that time, Liu Shih-tuan and Ts'ao Ti-li, were captured and executed, whereupon the society dissolved. The previous year (1898), in the intercalary third month (21 April–19 May), the Christians had falsely stated that the Great Sword was again stirring up trouble. At this juncture Yü-hsien was officiating as provincial judge and he received instructions by Imperial edict to proceed to Ts'aochou to suppress the disorders without delay. On arrival he made minute inquiries and concluded that the Great Sword Society had nothing what-ever to do with the troubles. But all along the Ts'aochou–Tanchou–Ch'engmu region the ordinary people and the Christians were at cross purposes. Yü-hsien discovered that the basic cause of this was that the Christians made a practice of cheating and insulting the ordinary inhabitants. From the former, the latter had to endure innumerable injuries. Thus it was that they, the ordinary people, had begun to organize the Boxer Society in order to protect their persons and their homes. Nevertheless, 'your slave' (Yü-hsien) had issued a proclamation forbidding the organization of this society and had given instructions to the local officials to restore peace between the parties, thus acting entirely without prejudice and refusing to take sides. All this had been reported by Yü-hsien to his superior, Governor Chang Ju-mei, who had transmitted the information to the throne, as was on record.

In April 1899, after Yü-hsien had assumed duty as governor of Shantung, he had set afoot a new and minute inquiry into the reasons for the disharmony between the people and the converts, and he had taken measures to pacify the region of Ichoufu where renewed trouble had arisen. On eight or more occasions he had issued proclamations forbidding the Great Sword or Boxer societies and the practice of 'spirit boxing'. These had produced some effect and the societies had dispersed. Every local official was enjoined not to allow trouble to arise between the ordinary people and the converts. At the same time Yü-hsien had sent military contingents to patrol the neighbourhood of the churches to suppress any disturbances, and to protect the Christian converts. No effort had been spared to restore good relations.

In the seventh month of that year (6 August–4 September 1899), the Boxer leader Ch'ên Chao-chü appeared in Chining, Chiahsiang, Wên-shang, Chüyeh, and neighbouring districts, collecting followers and causing a commotion. Yü-hsien had then ordered the district magistrate of Wênshang, Yeh Ta-k'o, to arrest him without delay, and the other local officials were to take energetic measures to suppress the Boxers. These orders were obeyed and order restored. However, early in the eighth month (5 September–4 October 1899) the district magistrate of Wênshang reported that the trouble-making temper of the Christians had increased. They had assembled over a hundred strong and had seized and bound several ordinary citizens, claiming that they were arresting members of the I Ho Ch'üan, whom they charged with raiding their church, with extortion from church members, and the like. In the ninth month (5 October–2 November) the 'highwaymen from outside', namely Chu Hung-têng, and his followers took advantage of the unrest to further their private ends. They robbed the converts of P'ingyüan. Thereupon Yü-hsien ordered the magistrate of Chinan,

Lu Ch'ang-i, to proceed with the local battalion commander to P'ing-yüan to investigate and take action. The robbers, relying on their numbers, resisted arrest, whereupon shooting took place and twenty to thirty of the bandits were killed. Thereupon Chu Hung-têng and his followers had broken ranks and fled in all directions. Orders were then given to run them to earth and seize them. Chu Hung-têng had made an alliance with the 'Ming Monk' from the Tingchia Temple, whose real name was Yang T'ien-shun. On 22 November 1899 (K 25/10/20) both Chu Hung-têng and the 'Ming Monk' were captured and sent to the provincial capital for trial and punishment.

Every possible precaution had been taken to prevent the Boxers reorganizing. Should they nevertheless reassemble, it would then be quite clear that they were rebels of their own free will and they must be dealt with accordingly. The fact that there was discord between the people and the converts all arose from the fact that the Christian missions had accepted converts without due inquiry as to their antecedents, as to whether in fact they were rascals or respectable citizens. The churches were thus corrupted by unworthy recruits and brought dishonour to the whole neighbourhood.

Yü-hsien gave a mass of circumstantial detail regarding the P'ing-yüan incident. He then added that the three bandit leaders, who had subsequently been captured, namely Chu Hung-têng, Yü Ch'ing-shui, and the 'Ming Monk', really were lawless rascals. He had ordered them to be sent to the execution-ground for decapitation. Now that the ringleaders had been disposed of the countryside had become peaceful again. Chiang K'ai's narrative may again serve as a corrective to Yü-hsien's apologia. In the remaining sections he insisted that Yü-hsien gave all encouragement to the Boxers and failed to support his subordinates in suppressing them, and Chiang added a defence of the 'burrowing worm', Ch'ên Tê-ho, especially in the matter of his alleged extortion of 300,000 cash (ch'ien).

Yü-hsien's apologia to the throne should also be considered in conjunction with the telegrams he sent to the Tsungli Yamen to answer the charges made against him by Mr E. H. Conger, the United States Minister.

Conger, writing to the Secretary of State (Hay) on 7 December 1899, reported the state of affairs existing among the missionaries and their converts in certain parts of Shantung.[1] Early in October, he said, a secret society called the 'Boxers', in the neighbourhood of Ch'ihping assembled with the avowed purpose of driving out foreigners and of extirpating Christians, but upon aid being requested by the American missionaries soldiers were sent and on 18 October a conflict ensued which resulted in the killing of some fifty or more of the Boxers and in dispersing them. The trouble then seemed to be over, but unfortunately a number of citizens of the village where the affair occurred were killed or wounded, in consequence of which the governor arrested the officer commanding the troops and memorialized the throne for his impeachment. This action of the government encouraged the Boxers and they had since rallied again and were doing much damage to the Christian converts, extorting money from them, threatening the missions, and giving ample cause for serious alarm:

It is generally understood that the governor, Yü-hsien, is strongly anti-foreign, and believed that he is by no means doing what he could and should do.

As you will see from my note to the Tsungli Yamen, I have, without demanding it, suggested the necessity and propriety of his removal, and I am glad to report that yesterday General Yuan Shih-kai, of the Imperial Guards, was appointed acting governor. He is an able, brave, and courageous man, has mingled much with foreigners, and it is believed that, if the right kind of orders are given him from the Throne the rioting will be stopped and order restored.

Enclosed with this despatch were copies of the correspondence between Conger and the Tsungli Yamen. With a letter from the latter dated 1 December 1899 was included a copy of a telegram from Yü-hsien to the Tsungli Yamen which (when translated) ran:

The said rioters commenced stirring up trouble at P'ingyüan. Soldiers were deputed to suppress the rioting. The rioters did not disperse and the soldiers opened fire and killed over thirty of their number. Some of the people of P'ingyüan were wounded by mistake. I memorialized the Throne, impeaching the officer for the mistake committed. The rioters then went to Ch'ihping and a battalion of soldiers from the brigade general's and Taotai's forces were despatched to suppress them. This was done. The Boxers then passed through T'angchuang and were met by the Christians who first opened fire on them and chased and tried to capture them. The Boxers returned the attack and burned a missionary chapel. Later, on account of this affair, the Boxers again assembled together. I devised a plan to buy a clue towards the discovery of the rioters, and to accomplish this end I was not sparing in spending money. Two of the leading rioters, Chen Hung-teng [Chu Hung-têng] and a priest of the Teng Chia Ssu [temple] were arrested. At Pop'ing and Kaotang there were soldiers patrolling with stringent orders to arrest rioters. The missionary cases brought to my notice are numerous, and immediate action is always taken. Whether by day or night every effort has been put forth.

In the Yamen's telegram of the 27th November the United States Minister, Mr Conger, remarks that the Governor of Shantung 'fails to obey' and is not protecting the people, and that he is reported to have arrested and threatened the officer in charge of the troops who dispersed the rioters with severe punishment. Who made these statements? The missionaries have believed rumours without foundation of fact. I beg the Yamen will tell his Excellency Mr Conger not to listen to the one-sided statements of the missionaries, but to instruct them to restrain and keep the native Christians in order, which is important.[1]

In his memorial to the throne dated 26 December 1899 (K 25/11/24),[2] Chu Tsu-mou, an Expositor of the Hanlin Academy, stated that the Great Sword and the Boxers were not officially organized but were self-established. He went on to say that since the acquisition of Kiaochow by the Germans and their usurpation of the hinterland the Christian missions had gone beyond all bounds in their invasion of the rights of the ordinary people—so much so that the latter were increasingly joining the Boxers for protection. In the P'ingyüan affair only three or four Boxers were killed, but over a hundred innocent persons who had no part in the disturbance, including more than thirty women and children, lost their lives. Now that Yüan Shih-k'ai had gone to Shantung he must display the benevolence of the dynasty. If the officials kept the balance, the Christian churches could not coerce people into joining them.

The following day, 27 December 1899, the Imperial censor, Huang Kuei-chün, memorialized the throne on the same subject.[3] He found that the Boxers and other societies in Shantung had no wish to create disorder, but being day by day exposed to the insults and injuries of the Christian churches they were tried beyond endurance. And, with the German aggression, the Christians had become even bolder and more demanding. Now that Chu Hung-têng and his followers had been captured it ought to be easy to pacify the remainder of the sect. The Boxers were hand in glove with the militia. The dynasty should show their sympathy with them, treating the people as the foundation of society. The militia in every province were constituted to aid the regular troops in the protection of the people. Why should the Christians alone be protected? As for the P'ingyüan affair, the magistrate Chiang K'ai had been guilty of an error of judgment in the first place, and Yüan Shih-tun had followed this up by reckless firing. Yüan Shih-tun, the censor pointed out, was Yüan-Shih-k'ai's younger brother, but he hinted that this should not prevent him being dealt with according to his deserts.

Yüan Shih-k'ai, in his telegram to Peking dated 5 January 1900 (K 25/12/5), was careful to say that although the first priority was to disperse the Boxers, he would be careful to discriminate between the guilty and the innocent. He made a discreet reference to the military officer who has been charged with acting with excessive severity ('like savage waves') but did not mention that he was his own younger brother and he was careful to delegate the disposal of his case to others.

Yü-hsien's influence made itself felt at the right psychological moment. His appointment as governor of Shantung had itself marked a stiffening of policy towards the Powers under the pressure of the victorious reactionaries; now his advice was to decide the Court in favour of lenience towards the Boxers. T'zŭ Hsi was bent on de-throning the Kuang Hsü emperor for his part in the plot to remove her from power in 1898, but she had been thwarted by the action of the Diplomatic Body, led by the British Minister. On 13 October 1898 Sir Claude MacDonald had conveyed semi-officially to the Tsungli Yamen his firm conviction that, should the Emperor die at this juncture of affairs, the effect produced among the Western nations would be most disastrous to China.[1] The Empress Dowager and her advisers hesitated in their course and eventually contented themselves (for the time being) with having Prince P'u Chün, the son of Prince Tuan, set up as heir apparent on 24 January 1900. But this setback to their plans only made T'zŭ Hsi and the reactionary party more anti-foreign than ever. The policy of the Court hovered between suppression and pacifi-cation of the Boxers until the turn of events brought the government forces and the main body of the Boxers under a single standard (June 1900). The setback they received at P'ingyüan and the execution of their principal leaders made the Boxers, for their part, more willing to adopt the 'pro-dynastic' line. Nevertheless, as we shall see, the parent sect from which they had sprung, including, no doubt, many of the sup-porters of Chu Hung-têng, remained faithful to the traditionally anti-dynastic aims of the 'White Lotus'.

CHAPTER X

'PRO-DYNASTIC' OR 'ANTI-DYNASTIC'? II

The correspondence summarized in the last chapter would seem to establish that the Boxers in 1899 consisted both of out-and-out anti-Manchu rebels and of ordinary people who had joined the sect as a rallying-point against the universally hated foreigner. The motive of the first element was to remove the Ch'ing and the foreigner simultaneously, and of the latter to remove the foreigner purely and simply. The out-and-out rebels the local mandarins would obviously have to suppress; the others might be brought under control by absorbing them into the militia or *Pao-chia* (as proposed by Chang Ju-mei). The question was how to discriminate between the two kinds of Boxer. Those of Li Ping-hêng's and Yü-hsien's school of thought clearly believed that this could be effectively done, and that the widespread resentment against intolerable economic and social conditions could be diverted from the government and directed exclusively against the foreigner. On the other hand, mandarins of Yüan Shih-k'ai's school of thought saw the grave danger of allowing any popular direct action which might easily get out of hand and would almost certainly be diverted against the Manchus and the mandarinate once the rebels were powerful enough.

At least a section of the movement was anti-government as shown by some of the Boxer posters even after the Boxers in general were definitely committed to the support of the dynasty. Here is one which is not precisely dated, but presumably belongs to the early months of 1900:

The Chinese Empire has been celebrated for its sacred teaching. It explained heavenly truth and human duties, and its civilizing influence spread as an ornament over rivers and mountains. But in an unaccountable manner all this has been changed. For the past five or six generations bad officials have been in office, bureaus have been opened for the sale of offices, and only those who have money to pay for it have been allowed to hold positions in the Government. The graduation of scholars has become useless, and members of the College of Literature (Hanlin Academy) and scholars of the third degree remain in obscurity at home. An official position can be obtained as the price of silver. The Emperor covets the riches of his Ministers, these again extort from the lower ranks of the mandarinate, and the lower mandarins in turn (by the necessity of their position) must extort from the people. The whole populace is sunk in wretchedness, and all the officials are the spoilers of their food. The condition of the yamens is unspeakable....The officials must be bribed...lawsuits are unnumbered...there is no one to whom the aggrieved may appeal. Now in their anger the heavenly powers are sending down multitudes of spirits to earth to make enquiry of all, both high and low. The Emperor himself, the chief offender, has had his succession cut off and is childless. The whole Court, both civil and military, is in an unspeakable condition. They indulge blindly in mere amusement, and disregard the cry of the widow, repenting of nothing, and learning nothing good.... Greater calamities still have overtaken the nation. Foreign devils come with their teaching, and converts to Christianity have become numerous. These [churches] are without human relations, and being most cunning have attracted all the greedy and covetous as converts, and to an unlimited degree they have practised oppression until every good official has been corrupted, and, covetous of foreign wealth, has become their servant....[1]

According to Lao Nai-hsüan, the Boxers of 1899 were above all nationalists and isolationists. Here is a summary of what he says regarding them.

The Boxer leaders declared that their object was solely to oppose foreigners and Christianity, and that they would never cause any disturbance among peaceable people or against the government and the officials. Thus it was in areas where the Christians and the ordinary people were hostile to one another that the non-Christians were finally misled and induced to support the movement. They were impressed by the righteous indignation of the Boxers against the common enemy, and disregarded the Boxers' dependence on magic and their use of incantations. Even the government officials undertook no investigations into their activities and issued no prohibitions against them. Indeed, some of the latter went so far as to applaud the Boxers as patriots and righteous people. The Boxers' claim, however, that they practised boxing solely as a means of self-defence was merely a cover for their exercise of the ritual boxing of the *Pa Kua* sect.

The secret of their plot to rebel against the dynasty (said Lao Nai-hsüan) and the mysteries of their cult were known only to a few of the principal leaders. Not only were outsiders kept in complete ignorance of these things, but so were also the majority of those who were inducted into the movement. In consequence of this, evil-doers who saw an opportunity for mischief or gain joined the ranks of the Boxers, besides ordinary credulous members of the public. Thus the Boxer ranks contained gentry and members of rich official families as well as poor and desperate characters.

The great mass of the people (Lao went on) had now come to believe in the Boxers and called them the *I Min Hui* (Society of the Righteous), regarding them as representatives of justice and not of evil. Last year (1898) a committee in Shantung had investigated their activities and had reported that the purpose of their pugilism was simply to protect themselves and their property. Their skill in boxing (the committee said) was excellent. Hitherto they had caused no trouble in spite of their growing strength and influence in the community. They respected the *I Ch'i* (Principle of Righteousness) and always manifested a frank and open disposition. When they saw any injustice they at once attempted to remedy it, even at the risk of their own lives. So (the committee concluded) if by any means their energies could be directed to serve the public interest, giving their courage a proper outlet, one could expect them to be of considerable use in a national emergency. The committee's report (said Lao) was proof that the Boxers were regarded as fundamentally sound by Government officials.[1]

The aim of the Boxers (according to Lao) was to 'Support the Chinese Dynasty; destroy the Foreign Religion' (*Fu Chung Ch'ao; Mieh Yang Chiao*).[2] *Chung* is 'Chinese' (the 'Middle Kingdom'); Ch'ao means a 'dynasty', but, unlike the slogan 'support the Ch'ing', which is specific, it is a little vague as to which Chinese dynasty was to be supported.

I would now call attention to two biographical entries in *IHT* which are of considerable importance to our inquiry. They relate to two outstanding Boxer leaders of the earlier stages of the uprising, namely Chu Hung-têng and Li Lai-chung.[3]

Of Chu Hung-têng the first entry says that his origins were uncertain. Some said that he came from the village of Lichiachuang in the Ch'angch'ing district. His surname and other names were alike uncertain. In the 25th year of Kuang Hsü (1899) he appeared under the standard of *Fan Ch'ing Mieh Yang* ('Overthrow the Ch'ing; Destroy the Foreigner'), and gathered round him a crowd of followers at P'ingyüan in Shantung. His assumed title (*hao*) was 'Heavenly Dragon'.[4] The people followed him in large numbers and burnt churches and killed foreigners. In the seventh month (6 August–4 September 1899) they defied the government army in the Ling district. In the ninth month (5 October–2 November 1899) they were again in revolt, and this time their operations extended into Chuang-p'ing, Ch'angch'ing, etc. (near P'ingyüan). Chu's followers now numbered about 8000. The authorities of the Ên district reported the emergency to the governor of Shantung who sent Yüan Shih-tun with a force of cavalry and infantry to stop him. In the subsequent action at Senlotien both sides suffered considerable losses, but Chu rallied his followers only to be defeated at Chuangp'ing by General Ma T'ung-ling, who captured him by a stratagem and sent him to Chinan. The governor, Yü-hsien, then put him in prison. His fate, however, was not yet decided, but in the eleventh month (3–31 December 1899), Yüan Shih-k'ai replaced Yü-hsien, being appointed acting governor, and on 24 December 1899 (K 25/11/22) Chu Hung-têng was executed.[1]

The second entry relates to one Li Lai-chung. Li came from Shansi and was said to be a sworn-brother of Tung Fu-hsiang (the Kansu Muslim general). He was of a mercurial and gregarious temperament. At the time of his birth his mother dreamt of a spirit-dragon. He was deeply trusted by the local people, and exploited this to gather a band of followers to overthrow the Ch'ing. Then he heard that Yü-hsien was resentful of the foreigners so he led his band into Shantung where they joined the rebel leader, Wang Chan. Li then adopted Wang's ritual of magic and incantations and people came in crowds from near and far to join them. The governor, Yü-hsien, who wanted to make use of the I Ho Ch'üan against the foreigners, often sent them presents of beer, wine and weapons. Then, all of a sudden, the slogan *Fu Ch'ing Mieh Yang* ('Support the Ch'ing; Destroy the Foreigner') was heard in unison from 10,000 mouths. Li thereupon secretly returned to Shansi to propagate this new idea, but he failed in his purpose. When the army of the Eight Allied Powers entered Tientsin and moved towards Peking, Li joined Li Ping-hêng's troops. When they reached Peich'iang, however, their resistance crumbled, and no one knows what became of Li Lai-chung after this.

It happens that a slogan very similar to the one mentioned by Lao Nai-hsüan and belonging to the same period is recorded by A. H. Smith. He says:

During the early part of the eighth moon (5 September–4 October 1899) there began to be talk of a general rising on the part of the I Ho T'uan in that region [Hsiaochang, about 50 miles south-west of Techou on the Grand Canal], as well as in Shantung over the border. They were said to be about to act on the motto of their flag, 'Protect the Empire; exterminate foreigners'.[2]

I now come to the earliest reference to the slogan 'Support the Ch'ing; Destroy the Foreigner' that I have been able to trace so far in a Chinese source. It occurs in 'A Record of Religious Cases of Tung-p'ing' (*Tungp'ing Chiao-an Chi*), by Liu T'ang, the Prefect of Tung-p'ing at the time, under the date of 23 September 1899 (K25/8/19). Liu says:

I received written instructions from the Governor Yü-hsien in which he says, 'I have just received a letter from the assistant bishop(?) T'ao-wan-li [a foreign missionary] in which he states that in several villages of the Tungp'ing Prefecture there is disorder, and the slogan of the mob is, "Support the Ch'ing; destroy the foreigner"' (*Fu Ch'ing Mieh Yang*)....[1]

Then Chih Pi-hu, in his *Hsü I Ho T'uan Yüan Liu K'ao* (1901),[2] says that after Chu Hung-têng and his friend the Ming Monk Yang and their followers had been defeated and wiped out, a few detachments from Tungp'ing, etc., escaped over the border into Chihli and joined up with a turbulent rascal named Wang Ch'ing-i and together they exploited their magic in battle with the Christians and burnt their houses. The officials were ineffective and, treating the rebels as 'righteous people', neglected to bring out the military against them. Thereupon the rebels, calling themselves 'spirit-soldiers', created a square flag on which was incribed, 'Support the Ch'ing; destroy the foreigner'; thus adopting a loyal aim. It will be noted that the appearance, or first adoption, of this slogan is put *after* the defeat of Chu Hung-têng in October 1899.

From early in 1900 onwards there are scores of references to the slogan, either in this form or with *pao* (protect) substituted for *fu* (support) as the first character. Occasionally the character *fu* with the 'chariot' radical and the 'begin' phonetic, with much the same meaning, is substituted for the usual *fu* with the 'hand' radical.

Contemporary Chinese historians, with the exception of Jerome Ch'ên, do not appear to have paid close attention to this very important question of the process of transformation of the Boxers from an 'anti-' to a 'pro-dynastic' movement, but the communist historian, Fan Wên-lan, makes a statement on the subject of the first appearance of the slogan just referred to, which we are bound to consider carefully. He says:

As a result of the fighting with the Government forces, the I Ho T'uan was transformed from a secret, underground organization which was afraid of being known to the Government, into an open and legitimate society. At first, the Shantung I Ho Ch'üan leader, Chu Hung-têng, a man of Ts'aochou, claimed to be a descendant of the Ming Imperial House and in his rebellion aimed at 'overthrowing the Ch'ing in order to restore the Ming' (*Fan Ch'ing Fu Ming*)....In order to attract more people into the ranks of the I Ho Ch'üan Chu Hung-têng changed the slogan to 'Support the Ch'ing; Destroy the Foreigner' (*Fu Ch'ing Mieh Yang*), with the result that the movement went from strength to strength. At that time, Yü-hsien was unable to cope with the situation. Fortunately for him, Nala [the Empress Dowager] issued a decree after the 1898 Reform which authorized the setting up of local militia units. Yü-hsien seized upon this as an opportunity to give the name I Ho T'uan to the I Ho Ch'üan thereby recognizing the I Ho Ch'üan formations as official militia units.[1]

A European writer who ventures to question the statements of a Chinese authority must do so with considerable diffidence, but it is obvious that the above was written before the documents published in *IHTTA* were available. If Yü-hsien gave the I Ho Ch'üan the title I Ho T'uan, then it must have been before May 1898 (which is unlikely), and from the extracts we have given from the *IHT* (1951) above it seems quite clear that it was not Chu Hung-têng who abandoned his anti-dynastic slogan for the pro-dynastic one. And, in any event, at what moment (we may ask) is Yü-hsien supposed to have seized the opportunity offered by the decree?

The authorities in *IHT*, however, seem to be united in agreeing that it was Yü-hsien who changed the name of the I Ho Ch'üan to I Ho T'uan. Liu Mêng-yang, for example, the author of an account of the Boxers in Tientsin (1901) states:

In the winter of the 25th year of Kuang Hsü [1899], the rebels rose in the prefectures of Chinan and T'aian in Shantung. They called themselves the I Ho Shen Ch'üan [I Ho Spirit Boxers], and their aim was to fight the Roman Catholics and the Protestants. They adopted 'Support the Ch'ing; Destroy the Foreigner' as their slogan, and many suffering from oppression were attracted to their ranks. When he learnt of their existence, the Governor, Yü-hsien, challenged them, saying, 'If gods and men are inspired by a single aim, the foreigners will certainly be destroyed'. Because he disliked their name as being unrefined, he changed it to I Ho T'uan.[2]

Let us see what more Fan Wên-lan has to say on the subject:

In Chihli, the headquarters of the I Ho T'uan was at Tamingfu in the south-east....The I Ho T'uan was a conglomeration of secret sects with no agreed programme or doctrine, and therefore it was practically impossible for it to have a paramount leader or any real unity. These sects agreed, however, on 'Destroying Foreigners', but disagreed as to 'Supporting the Ch'ing'.

Roughly speaking, there were three different opinions with regard to the latter aim, namely anti-Ch'ing (*Fan Ch'ing*), supporting the Ch'ing (*Fu Ch'ing*), and preserving the Ch'ing (*Pao Ch'ing*). The 'supporting' and 'preserving the Ch'ing' groups were inspired by the Manchu nobility; the 'anti-Ch'ing' groups belonged to White Lotus. The 'white' I Ho T'uan upheld the White Lotus orthodoxy....The name of the leader of the latter group is unknown, and the group remained semi-secret throughout the uprising.[1]

The support-the-Ch'ing group, the Chu Hung-têng branch, was the first to put forward the slogan, 'Support the Ch'ing; Destroy the Foreigner'. After Chu's death this branch developed its strength in Chihli under the leadership of Li Lai-chung, Chang Teh-ch'êng, and Ts'ao Fu-t'ien...(for the above information see *Ch'üan Fei Chi Shih*).[2]

Later on Fan Wên-lan speaks of the situation as it developed after the entry of the allied troops into Peking and the flight of the Empress Dowager:

Nala (the Empress Dowager) began to flatter the allied troops by killing the Boxers after her exodus from Peking. Ching T'ing-pin [the Boxer leader] then proposed a new slogan for the Boxers, namely, 'Sweep away the Ch'ing; destroy the foreigner', and established an anti-Manchu I Ho T'uan in the Kuangtsung and Chülu Districts of Chihli in 1901. In passing from 'supporting' to 'sweeping away', the I Ho Ch'üan had, in fact, re-covered its original nature.[3]

It is not possible to accept Chu Hung-têng as being the person who changed the slogan from 'anti-' to 'pro-Ch'ing' for the reasons already given. If his supporters had carried a pro-Ch'ing banner at the time of the P'ingyüan affray Chiang K'ai would certainly have mentioned it, but as it is he refers only to 'two small red flags' carried by the leading files of Chu's followers, and these were undoubtedly the religious banners of the First Division of the *Pa Kua* sect, and not political ones. Moreover, Chiang K'ai is careful to mention the *Fu Ch'ing Mieh Yang* slogan only on the hearsay evidence of an Italian priest.

But the identity of the Boxer chief who first adopted the pro-Manchu slogan is of less importance than the date of its appearance for the first time. That it was closely associated with Yü-hsien there can be no doubt at all, and he may even have invented it. It has a somewhat synthetic air about it. Even after its adoption by the Boxers it was never fully integrated with the Boxer programme. The collection of fifteen Boxer placards and incantations in *IHT* has only two items which contain any reference to the ruling dynasty.[1] One (p. 150) speaks of the 'heterodox creed (Christianity) excessively oppressing our great Ch'ing dynasty', and the second (p. 151) refers to 'the more than two hundred years' rule of *Ta Ch'ing*'. But the notices generally (when they are not actually anti-government, as in the one quoted earlier) are concerned with the religious side of the movement, with appeals to the Jade emperor, to Buddhas, to the Goddess of Mercy, and other supernatural beings. The mention of the Ch'ing suggests an afterthought.

Ch'ai O, in *Kêng Hsin Chi-shih* (A Recollection of the Years 1900 and 1901),[2] writing of the spring of 1900, refers to the divided counsels at Court. The Empress Dowager wanted to get rid of the Kuang Hsü emperor and to install a successor in his place, but was frustrated by the opposition of the foreign Ministers. The Boxer bandits at this time had the two characters *Mieh Yang* (Destroy the Foreigner) on their flag, but 'they received a secret Imperial Decree instructing them to add the two further characters *Fu ch'ing* (Support the Ch'ing dynasty) to these, and the consequence would be an access of power like a billow rising to heaven'.

There can be no doubt that at the time the Boxer slogan was authorized in its final form by the Court, but *Mieh Yang* had never, it seems, appeared as a separate device, and the full slogan had been recorded at least as early as the previous September.

I now come to a piece of evidence which does not fit in at all well with that from the Chinese sources.

P. Remy Isoré, S.J., who was stationed at Tchao-kia-tchuang (in south-western Shantung—Ts'ao-chia-chuang in the Wade–Giles romanization), recorded in his journal as follows:

Wednesday, 25 October 1898. At ten [six in Steiger] o'clock this morning I was informed of the uprising of the *Ihonokinen* (a hostile sect). These rebels have as their insignia a sort of turban and boots; their weapons are muskets or lances; their ensign, a yellow flag with a black border, carrying the motto, 'Obedience to the Tsing; Death to the Europeans'; their object, to provoke a general revolution at the beginning of the year; in the meantime to recruit, to drill, and to conciliate the officials by attacking only the Christians.[3]

Father Isoré also contributed a postscript to a letter from Father A. Wetterwald (at Weitsun) to the editor of *Chine et Ceylan*, published in that journal (p. 215—Steiger, p. 171), in which he says: 'Two or three individuals were put in prison or in the cangue; and thereupon ensued a sauve-qui-peut among our brave *Shokiun*; they believed that the moment had come when they were to pay for their audacious exploit of last November.'

Steiger thinks that *Kinen* (in Ihonokinen) is a misprint for *K'iuen*, the French form of *Ch'üan*—and he is almost certainly right. The 'Ihonokinen' are therefore the Boxers. (What the *no* in the middle of the word represents is not clear.) The *Shokiun* are also the Boxers. In this *K'iuen* is more correctly spelt. (*Sho* is probably a misprint for *I ho*.)

So here we have evidence of the appearance of the standard slogan of the crisis period, *Fu Ch'ing Mieh Yang*—nearly a year before we should expect to see it! The evidence certainly calls for close scrutiny.

It happens that 25 October 1898 was not on a Wednesday (as given in the reproduction of Father Isoré's journal in *Chine et Ceylan*), but a Tuesday. Since 25 October 1899 (the more likely year) *was* on a Wednesday, one is tempted to jump to the conclusion that a mistake of a year has been made in the date, but the succeeding entries in the journal are attributed to the correct days of the week, and the fact that the journal appeared within a month or two rules out this explanation. We could, of course, suppose Father Isoré to have made a mistake in recording the slogan (as he did make one in recording the exact name of the I Ho Ch'üan) or to have been gifted with prophetic vision—but these explanations are unlikely, though his evidence is not confirmed from any other source either Chinese or foreign. We must assume it to be possible, then, that as early as 25 October 1898, at least one band of Boxers was experimenting with the idea of an alliance with the reigning dynasty. However, even if this evidence is accepted, there is no reason to depart from what we have already established—namely that the I Ho Ch'üan was composed of several different elements and that the pro-dynastic ones obtained an ascendancy over the others only after the P'ingyüan setback to the 'pro-Ming' leadership, and that the developments at Court made 'Support the Ch'ing; destroy the foreigner' the only slogan which promised success, and was therefore adopted by most of the surviving Boxer leaders. The exceptions were the adherents to the White Lotus who remained pro-Ming and anti-Ch'ing.

There can be no doubt that the Boxers originated spontaneously and independently of the government and that they belonged to the secret societies (*Hui T'ang*) and heterodox cults (*Chiao Mên*) which had always been looked upon by the government as centres of revolutionary danger. They organized on their own and drilled with arms, and they intervened in disputes between farmers and converts or landlords and foreigners, taking no account of the Ch'ing Penal Code, which had proved quite ineffectual in countering the invasion of foreign power. They had established a patriarchal order of their own with a precedence of *Ta Shih Hsiung* (Eldest Teacher-Brother), *Êrh Shih Hsiung* (Second Teacher-Brother), etc. These facts are sufficient to establish that the Boxers belonged to the traditional Chinese secret and revolutionary societies and, as such, competed with the authority of the established government.

Ichiko agrees with Lao Nai-hsüan in regarding the Boxers as a branch of the White Lotus or *Pa Kua* sect, and as a group that was potentially dangerous to the Manchu government, but is of the opinion that the Boxers and the government were hostile to one another from the beginning and that there could therefore be no connection at all between the I Ho T'uan and the village militia since they had opposing aims. Muramatsu does not accept this opinion. He points out that Chang Ju-mei, in his memorial of May 1898, had declared his intention of including the Boxers in the *Hsiang T'uan* and that, moreover, the decree of 6 June 1900 (K 26/5/10) says: 'Recently the I Ho Ch'uan have guarded their persons and their villages with skill, demonstrating a talent for self-defence that has never caused any trouble heretofore.'[1]

The decree of 29 June 1900 (Muramatsu says) blames the officials for the spread of the Boxer movement, thus confirming that there was no initial disagreement between the Boxers and the authorities. It runs:

Before this there was a species of rebel (*Luan Min*) in Shantung and Chihli who were training in boxing and the use of the quarter-staff in each village, and to this they added a mysterious doctrine. Owing to the negligence of the local officials in investigation and observation they then embarked on an agitation which spread over a wide area in a short space of time and eventually reached Peking itself.[2]

But these two last decrees relate to a late period, long after the switch of the Boxers to the support of the dynasty, and from the evidence available to date it seems that Ichiko's theory is nearer to the facts than is Muramatsu's in this particular respect.

Foreign writers such as A. H. Smith and H. B. Morse have insisted that there was an intimate connection between the Boxers and the government, but they had no real knowledge of the history of the movement prior to the time when it was diverted from its original objectives. A. H. Smith says:

If Yü Hsien had done his duty as the Governor of a great and populous province for the welfare of which he was responsible, that Society would have been put down by simply following up the crushing defeat which the Boxers had met at the village of Sen Le Tien. The fact that he repudiated the success which his troops had won, and threw away its results, could only be accounted for upon the supposition that he had good reasons for his conduct, and in China no better reason for any act can be assigned than that it is commanded by the Throne.[1]

Opinions regarding the Boxers written before the appearance of the recent collections of documents are liable to be 'dated', but those of Sheeks and de Groot deserve at least a passing mention. Sheeks accepts the statement of the *Ch'ing Shih Kao* which states that it was Yü-hsien who changed the name of the I Ho Ch'üan to I Ho T'uan, but holds, as against Steiger, that major clashes of the sort that took place at P'ingyüan would not be likely to have occurred between the regular troops and an authorized militia—which certainly has force.[2] J. J. M. de Groot's view of the Boxers (a contemporary one) is interesting as demonstrating the lengths to which even a scholar conversant with the original sources will go in attempting to substantiate a pet theory of his own. De Groot's theory was that the Chinese government had always been intolerant in matters of religion (a proposition which was the direct opposite of the one to which he had himself subscribed for most of his career in China). The Imperial authorities, he holds, were bent on suppressing *all* unorthodox sects, and the Boxers and the Christians were in fact co-victims of the Manchus. He quotes the opinion of the Prefect of Wuch'iao, recorded by Ignace Mangin, a Jesuit priest who was afterwards killed by the Boxers, that the Boxers were nothing more or less than a ramification of the White Lotus sect which had been persecuted in the Chia Ch'ing reign, but since at that time there was little Christianity in China, the sect therefore could not have been the outcome of hatred against the Christians. 'After this [comments de Groot] it is certainly hardly possible to believe in the alleged conspiracy between the Boxers and the Chinese Government against the foreigners. Confucian patriotism co-operating with heresy. Mice with the cat! It is rather ludicrous.'[3] Nevertheless, the 'Mice and the Cat', did co-operate for a period in a way which alarmed the world.

'The Boxers' slogan of "Upholding the Ch'ing and exterminating the foreigners" caught the imagination of the people', says Chester Tan. This is unquestionably true, but it did not take place until some time after their general adoption of the slogan. We are concerned here to pin-point the change-over from 'anti-dynastic' to 'pro-dynastic' as precisely as possible. Jerome Ch'ên gives reasons for believing that the P'ingyüan affair marked the moment when the support of the reigning dynasty was first adopted as the aim of the movement. He writes:

Generally speaking, the officials in the Court were in favour of a compromise which was eventually achieved. The reason I say that the compromise came after Chu Hung-têng's arrest and the 'Ming Monk's' disappearance is that they were the last of a series of arrests and executions. Chronologically, this coincided with the change of policy of the Ch'ing Court and should also synchronize with a change in the Boxers' political aims if we grant their leaders a normal share of political alertness.[1]

This judgment is, I feel, correct, and it is from this time that we must date the beginnings of the ascendancy of that element of the Boxers which decided to throw in their lot with the Manchus.

Knowing that the Boxers consisted of diverse factions, it would be a matter of surprise if all of them unanimously accepted this change of aim. A majority, perhaps, whose basic inspiration was to get rid of the foreigner, would find no great difficulty in accepting the Emperor as their new ally in achieving this end, but the real revolutionaries could scarcely be expected to acquiesce willingly in the abandonment of their purpose to restore the Ming. We know, however, that they were not united or powerful enough to continue their original movement on their own, and we might even be tempted to doubt their continued organized existence, were it not for the recent researches of Jerome Ch'ên who has shown from the evidence of a new collection of Boxer documents that not only did the old White Lotus continue to exist throughout the crisis but became the object of the pro-Manchu Boxers' wrath when the latter were being defeated by the allied troops in the late summer of 1900.

One piece of evidence is an extract from a diary of one Shih Chung-fang, which runs: 'On the 29th day, 6th month [25 July 1900], more than seventy men and women of the White Lotus Sect were executed by the Boxers at Ts'ai Shih K'ou [Greengrocers' Market in Peking].'[2] And again: 'On the 6th day, 7th month [31 July 1900], more than thirty men were killed at Ts'ai Shih K'ou.'[3]

Another diarist, one Yang Tien-kao, writes:

On the 19th day, 6th month [15 July 1900] there were executions at the Greengrocers' Market. The victims were men and women of different ages, altogether seventy-eight of them. Earlier, the I Ho T'uan had issued a statement saying that when they had 'burnt a church they had discovered paper-men and horses as well as a list of names of members of the White Lotus Sect. The Sect conspired with the Roman Catholics to revolt on the 15th of the 8th month [8 September 1900]. Arrests were subsequently made according to the list. Altogether seventy-eight were arrested.[1]

The diary of another person, one Kao Nan, gives a similar description of the incident of 15 July, but in somewhat greater detail.

Another diarist (who is, however, anonymous) has the following: 'On the first day of the 7th month [26 July 1900], I stayed overnight at an inn in P'ingyangfu. At midnight, I heard Boxers and armed men shouting in the street and searching for the followers of the White Lotus Sect.'[2]

With its very long history, the White Lotus (or White Lily) sect is mentioned scores of times in the Chinese histories, but after the great revolutionary outbreaks with which it was associated during the reign of Chia Ch'ing, it disappears from the official documents, though many other sects, such as the Great Sword and the Boxers, are stated to be offshoots of its parent stem. But there could be little doubt that it was continuing to exist underground, and these diaries of ordinary people are not unexpected places in which to find renewed mention of it. The alliance between White Lotus and Roman Catholics is, however, somewhat more surprising, and was probably due to the fact that they were fellow victims of the Boxers and therefore the allies of the moment. It has, however, been suggested to me by a Chinese friend that the alliance may also have been due to the strain of Manichaeism still alive in the White Lotus which connected it eventually with orthodox Christianity. (St Augustine was a Manichee before his conversion, and Chu Yüan-chang, the founder of the Ming dynasty, is also said to have adhered to the remnants of that religion.) But this, I confess, brings us into the realms of pure speculation.

Jerome Ch'ên divides the development of the Boxer movement into three stages.[3] In the first stage the sole object of the Boxers was to exterminate the foreigners ('When the foreigners are wiped out, rain will fall and visitations cease').[4] 'The Roman Catholic and Protestant churches deceive our gods, destroy our belief in the saints, and repudiate the precepts of Buddha. Consequently we are assailed by famine and other afflictions.'[1] Only after the setback to their cause late in 1899 did the Boxers adopt their slogan of 'Support the Ch'ing; Destroy the Foreigner'. In the third stage they added to their programme the aim of 'protecting the people', taking over this duty, in fact, from the bureaucracy which had failed to fulfil it. Throughout (says Mr Ch'ên) they manifested a strong distrust of the ability of the officials to repel foreign interference in China and at heart they were always more 'anti' than 'pro' the Manchu government.

And this, I am sure, is a fair assessment.

CHAPTER XI

BOXER BELIEFS AND ORGANIZATION

The great mass of the Boxers were illiterate or semi-literate at most, but they were essentially 'Chinese' and their outlook was part and parcel of the Chinese ethos. This outlook they derived to some extent from tradition and to some extent from the ideas which percolated through to them from the literati. But since few of them (the exceptions being the scholar-recruits to their cause) had any direct access to, say, the *Chung Yung* or the *Tao Tê Ching*, from what sources then did the majority of them derive their ideas of the sages? The answer seems to be—from popular novels and plays.[1]

In the China of this period, Confucianism (or rather neo-Confucianism) was the orthodoxy of the educated, while the practice of the other religions was generally left to the people at large. In the minds of the peasantry, their ethical judgments were mainly Confucian, while matters of divine guidance, reward and retribution, the after-life, and immortality belonged to the other religions. But the several spheres were by no means clearly separated. The common people derived their interpretation of these faiths less from the literati and the priests than they did from tradition as disseminated by the popular novels and the operas based on them. During the second half of the nineteenth century the output of the latter increased by leaps and bounds. They offered an escape from the ugly facts of life in general and from national humiliation in particular.

The religious ideas of the Boxers can be traced back from their incantations and ritual to novels and operas such as *The Romance of the Three Kingdoms* (*San Kuo Chih Yen I*), *The Water Margin* (*Shui Hu*), *Pilgrimage to the West* (*Hsi Yu Chi*), *The Enfeoffment of the Gods* (*Fêng Shên Yen I*), *Prefect P'êng's Cases* (*P'êng Kung An*), *Prefect Shih's Cases* (*Shih Kung An*), etc., etc. The last two named were of especial importance as referring to the province of Shantung where the Boxer troubles started. The harmonious triangular alliance of Confucianism, Taoism, and Buddhism, for example, is the main theme of *The Enfeoffment of the Gods* in which the Three Religions score a resounding victory over heresy (the 'heresy' in question being, of course, Christianity). As Mr Ch'ên says:

This and other novels also furnished them with the names of the gods, with the sources of magic powers, and suggested to them their hierarchy in the celestial world, just as modern thrillers give ideas to would-be law-breakers. ...Frequent repetition of propaganda of this kind would certainly lead the uncritical mind to believe in the impossible and the fictitious.

A number of the incantations, songs, etc., of the Boxers are reproduced in *IHT*. For example, a divine rhyme said to be composed in Peking on 17 July 1900, by the demi-god Chi Kung (the hero of three novels published in the Ch'ing dynasty) stated the Boxer aims concisely. It runs:

> There are many Christian converts
> Who have lost their senses,
> They deceive our Emperor,
> Destroy the gods we worship,
> Pull down their temples and altars,
> Permit neither joss-sticks nor candles,
> Cast away tracts on ethics,
> And ignore reason.
> Don't you realize that
> Their aim is to engulf the country?
>
> No talented people are in sight;
> There is nothing but filth and garbage,
> Rascals who undermine the Empire,
> Leaving its doors wide open.
> But we have divine power at our disposal
> To arouse our people and arm them,
> To save the realm and to protect it from decay.
> Our pleasure is to see the Son of Heaven unharmed.
> Let the officials perish,
> But the people remain invincible.
> Bring your own provisions;
> Fall in to remove the scourge of the country.[1]

The public notices of the Boxers also declared these aims. Here are three examples:

We support the Ch'ing regime and aim to wipe out foreigners; let us do our utmost to defend our country and safeguard the interests of our peasants.
    Protect our country, drive out foreigners, and kill Christians.
    The heresy [Christianity] has no respect for either gods or Buddhas. It does not allow the burning of joss-sticks; nor does it obey the Buddhist

precepts. Its followers are arrogant towards our great Ch'ing Empire...the Buddhist I Ho T'uan on the other hand can defend the country and deliver our people from suffering.[1]

These aims were faithfully echoed in the Ch'ing Government's declaration of war of 21 June 1900:

The foreigners have been aggressive towards us, infringed upon our territorial integrity, trampled our people under their feet....They oppress our people and blaspheme our gods. The common people suffer greatly at their hands, and each one of them is vengeful. Thus it is that the brave followers of the I Ho T'uan have been burning churches and killing Christians.[2]

Among contemporary interpretations of the name I Ho T'uan were the following: 'Friends allied by their common belief in righteousness. For this reason they address one another as *Shih Hsiung* [fellow students of the same master]', and '*I* implies kindness, and *Ho*, rites. Neighbours should be kind and polite to one another. They should uphold the basic moral principles, pursue farming as their avocation, and obey the Buddhist doctrines. They must not allow personal antagonism to interfere with their public duties; they must not oppress the poor, bully the weak, or regard right as wrong.'[3]

That 'the foreigner' was the source of all the ills from which China was suffering, and was the primary, if not the sole, enemy to be obliterated, the people who read the Boxer notices were not to be allowed to forget. For example, 'When the foreigners are wiped out, rain will fall and visitations disappear.'[4]

A Boxer notice posted in T'aiyüan in July 1900 said: 'The Roman Catholic and Protestant churches deceive our gods, destroy our belief in the Sages, and disobey the precepts of Buddha—hence the famine and other disasters.'[5]

To disseminate their propaganda, the Boxers resorted to the 'chain letter' method, prophesying retribution to those who failed to pass on the message: 'If you do not pass on this message from Buddha, you will not be able to escape unnatural death. If, on the other hand, you copy this once and give it to another man, your family will be safe. If you copy it ten times and hand the copies to others, your whole village will be safe....'[6]

The gods whom the Boxers worshipped and the incantations they recited varied from place to place. All of them came from the popular novels. From *The Romance of the Three Kingdoms* came Liu Pei, Kuan Yü (the God of War), Chang Fei, Chu-ke Liang, Chao Yün, etc., from *Pilgrimage to the West* came 'Monkey', the Pig, and the Êrh-lang Shên; from *Prefect P'êng's Cases* came Huang San-t'ai and Tou Êrh-tun; from *Tung Chou Lieh Kuo* came Sun Pin; from *Hsüeh Chia Chang* came Fan Li-hua, and from *The Enfeoffment of the Gods* came Lao Chün and many others. The Boxers even deified and worshipped their contemporaries such as Ch'i Chün-tsao and Li Ping-hêng, the anti-foreign ex-Governor of Shantung. When these gods manifested themselves they spoke in exactly the same way as opera actors delivered their lines.[1]

Some of the gods were Buddhist, such as Bodhidharma and Chi Kung: some were Taoist, such as Hung Chun Lao Tsŭ and Li Shan Lao Mu, and many others were historical figures like Li Po (the T'ang poet) and Huang Fei-hu ('Flying Tiger Huang'). When one of the gods entered into him, a medium was supposed to acquire certain magic powers, as, for example, those that would make him invulnerable or would enable him to block the barrels of the enemy's rifles or cannon.

In order to summon one or several of these supernatural beings to manifest himself in him, the medium had first to recite one of a number of incantations, the nature of which will in due course be described.

Once we accept the fact that the Boxers derived a great deal of their inspiration from the popular novels and operas, we should be able to obtain a fair insight into their beliefs by a study of a few of the novels and operas they particularly favoured.

The *San Kuo* (Three Kingdoms) is a historical romance, 'seven parts truth and three parts fiction', as one critic describes it, but apart from wishing to entertain, the author also had a serious purpose.[2] The novel relates to a period of nearly 100 years, from A.D. 168, when the massacre of the eunuchs heralded the downfall of the Han dynasty, to A.D. 265, when the empire was reunited by the founder of the Ch'in dynasty. This troubled and confused period is known as the Three Kingdoms, in reality an age of strife and misery, but the author, Lo Kuan-chung, transmuted it into an age of romance and chivalry. It was written in the early years of the Ming dynasty, is the first Chinese novel, and is still the most popular book in the Chinese language.

The *San Kuo* is extremely long, running to 120 chapters. Its heroes are Liu Pei, who founded the Shu Han Kingdom in Szechwan, Kuan Yü, who was later deified as Kuan Ti, the God of War, and Chang Fei. These heroes, like the chief villain of the book, Ts'ao Ts'ao (who was the first Emperor of the Wei), were historical personages. But while the chief characters and the main lines of the story follow authentic history, the author has enlivened the tale by introducing romantic and dramatic adventures which have no foundation in fact, and has arbitrarily divided his characters into the 'sheep and the goats'. Ts'ao Ts'ao, who was no more of a usurper than Liu Pei, is represented as a double-dyed villain, while Liu Pei and his two friends are put forward as models of fidelity, courage and honour.[1] But the behaviour of Chinese gods and heroes no more complies with our modern ideas of morality and fairness than do the love-affairs of Zeus or the business transactions between Jacob and Esau.

The apotheosis of the historical Kuan Yü affords an interesting case-history. He was originally known as Kuan Yü, was born in Shansi, and lived from about A.D. 160 to 220. He is said to have had to flee his home after rescuing a girl from the clutches of the local magistrate and killing the latter in the process. Later on he fell in with Chang Fei and Liu Pei, one a butcher and the other a seller of straw-shoes, and they formed a partnership, swearing everlasting friendship in the afterwards famous Peach Garden. After this, they sacrificed a black ox and a white horse to Heaven and Earth, and sealed their bond by getting drunk. Then they armed themselves to fight the Yellow Turban insurgents. Kuan Yü's conduct in the wars was decidedly equivocal. He was taken prisoner by the Prime Minister and then changed sides. (Tradition adds to the romance by stating that, coveting the wife of a certain Ting I-lu, Kuan Yü persuaded his superior to seize her and thereupon made her his own concubine.) Once more a rebel, he tried to retake the fortified city of Chingchow, failed in the attempt, and fled. He was run to earth and captured. Refusing to change sides a second time and to rejoin the Prime Minister, he was put to death.

Kuan Yü is described in Chinese legend as having been nine feet tall with a beard two feet long, his face being the colour of dark jujube and his lips rose-carmine. His eyebrows, which were like sleeping silk-worms, shaded eyes that were bloodshot like those of a phoenix. His demeanour struck terror into the hearts of all who beheld him. In A.D. 260, Liu Pei's son bestowed on him the posthumous title of 'Brave and Faithful Marquis'; in 583 he became a 'Sincere and Merciful Duke'; in 678 the Buddhists made him tutelary guardian of their monasteries at Yuchun; in 1096 a tablet was presented to his temple at Kiaochow with the inscription 'Prayer-answering Illustrious Prince'. Thereafter there was no end to his posthumous honours. The Taoists recognized his power against demons. Kuan Ti was worshipped in practically every household in China and temples were dedicated to him in many places.[1] His image was placed in the first hall of a Buddhist monastery. He was adopted as a patron-saint by various trades and professions, gradually developed into a god of wealth as well as of war, and was regarded as a god of literature besides.[2]

Kuan Yü's companion, Liu Pei, was a native of the Cho district in Chihli and was a descendant of the Emperor Ching Ti. Rising from humble circumstances as a seller of straw-shoes, he took command of a body of volunteers and fought against Ts'ao Ts'ao, and later proclaimed himself Emperor of the Shu Han (or Minor Han) dynasty, considered by Chinese official historians to be the legitimate successor of the Great Han. The third one of the trio, Chang Fei, is also credited with many romantic exploits in the wars, but at length met his death at the hands of an assassin. Like Kuan Yü, he too is described as of astounding appearance. He was said to be eight feet in height, with a head like that of a panther, round eyes, swallow-like chin, and a beard like a tiger. His voice resembled the roar of distant thunder and his impetuosity that of a runaway horse. Until A.D. 184 he had been a farmer, butcher, and wine-merchant. There is a strong democratic strain in these popular heroes.

It is worthy of note that, at one time in his career, Liu Pei was magistrate of P'ingyüan in Shantung (the scene of the clash between the Boxers and the government in October 1899), and therefore a predecessor (by some seventeen hundred years) of the unfortunate Chiang K'ai.[3]

Another novel of great popularity with the Boxers, and even more important as a source of inspiration to them, was *Water Margin* (Shui Hu) or more precisely, 'Stories of the Fringes of the Marsh'. This book in its earliest form was attributed to Lo Kuan-chung of the early Ming dynasty, but was reshaped in the first half of the sixteenth century by 'Shih Nai-an', a pseudonym concealing the identity of some scholar of the age.

If the *San Kuo* can be compared to the Morte d'Arthur of Malory (with the differences that the personages in the Chinese novel had a real recorded historical existence), the *Shui Hu* is a saga similar to the cycle of Robin Hood tales, worked up into a novel centring round the personality of Sung Chiang, a bandit leader who lived in Shantung in the last years of the Sung dynasty, immediately before the Kin [Juchên Chin] invasions (*circa* 1100).[4]

The story relates to the adventures of 108 companions of Sung Chiang, and the plot, unwinding from chapter to chapter, tells how each of these men came to 'hide in the grass' (that is, became outlaws) and to join the band on the mountain passes of Liang Shan Po. Sung Chiang is, like each member of the Peach Garden Trio, also a historical character. Throughout the book it is the bandits who are the heroes—courageous, loyal and honourable men—while the officials, ministers and princes of the Sung dynasty are uniformly represented as vile oppressors, sordid scoundrels, and degenerate cowards.

One by one the bandit heroes in the novel are driven to outlawry by the gross injustice of the officials and the cupidity of the Court: they are honest men, with no thought of crime in their heads until they suffer unbearable wrongs. But, once they are outlaws, they avenge their miseries upon the officials, over whom, and the cowardly soldiers of the government, they score easy triumphs. Hu Shih remarks that such a book could only have been produced in an age when the government was bad and weak, and is really directed, not against the Sung dynasty, which had disappeared, but against the actual Ming government of the later fifteenth and early sixteenth centuries.[1]

The *Shui Hu* is a frankly revolutionary work, and it is not surprising that the governments of the Ming, and later of the Manchu dynasty, frowned upon it. Pearl Buck, who translated *Shui Hu* into English as 'All Men are Brothers', quotes the Laws of the Ch'ing dynasty under the date March 1799, as ordering that 'all bookshops which print the licentious story *Shui Hu* should be rigorously sought out, the woodblocks and printed matter burned, and the officials who have failed to prohibit its production severely punished'.[2]

Pilgrimage to the West (Hsi Yu Chi) is quite different in tone from the other novels; its English translator says of it:

Monkey is unique in its combination of beauty and absurdity, of profundity with nonsense. Folklore, allegory, religion, history, anti-bureaucratic satire and pure poetry...the bureaucrats are the saints in Heaven, and it might be supposed that the satire was directed against religion rather than against bureaucracy. But the idea that the hierarchy in Heaven is a replica of the government on earth is an accepted one in China. Here as so often the Chinese let the cat out of the bag, where other countries leave us guessing.[3]

The story centres round the pilgrimage to India in the seventh century A.D. of an actual person, Hsüan Tsang, or Tripitaka. 'Monkey' himself was born when a rock, which since the creation of the world had been worked on by the pure essences of Heaven and the fine savours of earth, the vigour of sunlight and the grace of moonlight, at last becomes magically pregnant and one day splits open, giving birth to a stone egg about as big as a play-ball. Fructified by the wind, it develops into a stone monkey, complete in every organ and limb. The Pig, or 'Pigsy', had received a call from Kuan Yin, the Goddess of Mercy herself, and had become a Buddhist monk. He and Monkey then join Tripitaka to form a trio to go to fetch the scriptures from India. Their mission completed, they appear before the Buddha to be rewarded. Tripitaka and Monkey are made into Buddhas, but Pigsy, because (as Buddha says) 'your conversation and appearance still lack refinement and your appetite is still too large', has to be content with the job of cleaning up all the Buddhist altars where offerings are made.

Êrh-lang Shên was the Jade emperor's nephew, sent by him to arrest Monkey for his misbehaviour, and hence there ensues an epic battle between the two, both making the fullest use of their magic powers. Eventually Monkey is captured, bound, and brought to the place of execution—but escapes the supreme penalty.

Bodhidharma (Ta-Mo), yet another of the supernatural beings worshipped by the Boxers, was a Buddhist saint who fell asleep over his devotions and, on awakening, cut off his eyelids and threw them on the ground where they took root and grew into a bush, the leaves of which infused with hot water would banish sleep, namely *tea*. Huang Fei-hu (Yellow Flying Tiger) comes from the novel *Fêng Shên Yen I* ('The Enfeoffment of the Gods') and was a hero of the Legend of the Diamond Kings. This relates to the eleventh century B.C., when the Chou dynasty was consolidating its position at the expense of the Shang. The supporters of the house of Shang appealed to the Four Genii, praying them to come to their aid, which they did with an army of 100,000 spirit-soldiers, who in less than a day traversed towns, fields, and mountains from Chiamênkuan to Hsich'i (most likely the proto-types of the spirit-soldiers whom the Boxers expected to descend to their aid). At the time General Huang Fei-hu was defending Hsich'i.

So much for the traditional gods of the Boxers—or a selection of them. Among the contemporary persons who were deified by the Boxers, we recognize, of course, Li Ping-hêng. We have already en-countered him as the governor of Shantung who incurred the wrath of the Germans, and in the next chapter he will turn up again, first as the implacable enemy of the foreigner, urging the continuation of the war, and then as the defeated general who committed suicide. It was probably he, even more than Yü-hsien, who gave the Boxers their first encouragement, and it was not unnatural that they should deify him in his lifetime.

The other modern saint, Ch'i Chün-tsao (1793–1866),[1] was an official and poet. He was born in Shouyang, Shansi, the son of the historian, Ch'i Yün-shih. In 1810 he became a *chü-jên*, and in 1814 a *chin-shih*. In 1821 he was ordered to serve in the Imperial Study; in 1822 he officiated as an assistant examiner at the metropolitan examinations and then as provincial examiner in Kwangtung. After holding other appointments, in 1837 he became Vice-President of the Board of War, and from 1837 to 1840 Director of Education for Kiangsu. He was also charged with coastal defence and the suppression of opium smuggling in Fukien. This was the time when the Fukien ports were attacked by the British. During the period of conflict and tension with Great Britain, Ch'i advocated war, which was no doubt the main reason for the reverence in which he was held by the Boxers. He later became a guardian of the heir apparent, but thwarted in his policies over coinage and military matters, he retired in 1855. Ch'i was also one of the leading poets of his time.

The above is enough, I hope, to give an idea of the gods revered by the Boxers. What sort of social philosophy can they have derived from the popular novels and from the plays and operas based upon them? Nothing, it seems, of the order of Plato's *Republic*, of More's *Utopia*, or even of Erasmus's *Adagia* or *Colloquia*, though *Pilgrimage to the West* might claim some resemblance to *Candide*. And of any modern system there is, of course, not a hint. *Water Margin* is the most revolutionary in fervour of all the novels, but it would not be easy to extract a social moral from it. 'My friends are all contemptuous of high places', says the author in his Preface, but this is merely a Taoist sentiment. 'When the desire for fame is over, the heart grows languid', he goes on. 'Of all joys nothing brings more joy than friendship and the most joyful part of friendship is quiet talk together among friends.'

What we talk of is not the affairs of the nation. This is because not only do I feel it right to keep my humble position, but also because our place is far distant from affairs of state, and political news is only hearsay, and since hearsay is never true it is a waste of saliva to talk about it. Never should we talk of people's sins. Men under Heaven have no original sin [an echo of the Trimetrical Classic] and we ought not to malign them.

Oppression came from the reigning dynasty and its officials, but not all dynasties and officials were bad. After the confusion of the Five Kingdoms, there came the Sung to restore peace. The first Emperor of the Sung, the Great Conqueror, was a 'great wise man...in truth he was the God of Thunder and Lightning himself, born above into human flesh.... The Emperor indeed swept clean and washed away all evil from the Empire.... Men walked in silk robes everywhere at will.' The remedy, then, under the oppressive Ming, was to restore the Sung; under the oppressive Ch'ing, it was to restore the Ming—if there was a political remedy at all!

The magical and the supernatural figure prominently in the novels and in the incantations and slogans. Chang, the Heavenly King, Chief of the Taoists, beseeches the Gods to drive away the evil flux; the Commander Hung, in his heedlessness, frees the spirits (like so many bottle-imps); Ch'ên T'uan the Taoist hermit, a man of deep religion and great virtue, can change the winds and shape the clouds; Heaven will send down the stars of Wisdom and of War to aid the Emperor. The Boxers appealed to the Taoist Temple of Upper Cleanliness in the Mountain of Dragons, to the Halls and Temples of the North Star, to Heaven, to Earth, to Water, and to the Subjugated Magic Devils.

The 'Golden Age' presented in *Water Margin* is that of the reign of Chên Tsung (997–1022). Then the country was at peace and the harvests of the Five Grains were plentiful; the people went merrily to their work; if anything of value was dropped on the roads no one picked it up, and doors were not locked at night. Who could see, however, that joy must end and sorrow come?

What Manichaean element can be traced in White Lotus-Boxerism? The Manichaean system was one of consistent, uncompromising dualism. The physical and the ethical are not distinguished, and when Mani co-ordinates good with light, and evil with darkness, this is no mere figure of speech, but light is actually good and darkness evil. But the native Chinese world-picture was essentially different: 'Undertones of good and evil were in fact *not* present in the Chinese formulations of Yin-Yang theory. On the contrary, it was only by the attainment and maintenance of a real balance between the two equal forces that happiness, health, or good order could be achieved.'[1]

So it seems that any similarity between the systems must be sought for outside the basic assumptions of either. Certainly a reverence in common for the cross (which has been suggested as a bond of union between the orthodox White Lotus and the Roman Catholics in July 1900) was insufficient by itself to join Boxers and Christian converts. The cross was exclusively a Christian symbol in 1899–1900. A Christian either had a cross on his head invisible to a non-Boxer, or a pair of staring eyes, or his joss-sticks would not burn.[1]

Membership of the I Ho T'uan was confined to men; the parallel (and much later) organization for women was called the Hung Têng Chao (Red Lanterns). The members of both organizations were mostly peasants, but right from the beginning there were, among the rank and file, scholars, tradesmen, merchants and Buddhist monks. Among the members are mentioned also, Chang Tê-chêng, a sailor, Ts'ao Fu-t'ien, a gambler, and Huang-lien Shêng-mu (Yellow Lotus Holy Mother), the daughter of a Grand Canal boatman, who became supreme head of the Red Lanterns.[2] The great majority of the members were adolescents.

The I Ho T'uan is believed to have been divided into eight groups according to the Eight Trigrams (*Pa Kua*), but only the first and fourth, and later the second, the *Ch'ien* (Heaven), *K'an* (water), and *K'un* (earth) groups, are actually known to have been in operation. The *Ch'ien* group were identified by their use of the colour yellow—yellow banners, turbans, sashes or belts, armbands and puttees. The *Ch'ien* group were identified by their use of the colour red. In the latter stages of the movement there was also a black (*K'un*) group in Chihli, which was supposed to possess greater magical powers than the other two. Yellow was the Imperial colour of the Ch'ing dynasty, and consequently the *Ch'ien* group was higher in rank than the *K'an* group and had fewer members.

An apparent difficulty arises here regarding the relative status and the distinctive 'colour' of the various *Kung*, or 'Mansions', of the trigrams. As has been mentioned in chapter VII, deep red was the traditional colour of the *Ch'ien* trigram, of which Chu Hung-têng was undoubtedly the chief (that of the *K'an* was blood-red), and as a Pretender to the Throne he would naturally assume command of the *Kung* associated with 'King' (his style of 'dragon' is also an attribute of the *Ch'ien* trigram). Chiang K'ai describes the colour of his insignia as red. The description of 'yellow' as the Ch'ien colour belongs to a later date, when the Boxers had definitely turned over to 'supporting the Ch'ing', and had adopted the Imperial yellow as a consequence.[3]

The basic unit of either group was called a *T'uan* in the countryside and a *T'an* in urban areas. A *T'uan* controlled a village. Its head was called a *Ta-Shuai* or *Lao Shih-fu*, and his unit might consist of anything between twenty-five and a hundred men. His headquarters were usually in the village temple. In the cities, a *T'an* (also called a *Lu*, or hearth) meant three things—the altar, the headquarters of a unit, and the area under the control of the unit.[1] Inside the headquarters there were idols and tablets which the Boxers worshipped, as well as incense-burners, candlesticks, etc. The head of the *T'an*, accompanied by the members on duty, worshipped the gods both in the morning and in the evening. Attached to the headquarters was a boxing-ground (*Ch'üan-ch'ang*) where the members of the unit practised their boxing.

The boundaries of the several *T'an* do not appear to have been clearly drawn and, apart from Tientsin, there was little co-ordination of their operations. That is to say that, except in Tientsin, there was no overall leader of the Boxer movement. One advantage of having no supreme leader was that no one could claim sole credit for a victory or be called upon to accept full responsibility for a failure. Moreover, although 'Support the Ch'ing' was now a leading publicized aim of the Boxers, a unified leadership might well have excited the suspicions of the Manchu government. It is also likely that the Boxers were aware of the strife that had ensued among the Taipings when a supreme leadership was established. Says Mr Ch'ên: 'This lack of uniformity in the organization of the Boxer Movement was a sign not only of its political backwardness but also of its political wisdom.' The 'political wisdom' in question was rather, perhaps, the instinctive realization that with many heads instead of one there was a better chance for the survival of the sect.

Under the *T'an* leader there were officers called *Hsien-Shêng* in charge of administration and *Shih-Hsiung* responsible for training new Boxers. The *T'an* made itself responsible for the provision of supplies for its members, and, for their part, the members had to perform certain duties in addition to their main work of wiping out foreigners and Christians.

In the early stages, the requirements for initiation were very strict. The name of the candidate for recruitment was written on a piece of paper and burnt. If the name was still recognizable in the ashes the candidate was accepted; if not, he was rejected. Later on, this test was dispensed with, and the Boxers on patrol duty accepted any applicant for enrolment who seemed eligible to them. In most cases the recruits were youths.

Discipline was strict. From the moment of their entry into Tientsin the Boxers were absolutely forbidden to accept any gifts of food, etc., from the local inhabitants. During the first period this rule was obeyed, but later it was relaxed. Nevertheless, throughout their existence the Boxers were subject to restrictions of diet; they were not allowed to eat meat or drink tea, and were confined to a diet of plain wheat cakes and water. They were also instructed to avoid contacts with women and to obey the conventional moral law. When walking in the streets they were enjoined to hang their heads instead of staring at people. When two Boxers met they were to bow.

The Boxers also had their own colloquial usages. *Yang*, meaning 'foreign', was to be avoided, so that 'foreign guns' became 'devil guns', 'railway' became 'iron centipede', 'locomotive', 'iron bull', and 'dynamite', 'smoke powder'. The local people imitated this practice and called foreign goods *Kuang-huo* (the *kuang* being short for *Kwangtung*).

The companion women's organization to the Boxers, the Hung Têng Chao ('Red Lanterns'), was composed of girls between twelve and eighteen years of age who carried red handkerchiefs and red lanterns in their hands. This organization was first reported in a letter from Tientsin of 6 May 1900 (K 26/4/8) as having come into being in a certain village near Paotingfu.[1] For widows, there was the Ch'ing Têng Chao ('Green Lanterns') and Lan Têng Chao ('Blue Lanterns'). The function and aims of the women's groups were identical with those of the Boxers, but, unlike them, they possessed a supreme leader in the person of a woman, Huang Lien Shêng Mu (already mentioned), who possessed tremendous magical powers. It was quite likely she who founded the Red Lanterns.

This association of women, on an equality, at least of effort, with men, the Boxers shared with the White Lotus sect, and it set them apart from the Chinese community in general. And it was all the more remarkable since 'woman' according to Boxer beliefs, was 'unclean'— that is to say that the presence of any impurity of the *yin* type would render their spells ineffectual, driving away the gods who would otherwise have manifested themselves.[2]

There were also the Sha Kuo Chao ('Cooking-pan Lanterns'), a kind of heavenly commissariat on the principle of 'Fortunatus' Purse' which provided the Boxers with food from magic saucepans that automatically supplied themselves with provisions and replenished themselves when empty.

To summon the aid of one or other of their many gods, the Boxers had recourse to incantations. These were divided into three categories —the esoteric, those intended to persuade the gods to manifest themselves, and those merely intended to bring luck. The esoteric was allegedly the most powerful, but was somewhat limited in effectiveness by the fact that no one knew exactly what the formula was. Chang Tê-ch'eng, the Boxer leader of Tientsin, was said to have known two or three words of it, but this it seems was less than the operative minimum.

The incantations of the second category were sometimes intelligible, sometimes not. Here are some examples of the first sort:

Righteousness wins many supporters: Gods, please descend.

Fast horse and whip. The Gods of the Mountains point once and the Gate of Heaven opens; they point twice and the Gate of Earth yields entry. To teach you boxing, pray the Master to come.

Your disciple is resolved to work hard and to turn weeds and grass into an army. He is honoured to be your medium to wipe out the foreign devils and to safeguard the Great Ch'ing dynasty.

The sun rises in the east. A drop of oil bestirs our brethren to travel from one side of the Empire to the other: once in motion, they arouse Lao Tzŭ: Lao Tzŭ, once aroused, awakes Êrh-lang Shên; Êrh-lang Shên once awakened, stirs into action, the god who can block gun-barrels and calls on Lao Tzŭ to manifest himself.[1]

On 18 July 1900 a Boxer poster displayed in Peking enjoined its readers to wrap their heads in red cloths and worship the Herd Boy and the Weaver Girl (star gods) on the seventh day of the seventh month (1 August). They were not to sleep or to cook during the night or the gods would refuse to descend to save the lives of the people. From the first to the fifteenth of the eighth month everyone must abstain from eating meat or drinking wine. They should worship the gods three times a day. Only if these things were done could the Boxers block the foreigners' gun-barrels.[2]

This brings us back once more to the cult of invulnerability, to the Western mind the most absurd of the Boxer pretensions. But leaving aside for a moment the question of its absurdity, it can be said that the source from which it derives cannot be in doubt, namely *hsien* Taoism.

This kind of Taoism (says Creel)[3] in its varying manifestations is marked by one constant aim—the achievement of immortality. The goal is to become a *hsien*, or Taoist immortal. In Chinese works written as early as the first century B.C. we find its practices called the *hsien tao*, 'The way of *hsien*'.

The immortality in question was the perpetuation of the physical body. It might be possible, by special means, for one already in the tomb to be resurrected, but best of all was during life to become a *hsien*, for ever deathless and ageless. Many ways, too, were believed to conduce to that happy state. One of the most important was to take drugs, sometimes herbal but more frequently, it seems, the products of alchemy. Complex techniques involving breath control and gymnastics, which have been compared to the Hindu *yoga*, are prominent. One should not eat any of the Five Grains; one must repent one's sins, practise virtue (including such Confucian virtues as filial piety and *jên*, benevolence), and give to the poor. A single bad action would wipe out an accumulation of 1199 good ones. Varying emphasis was given to sexual practices which combined licence with austerity. Feats of magic and charms played a prominent part in *hsien* Taoism: mirrors were potent talismans, and many of the bronze mirrors that have come down to us were no doubt considered magical. In a series of heavenly palaces, deities (in many cases identified with the stars) function as *T'ien Kuan* ('Heavenly Officers') in a graded hierarchy. A *hsien* who goes to heaven must take the lowest place to begin with since he has as yet no seniority—that is why some prefer to stay on earth. Furthermore, this whole spiritual hierarchy has its exact counterpart in spirits living inside the body of every human being. There were collective ceremonies designed to achieve various ends. One important objective of *hsien* Taoism was to avoid, or to abbreviate, the tortures of hell.

The differences between *hsien* Taoism and philosophic Taoism are striking, to say the least. The mere idea of all this toiling for immortality is repugnant to that of *wu wei*, not striving. The Confucian moral tone and concern with rank in a heavenly hierarchy conflict with the moral indifference and robust anarchism of Taoist philosophy. As for the idea of hell, it is doubtful if the authors of the *Chuang Tzŭ* had ever heard of it, but if they had it would undoubtedly have struck them as exceedingly funny. Yet both doctrines are called Taoism, and the distinction between them is sometimes made poorly if at all.[1]

'Immortality' and 'invulnerability' were different aspects of the same thing. If you had achieved immortality as a *hsien*, it was obvious that shot and shell could have no effect on you. But a Boxer could attain temporary *hsien*-hood only when he was possessed by a spirit or god. Then he became invulnerable to either guns or swords, and he could in this state, moreover, block the enemy's gun-barrels and command the divine fire to burn down churches or houses belonging to Christians.

To induce the gods to possess them, Boxers had recourse to a ritual known as *lien-ch'üan*, or 'boxing'. This was performed on the boxing-ground, and the details varied from one ground to another. A typical ritual would proceed as follows. A few days beforehand a new recruit was taught a 'manifestation' spell, and on the appointed day he went to the boxing-ground to recite it. This he did three times, whereupon he became short of breath and began to froth at the mouth, upon which a fellow Boxer would shout 'God descends!' At this point the recruit became possessed and acquired invulnerability, supernatural skill with sword and lance, and all the other qualities of the Boxer. The ritual needed practice (especially in the matter of keeping one's teeth clenched while breathing), but while some reports said that a single day was sufficient to acquire proficiency, others gave three months or 180 days as the requisite time.

The Red Lantern recruits also had to undergo a period of training ranging from 48 days to five months. To begin with, they were taught an incantation and, when possessed, practised walking on water on the surface of a river or pond. As their training proceeded, the women recruits (who for some supererogatory reason had to be pretty) would find that their weight was progressively reduced until in the end they were able to fly! Their magic was supposed to be less fallible than that of the Boxers, and their supreme leader, Huang Lien Shêng Mu, as well as possessing miraculous healing powers, had mastered the uncanny art of undoing the screws of the enemies' cannon at a distance of some miles.

This magic, of course, was soon submitted to the test of experience, but when it proved clearly ineffectual excuses were ready at hand. Interference with the spirits by the impurity of the *yin* was often put foward as the reason, or else disobedience to the rules of the Boxer sect. A simpler explanation was to say that a person who had succumbed to arrows or bullets was not a Boxer at all but one who had been masquerading as one. To counter the influence of women or other unclean agencies the aid was sought of the special species of Boxer known as the 'Black Boxers', who were unaffected by these particular impurities. But when, in spite of all these precautions, the movement suffered serious reverses, notices were posted up to explain that the 'Old Boxers' (*Lao T'uan*) would soon come to the rescue, or (as a last resort) to announce that the time for salvation and victory had been postponed.

It was only gradually that the people became disillusioned. In Shantung, Yüan Shih-k'ai, the governor, and Hung Yung-chou, the prefect of Tungch'ang, put the invulnerability of the Boxers to the test, and reported its ineffectiveness. In Tientsin, another test was again unfavourable. But the worst failure of all was on 2 July 1900, when a Chinese commander, General Ma Yü-k'un, relied upon the Boxers to block the foreign big guns for a period of six hours—with the result that his division was put out of action! But, once a myth is established, it takes more than ocular demonstration to refute it, and in large parts of Chihli people still believed the Boxer claims long after they had been exploded elsewhere.[1]

CHAPTER XII

TRIUMPH AND FIASCO

The preceding chapters describing the 'pro-' or 'anti-dynastic' nature of the Boxers have been, comparatively speaking, in slow-motion cinematography; this chapter, intended merely as a sequel to our main inquiry, will be in quicker motion, attempting to reduce an intricate complex of events to a short, generalized narrative. The time-scale will now be about fifteen minutes of reading to a year of historic time.

In the last months of 1899, the depredations of the Boxers in killing Christian converts and burning churches now became the subject of a protest from the French Minister in Peking to the Tsungli Yamen. As a consequence Yü-hsien was called to Peking for consultation and Yuan Shih-k'ai was appointed to Shantung as Acting-Governor. The new Acting-Governor actively suppressed the Boxers, executed Chu Hung-têng, and drove his followers from Shantung into Chihli.[1]

Meanwhile, Boxer activities had so increased in the districts of Fuch'êng, Ch'ingchou, Kuch'êng, Wuch'iao and Tungkuang that the five magistrates of these districts called a conference and resolved that the programme of six points recommended by Lao Nai-hsüan for the suppression of the Boxers be adopted and submitted to the Viceroy of Chihli for approval. On 13 December Yü-lu ordered that Lao Nai-hsüan's pamphlet on the origin of the Boxers be printed and distributed in the districts where the Boxers were active. Yü-lu, however, found Lao's six points too drastic for his taste and made no effort to implement them. When pressed by Yüan Shih-k'ai to memorialize the Throne to issue a decree explicitly ordering the suppression of the Boxers, he replied evasively and remarked that they could not cause any great trouble. Yü-lu was being subjected to pressure from the reactionary party in Peking, and was not in any case a man of great resolution so that his neglect to memorialize the Throne at this juncture gave the reactionaries a chance to weight the scales in favour of the Boxers. But he did, nevertheless, make an effort to crush the insurgents by force and sent an expedition of six battalions against them.

In the meantime Yü-hsien's reports and advice in Peking had been producing the results he had hoped for. His general attitude had already been clear from his memorial of 6 December, and he amplified it later in that of 26 December (both of these documents have been quoted at length in chapter x). He now gave a glowing account of the loyalty, bravery and dependability of the I Ho T'uan to Prince Tuan (Tsai-i) and the Grand Secretary, Kang-i, who conveyed his opinions to the Empress Dowager. In consequence of this he was not degraded in rank (as some of the foreign ministers would have wished) but was transferred to Shansi as governor a few months later where he was to be responsible for the massacre of some hundreds of missionaries and converts during the crisis of the summer months. In Shansi he is said (by Li Chien-nung) to have declared to his subordinates: 'There are two leaders of the I Ho T'uan—one is Li Ping-hêng and I am the other.'

Tz'ŭ Hsi's attitude during these months varied with her evaluation of the situation in the light of the information and advice she received from those around her. In October 1899, over the matter of the Italian demands for Sanmen Bay, she had adopted an attitude of resolute resistance as counselled by her advisers—and with success. If she was now willing to listen to Yü-hsien's counsels it was because the way had been prepared by the reactionary party at Court, and because the execution of Chu Hung-têng and the other 'pro-Ming' leaders had crippled the anti-Manchu wing of the Boxer movement and it was now definitely turning towards support of the reigning dynasty. Thus encouraged from above, the Boxers, from Hochienfu as well as the two counties of Shên and Chi in south-east Chihli, spread northwards to Tientsin, Ichoufu, and Paotingfu, burning, pillaging and kidnapping, and in some places they were able to assemble several thousand men.

But there was no question yet of official recognition. Yuan Shih-k'ai and other mandarins were well aware of the threat to the dynasty and to themselves constituted by the uprising and they wished therefore to suppress it. Tz'ŭ Hsi thus found herself forced to play an ambiguous role. This is clearly reflected in the edict of 11 January 1900, which declared that the members of societies were of different kinds, the good and the bad, and that those who were drilling for the protection of their village should not be regarded as bandits. The edict said: 'We strictly enjoin the local officials in dealing with cases of this kind to inquire whether the persons involved are rebels or not and whether they are planning trouble or not, regardless of whether they are members of societies or sects or otherwise.'

On 17 April another decree declared that in organizing the T'uan for the preservation of their families the people were acting in accordance with the ancient principle of 'keeping mutual watch and giving mutual help'. This decree was quite naturally interpreted by the Boxers as a signal to go ahead.

The first major collision between the Boxers and the government troops in Chihli took place in May 1900. Riots broke out in Kaolo village in the district of Laishui where 75 houses of Christians were burned down and 68 Christians killed. Troops were despatched to the scene and arrested 20 Boxers. The troops then attacked the main body of the Boxers, and in the ensuing battle the commander of the government forces, Yang Fu-t'ung, was killed. This was the first time that the Boxers had killed a government commander. The Viceroy, Yü-lu, however, was irresolute. He did indeed recommend the arrest of the leaders, but wished merely to disperse their followers, being unwilling to 'resort to severe measures unless the Boxers resist again'. And once more in its acknowledgement of his report the Court urged 'moderation'.

Whilst all this was happening, the foreigners in China were becoming gradually aware of the gravity of the situation. It was fully seventeen months, however, after the first official notice of the Boxers in May 1898, before their existence began to impinge on the consciousness of the foreign community as a whole. On 2 October 1899 the Boxers were mentioned for the first time in a foreign newspaper, namely in the 'outport news' of the *North China Daily News* in items from correspondents in Tientsin and Lincheng, Shantung, dated 21 September. As was to be expected, the missionaries in the country districts were the first to feel the effect of the civil commotion, and there were reports from them of isolated incidents from April 1899 onwards. But they were slow in realizing that a great movement was afoot of a new and original character. In May there was a rumour of a threatened attack on a station of the London Missionary Society at a market-town named Hsiaochang in Chihli, about fifty miles south-west of Têchou on the Grand Canal, and for six weeks the station was under a kind of siege by the Boxers which was terminated at length by the intervention of the authorities from Paotingfu. Dr A. H. Smith, stationed at P'angchuang in the Ên district of Shantung, relates that during the early part of the eighth month (5 September–4 October 1899), there began to be talk of a general rising of the I Ho Ch'üan in the Hsiaochang region of Chihli as well as in Shantung over the border. 'They were said [he writes] to be about to act out the motto on their flag: "Protect the Empire; Exterminate Foreigners".' But it was not until the P'ingyüan affray of 18 October that the missionary body as a whole became aware that they were witnessing what might well become a general uprising.

The Diplomatic Body in Peking, meanwhile, were preoccupied with the business arising from the 'Battle of the Concessions' and it was the murder of the British missionary, Brooks, of the Society for the Propagation of the Gospel at a place fifty miles south of Chinan on 31 December 1899 which first aroused them to the real seriousness of the trouble.[1] On 5 January 1900 Sir Claude MacDonald, the British minister, addressed a despatch to the Marquis of Salisbury (it was sent by sea and was received on 19 February) in which he stated:

For several months past the northern part of the Province of Shantung has been disturbed by bands of rebels connected with various Secret Societies, who have been defying the authorities and pillaging the people. An organization known as the 'Boxers' has attained a special notoriety, and their ravages recently spread over a large portion of Southern Chihli, where the native Christians appear to have suffered even more than the rest of the inhabitants from the lawlessness of these marauders. The danger to which, in both provinces, foreign missionary establishments have been exposed has been the subject of repeated representations to the Chinese Government by others of the foreign representatives—especially the German and United States Ministers—and myself.

In his further despatches of 16 and 17 January MacDonald reported the pressure he had brought to bear on the Tsungli Yamen to recommend strong measures for repressing the Boxers. The whole of the present difficulty (MacDonald said) could be traced to the attitude of the late Governor of Shantung, Yü-hsien, who had secretly encouraged the seditious secret society known as 'the Boxers'. The Imperial edict expressing sorrow for the murder of Brooks and enjoining strong measures was satisfactory as far as it went, but Her Majesty's Government required more than mere words. MacDonald enclosed a translation of the Imperial decree dated 11 January, remarking that it was 'regarded in some quarters with misgiving' since it was liable to be read as admitting the possibility of excuse for the existence of such 'societies' as the 'Boxers'. 'If the promise of the first edict (5 January) is not fulfilled, I may then use it as a proof of want of sincerity on the part of the Chinese Government.'

16-2

Joint representations were made to the Tsungli Yamen on 27 January, 27 February, 5 March, 16 March and 3 April, by the Diplomatic Body protesting against the inadequacy of the measures taken to suppress the Boxers, to which MacDonald added complaints of his own regarding the government's management of the situation and the neglect to punish all who were directly or indirectly responsible for Brooks's murder. The wording of these representations could scarcely have been more exigent than it was. Up to the middle of April MacDonald sent his longer despatches by sea, and it is only after this time that he began to resort to the telegraph for this purpose. But the telegrams included in the published records are only a selection of the many sent (for example his published telegram of 16 April on the Boxers refers to previous unpublished telegrams on the subject preserved in the Public Records Office of 10 and 23 March). On 17 May he telegraphed to Lord Salisbury to inform him that the French minister (M. Pichon) had called that day to inform him that the Boxers had destroyed three villages and killed sixty-one Roman Catholic converts at Paotingfu, 90 miles from Peking.

The diplomats have been criticized for their failure to realize the gravity of the situation and for not taking effective measures to avert the danger, but it cannot be said that they neglected either to press the necessity of urgent measures on the Tsungli Yamen or to keep their governments informed of the seriousness of the happenings. Yet they have frequently been condemned for behaving as 'ostriches'.[1] An extract from 'Putnam Weale' (Lennox Simpson)'s lurid description of the siege of the legations and the events leading to it, purporting to be an extract from his diary for 12 May 1900, has often been quoted (by Chinese writers as well as European) as evidence of the ignorance of the Diplomatic Body as to what was going on. It runs: 'Meanwhile the cloud no bigger than your hand [the Boxer uprising in Shantung] is quite unremarked by the rank and file of Legation Street—that I swear.'

If by 'rank and file of Legation Street' Simpson means the legation staffs it can be stated with confidence that, in the light of the records, this does not represent the truth.

But what additional action could the diplomats have been expected to take? They could only represent to the government the urgent necessity of suppressing the Boxers and point out to them the consequences of failing to do so—which they repeatedly did. In fact a charge of quite a different kind might be levelled against them with far greater justice, namely that by calling up the legation guards from Tientsin on 30 May they precipitated a general rising which might otherwise not have taken place.

If a charge of this nature were to be preferred against the Diplomatic Body, the first item in it would undoubtedly be the proposals they had made earlier for a naval demonstration. On 7 March the ministers sent telegrams to their respective governments suggesting that, in case of continued refusal on the part of the Chinese government to publish a decree against the rebellious societies in the terms required by them, a few warships of each nation concerned should make a demonstration in North China waters. The intention was, of course, to frighten the Manchu government more by this demonstration than they were already frightened by the Boxers, to induce them to comply with their own demands. But what was likely to be the effect on the population of these maritime regions whose feelings were already at fever pitch? Their reaction to the Italian naval demonstration in 1899 might have given some hint of the consequences of an even larger one.

As it happened, the home governments did not view the proposals of their ministers in Peking with any great enthusiasm. Lord Salisbury expressed his opinion that naval force should be used only after all other means had failed, and it was not until Sir Claude had informed him of the intended despatch of American, German, and Italian warships to Taku that two British ships were ordered to that port. An American ship arrived on 7 April and left on the 30th. The Germans also sent ships to Taku, but the French did no more than order their admiral to hold his fleet in readiness.

The presentation of their third 'identic' note (as above mentioned) was also the occasion for the proposal that the legation guards should be brought up to Peking.[1] On 10 March the American minister, Mr Conger, expressed the opinion that a naval demonstration would quickly make the Court comply with the foreign demands, but if it did not, then as a last resort he would agree to the guards being brought up in order to bring the Court to its senses. Nothing (he argued) could chagrin the Chinese government more than for word to go forth that they could not preserve order or protect their Imperial capital, and they would do almost anything rather than this should happen once again.

What the five foreign envoys (of Great Britain, France, Germany,

Russia and the United States) had demanded in their identic note of 27 January, namely that membership of the I Ho T'uan be declared a criminal offence against the laws of China, amounted to a demand that the Throne should repudiate its own earlier decrees and make new laws for the empire to suit the wishes of foreign diplomats.[1] The whole temper of the Manchu government at this juncture was unfavourable to compliance with such a demand, for they regarded the threat from the foreigners as a more real and unendurable one than that from the Boxers. The Diplomatic Body, therefore, should have weighed the chances of forcing the Manchu government to concede to their wishes by means of threats of this sort and have taken into account the risk of further inflaming public opinion by naval demonstrations and the movement of troops across Chinese territory.

The bringing up of the legation guards to Peking does not seem to have been accorded by historians the weight it deserves as a factor in precipitating the final crisis, for doing so made the despatch of re-inforcements (under Admiral Seymour) necessary, and, to secure their retreat, the Taku forts had to be taken, which in its turn led to war.

At the end of April the Boxer bands still existed, were still drilling, and were still recruiting, but there were few actual disturbances and the danger of a serious outbreak seemed to be disappearing. At the beginning of May the Court even contemplated the organization of the Boxers into a militia (a course scarcely necessary if, as Steiger holds, they had already been a militia since 1898). Jung-lu was against the proposal, largely because the Boxers had been found to be useless as soldiers and because their leaders were drawn from unreliable elements of the population. The better gentry, he knew, would refuse to lead such material. Yüan Shih-k'ai was even more hostile to the idea. The policy of suppressing the wicked sheep and tolerating the virtuous goats was still therefore theoretically adhered to. The situation did not yet appear to be utterly beyond control.

It was not until Bishop Favier depicted the state of the countryside in terrifying colours on 19 May that the Diplomatic Body as a whole became genuinely disturbed. The *known* intention of the Boxers, according to the Bishop, was to enter Peking at a given signal, and he asked the French minister for forty to fifty sailors for the immediate protection of his cathedral (the *Pei T'ang*).

On 28 May, at a meeting of the diplomats, it was decided that the legation guards should be brought up from Taku to Peking without waiting any longer. The Tsungli Yamen was asked for formal permission for this, but they demurred, asked for delay, and then reluctantly gave their consent on the condition that the number of guards for each legation should not exceed thirty. This condition, however, was ignored by the Powers. But before any action could be taken by the other Powers, M. Pichon, the French minister, had already ordered up his guards to the capital. The first detachment, which arrived in Peking on 1 and 2 June, consisted of 75 Russians, 75 British, 75 French, 50 Americans, 40 Italians, and 25 Japanese.

How desperate was the situation? Says Steiger:

At the moment when the diplomatic body reached its decision to summon the legation guards, the Boxer disturbances had resulted in no loss of foreign life since the murder of Mr Brooks, five months earlier in Shantung: in Chihli, the only foreigner who had suffered personal injuries of any sort was the French railway official at Fengtai.

It is perhaps not over-cynical to remark that if the Boxers really meant what their slogan said, 'Destroy the foreigner', so far they were not even trying.[1] If the diplomats were alarmed for the safety of their legations, it was not on account of any violence suffered by their nationals elsewhere to date, but on account of the violence they believed they would inevitably be subjected to if the guards were not called up. For this state of mind the report of Bishop Favier and the alarm of M. Pichon were undoubtedly mainly responsible. But what actually provoked the ministers to act was the news of Boxer attacks on the railways.

Before the guards reached Peking, other foreign lives had been lost. On the morning of 31 May a party of French and Belgian railway engineers, making their way by boat from Paotingfu to Tientsin, became involved in a fight with bands of armed Chinese about twenty miles from Tientsin. Four of the Europeans were killed and several injured.

Assuming that the government forces were inadequate to protect the legations, or unwilling to do so, and presuming that the Boxers would shortly enter Peking and threaten the legation quarter, a small garrison of a few hundred marines and volunteers might well have been considered inadequate to withstand the onslaught of a huge horde of armed Boxers (that the garrison *did* in the event withstand such an onslaught was due to political accident rather than to military sufficiency, as we shall see). The threat to call up the guards, however, was intended primarily not for defence but to bring pressure on the government to outlaw the Boxers. In this main purpose it failed the moment that the guards were actually called up, and it is at least arguable that the bringing up of the guards added fuel to the fire of anti-foreignism and thus endangered the very individuals it aimed to protect. Nevertheless, adequately to justify such a verdict, many more pros and cons would have to be examined, and this is beyond the scope of the present outline.

In the meantime the government had issued another two decrees regarding the Boxers, continuing as before to make a distinction between the 'good and the bad elements'. A number of serious incidents now occurred in quick succession which produced a strong demand from the provincial officials that the Boxers should be suppressed by force. On 4 June the Boxers, who had set fire to Huangts'un railway station, were engaged by General Nieh Shih-ch'êng's troops and a pitched battle took place in which several hundred Boxers were killed. Chang Chih-tung telegraphed from Hankow that the 'Boxer bandits' who were resisting government troops, killing military officers, and stirring up riots at the very gates of the capital, should be executed in accordance with the law. These people, he said, 'are staging a rebellion under the cover of anti-Christianity'. Even Yü-lu wired that unless the Boxers were quickly suppressed the fire would soon become a conflagration.

In spite of this, the Court still refused to take forcible measures. General Nieh was strongly reproved for fighting and killing the Boxers. A decree of 6 June laid down a compromise between appeasement and suppression, the former to be preferred. By this decree the Grand Councillor, Chao Shu-ch'iao, was appointed to convey the Imperial message to the Boxers, and to exhort them to obey it, disperse, and to resume their normal peaceful occupations. If after this they still refused to reform themselves, the Grand Secretary, Jung-lu, should order Generals Tung Fu-hsiang, Sung Ch'ing, and Ma Yü-k'un to exterminate them. It was important, however, to distinguish between leaders and followers and to disperse the followers. Chao was accompanied on his mission by Ho Nai-ying, who, on account of his pro-Boxer leanings, had been promoted to be Vice-President of the Censorate.

Then, having despatched Chao and Ho, the Court immediately sent the pro-Boxer Kang-i on precisely the same mission, as if to ensure that the Boxers would receive favourable treatment whatever happened.

On 8 June Kang-i ordered General Nieh's troops to withdraw from Kaopeitien and the troops at Laishui were similarly withdrawn from Tientsin. Instead of being dispersed, the Boxers had won a bloodless victory.

During the afternoon of 13 June a large force of Boxers entered Peking. By nightfall the churches in the East City were in flames and a great number of converts were massacred. By 15 June the reactionaries had obtained a firm grip on the government in Peking and were energetically preparing for war. On 10 June Prince Tuan and Ch'i-hsiu, together with two others, were appointed to the Tsungli Yamen, with Prince Tuan succeeding Prince Ch'ing as President.

In the meantime, on 4 June twenty-four men-of-war had arrived at Taku, including British, French, Japanese, and Austrian vessels. By 6 June Admiral Seymour had ordered the *Aurora* and *Phoenix* to Shanhaiwan since it had been reported that several Europeans in isolated places had been murdered and the anti-foreign feeling was rising everywhere. It was expected that communications between Tientsin and Peking might be cut at any moment and the British Consul at Tientsin, Carles, took it upon himself to telegraph Lord Salisbury informing him that the local consuls had passed a resolution asking for strong reinforcements.

The ministers had in the meanwhile come to a decision to telegraph their governments, asking them to instruct their naval officers at Taku—that is, of Great Britain, Austria, Italy, Germany, France, Japan, and Russia—to take concerted measures for the defence of the legations. In consequence, the commanding officers of the several squadrons and vessels received instructions to take what joint action they saw fit. On 10 June Admiral Seymour reported to the Admiralty, having received an urgent telegram from Sir Claude MacDonald saying that the situation was extremely grave and that unless arrangements were made for an immediate advance on Peking it would be too late. That morning Seymour left Tientsin by train with 300 British, 100 Americans, 60 Austrians and 40 Italians. Other detachments, including Russian, French and German, were to follow at once.

By 13 June Seymour had 1876 men under his command. His progress, however, was very slow. On 15 June he was attacked by a large force of Boxers and on 18 June he came into collision with Nieh Shih-ch'êng's front division and Tung Fu-hsiang's rear division, and was compelled to fall back on Tientsin to avoid being surrounded.

The passage of the few hundred marine guards by train through the midst of agitated Chihli had increased the popular unrest, but the advance of Seymour's much larger force over the same line aroused the people in the region to a new pitch of fear and resentment. Now, for the first time, the telegraph line between Tientsin and Peking was cut, and what the diplomats and missionaries had foretold would happen now began in earnest. Riots occurred in many places. On the night of 10 June the British summer legation in the western hills was burnt; on the 11th Mr Sugiyama, chancellor of the Japanese legation, was killed at the main gate of the Chinese city of Peking. By nightfall on the 13th (as already related) a large force of Boxers had entered the capital.

On 11 and 12 June the members of the Tsungli Yamen called upon the British minister to urge strongly that the reinforcements should not advance. Since these representations brought no response, the Chinese government prepared for war.

If the Chinese government had not consented to the bringing up of the guards to the number which actually came, neither had it offered armed resistance to their passage, but the continued advance of the reinforcements towards the capital was a thing which they felt could not be permitted. On 13 June a decree was issued to Yü-lu to order the whole army of Nieh Shih-ch'êng back to guard the strategical points in the railway area near Tientsin. If any more foreign troops attempted to go north by train, Yü-lu was to stop them. As for the Taku forts, General Lo Jung-kuang was to be on the alert against a surprise attack.

Two days later Yüan Shih-k'ai was ordered to Peking with his troops, but contrived to keep back his modern army of 7000 men (a move not without its significance in the post-Boxer events leading to the reign of the 'War Lords').

A fateful meeting of the Imperial Council took place at noon on 16 June, attended by all the Manchu princes, dukes, nobles, and high officials of the Boards and ministries. The Empress Dowager asked the meeting what policy should be adopted in face of the allied advance on Peking. There then ensued a violent debate between 'pro-Boxers' and 'anti-Boxers'. When the 'anti-Boxers' spoke of the Boxers as 'rebels' whose invulnerability was a fiction, Tz'ŭ Hsi interrupted to inquire, 'If we cannot rely upon magic charms, can we not rely on the heart of the people? If we lose it, how can we maintain our country?'

The upshot was that Na-t'ung and Hsü Ch'ang were ordered to proceed to the front to dissuade the foreign force from advancing any further. Furthermore, the Boxers were to be pacified and a decree was issued after the meeting ordering the recruitment of 'young and strong' Boxers into the army.

At a further Grand Council meeting the following afternoon, the Empress Dowager announced that she had received a 'Demand of Four Points' from the foreign ministers—(1) a special palace was to be assigned to the Emperor as a residence, (2) all revenues were to be collected by the foreign ministers, (3) all military affairs were to be committed to their hands, and (4), though Tz'ŭ Hsi did not mention it, was 'the restored rule of the Emperor'. This 'Demand of Four Points' is believed to have been forged by Prince Tuan in an attempt to infuriate the Empress Dowager into declaring war.

If the 2000 Chinese troops which were stated to be trying to cut Tientsin off from Taku advanced, the Council of Senior Officers of the foreign squadrons and ships had decided to shell the Taku forts. On 18 June the commanding officer of H.M.S. *Endymion* telegraphed to the Admiralty saying that at 1 o'clock in the morning of 17 June the Taku forts had opened fire on the ships of the allied squadron. After six hours' engagement the forts had been silenced and occupied by the allied forces.

On 19 June the Court received Viceroy Jung-lu's memorial reporting the allied senior naval officers' ultimatum demanding the surrender of the Taku forts. The decision was thereupon taken to break off diplomatic relations. Another memorial followed on 21 June giving a somewhat encouraging picture of the three days' fighting, both in Taku and Tientsin, and on the strength of this report an Imperial edict was issued the same day declaring war on the Powers.

On 19 June identic notes from the Tsungli Yamen were received at each legation, saying that in consequence of the commencement of hostilities by the naval forces at Taku it would no longer be possible to guarantee protection to the ministers and their families at Peking. They were therefore requested to prepare for departure within twenty-four hours and to be escorted to the coast. The Diplomatic Body protested, urged the impossibility of leaving Peking at such short notice, and requested an interview with the Yamen the following morning (20 June) at nine o'clock. No answer being received by the following morning, Baron von Ketteler, the German minister, set out for the

Yamen, and had almost reached his destination when he was shot and killed by a Chinese soldier. A new note was now received from the Yamen (containing no mention of the German minister) offering an extension of the twenty-four-hour time limit, but in spite of this, at 4 p.m.—promptly on the expiration of the time limit set in the first note—the Chinese troops opened fire on the legations. The siege of the legations had begun. That of the Roman Catholic Cathedral in the north of Peking commenced simultaneously. The sieges were to last, in varying degrees of intensity, until 14 August, a period of fifty-five days.

The siege of the Peking legations is an episode in the Boxer Uprising that has received tremendous publicity in the Western world. Sixty-six foreigners were killed whilst it lasted and 150 wounded. To those beleaguered it must have been a terrifying experience, and to those actually engaged in the fighting a dangerous one, but participants in the two great wars of the subsequent generations may be forgiven if they smile at the often portentous accounts of the hostilities and the heroics in which some of the civilian defenders indulged. Dozens of those besieged wrote accounts of their experiences, with the result that it is among the best documented episodes in the history of the Far East. But if it is not reduced to its proper proportions as a small incident in the vast history of China, the present book at least will have failed in its purpose.[1]

The total strength of the legation guards was twenty officers and 389 men of eight nationalities, to which must be added about 125 volunteers. The outlying legations, the Belgian and the Dutch, were abandoned on the first day of the siege, and on the second day the Austrian legation was unaccountably abandoned by the Austrian commander in charge of the entire garrison of the legations. The Chinese, however, failed to exploit their advantage: the Austrian commander was superseded, and Sir Claude MacDonald assumed command of the defences. On 24 June fire broke out in the adjacent Hanlin Academy, extending to its famous library, and, for a while, until the flames were brought under control, they threatened to consume the British legation.

To arrest the advance of the Seymour expedition, the Court was disposed to use the Boxers, but their protégés were already well out of hand. Decree after decree was issued directing that their ringleaders should be arrested and their followers dispersed, but with the receipt of a report from Yü-lu that victories had been won in Tientsin by the government troops and the Boxers in alliance, the latter came into their own. Decrees were now issued to Yü-lu commending their patriotism and attributing their success to the assistance of their ancestors and the blessings of their gods. The viceroys and governors in the several provinces were ordered to organize the Boxers to resist the foreign aggressors. In Peking, Prince Chuang and Kang-i were appointed to command them. Here they totalled some 30,000, and 1400 bands of them were organized under the leadership of Prince Tuan.

However good the discipline of the Boxers may have been in the earlier stages of the movement, with their numbers swollen by new recruits it had now declined to almost nothing. Each band had its own leader and made its own laws. Anyone wearing something red (usually a sash) could claim to be a Boxer, 'and any Boxer seemed to be invested with authority to kill, burn and plunder at will' (Chester Tan). Even notables, such as the Grand Secretary, Sun Chia-nai, himself a supporter of the Boxers, the Hanlin chancellor, I Ku, and the Vice-President of the Censorate, Tsêng Kuang-luan, were robbed by them and subjected to personal violence. The newly appointed governor of Kweichow, Têng Hsiao-ch'ih, was dragged from his sedan-chair, forced to kneel down, and robbed of all his clothes. As to assaults upon and ill-treatments of lesser officials and the population in general, no figures exist, but at one time the capital was so littered with dead bodies that the Court had to order the commanders of the Peking Field Force to have them removed from the city. Soon the Boxers were joined by the soldiers in their depredations.

There can be no doubt that the attack on the legations was authorized by the Imperial Court. Its motives were complex but probably included (a) the desire to give vent to its hatred and anger against the foreigners, (b) its wish to stimulate the patriotism of the people, and (c) to dispose of the foreign menace within the capital—and perhaps also (d) to implement the principle that 'dead men tell no tales'.

The military and personal aspects of the siege of the legations have been dramatically exploited by Mr Fleming; the diplomatic history of the siege from the Chinese angle has been illuminated by the researches of Mr Chester Tan; but the account of the latter from the angle of the besieged diplomats as given by Sir Claude MacDonald in his despatch to Lord Salisbury of 20 September cannot even now be improved upon, and for our present purposes can be compressed into a paragraph or so.

From 20 June until 14 July the events were almost purely military, but on the latter date a correspondence with the Chinese began which lasted until the end of the siege. In answering the Chinese communications the Diplomatic Body assumed that there must be different degrees of hostility towards the foreigners, and their motive was to strengthen the hands of those who, for whatever reason, were opposed to extreme measures, thus improving the chances of the legations' holding out by diminishing the vigour of the attack. The ministers thus allowed the Chinese to indulge the belief that there was a chance of their placing themselves and their families at their mercy by proceeding under Chinese escort to Tientsin. On the 16th a messenger brought a letter to MacDonald, the tone of which was different from that of the 14th and which invited the ministers to transfer themselves and their staffs and families to the Tsungli Yamen for their better safety. The refusal of the ministers to proceed to the Yamen, however, was accepted without demur and assurances were given that in future the legations would be better protected, from which the ministers concluded that something alarming to the Chinese government had happened in the outside world. This proved to be the fall of Tientsin on 14 July. A truce now ensued. Some shells were fired the following morning but they were the last until the end of the siege, and for ten or twelve days there was no heavy rifle fire. On 18 July the Japanese minister received a letter from Tientsin in answer to one sent out on 30 June from which it was learnt that a relief force was being organized. This was the first assurance the ministers had received that the situation in Peking was known outside. On 20 July a supply of water-melons and vegetables was sent into the legations by the Chinese government as a present, and on the 26th a further supply arrived together with some rice and 1000 pounds of flour. On the 26th and 28th, however, there were ominous signs that the truce was already nearing an end. Guns were moved, changes were made in the troops on the city wall, and sniping at night recommenced. The 29th marked the definite resumption of the hostilities. The ministers afterwards ascertained from the *Peking Gazette* that Li Ping-hêng, 'the notoriously anti-foreign ex-Governor of Shantung', had arrived in Peking and had an audience of the Empress Dowager. But, in spite of the renewal of hostilities, communications continued to be received from the Chinese, pressing the ministers to leave for Tientsin. On 7 August the Tsungli Yamen wrote to the British minister to communicate the sad news of the death of his Royal

Highness the Duke of Saxe-Coburg and Gotha; on 10 August news was received from the British and Japanese generals, dated from Nants'ai-ts'un on 8 August, that relief was actually on its way and might be expected on 13 or 14 August. On 13 August a letter came from the Chinese stating that after the orders which had now been given to the Chinese troops 'it was hoped that, dating from today, neither Chinese nor foreigner would ever again hear the sound of a rifle'.

Sir Claude's report concludes:

I read this sanguine aspiration to the accompaniment of a violent fusilade from the Chinese troops, which began shortly after a shell had burst in my dressing-room. Three times during the night it was necessary to call up the reserves in support of the firing line, the attacks being more frequent than on any previous night. But at two in the morning there were other sounds with those of the Chinese rifles. From the east we heard Maxim fire and heavy guns, and no one doubted that they were those of our relief. We listened to their music all the forenoon, until at half-past two the 7th Rajpoots found their way into the Legations, the first of the allied forces to arrive, and our eight weeks of siege was over.

Let us now see what had been happening in the meantime on the Chinese side of the curtain.[1]

While the war in the north was in full swing, to carry out the declaration of war by the Court effectively it should simultaneously have been extended to the south. That this was not the case was due to the action of the southern viceroys in co-operation with the foreign Powers who were only too glad to limit the conflict—the only alternative to undertaking the complete conquest of China. The formula which made it possible for the viceroys to confine to a token gesture their obedience to the Court's orders to despatch the provincial troops in force to Peking was that devised by the Director of Railways and Telegraphs, Shêng Hsüan-huai. As soon as hostilities broke out at Taku, but before the declaration of war, he suggested to Li Hung-chang that 'hostilities had started without orders from the Throne, and therefore peace should not be considered broken'. Li telegraphed to the Chinese ministers abroad that 'fighting at Taku was not ordered by the Throne', and asked them to inform the foreign governments and to request a truce so that the conflict could be settled by negotiation. After the actual declaration of war, the southern viceroys, Li Hung-chang, Chang Chih-tung, Liu K'un-i, and the governors associated with them, decided to ignore it. To do this without overt disobedience to the Throne, they seized on a sentence in a decree of

20 June which ordered that the viceroys 'should unite together to protect their territories' and interpreted it to mean that they should decide how to save the territories under their jurisdiction from peril, and this was the course adopted also by Yüan Shih-k'ai in Shantung. This bold decision proved to be a wise one, for it saved the southern and eastern provinces from the devastation of war and paved the way to peace between the Powers and the reigning dynasty by creating the fiction that at the time of the siege the Boxer forces were still in rebellion against the throne and the Chinese government had lost control of its own troops.[1]

The one great danger to the policy of the southern viceroys was the attitude of Li Ping-hêng. Li was now the Imperial inspector of the Yangtze naval forces, having been appointed to that post some time after being relieved of his governorship of Shantung. Upon receipt of the news that hostilities had started at Taku, he declared that foreign warships would be fired on if they passed near the Kiangyin fort near Shanghai. The southern viceroys, however, were able to restrain him from frustrating their plans until he left for Peking on 30 June.

Although the siege of the legations was already in progress, after the receipt of memorials from the southern viceroys dated 20 and 21 June, which urged that the Boxers be suppressed, the Court became conciliatory towards the Powers. But reports from Yü-lu in early July of victories over the foreign forces at Tientsin hardened its attitude again. On 9 July General Nieh was killed, and on 13 July the allies took Tientsin. Again the Court had to reshape its policy, and, urged by further memorials from the southern viceroys, tended once more towards conciliation. On 17 July the Court issued an edict embodying all the recommendations in a joint memorandum from the southern viceroys, including the offer of protection to foreign merchants and missionaries, the sending of an Imperial letter to Germany expressing regret for the death of Baron von Ketteler, and the issue of a decree to the Viceroy of Chihli ordering him to suppress riots on the part of rebellious 'bandits' or troops by force. On 14 July, the day after the fall of Tientsin, the Tsungli Yamen sent a memorandum to the legations stating that if in accordance with the previous agreement (which had never been accepted, however, by the foreign ministers) the Chinese government were to escort the foreign ministers out of the capital, there might be a misadventure since there were so many Boxers on the road to Tientsin, and they tried to persuade them to remove with families and staffs to the Tsungli Yamen. This offer, too, was refused as we have already seen. A conciliatory attitude, however, was maintained by the Chinese government and on 16 July a suspension of hostilities was ordered which lasted for 12 days. It was then to show their good-will that the present of fruit and vegetables was sent by the Chinese to the legations.

Because of the lack of confidence of the diplomatic corps in the bona fides of the Chinese, the effort of the latter to deliver them from danger was frustrated, but (says Chester Tan) there can be no doubt that, at least so far as the Tsungli Yamen was concerned, the offer was a genuine one.

The conciliatory phase was ended by the arrival of Li Ping-hêng at the capital on 26 July. In his audience with the Empress Dowager his theme was, 'Only when one can fight can one negotiate for peace'. His intervention greatly encouraged the reactionaries, especially Hsü T'ung and Kang-i. On 28 July, Hsü Ching-ch'êng, ex-minister to Russia, and Yüan Ch'ang, minister of the Tsungli Yamen, were executed by Imperial order, and two weeks later Hsü Yung-i, president of the Board of War, Lien-yuan, sub-chancellor of the Grand Secretariat, and Li Shan, president of the Board of Revenue, were also executed. This terrorism was resorted to by the reactionaries to consolidate their position and to silence those who advocated a peaceful settlement. The five executed ministers were singled out as being friendly to the foreign Powers and hostile to the Boxers.

After the ending of the truce at the beginning of August (though the diplomatic correspondence continued) hostilities were recommenced and lasted until the relief of the legations on 14 August. On 6 August Li Ping-hêng left Peking for the front. That day the allies had attacked Yangts'un and defeated the Chinese army, whereupon Yü-lu had committed suicide. The next day the two armies under Li Ping-hêng were also quickly defeated near Hosiwu. On 11 August, as the Chinese forces collapsed before the attack of the allies at T'ungchou, Li Ping-hêng took his own life.

The allies had entered the capital on 14 August and the next morning at dawn the Court left the capital by a northern gate and fled towards the west.

In the final stages, as the military situation had deteriorated, the Imperial Court had made one last effort for peace. In an edict of 11 August it declared that Li Hung-chang had been appointed plenipotentiary to negotiate with the Powers, and that telegrams had been sent to the foreign governments asking for a truce.

Many of the innumerable strands of the web of international relationships in which China was caught up have been sorted out elsewhere, and many still remain to be sorted. No attempt will be made here to contribute to this very specialist task, nor shall we repeat the dismal story of the sack of Peking by foreigner and native, nor of the brutal pacification of Manchuria by the (Tsarist) Russians. It will be convenient, however, to bring this summary to a conclusion in terms of the international situation.

Witte says in his *Memoirs* that, when news of the Boxer Uprising reached St Petersburg, Kuropatkin, minister of War, exclaimed, 'I am very glad. This will give us an excuse for seizing Manchuria. We will then turn Manchuria into a second Bokhara.' When the question of an international expedition to relieve the legations became a burning one, Witte and Lamsdorff were flatly opposed to Russian participation on the plea that China's friendship could be regained by a tolerant attitude, but Kuropatkin convinced the Tsar, and in the end Russia contributed 4000 men to the relief forces. The Russian commander was ordered, however, not to advance beyond Yangts'un. The fact that the Russians nevertheless entered Peking on 14 August in the van with the other troops was entirely due to accident—the order did not reach the commander until it was too late to obey it. But hardly had the legations been relieved when the Russian Foreign Office surprised the world by an invitation to the other Powers to withdraw their ministers and forces to Tientsin, since it was clear, they said, that the Empress Dowager and her Court, which had fled to Sianfu, would not return and negotiate so long as Peking was occupied by foreigners. But the Russian circular did not make a great impression on the other Powers, who were generally agreed that withdrawal from Peking would be premature. The French government alone gave the suggestion its support.

The German cabinet felt itself more directly touched than any other by what it regarded as Russia's perfidy in making the proposal. The Emperor Wilhelm had all along been obsessed by the idea of the 'Yellow Peril', had taken a vigorous line against the Boxers, and having sent out German troops to China on his own responsibility, had bidden them farewell in his celebrated speech of 27 July, when he had instructed his men to be ruthless.

Let all who fall into your hands be at your mercy. Just as the Huns a thousand years ago, under the leadership of Attila, gained a reputation by virtue of which they still live in historical tradition, so may the name of Germany become known in such a manner in China, that no Chinese will ever again dare to look askance at a German.[1]

The Kaiser now induced the Russians to acquiesce in the appointment of Field-Marshal von Waldersee as commander-in-chief of the allied (or rather associated) forces. The proposal gained the grudging approval of the other European Powers. Since at the time it was generally agreed that no expedition could start for Peking before the middle of September, it was therefore taken for granted that the Germans would play a very prominent part in it. But the sudden and successful relief of the legations under Russian leadership, with no German participation at all, took the Kaiser by surprise and caused him bitter disappointment.

To counteract Russian plans, the Germans sounded out the British. Lord Salisbury did not react favourably to the idea of an agreement with Germany, and the doubling of the German fleet had started an anti-German campaign in the British press. But fear of Russia eventually brought the two Powers to an arrangement. The object of this was to maintain the 'Open Door', but in order not to appear involved in a move against Russia, the Germans wished to exclude the Amur River and Port Arthur. In the end the principle of the 'Open Door' was to be upheld in all Chinese territory 'so far as they [Britain and Germany] could exercise influence'. Germany obtained the advantage in this agreement for while it forestalled any attempt by the British to establish themselves in the Yangtze basin and committed Britain to continuing the Open Door in that region, all this was without any commitment on the part of Germany to oppose Russian designs.

Whilst this wider rivalry was developing over the prostrate body of China, the Powers had to come to an understanding with regard to negotiations with her *de jure* rulers, against whom the Boxers had so wantonly 'rebelled'. The Germans, supported more or less by the British, favoured the stiffest possible terms, while the Russians, and to a certain extent the Americans and the Japanese, advocated gentler treatment for reasons of their own. After a great deal of international wrangling, a joint note was presented to the Chinese plenipotentiaries, Li Hung-chang and Prince Ch'ing, on 24 December 1900. Discussions in detail then began. The negotiations, which dragged on during the winter and spring, became at times very heated, and it was only in September 1901 that the final agreements were signed.

In an attempt to forestall the anticipated demands of the allies, the Chinese Court had already decreed punishments for individuals who were likely to have incurred the allied wrath. On 13 November 1900 a decree ordered that Princes Tuan and Chuang should be immured for life at Mukden; Prince I and Tsai-ying were to be handed over to the Clansmen's Court for imprisonment; Prince Lien was to be confined to his house; Duke Tan was to be reduced one degree in rank and deprived of his emoluments; Yü-hsien was to be banished to the remotest frontier and be sentenced to hard labour for life. But these punishments did not satisfy the allies. Finally, after much exchange of correspondence, the Court agreed that Prince Tuan and Duke Lan should be condemned to imprisonment pending decapitation, Ying-nien and Chao Shu-ch'iao were to be allowed to commit suicide; if Kang-i, Li Ping-hêng, and Hsü T'ung had still been alive they would have been condemned to capital punishment, but being dead, they would merely suffer the legal consequences of such punishment: Yü-hsien was to be beheaded. Difficulties remained only in the case of Tung Fu-hsiang. Before deciding on his ultimate punishment, it was necessary first to deprive him of his command.[1]

The final protocol of 7 September 1901 consisted of twelve articles. These included provisions for Prince Ch'un to proceed to Berlin to convey to the German Emperor the regrets of the Chinese Emperor and Grand Council for the murder of Baron von Ketteler, and for the erection of a monument on the spot where he was killed:[2] the suspension of the official examinations for five years in all cities where foreigners had been massacred or maltreated: Na T'ung, vice-president of the Board of Revenue, was to proceed to Japan to convey the regrets of the Chinese Emperor and government for the murder of Mr Sugiyama: China was to erect an expiatory monument in each of the foreign international settlements that had been 'desecrated': the importation of arms and ammunition were to be prohibited for five years; the legation quarter in Peking was to be reserved for the exclusive residence of foreigners: the Taku and other forts which might impede free communication between Peking and the sea were to be razed: certain specified points were to be occupied by the Powers: an edict prohibiting membership of any anti-foreign society for ever upon pain of death was to be issued and there were other provisions including the negotiation of amendments to the existing Treaties of Commerce and Navigation and the establishment of river conservancy boards with foreign participation; the reformation of the Tsungli Yamen and its promotion to be a Ministry of Foreign Affairs (*Wai Wu Pu*) with precedence over the six other ministries of State.

What amount could China afford to pay as an indemnity? After much discussion between the Powers, this was fixed at 450 million taels or 67 million pounds. All the foreign ministers approved this sum except the American minister who, on the instructions of his government, wished to keep the total within £40 million. On 26 May 1901 an Imperial edict was issued to pay the allied Powers the former sum.

The methods of payment decided on by the Powers involved further very extensive invasion of China's sovereignty. The following resources were to be taken as security for the indemnity—the maritime customs and that part of the *likin* (internal customs) already under foreign control, that part of the *likin* hitherto under Chinese control, and the salt gabelle. Import duties were to be increased to an effective 5 per cent ad valorem, and there was also to be an impost on goods hitherto free of duty.

The indemnity, then, was to be of 450 million taels of silver (with accrued interest over the period of thirty-nine years, the sum exceeded 980 million taels). An addition of 20 million pounds a year was thus added by the protocol to the burdens of the impoverished Chinese people.[1]

I have recited these humiliating and crippling terms at some length since they bring home the fact 'that the function of the Manchu Government was now little more than that of a debt-collecting agency for the Powers' (Chester Tan).

China was indeed 'in eclipse'. Europe's treatment of China in the whole period from 1895 had been devoid of all consideration and all understanding.

Hardly anywhere in the diplomatic correspondence [says Langer] does one find any appreciation of the feelings of the Oriental or any sympathy for the crude efforts made at reform. The dominant note is always that force is the father of peace and that the only method of treating successfully with China is the method of the mailed fist. The Boxers were considered to be so many ruffians who deserved no better treatment than is ordinarily meted out to common criminals. When the trouble began, legation guards were rushed to Peking, where evidently they took the initiative in shooting at Chinese troops. The American Minister thought that these 'exhibitions of skill and courage' would serve as 'good object lessons'. In their negotiations with the Yamen the foreign ministers rarely bothered with the facts. Indeed, a careful student of the problem [Steiger] has put on record his opinion that each of the decisive steps taken by the diplomats of Peking, or by their naval commanders at Taku, was taken on the strength of rumours which have never been substantiated: each has been justified only by appealing to subsequent events as 'evidence of the wisdom and necessity of the act'.[1]

After a reconsideration of the evidence, there seems to be no reason to dissent from this judgment.

CONCLUSION

I have lived amongst men of letters who have written history without mixing in affairs, and amongst politicians who have been occupied with making things happen without ever troubling to write about them. I have always noticed that the former see general causes on all sides, while the latter, living in the haphazard of daily events, prefer to think that everything that happens must be attributed to particular accidents and that their daily string-pulling represents the forces that move the world. I believe that both are mistaken. For my part I hate these absolute systems which make all the events of history depend on first great causes by a chain of fatality, and which, as it were, exclude man from the history of mankind. I believe, with all due deference to the writers who have invented these sublime theories to nourish their vanity and facilitate their work, that many important historical facts can only be accounted for by accidental circumstances, and that many others remain inexplicable, and that, in fine, chance, or rather that network of secondary causes which we call chance since we are unable to unravel it, counts for much that we see in the theatre of the world. Antecedent facts, the nature of institutions, mental attitudes, the state of morals—these are the materials from which are composed those impromptus which amaze and terrify us.

ALEXIS DE TOCQUEVILLE, quoted by J. P. Mayer, *Alexis de Tocqueville; a Biographical Study in Political Science* (New York, 1960), pp. 91–2.

The Boxer movement was anti-foreign and therefore anti-Christian. Any attempt to apportion the responsibility for arousing the popular resentment as between the foreign governments, the diplomats, and the merchants on the one hand and the missionaries on the other is bound to be inconclusive, and any attempt to apportion the blame as between the Roman Catholics and the Protestants is likely to be equally unhelpful. Although the Chinese were disposed to regard Catholicism and Protestantism as two different religions (with two different self-given names), they regarded them both indifferently as enemies.

Steiger argues that the Boxers could not have been both a religious sect and hostile to Christianity since this was against Chinese tradition, but the fact is that they were both a religious sect and anti-foreign and anti-Christian. Says Jerome Ch'ên: 'It was a religious uprising—the

263

most important religious uprising in the world as a whole to take place this century.'[1]

In chapter VI I have summarized the arguments in their defence put forward by the two main divisions of Christianity in China. Regarding the specific part played by them in causing the Boxer Uprising, Dr A. H. Smith says:

For the precipitation of the tremendous crisis which has occurred, the proportion of the responsibility of the Protestant missions is undoubtedly real, but it is a small and relatively insignificant factor.[2]

Its [the Boxer Movement's] sources were race hatred and the political aggressions of Western nations. Yet the universal and deep-seated animosity to the claims and the practices of the Roman Church throughout the Empire have added greatly to the fury and bitterness of these attacks, and will contribute materially to the difficulty of a permanent settlement.[3]

It is true that the claims to authority advanced by the Roman Catholic Church were bound in the long run to bring it into head-on collision with the civil government (as happened with the Emperor in the seventeenth and eighteenth centuries and with the communists in the twentieth), but, like the Protestant churches, it could not altogether free itself from national affiliations. But both religions had equally uncompromising aims, and both involved the complete surrender by the Chinese of their traditional methods of thought. Dr Smith himself said:

What China needs is righteousness, and in order to attain it, it is absolutely necessary that she have a knowledge of God and a new conception of man, as well as of the relation of man with God . . . the manifold needs of China we find, then, to be a single imperative need. It will be met permanently, completely, only by Christian civilisation.[4]

This was a surrender that the Chinese had never been willing to make, and when the real Revolution did eventually come about in 1949, the great endeavour of the communists was to persuade the Chinese people that even the most revolutionary communist reforms now being introduced were basically developments of the traditional institutions of Chinese society.

The first large-scale secret society movement after the Sino–Japanese War, that of the Great Sword, was anti-foreign and, in particular, anti-German. It was an offshoot of the White Lotus and, like the Boxers, it had the cult of invulnerability. But although Yü-hsien was later credited by some foreigners with having organized this society, there is no evidence to support this assertion. The outbreaks of the Great Sword were accompanied by rebellions of an anti-dynastic nature, but whether any of them openly aimed to 'overthrow the Ch'ing and restore the Ming' we do not know. But we can say with some certainty that they had no 'pro-Ch'ing' slogan, and no aim to support the ruling dynasty.

When the Boxers first reappeared in May 1898 they were not openly, and probably not actually, anti-dynastic. If they had been, they could not have been regarded as harmless by Governor Chang Ju-mei and he would surely have recommended their suppression rather than their absorption into the militia. Li Ping-hêng, Chang Ju-mei and Yü-hsien aimed in turn to direct the ever-growing popular discontent and agitation away from the government and against the foreigner. It was quite obviously a hazardous manœuvre of which Yüan Shih-k'ai and other mandarins fully realized the dangers. If ever the rebels had obtained full control, the anti-government elements would undoubtedly have taken charge and the Manchus would have been overwhelmed (as actually happened in 1912, when the mainspring of the Revolution was the widespread anti-Manchu feeling).

Father Isoré's evidence of the existence of the slogan, 'Support the Ch'ing; Destroy the Foreigner' in October 1898, is unsupported (though it may conceivably be true), but we can accept the Chinese sources as evidence that the slogan first came to the forefront about September 1899. By this time Chu Hung-têng had been in the field for some months, and there is no reason to doubt the statement made in *IHT* that his aim was to 'Overthrow the Ch'ing; Restore the Ming' (although no report of an actual banner bearing these words appears to have survived). But it is impossible to accept Fan Wên-Lan's statement that it was Chu Hung-têng himself who changed the slogan of the Boxers to 'Support the Ch'ing; Destroy the Foreigner'. For one thing, we have the statement in the *IHT* biography that it was the Boxer leader, Li Lai-chung, who actually *did* adopt the slogan, and that he later, with his followers, joined Li Ping-hêng's army against the Powers. If Chu had succumbed to Yü-hsien's blandishments, it is scarcely likely that the latter would have left him in prison to be executed by his successor, Yüan Shih-k'ai.

But the actual moment of the changeover is not a matter of the first importance; the crucial question to decide is the precise *phase* in the movement when the changeover did take place. There can be no doubt that it was after the setback to the anti-dynastic elements at P'ingyüan in October that the Boxer leaders who had not been arrested or dispersed did adopt the pro-Ch'ing slogan since it now offered the only promise of success. And at this same moment it happened that the reactionaries at Court who wished to exploit the anti-foreign sentiment of the Boxers were in power.

Nevertheless, we also know now that the parent body of the White Lotus remained faithful to their traditionally anti-dynastic aims, with the result that considerable numbers of them were put to death by the Boxers in the Greengrocers' Market in Peking in July, that is, after the entry of the Boxer hordes into the capital.

Apart from their single pro-Ch'ing banner, the Boxer insignia seem to have been exclusively those of the Eight Trigrams sect. Their prayers and incantations, however, were directed towards Buddhist deities as well as towards Taoist gods and legendary heroes with Confucian allegiances. These gods and heroes, as we have seen, were all drawn from the popular novels and plays, but the legends concerning them were no doubt reinforced by folk-tradition.

What resemblance, if any, had the Boxers to rebels in other parts of the world? They certainly belonged to what the sociologists call the 'primitive' or 'archaic' forms of social agitation. These have been classified for Europe as 'banditry of the Robin Hood type, rural secret societies, various peasant revolutionary movements of the millenarian sort, pre-industrial urban riots, some labour religious sects and the use of ritual in early labour and revolutionary organizations'.[1]

There was a 'Robin Hood' element in the Boxer creed represented by the novel *Water Margin*, etc.; they belonged to the 'rural secret societies', they were for the most part (but not entirely) 'pre-industrial', and they certainly relied heavily on the use of ritual. 'Millenniarism', however, namely 'the hope of a complete and radical change in the world which will be reflected in the millennium, a world shorn of all its present deficiencies', was not entirely reproduced in the Boxer desire for reversion to a 'golden age'. It seems (says Hobsbawm) that classical millenarian movements occur only, or practically only, in countries affected by Judaeo-Christian propaganda—

This is only natural, for it is difficult to construct a millenarian ideology within a religious tradition which sees the world in a constant flux, or series of cyclical movements, or as a permanently stable thing. What makes millenarians is the idea that the world as it is may—and indeed will—come to an end one day, to be utterly remade thereafter, a conception which is alien to such religions as Hinduism and Buddhism.[1]

There was certainly nothing like this in Boxerism; nor did Utopianism appear. The Boxer standards were firmly rooted in the past; they did not deny constituted authority though they tended to supersede it when it became ineffective (as in their 'protect the people' phase); their moral code, though modified by Taoist sexual egalitarianism, was orthodox.

There are some general points of resemblance between the Boxers and the Lazzarati, the Andalusian anarchists, the Sicilian Fasci, the Mafia, etc., but it would be hazardous to pursue them too far outside the context of Chinese civilization. One notable similarity should nevertheless be mentioned, namely the cult of magical invulnerability. Angiolillo, the leader of the Neapolitan bandits of 1799, was supposed to possess a magic ring which turned away bullets. Oleksa Dovbush, the legendary eighteenth-century Carpathian bandit-hero, could be killed only with a silver bullet that had been kept one year in a dish of spring wheat, blessed by a priest on the day of the twelve great saints and over which twelve priests had read twelve masses.

Quite apart from its organizational and other weaknesses, the Boxer movement could not have succeeded in establishing a successful regime in China because its ideology was inadequate to fill the vacuum created by the decline in State Confucianism. It had no programme of reform comparable even to that of the Taipings. Its sole progressive principle was the equality it accorded to women (even though it associated them with the somewhat sinister qualities of the *Yin*). It advocated strictly moral behaviour (in the Confucian sense) and insisted on the asceticism of its followers, and, in its later stages, assumed the role of the 'protector of the People', in place of the ineffectual mandarins. But, although patriotic, it had not a word to say about such things as 'land reform', or how China should adapt herself for entry into the modern world. All modern inventions and innovations from vaccination to paraffin lamps were condemned as *yang* ('oceanic' or 'foreign'). Apart from their love for China and their anti-foreign animus, the only force binding the Boxers together was their common adherence to a Taoist–Buddhist–Confucian amalgam of religions. The *hsien* Taoism did indeed promise immortality but, in the interim, the only solace offered to the aspirants was ritual exercise and prayer—

a poor substitute for a full life of the body and the emotions guided by the intellect (*pace* the modern Western poets).

But notwithstanding these deficiencies, the general ridicule of the Boxer religion by Western writers is justified neither by its own complete absurdity nor by the comparative reasonableness of European beliefs. Nor can the intricate history of Boxer origins, implicated as it is with that of a great civilization, be dismissed as trivial or irrelevant. Yet this is what Mr Peter Fleming appears to do.

To explain, therefore, as several authorities have, that the Boxers were an offshoot of the Eight Diagram Sect, were associated with the White Lotus and the Red Fist societies, and had affiliations with the Ta Tao Hui or Big Knives, will scarcely enlighten the most learned reader. It seems best to leave the Boxers' cloudy pedigree on one side, and to set down such facts as are known about their eruption in 1898.[1]

Of Chinese religion in general the same author says, 'A marzipan effect is produced by the superimposal, on a basis of Shamanism and myth, of Buddhism, Taoism, and Confucianism'. The Boxers' incantations are 'abracadabra'; their ritual is 'magical goings-on'. This attitude is that of Macaulay, who dismissed Indian history and religion *in toto*, with its 'seas of treacle, and its reigns thirty thousand years long', but swallowed Jonah and the Whale entire as part of Holy Writ.

The height of the ridiculous in European eyes was, of course, the Boxers' claim to invulnerability. It was ridiculous because it was unfounded, but (unlike many Western superstitions) it had the merit that it could be disposed of by a practical test. Nevertheless, the *hsien* Taoism from which the notion derived had a factual basis, and the exercises and breathings (like those of *yoga*) have been adopted by modern Western therapy with profitable effect. Nor is *judo* (which is cognate with Chinese boxing and not very distant from it) despised in modern Europe as a discipline for both the body and the mind, and an approach to immortality through an extension of longevity is at least as reasonable as mere wishful-thinking.

Credulity is regrettable wherever it is found. As Bertrand Russell says, 'It is undesirable to believe a proposition when there is no ground whatsoever for supposing it true.' But to do so is not an exclusively Chinese failing. Without mentioning more controversial examples, witchcraft was a Christian heresy, invented by theologians, maintained by the orthodox creeds up to 1750 and frequently revived in more modern forms. It is easy to ridicule the Boxers as 'ignorant coolies' dressed in long baggy trousers tied at the ankles and wielding obsolete, scimitar-like sabres decorated with ribbons, relying on an absurd 'invulnerability', and conjuring up millions of 'spirit-soldiers' to help them in their fighting. It is more justifiable to arouse indignation at their bloodthirsty deeds, but even these were on a very small scale as compared with the historic massacres of Asia or the more recent ones of modern Europe. But when one reads of the excesses of the allied soldiery after the relief of the legations and of the greedy banditry of the Powers, one may be excused for wondering whether the Europeans (especially the Russians) were not equally barbarous.

When we come to reconsider the international scene and the wider issues, Mr Fleming again provides a handy and topical point of reference, for not only is his a recent reassessment but it faithfully reflects the 'Old China Hands'' point of view (which they no doubt derived from our Public Schools).

They [the foreigners] came to China to trade; their motive may not have been lofty, but it was natural and legitimate. When the Chinese refused to let them trade, the foreigners could hardly be expected to understand, let alone sympathize with the reasons for this refusal. They were in hard fact very silly reasons, based on a conception of the world which was self-centred, obsolete and doomed, and they were normally explained—if at all—in a gratuitously offensive manner....It was inevitable that the Powers would come with selfish aims to China. It was inevitable that they would be prepared to use force to further their aims. What, as we look back down history, does not seem wholly inevitable is that China's rulers should have immured the country for so long in a cocoon of childish bigotry that her first important encounters with younger civilisations were bound to end in tears.[1]

The Chinese, in fact, were 'cads who didn't play the game'. When opium and brummagem goods were forced down their throats, and their country was carved up like a joint they responded in a 'gratuitously offensive manner' which showed them up as the bounders they really were.

It is pertinent to reflect on the consequences of the action of the European Powers at the present day. The Europeans may or may not have had the right to force the Chinese to trade (and in another passage Mr Fleming concedes the Chinese their right to isolation), but the ultimate consequence of insisting on the 'opening up' of China in this way is that she has now closed her doors to trade except on a State to State basis. She has also decided to dispense with private enterprise and to follow a communal road towards capital formation. To discuss the merits of this decision is outside the scope of this book, but one may perhaps venture a regret that China's experience of capitalist enterprise and imperialism was so unfortunate that she has chosen to join the *bloc* of Powers hostile to our own, and to speculate whether a different line of approach on the part of the Powers might not have had happier results for the West.

How does the Boxer Uprising fit into the pattern of Chinese history worked out by the Chinese communist historians? My limitations as a Marxist theorist prevent me from attempting any expert answer to this question. I can disclaim, however, any partisan approach that would dismiss Marxism offhand; Marx was a great thinker and if the theory can be made to fit I am quite happy to accept it to the extent that it does so. Like Max Weber, however, I confess to a suspicion of *monocausal* explanations. It seems to me that the Peking historians are, in the interests of the theory to which they are committed, rather too anxious to show that the Boxer and other risings in China were 'anti-dynastic' through and through. As I have said above, I do not think that the evidence shows that in 1898 (at any rate in this traditionally loyal part of China) the majority of the Boxers were anti-Manchu; what was said of their scriptures in the Chia Ch'ing reign by the mandarins, namely that 'there was not one word in them relating to rebellion or opposition', was true of most of the Boxer scriptures in 1898. It was only later that the traditionally anti-Ch'ing elements temporarily gained the upper hand, but even then there is no reason to believe that the movement, in essence 'anti-foreign', at any time was uniformly subversive of Manchu rule.

The motive of the communist historians in insisting on the rapacity and lack of conscience of the Powers before, during and after the Battle of the Concessions is sufficiently obvious. It is to infer that 'capitalist imperialism' was by its very nature compelled to take the course it did, that it is incapable of changing its nature to meet changing conditions, and that the different appearance that it presents in the world of today is only a cover for its unchangeable character and objectives. The facts do not bear out this proposition. The policy of Great Britain, for example, underwent a complete transformation during the first half of the twentieth century resulting in the surrender of extraterritorial powers everywhere and the rendition of the 'settlements' in the Treaty Ports of China. Nor can it be fairly maintained that the British

'Empire', which has so successfully transformed itself into the Commonwealth consisting of equal and friendly partners, is no different from the Empire of Curzon, Kipling, or the concession-hunters in China. The communist thesis, however, is the 'necessity of revolution', and history seemingly must be made to conform to it.

Sir Robert Hart held that in spite of all their mistakes and crimes and superstitious follies, the Boxers were animated by a true spirit of patriotism, and Sir Reginald Johnston said:

In some ways it would not be unfair to describe the Boxers and their Manchu patrons as the real founders of the new Nationalism in China which has recently [1926] forced itself on the attention of the whole world, and the leadership of which definitely passed into the hands of the Students, in May, 1919.[1]

These judgments, I feel, are correct. Modern Nationalism has defects (and its dangers) as we know, but Mazzini was probably right when he insisted that 'Nationalism must precede Internationalism'.

Mr Chester Tan calls the uprising 'The Boxer Catastrophe', and, in contemporary terms, a catastrophe it undoubtedly was. Not only did it entail slaughter and suffering, but it resulted in the imposition of crippling taxation on the already impoverished Chinese people to pay the indemnities imposed by the Powers. At the same time, this mass uprising was a warning to the foreigner not to attempt the partition of China. The patriotic outburst of the North China peasantry, accompanied by outbreaks in many other parts of China, signalized the birth of Chinese Nationalism. But even if this happening forestalled a French Yunnan and Kwangsi, a British Yangtze Basin, a Japanese Fukien, and a Russian Colony of North China, such a partition could only have been temporary, and it could scarcely have been worse than the partition of the country which actually took place after the Revolution of 1911. It is therefore of no profit to search for comforting compensations. The more important question is why China missed the Scientific Renaissance with all that that implied and had to enter the modern world in the painful way that has been her lot.

CHING-SHAN'S 'DIARY'

This 'diary' first came to public notice in *China Under the Empress Dowager*, by J. O. P. Bland and E. Backhouse, published in London in 1910. Chapter XVII is entitled 'The Diary of His Excellency Ching Shan' and is prefaced by a note by the authors giving a summary of Ching-shan's career and adding a statement that 'the Diary was found by the translator in the private study of Ching-shan's house on 18 August 1900, and saved in the nick of time from being burnt by a party of Sikhs. Many of the entries [the note continues] which cover the period from January to August, 1900, refer to trivial and uninteresting matters.' Before that of 1 June 1900 the only entries translated are those of 25, 30, and 31 January.

This document is no longer regarded as genuine, but the circumstances relating to its fabrication and discovery are of some historical interest, although the mystery attaching to them has not yet been dispelled.

In *Acta Orientalia* (III, 1924) the late Professor J. J. L. Duyvendak undertook a new translation of the diary since he felt that that given in Bland and Backhouse was 'to judge from the very fluency of the English...probably rather free', and, in the light of the examination by him of the original manuscript deposited in the British Museum by Mr Bland, incomplete. Duyvendak found that the MS., consisting of thirty-eight pages of very unequal length, was bound together in a linen cover. The binding had been so badly done and the proper sequence of the pages had been so upset that he had to re-order them by the dating of the entries.

Professor Duyvendak in his introduction called attention to the number of discrepancies between the account of the diary in Bland and Backhouse and the results of his own examination, but he does not seem at this juncture to have entertained any doubts as to the genuineness of the diary. He notes, *inter alia*, that in spite of the statement of Bland and Backhouse that Ching-shan 'gives a full account of the rise and spread of the Boxer movement, describing in detail their magic rites, their incantations, and their ceremonies of initiation', nothing of the sort is to be found in the diary. Later on when Duyvendak corresponded with Bland he was informed by him that the missing entries had been handed over to the publishers (Heinemann) in 1910 for reproduction. Again, Duyvendak remarks that in giving the speeches of the Empress Dowager, the text of the Imperial edicts was followed very closely, 'without, however, so closely resembling it that we might suspect plagiarism'. Bland explained to Duyvendak that the missing portions of the diary were in his possession and that he intended in due course to publish a translation of them.

Duyvendak also reveals some other noteworthy facts. For example (p. vi):

A comparison of the text with the translation given in Bland and Backhouse shows that the previous editors, writing for the general public, did not aim at literalness. As Mr Bland tells me, the translation was Sir E. Backhouse's work, but he himself revised it, without reference to the original, omitting those portions which seemed uninteresting and generally polishing up the style of the documents. The facts related in the diary have, however, practically all been given.

The Backhouse–Bland and the Duyvendak versions of the diary vary considerably in some places and the dating of the entries after 7 July is quite different. Moreover, a search by Mr Bland among his papers resulted in the discovery of a long extra sheet which proved to be the end of the diary. Parts of the original text are reproduced as illustrations to the article in *Acta Orientalia*.[1]

Thirteen years later Mr William Lewisohn published an article in *Monumenta Serica* (1936), entitled 'Some Critical Notes on the so-called "Diary of His Excellency Ching Shan"'. In it he says that considerable criticism and doubt were expressed at the time as to the genuineness of the diary, but that historians (such as Morse) had used the text in Bland and Backhouse 'with, as must now be said, a surprising lack of the critical faculty'. In the course of examining the MS. in the British Museum and comparing it with other Chinese and foreign records of the Boxer times, Lewisohn was struck by a number of strange previsions, inconsistencies, and errors which were most unlikely to occur in a real diary and which were also incompatible with its authorship by such a person as Ching-shan. The conclusion he arrived at was that it was not the diary of one person, but a compilation, probably by more than one person, made some time after the actual events mentioned in it. Lewisohn then proceeded to a detailed examination of the MS.

Lewisohn asks how it was possible for Mr Backhouse, presumably the 'translator' who found the diary, to recognize the value of this precious document since he had only arrived in China for the first time in 1899 (the previous year), and to learn Chinese, let alone the enormously difficult 'grass hand' in which the diary was written, several years were required (even an eminent sinologist such as Duyvendak had to call in the assistance of a Chinese). How did it happen, moreover, that no word of the finding of the diary is heard until the publication of *China Under the Empress Dowager*, ten years later?

Regarding the external evidence, Lewisohn points out that the diary was written on separate pieces of paper of different size and texture (certainly not the custom with regular diarists, even in China) and that the handwriting varied considerably on the different sheets. Besides, it was incredible that a person as deaf as Ching-shan proclaimed himself to be should have been able to reproduce in full detail not only the conversations he had heard but also the long speeches made at the War Councils that were retailed to him by third parties (Duyvendak had himself called attention to this point). The diary, moreover, had a great air of artificiality and no details were given in it of relatives, officials, or ordinary persons unless they were in some way connected with the Boxer affair. 'Yet, here and there, scattered throughout the diary, we find remarks about his chair-coolies or his barber which anyone, Chinese or foreigner, could easily have written.'

As for the internal evidence, there were many discrepancies in dates which invalidated several of the 'previsions' in the diary, and it contained information which could not have been in Ching-shan's possession when he allegedly made the entries in question. There were besides errors and slips of the pen which he would hardly have made. Two entries were clearly spurious (of one of these Duyvendak himself remarks on p. 59 of his translation, 'The style of this paragraph is rather muddled').

Duyvendak made a rejoinder to Lewisohn in an article entitled, 'Ching-shan's Diary: a Mystification' (*T'oung Pao*, XXXIII, 1937), in which he confirmed Lewisohn's conclusion, but rejected his reasons for coming to it. The majority of Lewisohn's arguments, he said, were based on points to which he himself, in his version of the diary, had already drawn attention. To these Lewisohn had merely added a few discrepancies of the same order, 'for which, so long as one's faith in the Diary is not shaken for more fundamental reasons, an explanation can be found'. He therefore considered Lewisohn's arguments 'inadequate as a basis for the serious charge against the Diary which he prefers'.

Nevertheless, Duyvendak acknowledged his obligation to Lewisohn for reopening the discussion because his doing so had induced him to undertake a fresh examination of the evidence. This renewed study (largely with the aid of Chinese material that was not at his disposal in 1924) had compelled him to the conclusion that 'the diary, as presented to the world, was *not* authentic'. He had arrived at this opinion 'by philological methods in face of very strong internal evidence to the contrary'.

Now that his own suspicions had been thoroughly aroused, Duyvendak found innumerable extra discrepancies. One was that the execution of Hsü Ching-ch'êng and Yüan Ch'ang, stated by the diary to have taken place on the seventh day of the seventh moon (1 August 1900) at the hour *wei* (1–3 p.m.), in the presence of Ching-shan's son, actually took place on 28 July, four days earlier. He calls attention to the coincidence that several passages from the so-called journal or 'letter' of Wang Wên-shao, published in the *Ch'ing-t'an* in 1916,[1] are identical with passages in Ching-shan's diary. Nor can the diary of Ching-shan be in his own handwriting, despite the fact that several credible witnesses recognized it as being so.

Duyvendak's conclusion is:

The diary then cannot be authentic, and we are fully justified in placing an unfavourable interpretation upon all the suspect passages. I am quite willing to believe that there does exist a real diary by Ching-shan, found by the first translator in his study, and that portions of it have been incorporated into the mystification....As an independent source for the history of the Boxer troubles the 'Diary' must in future be disregarded. It retains value merely as a literary fiction, which, in masterly fashion, expresses the atmosphere of those days.

It will be noted that Duyvendak, by his willingness to believe that the diary as found by Backhouse was genuine but had been turned into a forgery whilst in his possession, introduces an extra and somewhat baffling element into the mystery.

In *Monumenta Serica* (5), 1940, Lewisohn added to his arguments that the diary was not genuine (pp. 419–27) in refuting a 'Publisher's Note' to a new edition of *China Under the Empress Dowager* (Vetch, Peking, 1939), in which various explanations were offered for the fact that numerous passages in the diary were identical with those in other works. He concludes that 'to say the least, there is something very wrong about *The Diary of His Excellency Ching Shan*'.

In the *Yenching Hsüeh-pao*, 1940 (English summary at p. 274), Ch'êng Ming-chou adduced additional evidence in support of Lewisohn's and Duyvendak's charges against the diary's authenticity and argued that philological peculiarities in two-thirds of the text suggest that whoever forged this part of it (which was the part justifying Jung-lu) had in certain instances used words and phrases which were Japanese and not Chinese. Dr Arthur Waley, however, doubts whether Ch'êng is right in seeing a Japanese hand at work in the diary.

Fan Chao-ying[1] says that, according to Chin-liang, who took an active part in editing the official draft history of the Ch'ing dynasty (*Ch'ing Shih Kao*), the motive of those who fabricated the document was to make Jung-lu appear as a friend to foreigners and so clear him of any responsibility in connection with the attack on the legations. In his miscellany, entitled *Ssŭ Ch'ao I Wên* (1936), Chin-liang also states that he intended to include in the official history of the Ch'ing a biography of Ching-shan, because of the latter's wide fame as the author of the diary, but that on closer examination of the diary he discovered so many errors and discrepancies in it that he decided to omit the biography. A comparison of the diary with known memorials (says Fang Chao-ying) shows that many statements in it which criticize the Boxers and favour foreigners were culled from these memorials and put into the mouth of Jung-lu. In Chin-liang's opinion, friends or adherents of Jung-lu, anticipating that the wrath of the foreign Powers would fall on him, forged the diary in order to clear him, and then placed it where observant foreigners would find it.

Duyvendak is apparently concerned to defend (or at least not to attack) the bona fides of Backhouse and Bland, who were still alive at the time. J. O. P. Bland (1863–1945) joined the Imperial Maritime Customs in 1883, resigning in 1896 to become Secretary of the Municipality for the foreign settlements of Shanghai. Edmund (later Sir Edmund, on the inheritance of a baronetcy) Backhouse (1873–1944) first arrived in China as a Student Interpreter in 1898 (not in 1899 as stated by Lewisohn). He had thus had time in which to learn enough Chinese to enable him to form an opinion as to the importance of the diary. It seems that while at Oxford he had shown an unusual facility for languages and his biographer[2] says that 'eventually he was able to read and write Chinese perfectly and could even translate the difficult "bamboo" characters'. Certainly his subsequent career as a scholar and lexicographer suggests that two years was sufficient in his case for him to have learned enough Chinese at least to realize the importance of the document.[1] He died in Peking in 1944 during the Japanese occupation and his papers were burned, either by the Japanese or to prevent them falling into Japanese hands. (I have not, so far, been able to trace the whereabouts of any private papers of J. O. P. Bland.)

Using Duyvendak's version of the text, we find that the primary object of the diary was apparently to justify the conduct of Jung-lu. Certainly he appears to advantage in it as the protector of the foreigner. On 1 June he is represented as denouncing the 'supernatural bands' (the Boxers)—'Should Jung-lu maintain this point of view [writes Ching-shan], it is to be feared that the Empress will never believe in the Boxers'; on 30 June, in response to a request from Tung Fu-hsiang for the loan of his big guns, he is reported as replying, 'If you really wish to use my big guns, please go and ask the Old Buddha for my head'; on 4 July, 'The ministers severely criticize Secretary Jung's friendship for the foreigners, because he will not lend his heavy guns'; 7 July, 'Grand Secretary Jung has again memorialized the Old Buddha, requesting her to stop the fighting at once'—and much more of the same sort.

Kang-i is referred to favourably (as 'really worthy of respect', 1 June), but others do not come out so well. Prince Tuan is 'over-bearing and extravagant, licentious and idle' (30 January); 'the I Ho T'uan were raised in Shantung by Governor Yü-hsien' (25 January); while the Empress Dowager's policy is shown as fluid—'She does not yet approve of the Big Sword's plan to exterminate the foreigners, as she fears we are too weak' (1 June), but she 'is certainly not in favour of war' (1 June). But all this may have been inserted to create 'an artistic verisimilitude'.

It seems quite clear from this that Ching-shan's diary is based on other documents. Duyvendak shows convincingly, for example, that the Imperial edicts and Wang Wên-shao's journal are among these. This journal is quoted at length in *China Under the Empress Dowager* (pp. 342–5), where it describes the flight of the Court from Peking.[2] Backhouse (says Duyvendak) must have been aware of the identity of the text with that of Ching-shan's diary, for where at one place some words appear in the diary which are missing from the journal, he supplied some of them from the diary (that is, by adding the words 'entering a coffin-shop'). If so, why was the diary's first translator not suspicious?

The consideration of these facts must suggest two propositions to those with any acquaintance with 'protocol'—the first is that if Backhouse, a Student Interpreter attached to the British Legation, had discovered a document which he considered of importance it was his duty to inform the British Minister, presumably through his own immediate chief, the Chinese Secretary, and second, that had this been done and had Sir Claude MacDonald endorsed his opinion, Sir Claude himself was under an obligation to inform his colleagues of the Diplomatic Body of its purport. There is no evidence, however, that either of these things happened.

An examination of the published correspondence in Accounts and Papers, China (3) 1900, of the correspondence in the Public Records Office, namely that between Peking and London (P.R.O. F.O. 17 (China), 1410–14) and the papers of the Chinese Secretary's Office, Peking (P.R.O. Embassy and Consular, F.O. 228 (1350–2), 230 (143–4), 233 (124))[1] does not bring to light any mention of the diary, or of Backhouse or Ching-shan. Nor is there anything in the diplomatic correspondence I have been able to consult which suggests that this diary had any influence on the negotiations for the protocol. It can be postulated, moreover, that if any noteworthy change had taken place in the attitude of the Powers towards Jung-lu between August and December 1900, it might well suggest that they had been influenced by some confidential information. But this was not the case. Although Jung-lu had been given the credit (by MacDonald at least) for not pressing the attack on the legations, the foreign ministers generally were hostile towards him on account of his having taken part in the siege. He consequently disobeyed the order of the Court to remain in Peking to negotiate with the Powers and fled to Paoting. On 2 October Li Hung-chang memorialized the Throne, reporting the hostile attitude of the foreign ministers towards Jung-lu and requesting his recall to Court. He was recalled on 11 November.[2]

I sought the assistance of the Foreign Office in trying to get to the bottom of the mystery and it was freely given. It transpires, however, that there is no subsequent record in the Foreign Office that suggests that the authority of the diary was suspect. The British Minister, Sir John Jordan, in his annual report for 1910 devotes seventy-six foolscap pages to *China Under the Empress Dowager*, but his remarks read like a book-review. He does not (so I understand) expressly state in it his suspicions as to the genuineness of the diary.

A review of Bland and Backhouse's book in the *Times Literary Supplement* of 13 October 1910 says:

Had Ching Shan's diary been in the hands of the diplomatists who sat in conference at Peking in the winter of 1900–1, the irrefutable evidence of its pages would certainly, on the other hand, have added to the black list of expiation the name of the Chief Eunuch, and of others in the Empress Dowager's immediate entourage, whose share in the attack upon the Legations is now fully disclosed; and it is quite conceivable that Russian diplomacy would have been less inclined to exercise its condoning influence, with results which might well have affected the subsequent course of history in the Far East.

But in spite of all that is now known about it, the diary continues to be quoted as if it had been fully authenticated.[1]

The above represented the extent of my own information until I visited the British Museum on 8 July 1960 to inspect the Ching-shan MS. Mr Grinstead, the Chinese specialist at the Museum, then drew my attention to 'A Footnote to "China Under the Empress Dowager"' which is preserved in the same box as the MS. together with a covering letter from Mr J. O. P. Bland dated 26 December 1944, to the late Dr Lionel Giles of the Museum. I considered this of sufficient importance to be reproduced in full, and no doubt this is what Sir Edmund himself would have wished.

It will be seen that while it makes Sir Edmund Backhouse's part in the episode perfectly clear and adds some valuable facts to our information, it throws no light on the authenticity or otherwise of the original MS. discovered by him.[2]

The MS. is now in one continuous roll, the sheets being carefully pasted on paper of uniform depth. The original paper, however, is all more or less of the same depth, and it must be pointed out that when Duyvendak spoke of '38 pages of very unequal length', he must have been referring to their 'length' laterally and not vertically.

The 'grass hand' used in the MS. is not of the highly cursive sort, and would have offered no great difficulty to a student of the experience of Mr Backhouse at the time.

I noted that whenever the Empress Dowager was referred to (as such or as the 'Old Buddha') the characters were elevated above the column, as was *de rigueur*.

Brudenell House
Aldeburgh
Suffolk
26 *December* 1944

Dear Mr Giles,

I enclose a document which was sent to me by the late Sir Edmund Backhouse in 1937, referring to the text of the Diary of Ching Shan, the original of which diary is amongst your records. It occurs to me that this document might be filed together with the Diary, and that it may be of interest and value hereafter, owing to the controversy which has arisen lately over the authenticity of the Diary. If Professor Duyvendak is alive he will, I am sure, take a hand in the logomachy.

The pencilled annotations on this document are in Backhouse's writing.

Yours truly,

J. O. P. BLAND

Peiping, *April* 1937

A FOOTNOTE TO 'CHINA UNDER THE EMPRESS DOWAGER'

It has been suggested to me that a fuller narration of the circumstances in which I found the document, believed by me then and believed by me still, to be the Diary of Ching Shan, would be of interest.

After the occupation of Peking by the Allies on August 15th, 1900, I was living in temporary quarters in what is now called by Europeans Morrison Street, Wang Fu Ching. As this portion of the city was temporarily in Russian control, I decided to move into the British section inside the Imperial City. I applied for permission to occupy part of the house belonging to Ching Shan, on the banks of the now filled-in 'river' bed, called Yü Ho. Captain Rowlandson, of the Baluchistan Regiment, who was in command, readily gave his consent and I moved into my new quarters, accompanied by a small escort of Welsh [*sic*] Fusiliers, who had been sent by Sir Claude MacDonald's order to ensure my safety. They were under command of a Sergeant Burke and were instructed to protect me against roving soldiery or looters.

On arrival at Ching Shan's house I found a couple of Sikh sentries inside the main gate and a detachment of some eight men under a native officer in the inner courtyard. There was friction between Sergeant Burke and the native officer who objected to the presence of the Welsh regiment. A quarrel seemed about to develop when Lieutenant Woodhouse appeared on the scene and the Welsh Fusiliers, having fulfilled their mission, returned to the Legation. In the main room of the inner courtyard Madame Ching Shan lay moaning and murmuring on the *K'ang*: a maid was in attendance and her younger son and daughter-in-law were trying to persuade her to take some gruel.

Lieutenant Woodhouse was most kind in welcoming me to the quarter and took me up to the adjoining Temple, where were the British detachment under Captain Rowlandson. He confirmed his permission to me to reside in the Ching Shan house, told me that the family were under suspicion of having Boxer affinities, that the eldest son was 'wanted' on a charge of parricide and of harbouring Boxers, and that I could occupy the whole house, excepting that portion where the Sikh detachment was stationed. He added that the latter would be withdrawn if En Ch'u, the eldest son, was surrendered to the British for trial. He authorized me to take any books and papers (of which, he said, there were a great number) for my own use, requesting that I should inform him if I found any Boxer documents or evidence of the Boxers' occupation of the house.

I returned to my new quarters and found my servants fixing up the outer guest room which was in a state of great disorder. From it I entered by a door on the west side the small apartment which, I was afterwards told by Madam Ching Shan's maid, had been Ching Shan's private study. It contained a table, chairs, and two large cupboards. On the brick floor were several boxes, the contents of which had been rifled. The cupboards were practically empty, but the floor was littered with papers, some being tied in bundles but the majority scattered about pell mell in almost inextricable confusion. I am sure that it is no exaggeration to describe the litter of paper as several inches deep. Books, some of them of value, had been thrown among the papers. One of the boxes was full of ancient memoranda, relating to Ching Shan's official duties, rescripts on petitions, drafts of memorials and the like. I attributed the confused medley to a search for loot and thought that the looters had turned everything topsy turvy in the hope of finding silver hidden in the room. A side door led into the main courtyard and another into an adjoining corridor. The latter was also littered with papers, while in the courtyard there were signs of burnt paper, as if the looters, or perhaps the Sikhs, had had a bonfire of the accumulated debris.

My first task was to retrieve the books, many of which were interesting Sung philosophic works. I then proceeded to examine the papers and was at once struck by the appearance of numbers of loose sheets scattered about the room. The first thing that struck my eye was the date on a long sheet, because it was very recent. On examining further I perceived that it was a record of the Court's departure. It was written in running hand, and a recent hostile critic has been polite enough to cast doubt on my ability to read running hand, seeing that I had only reached China in 1898 (not 1899, as this gentleman states). He contrasts me with Professor Duyvendak who confessed difficulty in deciphering the running hand and says in so many words that I am lying in pretending to have read the document in August 1900. My critic does not know that I began studying Japanese in 1894 and had been working at it continuously for *four and a half years* before coming to China. The first task that confronts the Japanese student (as Professor Chamberlain says in his book on the written language) is to learn the Hiragana, or Japanese grass hand, syllabary. As the fifty syllables have many variant forms, the number that the student must master, as given in Aston's Japanese grammar, runs into several hundred characters. The study of these leads on insensibly to that of other grass characters in common use in Japanese letters and ordinary documents. When I came to China in 1898, I could certainly read over 4000 grass characters and I believe that friends such as Bishop Norris, who knew me then, would confirm my statement. *Pace* my hostile critic, the diary of Ching Shan is not written in difficult running hand, but I am free to confess that there were a few individual characters which puzzled me at the moment but were readily found on reference to a Grass-and-running hand dictionary, of which many exist both in Japanese and Chinese.

The more I looked into the litter of papers, the more convinced I became of their interest. As the handwriting tallied with that on various documents of another nature bearing Ching Shan's signature, I came to the conclusion that the records were undoubtedly by him. I at once informed Captain Rowlandson of the discovery, which greatly interested him, owing to Ching Shan's reference to Boxers being quartered on his premises. When, a few days later, the eldest son was arrested, reference was made at the Court Martial to the charge made by his father against him. He was found guilty of murder and of harbouring Boxers. The sentence of death by shooting was carried out under the wall of the Imperial City, just opposite Ching Shan's main gate.

So far from observing a mysterious silence regarding my find, I informed General Barrow (for whom I was acting as Interpreter), Colonel Tulloch of the Baluchistan Regiment, Captain Pell of the General Staff and other Officers. When Sir E. Satow arrived in Peking, I informed him of the document at my first visit to him. He was much interested in learning of the names of Boxer ringleaders such as Fen Ch'e and Kuei Ch'un. He strongly advised publication but recommended that it be deferred till after the Empress's death.

It took me some time to sort the papers, the untied bundles proved to be a mass of records of all kinds from previous years. The *format* was the same in each case, a series of loose sheets of different sizes and shapes. The bundles which remained intact and tied with coarse string were composed of private correspondence, petty accounts, records of the day's events. I should hazard a conjecture that the whole mass of papers contained well over a million characters.

After the Empress's death in November 1908, I began to think of publishing my find, but owing to financial circumstances, was not in a position to pay for the publication and I doubted if I could find a publisher. (My doubts were justified, as, even after Mr Bland's most brilliant collaboration, we had the greatest difficulty in inducing a publisher to take the work. Murray and Arnold both turned it down but Heinemann had the adventurer's spirit and accepted the book.) I was naturally much pleased when Mr Bland, whose acquaintance I had recently had the privilege of making, offered to collaborate with me in writing a biography of the Empress, whom, like myself, he greatly admired and reverenced.

I am anxious publicly to express my thanks to Mr Bland for his generosity.

I sold to him all my rights in the book in February 1910 in exchange for the sum of £150. In consideration of this amount, I surrendered to him all that portion of the document which was published for the book. It became his absolute property and it was on his initiative that the Manuscript was placed in the British Museum. Mr Bland most generously paid to me, as an act of grace, half the share in the profits of the book between 1910 and 1917. The untranslated portions as well as a small portion that had been translated but not published, remained in my possession until 1932. I had always hoped to publish a full and literal translation, with notes, but illness, eye trouble, and financial worries, all stood in my way. Publication would have been an expensive undertaking and profits vague and nebulous. My critic writes of 'historical' or 'bibliographical' interest, I do not deny the one or the other, but there is a higher and a more immediate interest, viz. BREAD AND BUTTER interest, and RES ANGUSTA DOMI. The MS. still remaining in my possession up to 1932 was offered by me to Professor Duyvendak in 1926, on condition that he would publish a facsimile. This gentleman very kindly wrote to Bishop Norris in March 1936, 10 years later, offering to purchase the MS., but it was too late, as I had already sold it, with other documents, books and household effects in my possession in order to keep the wolf from my door. My former comprador, Mr Chang Hochai, who effected the sales, was murdered in his home here before handing me a full list of the purchasers.

My Critic reproaches me with my translation. My object was to give the spirit of the original in a book intended for the general public and not for the student. The omissions are intentional, because I did not regard the entry, or entries, as of interest. There are one or two clerical errors. I admire Professor Duyvendak's rendering, but I do not always agree with his version, e.g. Jung Lu, which is a quotation from the Book of Rites, 'he who knows music, understands the minutest questions regarding ceremonies' i.e. Jung Lu understood the minutest phase of the affair, or, in other words, had prevision of the event.

My friends know that I am not a conceited man, but, if I were indeed the ignoramus that my malevolent enemies love to traduce and calumniate, I ask my readers whether men like Sir E. Satow, himself a great scholar, Sir J. Jordan, Sir S. Barton, would have employed me as a translator in most delicate work, where accuracy was essential? Would these men have paid me a sum of about £2000 over many years, if my translations, whether into or from Chinese, Mongol, Japanese, Russian etc. were of no value? I possess letters of commendation from Satow, Sir S. Barton, and in particular a letter of thanks from Jordan for deciphering for the Colombo Museum a Chinese Imperial tablet erected in Ceylon about 1420.[1] I possess a most cordial letter of thanks from Sir R. Clive for work done at his order for the Legation. Quite recently, when feeble from old age, poverty, and manifold infirmities, I have earned the authorities' gracious approval, for translations from the Japanese owing to their accuracy and faithfulness to the original.

Magna est veritas et prevalebit.

(*Signed*) E. BACKHOUSE

P.S.

I also possess an autograph letter from a very high personage in H.M. Government dated May 1937, thanking me for translations from the Japanese furnished to H.E. The Ambassador.

Why did not Backhouse report the finding of the diary to Mac-Donald, who was still British Minister in Peking for a month or two after its finding? Satow does not seem to have attached any great importance to the diary for there is no reference by him to it in the files in the Public Record Office that I can discover. In the Satow Papers,[1] however, there is a letter from G. E. Morrison to Satow dated 15 November 1901 from Shanghai (the address given being 'care of J. O. P. Bland') enclosing a copy of the Chinese text of an agreement on Manchuria, which says:

Tsai Ch'un, the Envoy to Japan, declares emphatically that whatever credit is due to Chang Chih-tung and Liu Kun-yi for the resistance they dared to make to the Extermination Edicts of June 1900, still greater credit is due to Jung Lu who privately wired to them both to disregard the Edicts. Tsai Ch'un declares that without this powerful backing neither Liu nor Chang would have dared to oppose the Imperial will.

No opportunity has been given me to verify this statement. If true, it puts Jung Lu in a more favourable light than he has been seen hitherto.

Neither Morrison nor Bland himself, it is clear, had any knowledge of the diary at this time (fifteen months after its discovery) and Satow wrote no remark on the letter (as he did in other cases).[2]

MISSIONARY ARCHIVES

Steiger has extensively utilized the records of the American Board, but British missionary archives have been drawn on only to a limited extent. I have therefore sought out references to the Boxers in some of the archives of the missionary bodies situated in London. All those missionary bodies that I approached (the C.I.M., L.M.S., S.P.C.K., C.M.S., and S.P.G.) expressed their willingness to allow me access to their records, but I have investigated only those of societies operating in the disturbed regions of Shantung and Chihli in the period relevant to my main study (1898–9).

The conclusion I arrived at after a study of the records of the London Missionary Society and the Society for the Propagation of the Gospel in Foreign Parts confirmed the opinion I had already formed, namely that the foreign missionaries in general were not very closely in touch with what was happening in the neighbourhood of their mission stations and were taken by surprise when the storm burst around them, involving 'their converts' and themselves.

The following extracts from correspondence impressed me as being sufficiently important to transcribe for inclusion here. I would stress once again that they relate only to the pre-1900 period and there is a mass of material in the archives of the societies in question relating to the events of 'Boxer Year'.[1]

The following extracts from letters of L.M.S. missionaries in North China to headquarters in London relate to the earlier stages of Boxer activity:

No. 7175, of 24 January 1899. Dr S. S. MacFarlane[2] (in Shanghai) writes to say that he has heard from Mr Rees that things are quiet at Hsiaochang.

No. 6886, of 28 May 1899. From Dr S. MacFarlane in Chichou to Mr Cousins (London). '...Rees has doubtless given you full details about this Secret Society rising called the I Ho Ch'uan. Things are getting very lively when three fellows have to sit up at night outside the ladies' rooms with loaded revolvers prepared to make a firm stand if necessity demanded it. It was a memorable prayer-meeting at 1.30 a.m. when we knelt round Miss Harré's bed (she had been in bed three weeks Peill says with lumbago) and commend ourselves to His protecting care, knowing that greater was He that was for us than all they that were against us. The fitful firing of guns periodically during our prayer-meeting rendered the occasion all the more serious. The telegram to Tientsin brought a very high official along to enquire into matters. He has been here a week and is still in the yamen thrashing the matter out to the core. . . .'

No. 6884. W. H. Rees, Chichou, 31 May 1899, to Cousins. 'We are passing thro' a storm—Secret Society men have been arriving and kidnapped one of our deacons, threatening an attack on us. Our place is guarded by armed Christians. But I am now writing to say that I hope to send you full particulars when I find time, and that you will please not give credence to any unfounded alarm that may reach you. . . .'

No. 6885. Rees to Cousins, Chichou, 8 June 1899. 'The following is a short account of the troubles that have assailed us recently.

'Early in May, a few ringleaders of the Secret Society, known as the "United Boxers", were present at a large fair at which a number of volunteers were preaching. The Boxers cut short the preaching by reviling and brandishing "seven pointed swords". Next day, two of our evangelists visited the fair, but they failed to secure a place for preaching purposes, and the Boxers assumed such a threatening attitude that the two helpers returned home. Dr Peill (Mr Meech and I were away attending committee meetings in Tientsin) wisely decided not to send preachers again until the opposition had ceased, as it was evident that a well planned and formidable attack on Christian teachers had been agreed upon.

'On the third day, a teacher from an out-station, knowing nothing of these troubles went to the fair with the intention of helping in the preaching. He was drinking tea in a tent, when a descendant of Judas entered. This man had been baptised nearly 25 years ago, but I had expelled him immediately on my arrival in this place 11 years ago, as his character and influence were vicious. Since then he had repeatedly worried us. On this occasion, he spoke to our deacon in a loud voice, which evidently was a signal as forthwith a gang of men entered. They proved to be leaders of the "Boxers" and this expelled convert said—"This is the man", pointing to our deacon. He was arrested at once.'

There then ensued a discussion among the ringleaders and the deacon was released on condition that he should pay £75 ransom. This amount was not paid, but the deacon nevertheless surrendered himself to his bail.

The fair continued for 3 days more. On each day the Boxers appealed to the people to help them to exterminate the foreign devils, to burn their residences, and then kill all the converts, declaring that they were acting in accordance with the secret instructions of the Empress Dowager. All this was said from the platform of the theatre, in the presence of a huge crowd, at a place just 3 miles from here, and then they—the Boxers—drilled openly, brandishing their arms and using the vilest epithets imaginable to hurl at the foreigners. And yet, we had never collided with them, neither had we given them cause to complain of us.

The missionaries mounted a guard of sixty converts with the addition of 'a few heathen who offered their services to protect us'. Firing was kept up at a distance for several nights. The ringleader was a young man of 30, cousin to the magistrate. 'No wonder the official was unwilling to protect us!'

The Commissioner, appointed by the Viceroy,....is a clearheaded man, keen and alert, and grasped the situation at once. He had been authorized to call in the aid of 1000 soldiers, if necessary. He acted promptly and vigorously, and succeeded in arousing our phlegmatic and opium-besotted magistrate, nicknamed by the people 'Stupidity'.

After thorough investigation the Commissioner proposed to us the following terms:

1. The magistrate's cousin to be put in irons in open court, and then to be deposted to a place 600 miles away. If he attempted to escape, or dared to return, he should be beheaded at once.

2. The other leaders to give a bond, acknowledging their guilt, and promising to abstain from further molestation. Should they or their followers cause trouble in future, they alone shall be held responsible.

3. 'Judas' to be beaten, and to be deprived of his button. The innkeeper to be beaten, and to find sureties for his good conduct hereafter.

4. The magistrate to issue proclamations declaring to all that in future, wherever a fair or a theatrical performance is to be held, the chiefs of the guild must give written guarantee that no Christians shall be molested; if they decline to give such guarantees, the fair and the theatre shall be prohibited.

5. The expense incurred by the missionaries in feeding the men who guard their premises, to be paid by the magistrates.

We accepted these terms without demur, and they have been honourably observed in every particular. We had no hesitation in agreeing to these proposals, as the alternative was the immediate execution of the four ringleaders, and the dismissal of the magistrate. No followers of Christ could desire such condign punishment, nor agree thereto.

And now peace reigns again, and we have liberty to carry on our work as of old, but it will take a long time to counteract the evil influences this set going. Converts from distant stations are coming here, and are surprised tho' glad to see our premises still unscathed, and the missionaries alive,— the rumours of our murder being now quite generally believed by people at a distance. Our members must inevitably suffer much persecution, as those who do not know the true facts of the case, will ruthlessly and persistently abuse and revile.—But such incidents are not uncommon in our mission centre, and they are parts of the programme of missions.

That we have been mercifully preserved from what threatened to be a very serious riot is beyond doubt. We owe a debt of gratitude to the Consul and the Chinese Commissioner. But above all in praise of Him whose unworthy servants we are. He has some work for us to do in this benighted region. With this I believe we shall go forward, seeking in all things to do His will.

With kindest regards,
Yours sincerely,

WM HOPKYN REES:

No. 6952. Rees, Chichou, 1 July 1899, forwards a balance sheet to Cousins containing a charge for the guarding of the mission premises during the recent troubles and which he hopes the Directors will grant.

No. 7172. Rees to Cousins, Chichou, 15 September 1899. 'Renewed antagonism of the "Boxers". We are having another struggle with the "Boxers". Our poor people are suffering bitterly, and we have all been in danger. I am hoping that this new outburst will soon pass away, but it is most detrimental to our work, not to say anything of the anxiety regarding our personal safety, when these reckless men combine to attack our converts and threaten to destroy us and our homes.—Our work is at a standstill, and the Romanists suffer with us.'

No. 7243. Rees to Cousins, Chichou, 13 October 1899. 'We are still hindered by the "Boxers", and there is much unrest throughout the district. We are expecting soldiers daily to guard our houses, and we must insist on arresting the ringleaders, there can be no peace until this is done....

'I wish it were possible to give you more reassuring news about the rioters. French, American and British missions are now affected and the unrest is extending. The Americans have 300 soldiers in their district, and several ringleaders have been arrested. 160 soldiers are here, and tomorrow morning the local official and the Captain of the Cavalry are coming to consult with me as to the best plan for putting an end to their widespread opposition. The ringleaders do not belong to our district, but have come from distant and unknown places, and have gathered around them some hundreds of dissatisfied loafers and reckless robbers. Our own neighbourhood is quiet, but 23 miles away there is a big row with the Catholics, and the people there are in danger. It is entirely due to palace intrigues as the country people believe that the Emperor was deposed because he had become a Christian. We are on the eve of great events in China. What a pity that Britain's name is no longer feared, that British prestige has been completely lost, and that Russia rules all but in name....'

No. 7247. Dr Thos. Cochrane, Chaoyang to Cousins, 16 October 1899. 'Things are quiet here now and the property undamaged. Our compound was threatened but fortunately a large detachment of soldiers arrived in time and about 100 of the malcontents were beheaded and the rest scattered and our work goes on as usual.'

No. 7176. J. Stonehouse, Peking, to Cousins, 17 October 1899. 'Indifference and enmity of the people. . . . With regard to general mission work, the attitude of the people is one of indifference and of enmity. Since the Emperor was put on one side, we have not had one Manchu enquirer, let alone a baptism. The reigning dynasty being Manchu, the people have feared to have anything to do with Europeans. The officials have been decidedly against us. Time after time I have been told that the officials used threats to keep people away from us.'

No. 7416. Rees, Chichou, to Cousins, 16 and 23 December 1899. '16 December. Just a short note to say that the rebellion is spreading like a prairie fire. Over the borders in Shantung, American Congregationalists, American Presbyterians, French Catholics and others have suffered severely. Many churches and chapels have been destroyed and hundreds of converts have been looted, and some names have been added to the long and ever growing roll of martyrs.—

'In our district a preacher has been captured and ransomed by the officials. One of our chapels has been cleared of all its furniture, but not destroyed as the enemy's drilling place is next door. A few of our converts have been looted, animals and grain taken away and all furniture smashed. One preacher has been hiding for a long time, but has at last managed to escape to us. Very many Catholic chapels have been destroyed, and Catholic gentry captured and have paid ransom money. About 30 counties are involved, and the officials are helpless now. They are to blame for not nipping the thing in the bud, and they blundered seriously when they paid ransom money. This only aggravated matters, and made the Boxers more arrogant and insolent. 1500 foreign drilled soldiers have arrived in Shantung and there must be a desperate battle soon in that region. The Governor of Shantung has been dismissed and his place taken by the well-known Yuan Shih-k'ai, resident in Corea at the time of the war. We have appealed for protection, and have 10 soldiers and about 20 opium sots known as Yamen runners. The Consul telegraphed that the Viceroy is sending soldiers. We trust they will soon be here, as the enemy is in strong force 6 miles away, and we hear from various quarters that he is to be attacked within 2 days. We have a number of Christians here as a guard, fairly well equipped, but we can never hope to drive off the hundreds of fanatical scoundrels, whose flags have characters *Mieh Yang* (extermination of foreigners) inscribed upon them. . . .

'Dec. 23rd Since writing the foregoing, we have felt the full force of the storm. Our compound has today over 80 refugees, who have lost all their earthly possessions—including grain, clothing, bedding, animals etc., and 5 of our chapels are of no use any longer. Battle fought last week. 70 killed and 100 captured of the enemy. 70 soldiers here now and more expected on Monday. It will be a sad Xmas for us all. . . .'

The next reference to the Boxers in the correspondence is on 25 May 1900 in a letter from D. S. Murray, Tsangchou, to Cousins: 'The whole province is in a very restless and inflammable condition. If the hand of the law does not make itself felt more there are great dangers ahead for all the Churches.' Thereafter, the accounts of the collision with the Boxers, including the Hsiaochang affair of May, are very full and deserve the notice of future students of the 1900 crisis.

Society for the Propagation of the Gospel, I, 94. No. 95.

Rev. Henry Mathews. P'ing Yin report for year ending 31 Dec. 1899.

'At present we are in a somewhat troubled condition through the disturbances being caused throughout this part of the province of Shantung by a semi-secret society called "The Society of the Big Swords". Its chief object seems to be to resist all things foreign and especially foreign teaching. During the last three months its members have burnt down several Roman Catholic village churches and plundered the Christians. The members number some hundreds and in one case they came to a regular battle with the Imperial troops with the result that they were defeated and lost many men. They have been particularly active about twenty miles from us, but have not crossed the Yellow River. All the Christians in the district are considerably alarmed but they are standing fast....'

8 Feb. Missionary Reports I, 98, Ping Yin, Mathews to Preb. Tucker. 'In December last I wrote a brief report to the Society of the year's work in the Ping Yin mission. I had to tell of progress and bright prospects. Since then a time of trouble and severe persecution has fallen on the church, and I have now one of the saddest stories in the history of missions in North China to record.

'During the autumn of 1899 a fanatical society composed of most of the bad characters in North-Western Shantung made professions of zeal for the government and hatred of everything foreign an excuse for attacking, plundering, and even murdering native Christians in a widely extended district north of the Yellow River. The Governor of Shantung of the time was a Manchu of strongly anti-foreign feeling. Instead of putting down with a strong hand the gangs of lawless ruffians who roamed about the country committing the most cruel and barbarous acts, he openly encouraged them, with the result that hardly a mission station or any little village community of Christians escaped being looted. Day after day in broad daylight Christian homes were burnt down and Christians robbed of all their possessions. Some were bound and held at ransom, and others were killed. The only terms of peace were apostasy....

'On Saturday[1] came the most terrible news of all. A man came running in to say that the Rev. S. Brooks had been taken prisoner after being wounded in a struggle on the road from Taian to Ping Yin.[2] It appeared that when my letter reached Taian with news of the trouble at Ping Yin, he at once felt it his duty to return. He could not bear the thought of my being alone to face the anxiety and trial, and set out as he had intended on Dec. 29th. He did not anticipate any danger on the road, but on the second morning when about twelve miles from Ping Yin he was attacked by a band of about thirty armed ruffians who after struggling with him and wounding him on his head and arms with their swords bound him and led him away towards Ping Yin. It was an intensely cold day and snow was falling. In spite of this they took from him all his outer garments and led him about for some hours. He endeavoured to ransom himself with promises of large sums of silver but they were unwilling. In the afternoon the band stopped at a little roadside food-shop for their afternoon meal and while this was being eaten Mr Brooks was bound to a tree close by. It is said that by some means he managed to escape and fled in the direction of Ping Yin. He was quickly pursued by three horsemen who cut him down when only a mile from our little church at Ta Kuang Chuang and there by the roadside the last act in this terrible crime was committed. His head was taken from his body and both thrown into a gully only a few feet away. It must have been just at this moment that the news of his capture reached me at Ping Yin, at the same time news came that the band from Shiu-li-p'u, two hundred strong, was only a few miles away and advancing on Ping Yin. The whole country-side seemed involved in a fierce storm of robbery and burning. Humanly speaking nothing could save our central station at Ping Yin....Since his death the ambassadors in Peking have been able to insist much more strongly on its [the I Ho Tuan's] suppression and thus in a very real sense he laid down his life for us all.'

NOTES

PAGE 2

1 E. H. Parker, in an unpublished official memorandum (included in a confidential despatch from the Secretary of State, Lord Knutsford, to Sir Clementi Smith, the Governor of the Straits Settlements, of 8 February 1889).
2 But the Manchu women at least had a distinctive head-dress which I saw some of them still wearing in Peking in 1923, and they were conspicuous otherwise since none of them bound their feet.

PAGE 3

1 Li Chien-nung, *The Political History of China, 1840–1928*, trans. Ssŭ-yü Têng and J. Ingalls (Princeton, 1956), pp. 2, 3; and Ssŭ-yü Têng and John K. Fairbank, *China's Response to the West* (Harvard, 1954), p. 7.
2 See Liang Ch'i-ch'ao, *Intellectual Trends in the Ch'ing Period (Ch'ing Tai Hsüeh Shu Kai Lun)* (1920), trans. by Immanuel C. Hsü, foreword by Benjamin I. Schwartz (Harvard, 1959).

PAGE 4

1 The titles of the Emperor and of all the princes and the officials of the empire are set out in W. F. Mayers, *The Chinese Government: A Manual of Chinese Titles*, 3rd ed. (Shanghai, 1897).
2 E. H. Parker, *China: her History, Diplomacy and Commerce* (London, 1901), p. 161.
3 He was writing in the Boxer Year.
4 The structure of the Ch'ing administration is set out in *Ta Ch'ing Hui Tien (Collective Statutes of the Ch'ing)*. See John K. Fairbank and Ssŭ-yü Têng, *Ch'ing Administration: Three Studies*, Harvard–Yenching Institute Studies, XIX (Harvard, 1960), for a detailed account of procedure in the Grand Council, Boards, etc.
5 See Alfred Kuo-liang Ho, 'The Grand Council in the Ch'ing Dynasty', *FEQ*, XI, 2 (February 1952).

PAGE 6

1 For justification of this slur, see Ch'ang-tu Hu, 'The Yellow River Administration in the Ch'ing Dynasty', *FEQ*, XIV (August 1955).

PAGE 7

1 John K. Fairbank and Ssŭ-yü Têng, *Ch'ing Administration* (Harvard, 1960), p. 69.

PAGE 10

1   G. Nye Steiger (*China and the Occident*, New Haven, 1927, p. 2) follows
    Parker and Douglas, and even goes further in calling China 'the only
    country in the world where essential democracy has been successfully
    worked out'.

PAGE 11

1   *T'ang-pao*, *Peking Gazette*, lit. courier news, was also called *Ching-pao*,
    Ti-ch'ao, *Ti-pao*, etc. It was not a type of document but one of the chief
    means of dissemination of important documents into the provinces,
    consisting of copies of documents sent from the capital to the high pro-
    vincial officials for their information; sometimes printed, and sometimes
    reprinted in the provinces for further circulation; also made up and
    distributed by private firms. The term '*Peking Gazette*' is thus a generic
    one, including many forms, both official and non-official. John K.
    Fairbank and Ssŭ-yü Têng, *Ch'ing Administration* (Harvard, 1960),
    p. 96.
2   Schuyler Cammann, 'The Making of Dragon Robes', *T'oung Pao*, XL
    (1950–1). European aniline dyes were used with vegetable dyes in the
    late nineteenth century for the imperial robes, thus helping the general
    decay of Chinese taste, most noticeable from Chia Ch'ing onwards.
3   John K. Fairbank, 'The Manchu–Chinese Dyarchy in the 1840's and
    '50's', *FEQ*, XII, 3 (May 1953).

PAGE 12

1   Alfred Kuo-liang Ho, *loc. cit.*
2   *Accounts and Papers* (1900), CV, p. 237. H. O. Bax-Ironside to Foreign
    Office. Of the sixty-two viceroys, governors, treasurers, and judges of
    the eighteen provinces and the New Dominion, twenty-four (says
    Bax-Ironside) were Manchus, whereas before the *coup d'état* only thirteen
    of them were Manchus.

PAGE 13

1   E. H. Parker, *China*, p. 169.

PAGE 15

1   *China*, p. 6.
2   E. H. Parker, *China*, p. 170. Morse (*IRCE*, I, 14) says that in 1906 there
    were 1443 *hsien* in the provinces and twenty-seven in Manchuria.

PAGE 16

1   *China*, p. 171.

PAGE 17

1   *Op. cit.* p. 89.

PAGE 18

1   Mary C. Wright, 'What's in a Reign Name?', *JAS*, XVIII, 1 (November 1958).

PAGE 19

1   Li Chien-nung, *op. cit.* p. 97, quoting Yün Yü-ting, *Ch'ung Ling Ch'uan Hsin Lu* (*A Veritable Account of the Crisis of the Kuang Hsü Reign*) (Shanghai, 1911).
2   See W. F. Mayers, *op. cit.* p. 84.

PAGE 20

1   John K. Fairbank (ed.), *Chinese Thought and Institutions* (Chicago, 1957), p. 217, says 169,000—more than half of them Chinese or Mongols.
2   Franz Michael, 'Military Organization and Power Structure of China during the Taiping Rebellion', *Pacific Historical Rev.* no. 4 (November 1949). K. S. Latourette, *The Chinese: Their History and Culture* (New York, 1946), p. 541.

PAGE 21

1   Robert K. Douglas, *Society in China* (1894), p. 363.
2   E. H. Parker, *China: her History, Diplomacy and Commerce*, pp. 198, 245.
3   Sir T. F. Wade, 'The Army of the Chinese Empire', *Chinese Repository*, XX (1851), 250, 300, 363.
4   S. Wells Williams, *The Middle Kingdom* (1883), II, 425–6.

PAGE 22

1   See p. 49.
2   Ho Ping-ti, *Studies on the Population of China, 1368–1953* (Harvard, 1959), pp. 67–8.

PAGE 23

1   E. H. Parker, *China*, pp. 257, 259.

PAGE 24

1   He perhaps reached the acme of the ludicrous in the comic opera *San Toy*, running at Daly's Theatre in 1899.

> Chinese sojer-man
> He wavee piecee fan,
> He shoutee Hip, hoo-lay for Empelor,
> He makee hollid yell,
> Bangee drum and lingee bell
> When Chinee sojer marchee out to war!

2 Andrew Wilson, *The 'Ever-Victorious Army'* (1868), pp. 136, 137, and *passim*.

PAGE 26

1 Ralph L. Powell, *The Rise of Chinese Military Power, 1895–1912* (Princeton, 1955), p. 42.
2 Wooden cannon balls were painted to resemble iron ones to cover misappropriation (E. T. Le Fevour, *Western Enterprise in China, 1842–1895*, p. 350 (unpublished Ph.D. dissertation, Cambridge University, 1961).

PAGE 27

1 M. E. Cameron, 'The Public Career of Chang Chih-t'ung, 1837–1909', *Pacific Historical Rev.* (September 1938), pp. 187–220, and Yung Wing, *My Life in China and America* (New York, 1909), pp. 225–6, quoted by Ralph L. Powell, p. 61.

PAGE 28

1 But see p. 30, note 2, below.
2 The efficiency of Chang Chih-tung's troops is much to be doubted. When the real test came in October 1911, they made a very poor showing. See Jerome Ch'ên, *Yüan Shih-k'ai, 1859–1916* (1961) (chapter III) for the military history of the Boxer period.

PAGE 29

1 Ralph L. Powell, *op. cit.* p. 84.
2 *The Times*, 25 July 1900, estimated that the Chinese troops mobilized against the allies in Chihli, excluding Boxers and Secret Society members, would not exceed 100,000 men (see Parker, pp. 253–4).

PAGE 30

1 C. Beresford, *The Break-up of China* (1899), pp. 270–5. Minute details of the organization and pay of Yüan Shih-k'ai's troops are contained in the confidential report of the British Military Attaché in Peking, Colonel Browne, of 24 May 1898 (P.R.O., F.O. 17 (China), p. 97). At 8 taels to the pound sterling, the pay of a battalion commander was 400 taels a month, of junior captains and lieutenants 30 taels, and of private soldiers 4.50 taels. Buglers were paid one tael a month more than a private. Colonel Browne, in recommending methods for forming a British Chinese battalion, points out that white could not be used for the soldiers' uniforms as it was the sign of deep mourning, and green was very objectionable (all the caricatures of missionaries showed them as wearing green hats). The coat should be red (a most auspicious colour) with blue trimming, and the trousers black.
2 Etienne Zi, *Pratique des Examens Militaires* (*Variétés Sinologiques*, 9) (Shanghai, 1896).

NOTES

PAGE 31

1 George Lynch, *The War of Civilisations* (1901), p. 281.

PAGE 32

1 J. Needham, 'The Past in China's Present', *Centennial Rev.* IV, 2, 3 (1960).

PAGE 34

1 Morton H. Fried, 'Community Studies in China', *FEQ*, XIV, 1 (November 1954).
2 Li Chien-nung, *op. cit.* p. 279.

PAGE 35

1 For Smith's other books, see Bibliography.
2 *Op. cit.* XV, 169.

PAGE 36

1 Joseph Needham has coined a non-pejorative word for the 'squeeze' system, namely nosphomeric (from *nosphizein*, to sequestrate; *meros*, a part).
2 *Village Life in China*, p. 226.

PAGE 37

1 *Ibid.* p. 132. Morse, *IRCE*, I, 2, says, '...autocracy and bureaucracy together govern, by oriental methods, a people, which, as manifested in the life of the gild and village, has the essentials of a democracy'.
2 *Village Life in China*, p. 227.

PAGE 38

1 *Society in China*, p. 169.

PAGE 39

1 Douglas describes Chinese farms as market-gardens rather than agricultural holdings. The implements used were primitive in the extreme—a plough that did little more than disturb the surface of the soil, a hoe, and a few rakes and bill-hooks. Apart from cereals, the main crops in the regions referred to were mulberries and a kind of oak for feeding silkworms, tea, and the opium poppy.

PAGE 40

1 The fact remains, however, as I can state from personal knowledge, scholars, even as late as the 1920's, preferred to endure great poverty rather than to turn to trade and thereby lose the prestige of their literary status.

PAGE 42

1   The European observers generally seem to have had no suspicion of the existence of social or economic 'classes' as they are understood today. They believed too in the 'equality of educational opportunity'. Here are a few more examples.

Chester Holcombe (U.S. Foreign Service), *The Real Chinaman*, 2 vols. (New York, 1895): 'For many centuries the practical government has been in the hands of those who have sprung from the common people' (I, 45).

Emile Bard, *The Chinese at Home* (n.d.) (translation and adaptation of *Les Chinois chez eux*, Paris, 1900): 'These [examinations] are open to all without regard to origin, the rich and poor being able to compete in them on a footing of the most perfect equality' (p. 103).

Rev. J. Macgowan (London Missionary Society), *Sidelights on Chinese Life* (1907): 'The mandarins are all sprung from the people without any reference to class or social position' (p. 273).

H. A. Giles, *China and the Chinese* (1902): 'Want of means may be said to offer no obstacle in China to ambition and desire for advancement' (p. 79).

2   Introduction to Chang Chung-li, *The Chinese Gentry* (Seattle, 1955), p. xiv.

PAGE 43

1   Karl A. Wittfogel, *Oriental Despotism; a Comparative Study of Total Power* (New Haven, 1957). Wittfogel's thesis that in 'hydraulic' societies there were no effective institutional checks on absolutism, has been criticized, for example, by E. G. Pulleyblank in the *Journal of the Economic and Social History of the Orient*, I (Leiden, 1958), who says that while this may have approximated to the truth at certain periods, nevertheless certain vested interests—clans, guilds, gentry as a class— did collectively obstruct the will of an autocrat. What was lacking was defence for the individual non-conformist, both against the State and against vested interest.

2   See note 2, p. 42.

3   Arthur Waley criticizes the use of 'gentry' to translate the term *chin-shên*. While welcoming Mr Chang's book as a 'fine piece of work, punctiliously documented and exhibiting an immense range of learning', he says that it suffers from the vagueness of the word *chin-shên* which has at least three meanings: (1) local people who held a degree, but who were not officials; (2) the class consisting of (*a*) officials, (*b*) holders of degrees who were not officials; and (3) officials, as opposed to those who merely held degrees. A more manageable study (Dr Waley considers) would have been the influence, in local life, of those holders of degrees who were not officials. These local (*hsiang*) *chin-shên* were a class that had no counterpart in other civilizations. A man might be well born, well off,

a learned Confucian and yet not count as belonging to it. An example was T'êng Yü, who planned the Gazetteer of Honan in 1767. He held no degree or official post, but he was emphatically in birth, education, and social status what we should call a gentleman. In Chinese terminology, however, he was a *pu-i* (cloth-jacketed person), not a *chin-shên* (*RASJ*, parts 1 and 2, 1956, p. 94).

Actually Chang Chung-li does not refer to *chin-shên* but to *shên-chin* (which is apparently the reversed form of the same expression), and then only once, and prefers *shên-shih* as a general term for 'gentry'. Franz Michael uses both *shên-chin* and *shên-shih* for 'gentry'.

PAGE 45

1   See analysis of the traditional Chinese social classes in T'ung-tsu Chü, 'Chinese Class Structure and its Ideology', in John K. Fairbank (ed.), *Chinese Thought and Institutions*, pp. 235 ff.

PAGE 47

1   *Op. cit.* p. 187. E. A. Kracke, Jnr., in 'Family versus Merit in Chinese Civil Service Examinations' (*HJAS*, 1947, p. 103), quotes François Quesnay, in *Le Despotisme de la Chine* (1767), as an example of the early European idealization of the Chinese examination system—'There is no hereditary nobility in China; a man's merit and capacity alone mark the rank he is to take'. Wittfogel (1938) says, 'Some fresh blood may have been absorbed from the lower strata by means of the examination system, but on the whole the ruling officialdom reproduced itself socially more or less from its own ranks'. Kracke concludes that under the Sung, 'graduates who had no family tradition of the civil service, played by virtue, both of their numbers and their official functions, a highly significant part'.

2   'Bureaucratic Constraints on Nepotism in the Ch'ing Period', *JAS*, XIX, 2 (February 1960).

3   Fei Hsiao-tung, *China's Gentry, Essays in Rural–Urban Relations* (Chicago, 1953).

4   *FEQ*, XIII, 3 (May 1954). Review of above.

PAGE 48

1   Hsiao Kung-ch'üan, 'Rural Control in Nineteenth Century China', *FEQ*, XII, 2 (February 1953).

2   Y. K. Leong, and L. K. Tao, *Village and Town Life in China* (1915), p. 4f. The book refers to China under the empire.

PAGE 49

1   Parker says 1300. See p. 15.

PAGE 50

1 Hsiao Kung-ch'üan, *loc. cit.*
2 Irene B. Taueber and Nai-Chi Wang, 'Population Reports in the Ch'ing Dynasty', *JAS*, XIX, 4 (August 1960).
3 G. Nye Steiger, *China and the Occident*, p. 2.

PAGE 51

1 See p. 36.
2 See p. 16.
3 Hsia Nai, 'The Land Tax in the Yangtze Provinces before and after the Taiping Rebellion', in E-tu Zen Sun and John de Francis (translators), *Chinese Social History: Translations of Selected Studies* (Washington, D.C., 1956), p. 361.

PAGE 52

1 Hsia Nai, *ibid.* p. 381.
2 See pp. 150-1.

PAGE 53

1 The phrase 'closing decades of the eighteenth century' of course had no meaning for China where there was no 'eighteenth century', but the corresponding period happens also to mark the end of a phase in Chinese history and the phrase can therefore be used appropriately in writing for a Western public.

PAGE 54

1 L. Carrington Goodrich, *A Short History of the Chinese People* (New York, 1959), p. 221.
2 Quoted by Hsiao Kung-ch'üan, *ibid.* p. 180, also p. 28 n.
3 I have italicized these words of Hsiao's since they will have a special bearing when we come to consider the causes of the Boxer rebellion in detail.

PAGE 55

1 *Selected Works of Mao Tse-tung* (Peking, 1955), I, 13 f. See chapter VII.
2 *Ibid.* I, 42-5.

PAGE 56

1 The important and comprehensive survey by Hsiao Kung-ch'üan, *Rural China: Imperial Control in the Nineteenth Century* (Seattle, 1961), came to hand after this book had gone to press. It contains much information relating to rural society, the White Lotus, etc.

PAGE 57

1 Benjamin Schwartz, Foreword to Immanuel C. Hsü (trans.), Liang Ch'i-ch'ao, *Intellectual Trends in the Ch'ing Period* (Harvard, 1959).

PAGE 58

1 Ho Kan-chih, *A History of the Modern Chinese Revolution* (Peking, 1960), p. 3.

PAGE 59

1 Tai I, 'Chung Kuo Chin Tai Shih Ti Fên Ch'i Wen Ti', *Li-Shih Yen-chiu*, XII, 6 (1956).
2 Wang Jên-ch'ên, 'Tui Chung Kuo Chin Tai Shih Fên Ch'i Wên T'i Ti Shang Chüeh', *Li-shih Yen-chiu*, XII (1956).
3 John K. Fairbank, 'China's Response to the West: Problems and Suggestions', *Cahiers d'Histoire Mondiale*, III-2 (Paris, 1956), 381–406. See also Ssŭ-yü Têng, John K. Fairbank, and others, *China's Response to the West, a Documentary Survey, 1839–1923* (Harvard, 1954), *passim*.

PAGE 60

1 Joseph Needham, *Science and Civilisation in China* (1954), and 'The Past in China's Present', *Centennial Rev.* IV, 2, 3 (1960).
2 *SCC*, I, 3.
3 *Ibid.* 242. Needham originally included clockwork in this list until he discovered that in A.D. 725 the Chinese had constructed what was essentially the first of all mechanical clocks (*SCC*, III, 350).

PAGE 61

1 Michael Greenberg, *British Trade and the Opening of China, 1800–42* (Cambridge, 1951), p. ix.

PAGE 63

1 Jean Escarra, *Le Droit Chinois* (Peking, 1936), p. 3, trans. J. Needham, *SCC*, II, 521. Needham remarks that Escarra exaggerates in saying that Chinese law is 'purely penal' as it is, above all, administrative law.
2 J. Needham, *SCC*, II, 575.

PAGE 64

1 The passage is taken by Prémare from Su Tung-p'o (1036–1101) (part II, chapter 10), who quotes in support of his statement the commentary of Tsoch'iu Ming on a passage in the *Spring and Autumn Annals* saying that Duke Yin's object was to cultivate the friendship his father had maintained with the Jung tribe, but declined to enter into a covenant with them as they wished (James Legge, *The Chinese Classics*, V, part 1, book 1, 2nd year, Hong Kong, 1861–72).

PAGE 65

1 *Hansard*, 8 April 1840, c. 818.
2 *Ibid.* c. 816. On 27 July 1840 Gladstone spoke for 1½ hours ('for the liberation of my conscience') on the subject of opium compensation, and in 1841 he wrote, 'I cannot be party to exacting by blood opium compensation from the Chinese' (Morley, *Life of Gladstone* (1903), I, 229, 239).

PAGE 66

1 W. F. Mayers, *Treaties between the Empire of China and Foreign Powers* (Shanghai, 1902), p. 6.
2 France desired that a clause granting toleration to Christianity should be included in her treaty, but although this was not agreed to, she did succeed in getting the Emperor to issue two edicts improving the position of Roman Catholicism in China.

PAGE 69

1 H. B. Morse, *International Relations of the Chinese Empire*, I, 570, 615, cited by K. A. Latourette, *A History of Christian Missions in China*, p. 274. Out of a total of $489,694.78 allowed to claimants from the indemnity allocated to the United States, $57,019.71 went to missionaries and missionary societies. This was chiefly in respect of property destroyed in Canton in 1856. Out of the large indemnity paid to the British for losses in Canton, $2466.63 was given to the Wesleyan Mission, $18,464.20 to the Church Missionary Society, $2839.98 to the Rev. J. H. Gray, and $8680.00 to the Seamen's Bethel.
2 The passages from Chinese sources cited in the following paragraphs are from Ssŭ-yü Têng and John K. Fairbank, *China's Response to the West*.

PAGE 71

1 H. B. Morse, *IRCE*, III, 390.

PAGE 72

1 Hu Shêng, *Imperialism and Chinese Politics* (Peking, 1955), p. 69.
2 *Annals of the Conduct of Foreign Relations* (in Chinese), 55, pp. 7–8, quoted by Hu Shêng, p. 70.

PAGE 73

1 Arthur Waley, *The Opium War Through Chinese Eyes* (1958), p. 56.
2 A. B. Freeman-Mitford, *The Attaché at Peking* (1865), pp. 77, 86.

PAGE 74

1 Mary C. Wright, *The Last Stand of Chinese Conservatism: The T'ung Chih Restoration, 1861–74* (Stanford, California, 1957), p. 21.
2 The Imperial Maritime Customs were also the first to build modern lighthouses in China, and to introduce other aids to navigation.

PAGE 75

1 K. S. Latourette, *A History of Modern China* (1954), p. 78.

PAGE 76

1 Hu Shêng, *op. cit.* p. 85.
2 Henri Cordier, *Histoire Générale de la Chine* (Paris, 1920), IV, 124.
3 Helmuth Stoecker, *Deutschland und China im 19. Jahrhundert* (Berlin, 1958), p. 66.
4 Quoted by Mary C. Wright (*op. cit.* p. 25). *Hansard*, 194, c. 933.

PAGE 77

1 *Ibid.* p. 25 from *Hansard*, 194, c. 933–7.
2 *Ibid.* p. 25 from *Hansard*, 194, c. 937–44.
3 *Parliamentary Papers* (China, 1870), no. 9, pp. 4–11, cited by K. S. Latourette, *A History of Modern China*, p. 474.
4 In *FC*, 147 of 31 October 1899, Bax-Ironside to Salisbury, correspondence with the Bishops of Anglican Communion is transmitted. The six bishops (Scott, Corfe, Graves (U.S.A.), Cassells, J. C. Victoria (Hong Kong), and Moule) 'do not wish to complicate their spiritual responsibilities by the assumption of political rights and duties, such as have been conceded to the Roman Catholic hierarchy'. They add, 'but we cannot view without alarm both on behalf of our own flocks and the Chinese population generally, the rapidly growing interference by French and other Roman Catholic priests with the provincial and Local Government of China'. At the same session, 21 October 1899, the Anglican bishops passed a resolution:
'To address a letter to the Representatives of Great Britain and the United States in Peking, setting forth the danger, both to the legitimate interests of the Anglican and other non-Roman missions in China and to the public peace, arising from the disregard of first principles of justice and charity exhibited by certain European priests, apparently with the support of the French Legation, and to deal with which the Chinese Mandarins have professed themselves powerless.'
Earlier the same year the project of appointing an Apostolic Delegate to Peking, which had long been entertained by the Pope, had been renewed under the influence of the French government who were endeavouring to obtain the appointment of a French priest, Father Battembourg, Secretary of the Order of Lazarists in Paris. Both Britain and Germany opposed this indirect extension of French power (*FC*, 65, Rome, Sir P. Currie to Salisbury, 17 January 1899).

NOTES

PAGE 78

1   In spite of the maximum import tariff of 5 per cent fixed by the treaties.

PAGE 79

1   Their slogan was, *Chung hsüeh wei t'i; hsi hsüeh wei yung,* 'let Chinese learning be the essence, and Western learning provide the material efficiency' (see chapter v).
2   Hu Shêng, *op. cit.* p. 93.
3   Liang Ch'i-ch'ao, Kang Yu-wei's principal lieutenant in the Hundred Days Reform of 1898, said that Li Hung-chang was a big shareholder in the China Merchants' Steam Navigation Company, the General Telegraph Office, the Kaiping Mines and the Commercial Bank of China. It was also said (added Liang) that he was proprietor of all the big stores and money brokerage firms in Nanking and Shanghai. Liang Ch'i-ch'ao, *Li Hung-chang* (in Chinese), p. 85. To this would be added the large bribes Li received from foreign governments—certainly from Russia in 1896—for his part in securing concessions for the Chinese Eastern Railway, and in 1898 (500,000 taels) for helping Russia to occupy Port Arthur. To secure a share in modern industry for China was considered 'patriotic', even if this took the form of enrichment of the individual.

PAGE 81

1   *Chambers's Encyclopaedia* (1950), VIII, 49.
2   Sir G. B. Sansom, *The Western World and Japan* (1950), p. 532.

PAGE 82

1   Albert Feuerwerker, *China's Early Industrialization: Shêng Hsüan-huai (1844–1916) and Mandarin Enterprise* (Harvard, 1958), p. 56.

PAGE 83

1   Feuerwerker, *op. cit.* pp. 250, 251. Norman Jacobs, in *The Origin of Modern Capitalism and Eastern Asia* (Hong Kong, 1958), suggests that the similarity of the system of land-tenure, labour-service, freedom of the market, the independence of the merchants from the ruling authority, the organization of the guilds, and the system of taxation in Japan to those of Western Europe facilitated her industrialization, while the corresponding features of China did not.
2   Ho Ping-ti, *Studies on the Population of China, 1368–1953,* p. 276.

PAGE 84

1   I have generally followed William L. Langer, *The Diplomacy of Imperialism, 1890–1902,* 2 vols. (New York, 1935), chs. VI and XII, as being the most reliable accounts available, but I have incorporated from vol. III,

ch. XIII (by F. H. Hinsley) of *The Cambridge History of the British Empire* (1959), overall judgments somewhat less condemnatory of Britain than those of Langer.

PAGE 85

1 Langer, *op. cit.* I, 386. Having condemned the existing regime in these terms, it might have been expected that the British writers would have shown some sympathy with the reformers. But they did not. Douglas (in the first edition of the *Cambridge Modern History* (1910), XII, 517), for example, is contemptuous of the 'Modern Sage', K'ang Yu-wei, 'who told so plausible a tale that Kwang Hsü adopted his views with enthusiasm.'

PAGE 86

1 Lo Hui-min, 'The Battle of the Concessions, 1895–1900' (Ph.D. dissertation, 1956–7, Cambridge University, unpublished), shows how the foreign loans were used by the Powers as a means to gain control of China's financial system and establishes that an attempt was made for the first time to bring China under joint domination by means of a 'Consortium'.

PAGE 87

1 Langer, *op. cit.* I, 399.

PAGE 88

1 Langer *op. cit.* I, 403.
2 *Ibid.* I, 407.

PAGE 89

1 Sir Valentine Chirol, *Fifty Years in a Changing World* (1927), p. 186, cited by Langer, *op. cit.* I, 408.

PAGE 90

1 Langer, *op. cit.* II, 448.

PAGE 91

1 See p. 191.
2 Langer, *op. cit.* II, 451, citing *Die Grosse Politik*, XIV.

PAGE 92

1 Langer *op. cit.* II, 452.

PAGE 93

1   *Langer, op. cit.* II, 459.
2   Saved from execution in 1898 by the intervention of Sir Claude Mac-Donald.

PAGE 95

1   Philip Joseph, *Foreign Diplomacy in China, 1894–1900* (1928). Langer says of this book, 'On the whole this is the best general modern account', but 'its viewpoint is conventional', and 'the great weakness of the book is the author's complete neglect of Russian material'.
2   The Salisbury Papers, preserved in the Library of Christ Church, Oxford, which I have briefly inspected, throw further light on the Weihaiwei episode and deserve the attention of future researchers.

PAGE 96

1   The existing British territory comprised the island of Hong Kong (1842), 32 square miles, and Kowloon with Stonecutters' Island (1860), $3\frac{1}{2}$ square miles.

PAGE 98

1   Langer, *op. cit.* II, 684, citing *Hansard*, LXII, c. 803 ff.

PAGE 99

1   John K. Fairbank, *The United States and China* (Harvard, 1948), p. 313.
2   *Ibid.* p. 321.
3   *Ibid.* p. 319.
4   *Ibid.* p. 322.

PAGE 100

1   Hu Shêng, *Imperialism and Chinese Politics*, p. 116. Russian communist writers have, not unexpectedly, supported their Chinese colleagues in this contention. A. A. Fursenko, for example (in *Bor'ba za razdel Kitaja i Amerikanskaja doktrina otkrytych dverej, 1895–1900* (Moscow, 1956), partly based on unpublished Russian archive material), concludes that the underlying purpose and final aim of the American Open Door policy (which was not British inspired) was the economic conquest of China by American capital.

PAGE 102

1   The main sources followed for the careers of K'ang Yu-wei and Liang Ch'i-ch'ao consulted are, Li Chien-nung, *China, 1840–1928*, ch. IV; A. Hummel, *Eminent Chinese of the Ch'ing Period* (Washington, 1943–4); J. R. Levenson, *Liang Ch'i-ch'ao and the Mind of Modern China* (Harvard, 1953); Fung Yu-lan, *A History of Chinese Philosophy* (Princeton, 1953); and T'ang Chih-chün, *Wu Hsü Pien Fa Shih Lun*, 2 vols. (Shanghai, 1955).

NOTES

PAGE 104

1 Chou Chên-fu, *Yen Fu Ssŭ Hsiang Shu P'ing* (Chungking, 1940),
p. 82, cited by Jerome Ch'ên in *Yüan Shih-k'ai, 1859-1916: Brutus
Assumes the Purple* (1961).
This formula was first applied to Sino–Western relations by Fêng
Kuei-fên about 1860.
'The *t'i-yung* bifurcation was an unrealistic one from the beginning.
The Western *yung* could not be imported without a considerable bit of
t'i coming with it, and the Chinese *t'i* could not survive once the Chinese
yung had been abandoned. It would be a mistake, however, to regard
this famous dichotomy as a *source* of official action or even of policies;
on the contrary, it was a formula which became widespread rather late,
after modern contact had begun its inexorable course' (John K. Fairbank
(ed.), *Chinese Thought and Institutions*, p. 229).
2 Laurence G. Thompson, *Ta T'ung Shu: The One World Philosophy of
K'ang Yu-wei* (1958), p. 55.

PAGE 105

1 See also, John K. Fairbank and Ssŭ-yü Têng, *China's Response to the
West*, p. 147.

PAGE 106

1 I owe these observations to Wang Gungwu, 'Chinese Reformists and
Revolutionaries in the Straits Settlements, 1901–1911'. (Academic
exercise, unpublished.)
2 J. R. Levenson, *op. cit. passim.*

PAGE 107

1 F. S. A. Bourne, article in *China Review* (1879–80), in which a full translation with notes is given. For an extended summary see the present
writer's *Problems of Chinese Education* (1936), p. 31. Themes for 'Eight-
legs' essays are given in *Variétés Sinologiques*, 5 (Etienne Zi, 'Pratiques
des Examens Littéraires', pp. 139–40).

PAGE 110

1 J. Needham, *SCC*, III, 450.
2 K. S. Latourette, *A History of Christian Missions in China*, p. 443. See
also, Liu Kwang-ching, 'Early Christian Colleges in China', *JAS*, xx
(November 1960).

PAGE 111

1 K. S. Latourette, *A History of Christian Missions in China*, pp. 338–9.
2 See Tsuen-hsuin Tsien, 'Western Impact on China through Translation', *FEQ*, XIII, 3 (May 1954). This valuable study covers the period
1580–1940.

PAGE 112

1   Tsuen-hsuin Tsien, *loc. cit.*, citing a report of the committee appointed to take charge of the preparation of the series of school and textbooks, by Alexander Williamson of 15 July 1878, published in the *Chinese Recorder*, 9 (1878), 307–9.

One Chinese scholar commented, 'Religious [Christian] books are all superficial and unworthy to be studied; the style of the translation is especially bad', Chao Wei-hsi, *Hsi Hsüeh Shu Mu Ta Wên (A Bibliography of Western Studies)* (Kweiyang, 1901), cited by Tsuen-hsuin Tsien, *loc. cit.*

PAGE 113

1   Dr Martin himself compiled a list of the books translated by the T'ung Wên Kuan. This comprises twenty-two titles including *Wheaton's International Law* and *Natural Philosophy* (translated by himself), *Woolsey's International Law*, *Chemistry for Beginners*, *Advanced Chemistry*, *English Grammar*, *Fawcett's Political Economy*, *History of Russia*, *Outlines of the World's History*, *Bluntschli's International Law*, *International Law in Ancient China* (Martin), four books on astronomy, the *Penal Code of the Straits Settlements*, and a *Franco–Chinese Dictionary* (the emphasis on international law, four titles out of twenty-two, will be noted). Appendix F to Morse, *IRCE*, III, 478.

PAGE 114

1   J. R. Levenson, *op. cit.* p. 27, n. 63.

PAGE 115

1   R. Mackenzie, *The Nineteenth Century, a History*, p. 460.

Mackenzie's book was translated by Richard as *T'ai Hsi Hsin Shih Lan Yao*. Richard published several other works including *Shih-shih Hsin-lun (Tracts for the Times)*.

2   The actual distance is not half this, but this is perhaps what it seemed like from Dundee.

PAGE 116

1   William E. Soothill, *Timothy Richard of China* (1924), p. 221. Richard was hired by Jardine Matheson in 1895 to report on Li Hung-chang's intentions regarding railway construction (E. T. Le Fevour, *Western Enterprise in China, 1842–1895*, p. 332. (Unpublished Ph.D. dissertation, Cambridge University, 1961.)

PAGE 117

1   Robert S. Schwantes, 'Christianity *versus* Science', a Conflict of Ideas in Meiji Japan', *FEQ*, XII, 2 (February 1953).

1 The circumstances under which Yüan Shih-K'ai betrayed the Emperor to Jung-lu are fully narrated and discussed in *Yuan Shih-k'ai, 1859–1916*, by Jerome Ch'ên (London, 1961). This work also throws a considerable amount of new light on the Reform Movement generally.

1 S. L. Tikhvinsky, *The Movement for Reform in China at the end of the Nineteenth Century and K'ang Yu-wei* (Moscow, 1959) (in Russian).

1 *IHT*, II, 8.
2 *IHT*, I, 510.

1 A. H. Smith, *China in Convulsion* (New York), I, 200.
2 Ssŭ-yü Têng and John K. Fairbank, *China's Response to the West*, p. 190.
3 *China in Convulsion*, I, 53.

1 C. P. Fitzgerald, *Revolution in China* (1952), p. 123. See also, Paul A. Cohen, 'The Anti-Christian Tradition in China', *JAS*, XX, 2 (February 1961), and Paul A. Varg, *Missionaries, Chinese, and Diplomats* (Princeton, 1952), *passim*.

1 P.R.O., F.O. 17 (China), 1333, 'Notes on Manchuria', by Colonel Browne, dated 17 March 1898.

1 Fitzgerald, *op. cit.* p. 125 and *passim*.

1 Wên Ch'ing (edited by the Rev. G. M. Reith, M.A.), *The Chinese Crisis from Within* (1901). The book originally appeared as a series of articles in the *Singapore Free Press*. Mr Reith does not appear to have been aware of the author's identity, but he was Dr Lim Boon-keng (Wên-Ch'ing and Boon-keng are the same, the first being the Mandarin and the second the Hokkien form). He was well known to the present writer for many years, was trained as a doctor in Scotland, and was later Principal of Amoy University. At Cambridge, he did research in physiology with Sir William Hardy, one of the pioneers of modern biophysics.

PAGE 131

1 Wên Ch'ing, *op. cit.* p. 297. Lim Boon-keng was in close touch with Chinese affairs through his contacts with Fukien and elsewhere. It is worthy of note that he was emphatically *not* a revolutionary, and in 1900, as in years to come, believed that a revolution would be a great misfortune for China, and advocated gradual change.

PAGE 133

1 *Ibid.* p. 305.

PAGE 134

1 *Ibid.* p. 317.

PAGE 135

1 *Ibid.* pp. 320–1.

PAGE 136

1 Marshall Broomhall, *Martyred Missionaries of the China Inland Mission* (1901), p. 10.
2 A copy is in *China's Millions*, 1900 (China Inland Mission), p. 167. The statement was signed by the Rev. B. Warlaw Thompson for the L.M.S., the Rev. H. E. Fox for the C.M.S., the Rev. Alexander Connell for the English Presbyterian Mission; on behalf also of the C.E.Z.M.S., the China Inland Mission, the Baptist, Wesleyan, United Methodist, Methodist New Connexion and Friends Missions, and the Religious Tract Society.

PAGE 137

1 Columba Cary-Elwes, O.S.B., *China and the Cross* (1957), p. 221.

PAGE 138

1 See also, Paul A. Cohen, *loc. cit.*, and Paul A. Varg, *op. cit. passim.*

PAGE 139

1 S. Wells Williams, *The Middle Kingdom*, II, 221.
2 Howard S. Levy, 'Yellow Turban Religion and Rebellion at the end of the Han', *JAOS*, 76 (1956).
3 De Groot distinguishes the 'sects' (*chiao*) from the secret associations (*hui*) of political aim, but there is no justification for this in modern usage. Indeed, *hui* is the general term for the societies and sects in South China where *chiao* is not used.

PAGE 140

1 See p. 227.
2 Vincent Y. C. Shih, 'Some Chinese Rebel Ideologists', *T'oung Pao*, XLIV (1956), 150–226.

PAGE 141

1 In present-day Shantung.
2 North-west Kiangsu.
3 Hopei and Manchuria.
4 Hopei.
5 Hunan, Hupei, and south-west Szechwan.
6 Kiangsu, Anhwei, Chekiang, Kiangsi and Fukien.
7 South-west Hupei and north-west Shantung.
8 Honan.

PAGE 142

1 Henri Maspero, *Mélanges Posthumes* (Paris, 1950), I, 49.
2 E. G. Pulleyblank, *The Background of the Rebellion of An Lu-shan* (1955), v, 1 ff., 103.

PAGE 143

1 Slavery was of considerable economic significance from the Han to the T'ang dynasty and beyond, but 'at the same time there is little evidence that slaves formed a large part of the whole population at any time or at any time outweighed in economic importance the attached retainers, hired labourers, share-cropping tenants and unattached peasants' (E. G. Pulleyblank, *Journal of the Economic and Social History of the Orient*, I (1958), 220).
2 See W. Eichhorn, 'Zur Vorgeschichte des Aufstandes von Wang Hsia-po und Li Shun, Szechuan (993–995)', in *Zeitschrift der Deutschen Morgenländischen Gesellschaft*, 105, 1 (Wiesbaden, 1955).

PAGE 146

1 Sun Tsu-min, 'Chung Kuo Nung Min Chan Chêng Ho Tsung Chiao Ti Kuan Hsi', *Li-shih Yen-chiu* (1956), takes examples from a number of rebellions from the third century B.C. to the nineteenth century to illustrate his thesis that, as far as the religion of the lower classes is concerned and despite its inherently backward nature, the function of religion has been threefold—to organize the peasants, to rouse them to rebellion, and to keep secretly the power of resistance alive after a revolt had failed.

PAGE 147

1 Liu Yen, 'Ming Mo Ch'êng Shih Ching Chi Fa Chan Hsia Ti Ch'u Chi Shih Min Yün Tung', *Li-shih Yen-chiu* (1955).
2 See C. P. Fitzgerald, *Revolution in China*, p. 335.
3 P. 29, by Hsia Hsieh (fl. 1862), extracts, trans. by E. H. Parker, in *China's Intercourse with Europe*, p. 29.
4 Fan Wên-lan, *Chung Kuo Chin Tai Shih*, part I, vol. I (Peking, 1958), ch. 8, sect. 2, p. 355.

PAGE 148

1   Jerome Ch'ên, 'The Nature and Characteristics of the Boxer Movement —A Morphological Study', *BSOAS*, XXIII, 2 (1960). Mr Ch'ên informs me that Wu Han (historian and now deputy mayor of Peking) has written a learned article on this question, namely 'Ming-chiao yü Ta-Ming Ti-kuo', reproduced in his *Tu Shih Cha Chi*.

2   See P. Pelliot, 'La Secte du Lotus Blanc et la Secte du Nuage Blanc', *BEFEO*, III (1903), 304–27, for a history of the sect.

PAGE 149

1   L. Wieger, *Textes Historiques* (Hsienhsien, 1923), II, 1724, 1718; Shang Yüeh-chu (ed.), *Chung Kuo Li Shih Kang Yao* (Peking, 1954), p. 349.

PAGE 150

1   *wu wei* is the Taoist doctrine of 'non-activity', or 'non-interference'. See p. 64.

2   The Religion of the Luminous Venerable, and may refer either to some particular Buddha or all Buddhas collectively (De Groot, *Sectarianism and Religious Persecution in China* (Amsterdam, 1903), p. 150). Sir G. T. Staunton, *Ta Tsing Leu Lee*, renders the name of the religion as Mi-Le-Fo (Penal Code, CLXII, 175).

3   This translation is by De Groot, p. 13. Compare Staunton, p. 175.

PAGE 151

1   See Rev. William Milne (trans.), *The Sacred Edict* (Malacca, 1817), pp. 126 f.

PAGE 152

1   *Op. cit.* p. 587 (under Pah-Kwa Kiao in de Groot's index).

2   Joseph Needham, *SCC*, I, 228; II, 312 (with tables of the trigrams and hexagrams). A Boxer banner inscribed with the Eight Diagrams is reproduced in *IHT*, I, 4, facing list of contents.

3   *Op. cit.* p. 429.

PAGE 153

1   *Op. cit.* p. 420.

2   See J. Needham, *SCC*, II, 313.

3   *Ibid.* 304.

PAGE 154

1   De Groot, *op. cit.* p. 338.

2   De Groot (*op. cit.* p. 335) says that it was proscribed, together with the sects of the White and the Red Yang, in an article of Law against Heresy, 'which in its present form dates from 1821'.

3　In 1777 a mirror was found next to the heart of a chief of a sect, killed in battle, whose function was to reflect back an arrow, bullet, or a blow with sword or lance.

PAGE 155

1　The Chia Ch'ing emperor ordered Ho-shên to commit suicide and confiscated his property—thereby adding to his own income an amount ten times the annual revenue of the national treasury (Li Chien-nung, p. 7).

2　Arthur Waley (*The Opium War Through Chinese Eyes*, p. 14) gives a translation of Commissioner Lin's travelling pass which asserts the rights, not of the Commissioner, but of the officials, rest-houses, and relay-stations whose duty would be to receive him.

3　Wei Yüan, *Shêng Wu Chi* (*Description of the Military Operations*), a military history of the dynasty up to 1842, the year of its publication. The author was a high official of the Imperial Chancery and has previously been referred to (see Index).

PAGE 156

1　De Groot, *op. cit.* ch. XII, pp. 350 ff.

PAGE 157

1　*Niu* (ox) and *pa* (eight) were the constituent parts of Chu, the family name of one, Chu Hung-t'ao, who, having the same surname as the Ming emperors, was regarded as being a pretender to the throne. The simultaneous appearance of a Maitreya lent colour to the suspicion.

2　The barbarity of the Ch'ing punishments is exemplified by the edict of the Chia Ch'ing emperor of 1803 ordering that Chin Tê, 'the atrocious malefactor', who had attempted to assassinate Chia Ch'ing, should be put to death by slow and painful execution, and that his two sons, being of tender age, should be strangled (Sir G. T. Staunton, *Ta Tsing Lu Li*, p. 539).

PAGE 158

1　See pp. 152, 197.

2　De Groot, *op. cit.* pp. 146, 443, etc. (see his index under sects: Pah-Kwa).

PAGE 159

1　A minute account of this rebellion is given in *Ch'in Ting P'ing Ting Chiao Fei Chi Lüeh* (*Chronological Account, with Imperial Sanction, of the Pacification of the Religious Rebels*) (1817), by a committee of forty-four high officials (De Groot, *op. cit.* p. 418). (It is, incidentally, a beautifully printed work.)

PAGE 160

1　Li Chien-nung, *The Political History of China*, p. 8.

2　See p. 153.

NOTES

3 *IHT*, I, 356. See also Yuzi Muramatsu, 'The Boxers in 1898–1899', *Annals of the Hitotsubashi Academy* (April 1953), p. 252.
4 De Groot, *op. cit.* p. 420.

PAGE 161

1 *IHT*, IV, 123.
2 De Groot, *op. cit.* p. 429, n. 2.
3 *IHT*, IV, 431, 447, 475. Chester C. Tan, *The Boxer Catastrophe*, pp. 36, 43–5. Tan gives September, but the articles in *IHT* are dated 9th month of 25th year of Kuang Hsü (5 October–2 November 1899), K25/11/14 (16 December 1899), and 2nd month of 26th year of Kuang Hsü (1–30 March 1900). Besides being an official, Lao Nai-hsüan was a mathematician and an historian of mathematics.
4 De Groot, *op. cit.* p. 429.

PAGE 162

1 *Jên Tsung Jui Huang Ti Shêng Hsün.*
2 H. A. Giles, 'The Home of Jiu Jitsu', *Adversaria Sinica* (Shanghai, 1914), p. 132.

PAGE 163

1 Joseph Needham, *SCC*, II, 145–6.
2 Henri Maspero, *Les Religions Chinoises* (Paris, 1950), p. 16.
3 The *hsien* variety of Taoism from which these beliefs are derived is fully described by H. G. Creel in 'What is Taoism?', *JAOS*, 76 (1956), 139–52.

PAGE 164

1 Ho Ping-yü and Joseph Needham, 'Elixir Poisoning in Medieval China', *Janus*, XLVIII, 4 (1959).
2 See J. M. Amiot (ed.), *Mémoires Concernant les Chinois*, 'Note du Cong-fu des Bonzes Tao-sse' (Paris 1779), and John Dudgeon, M.D., 'Kung-fu, or Medical Gymnastics', *Journal of the Peking Oriental Society* (1895), 3, p. 341. Also Wang Tsu-yüan, *Nei Kung T'u Shuo* (Peking, 1955).
3 To exercise oneself bodily. The characters are also allusively rendered, *Kung*, Great Bear, and *fu*, a charm.
4 S. Couling, *The Encyclopaedia Sinica* (1917), p. 60.

PAGE 165

1 Ssŭ-yü Têng and John K. Fairbank, *China's Response to the West*, p. 188.
2 A. H. Smith, *China in Convulsion*, I, 197; *IHT*, I, 238; II, 145; IV, 152.
3 See G. Schlegel, *Thian Ti Hwui; the Hung League or Heaven–Earth League* (Batavia, 1866), Introduction.
4 Cantonese is rather an ancient form of Chinese that has survived than a 'dialect'.

PAGE 166

1 See Shang Yüeh-chu (ed.), *Chung Kuo Li Shih Kang Yao*, p. 395.
2 Wei Yüan, *Shêng Wu Chi*, vol. VIII.
3 Translated by Pearl Buck as *All Men are Brothers* (1934). The novel has a 'Robin Hood', anti-government theme.

PAGE 168

1 As far as is known, Mason was the only non-Chinese to have become a member—but the plotters needed him to smuggle arms and dynamite.
2 See M. L. Wynne, *Triad and Tabut* (Singapore, 1941), and L. Comber, *Secret Societies in Malaya* (Locust Valley, New York, 1959). Wynne attributes a dual origin of Chinese secret societies in Malaya from quite separate roots—the Han and the Hung—but W. L. Blythe (in his Foreword to the work, 1957) shows that they were all branches of the Triad.

PAGE 169

1 Li Chien-nung, *The Political History of China*, p. 62.
2 *T'ien-ch'ao T'ien-mou Chih-tu.*

PAGE 171

1 *T'ai P'ing T'ien Kuo Yi Shu*, Preface by Lo Erh-kang (Kiangsi People's Publishing House, 1960).
2 Kuo I-shêng in *Li-shih Yên-chiu* (1956), 3, pp. 1–25.
3 Li Ch'un, *T'ai P'ing T'ien Kuo Chih Tu Ch'u T'an* (Peking, 1956).

PAGE 172

1 See Wei Yüan, *Shêng Wu Chi*, VII.
2 Siang-tseh Chiang, *The Nien Rebellion* (Seattle, 1954), p. 10. A. Feuerwerker (review in *JAS* (1956), p. 165) says that the theory, while not a new one, is credible and helps to explain the ability of the Nien to knit together their own units, to assimilate outlying forces, and finally to turn Huai-pei into a solid fortress against the loyalists. See also S. T. Têng, *The Nien Army and their Guerilla Warfare, 1851–1868* (Paris, 1960).
3 A society, behind rebellions in neighbouring Korea, deserves a footnote. The Tong Hak (Eastern Learning) Society, established in Korea about 1860, had tenets composed of a mixture of Confucianism and Taoism, and was opposed to Western Learning (particularly Roman Catholicism). After 1864 it extended its objects to counter excessive taxation, government corruption, and foreign encroachment. It was behind short-lived revolts in 1893 and 1894.
4 Chün-tu Hsüeh, 'Sun Yat-sen, Yang Chü-yün, and the Early Revolutionary Movement in China', *JAS*, XIX, 3 (May 1960).

PAGE 173

1 A tael, a Chinese ounce of silver, varied in value with the price of silver. In 1899 it was worth about 2s. 9d. sterling.

NOTES

PAGE 174

1 See Yuzi Muramatsu, Professor of Economic History in the Hitotsubashi University, Tokyo, in *Annals of the Hitotsubashi Academy*, III,
2 (April 1953), 236–61.

PAGE 175

1 A. H. Smith, *China in Convulsion*, I, 90–1.
  Muramatsu (pp. 255–6) gives tables showing the growth of the trade
in Tientsin, Chefoo and Newchang from 1894 to 1899. For 1894 the
total exports from these three ports was valued at 8,771,000 taels, and
the total imports at 7,099,000 taels; for 1899, the total exports were
valued at 21,637,000 taels, and the total imports at 26,073,000 taels. The
import of cotton yarn into China as a whole increased from a value of
21,299,000 taels in 1892 to a value of 54,607,000 taels in 1899. Foreign
opium imported via Chefoo increased from 355 piculs in 1896 to
1413 piculs in 1899.

PAGE 176

1 *Tê-tsung Shih-lu*, 416, p. 3B.
2 *Ibid.* 411, p. 14B, cited by Muramatsu, p. 244.
3 *Loc. cit.* p. 247.

PAGE 177

1 A *yamên* was the 'public residence' or 'office' of an official.

PAGE 178

1 *China in Convulsion*, I, 88–101.

PAGE 179

1 *Foreign Relations of the United States* (1899), pp. 123, 170.

PAGE 180

1 See Appendix B.
2 *IHT*, IV, 431–9; Chester C. Tan, *The Boxer Catastrophe*, pp. 36, 43–6;
G. Nye Steiger, *China and the Occident*, ch. VII. Lao also published other
pamphlets on the Boxers (see *IHT*, IV, 447, 475).

PAGE 181

1 See p. 167.

PAGE 182

1 See Appendix B.
2 *IHT*, IV, 433.

PAGE 183

1 *IHT*, IV, pp. 433–9.
2 *Ibid.* pp. 4–8.
3 *Ibid.* p. 11.
4 *Ibid.* p. 11.
5 *Ibid.* p. 12.
6 *Ibid.* p. 12.
7 *Ibid.* p. 13.
8 *Ibid.* p. 16.

PAGE 184

1 Chester Tan, *The Boxer Catastrophe*, p. 37.
2 A. H. Smith, *China in Convulsion*, p. 171.

PAGE 186

1 See pp. 49–50.
2 Tan, *op. cit.* p. 43.

PAGE 187

1 Yuzi Muramatsu, 'The Boxers in 1898–1899; the Origin of the I Ho Chüan Uprising, 1900', *Annals of the Hitotsubashi Academy*, III, 1 (October 1952).
2 M. N. Roy, *Revolution and Counter-revolution in China* (Calcutta, 1948), pp. 144–6.
3 Chûjô Ichiko, 'Giwaken no seikaku', pp. 245–67 (included in *Kindai Chugoku Kenkyu*, compiled by Gakujutsu Kenkyu Kaigi (Muramatsu, *loc. cit.*)).

PAGE 188

1 *IHTTA*, I, 1 ff.

PAGE 191

1 H. Cordier, *Histoire Générale de la Chine*, IV, 204. Steiger (*China and the Occident*, p. 64) says 'the village of Yenchow', but Yenchow is a town, a prefectural capital, and Cordier's account is undoubtedly the correct one.

PAGE 193

1 *IHTTA*, I, 14.
2 See pp. 255 *et seq.*

PAGE 194

1 *IHTTA*, I, 14.
2 At this period a large number of new churches were being erected. Shantung was parcelled out among the Christian sects. The American

Board were allotted the area to the south between the Chihli frontier and the Yellow River; the American Presbyterians both sides of the river to the east of Chinan, the Baptists that to the west of it; to the south of these came a strip within the spiritual care of the Anglican Mission (with a small American Baptist enclave in its centre), then there was a strip of territory in which the American Methodists were paramount; and so on throughout the province. The Roman Catholics, of course, ignored these heretical frontiers and exercised ecclesiastical jurisdiction as opportunity offered. The tip of the Shantung peninsula, it appears, was the preserve of the Plymouth Brethren.

3   Chester Tan, *The Boxer Catastrophe*, p. 47.

PAGE 195

1   *IHTTA*, I, 17.
2   *Ibid.* p. 18.
3   *Chih Tung T'ien Ts'un*, I/3; quoted by Chester Tan, *op. cit.* p. 47.
4   *Chih Tung T'ien Ts'un*, I/11; quoted by Chester Tan, *op. cit.* p. 47.

PAGE 196

1   *IHT*, IV, 3.
2   *Ibid.* p. 5.
3   Decree of 6 April 1899 (K25/2/26). Chester Tan, *op. cit.* p. 31.

PAGE 197

1   Chiang K'ai, *P'ingyüan Ch'üan Fei Chi Shih*, *IHT*, I, 353–62.
2   See p. 158, note 1.

PAGE 199

1   *IHT*, I, 356.

PAGE 191

1   *Ibid.* I, 361.
2   See Harvard–Yenching Institute, *Sinological Index Series*, no. 9, 1/465/5a (*not* 1/471/5a as in the Index).
3   A. H. Smith, *China in Convulsion*, I, 165.

PAGE 200

1   *IHTTA*, I, 30.
2   *Ibid.* p. 34.
3   *Ibid.* p. 45.

PAGE 201

1   The traditional epithet for dishonest minor officials.

PAGE 202

1   *IHTTA*, I, 36.
2   *Ibid.* p. 37.

PAGE 203

1   *IHTTA*, I, p. 37.
2   Steiger, *China and the Occident*, p. 176.
3   *IHTTA*, I, 38, 41.

PAGE 205

1   *Papers relating to the Foreign Relations of the United States*, transmitted to Congress on 3 December 1900 (Washington, 1901), no. 289.

PAGE 207

1   A telegram from Dr A. H. Smith of 1 December, from P'angchuang, included in this correspondence, to Mr Conger, savours of panic: 'Boxer rebellion, twenty counties, Shantung, Chihli; rapidly spreading; pillage; arson; murders increasing; avowed object kill Christians, exterminate foreigners; Pang-chuang, Linching, Chinanfu Americans consider position almost hopeless; reply awaited. Smith'.
2   *IHTTA*, I, 42.
3   *Ibid.* p. 44.

PAGE 208

1   *Parliamentary Papers, China*, no. 1 (1899), p. 304.

PAGE 210

1   A. H. Smith, *China in Convulsion*, I, 201.

PAGE 211

1   *Ch'üan Fei Chi Lüeh*, compiled by Chiao Tê-shêng, part II, vol. 2, p. 2A (Muramatsu, p. 240 n.); *IHT*, IV, 451–74.
2   *IHT*, IV, 458.
3   *Ibid.* p. 504. The biographies are by Wang Ch'i-chü and Yang Ch'i-an.
4   No doubt from the associated attributes of the first of the trigrams of the *Book of Changes* (*I Ching*), namely *Ch'ien*, and connoting also 'father, metal, king, head', etc., and the colour 'red'.

PAGE 212

1   The authorities given by *IHT* for these statements regarding Chu and Li Lai-chung are *P'ingyüan Ch'üan Fei Chi Shih* and *Ch'üan Fei Chi Shih*. The first is by Chiang K'ai, and the second is presumably that by Sawara Tokusuke (Chester Tan, *The Boxer Catastrophe*, p. 250), included in *IHT*, I, 105–300, but in neither is there a reference to the *Fan Ch'ing Mieh Yang* slogan or to the association of Li Lai-chung with the 'Support the Ch'ing' slogan.
2   *China in Convulsion*, I, 166.
    S. Tikhvinsky, 'Two Different Points of View concerning the Purposes of Reform in China at the end of the Nineteenth Century' (in

Russian), *Bulletin of the XXVth International Congress of Orientalists* (Moscow, 1960), says that the agitation against the foreigner, spreading more widely under the slogan, 'Burn the churches; drive away the missionaries', began increasingly to be directed against the government. A new slogan, 'Expel the foreigner; liquidate the corrupt officials', was later widely adopted by the Boxers.

PAGE 213

1   *IHT*, I, 391.
2   *IHT*, IV, 443.

PAGE 214

1   Fan Wên-lan, *Chung Kuo Chin Tai Shih* (Peking, 1953), I, 357-8.
2   *IHT*, II, 7.

PAGE 215

1   *Ibid.* p. 361.
2   *Ibid.* p. 366.
3   *Ibid.* p. 368. No authority is given for this statement, and it would be very interesting to have it. I can trace no other reference to the slogan *Sao Ch'ing Mieh Yang* at this period, but it was one of the Nien slogans engraved on a seal (see p. 172).

PAGE 216

1   *IHT*, IV, 145-52.
2   From the author's *Fan-t'ien-lu Ts'ung-lu* (1929); *IHT*, I, 303-33.
3   Steiger, *China and the Occident*, p. 132, from *Chine et Ceylan* (a Jesuit magazine published at Abbeville), I, 106. The files of *Chine et Ceylan* are in the Bibliothèque Nationale, Paris, and I have consulted these.

PAGE 218

1   *IHT*, IV, 16.
2   *Ibid.* p. 27.

PAGE 219

1   *China in Convulsion*, I, 167-8.
2   R. B. Sheeks, 'A re-examination of the *I Ho Ch'üan* and its Role in the Boxer Movement', *Papers on China* (Harvard, 1947), pp. 75-135.
3   J. J. M. de Groot, *Sectarianism and Religious Persecution in China* (Amsterdam, 1903), p. 430 n.

PAGE 220

1   In correspondence with the author.
2   *Keng Tzŭ Chi Shih* (*Records of Kêng Tzŭ Year*), compiled by the Institute of Historical Research (Peking, 1959), p. 26.
3   *Ibid.* p. 27.

PAGE 221

1   *Keng Tzŭ Chi Shih*, p. 89.
2   *Ibid.* p. 263.
3   Jerome Ch'ên, 'The Nature and Characteristics of the Boxer Movement
    —A Morphological Study', *BSOAS*, XXIII, 2 (1960).
4   *IHT*, II, 8.

PAGE 222

1   *IHT*, I, 510.

PAGE 223

1   See Jerome Ch'ên, 'The Nature and Characteristics of the Boxer Move-
    ment—A Morphological Study', *BSOAS*, XXIII, 2 (1960). Mr Ch'ên is
    the first to draw attention to the Boxer reliance on novels and plays, and
    I have used his researches as a framework for this chapter.

PAGE 224

1   *IHT*, II, 188; Jerome Ch'ên, *loc. cit.*

PAGE 225

1   *IHT*, see also IV, 148, 149; V, 151, 152; Jerome Ch'ên, *loc. cit.*
2   *IHT*, IV, 125.
3   *IHT*, II, 183; IV, 148. See also *IHT*, I, 90.
4   *IHT*, II, 8.
5   *IHT*, I, 510.
6   *IHT*, II, 11.

PAGE 226

1   *Ibid.* p. 8.
2   See C. P. Fitzgerald, *China: a Short Cultural History*, pp. 500–10.
    Lu Hsün, *A Brief History of Chinese Fiction* (Peking, 1959), says that the
    earliest known edition is that of 1494.

PAGE 227

1   Ts'ao's Imperial honour, however, was posthumous. He had never been
    king. Liu Pei, on the other hand, did proclaim a kingdom, and in the
    San Kuo he represents legitimacy.

PAGE 228

1   One of the most famous of these is the Kuan Ling, a few miles south of
    the city of Loyang, recently restored at great expense as a national
    monument and an archaeological museum.
2   See *Variétés Sinologiques*, no. 39, *Recherches sur les Superstitions en Chine*,
    II, 6, *The Chinese Pantheon* (Shanghai, 1896).
3   Jerome Ch'ên comments: 'Liu Pei had not been considered the legitimate
    heir until the Sung dynasty. The compilers of *Chronicles of the Three*

Kingdoms and the History of the Chin (or Tsin) did not think much of him. The latter history was completed under the editorship of the second and most brilliant Emperor of the T'ang.'

4   C. P. Fitzgerald, *Revolution in China*, p. 507.

PAGE 229

1   But Lu Hsün, *op. cit.*, says (p. 158) that the original basis of the novel was the famous peasant revolt suppressed in 1121.
2   Pearl Buck, *All Men are Brothers*, 2 vols. (New York, 1933), I, p. vi.
3   Translated as *Monkey*, by Arthur Waley (1942), p. 9.

PAGE 231

1   A. Hummel (ed.), *Eminent Chinese of the Ch'ing Period*.

PAGE 232

1   J. Needham, *SCC*, II, 277.

PAGE 233

1   *IHT*, I, 497; II, 13.
2   *IHT*, I, 241; II, 146; IV, 512; Muramatsu, p. 252.
3   See *IHT*, I, 238, which relates to the spring of 1900.

PAGE 234

1   The root meaning of *T'an* is 'altar'. *IHT*, I, 238; II, 183; I, 270, 468.

PAGE 235

1   *IHT*, I, 112.
2   *IHT*, I, 346; II, 9. The Taoist attitude towards women was in advance of that of the rest of Chinese society as far back as the second century A.D. The ranks of Male Bonnet (*Nan-Kuan*), Female bonnet (*Nü-Kuan*), or, higher still, Father of the Tao (*Tao-fu*) or Mother of the Tao (*Tao-mu*) were accessible both to men and women. See Howard S. Levy, 'Yellow Turban Religion and Rebellion at the End of the Han', *JAOS*, 76 (1956).

PAGE 236

1   This catenary construction, or Sorites, is very common in Chinese classical writings. The most famous example is in the *Ta Hsüeh*, I, 4.
2   Steiger surmises that the Boxers used Christian phraseology at times in their incantations, etc., but (says Jerome Ch'ên) 'nothing can be further from the truth: the Boxers learnt from supernatural novels and operas, not from the Bible'.
3   H. G. Creel, 'What is Taoism?', *JAOS*, 76 (1956), 142f.

PAGE 237

1   Creel, *loc. cit.*

PAGE 239

1 When this book was ready for press my attention was called to the announcement of a forthcoming article in *T'oung Pao*, XLVII (1961), 'Religion et Magie dans le mouvement des Boxeurs d'après les textes Chinois', by G. G. H. Dunstheimer. Monsieur Dunstheimer has very kindly allowed me to see his valuable article in proof. It contains long translations of extracts from *IHT* and other Chinese sources and references to authorities, some of them additional to those quoted in this book, and should be consulted by future students of the Boxer movement.

PAGE 240

1 The first reference to the Boxers as such in F.O. correspondence is an indirect one. In *FC* 86, 15 November 1899, Viscount Gough to Salisbury quotes the 'North German Gazette' to the effect that an official telegram had just been received from Peking by the German government on the subject of the present situation in German missionary districts in Shantung, where the followers of the sects of the 'Red Fist' and the 'Great Knife' were in a state of revolt against the administration and the people in that province.

PAGE 243

1 See Appendix B.

PAGE 244

1 E.g. Peter Fleming, *The Siege at Peking*, 1959, chapter I, 'The Ostriches'.

PAGE 245

1 Legation guards had been brought to Peking during the troubles following the coup d'état of 1898. In a telegram of 10 March 1899 to Salisbury (*FC* 292) MacDonald stated that all the representatives except the German Minister agreed to their withdrawal. In reply (*FC* 293, telegram of the same day) Salisbury authorized MacDonald to send the British legation guard back to Tientsin. This was done.

PAGE 246

1 Steiger, p. 199.

PAGE 247

1 The fatal casualties inflicted on the Chinese by the foreigners were far greater than those inflicted on the foreigners by the Chinese during the uprising. In *FC* 107 of 13 March 1901, Satow gives the total number of missionaries and other persons of British, French, German, Italian, Belgian and Dutch, American and Swedish nationality, men, women and children, murdered during the Boxer troubles as 239. In the Liuchiatien (north of Talienwan) incident of October 1899 alone, the Cossacks

killed over a hundred Chinese who had come to petition the Russian authorities against the land tax (*FC* no. 170, MacDonald to Salisbury, 18 October 1899). On 17 July 1900 the Russians slaughtered several thousand Chinese in Blagoveshchensk, and many more in Harbin.

PAGE 252

1 Among the accounts the following may be singled out as of especial interest: W. A. P. Martin, *The Siege in Peking* (1900); Arthur H. Smith, *China in Convulsion* (2 vols., 1901); Sir Robert Hart, *These from the Land of Sinim* (1901). The first two were by American missionaries; the third is by the celebrated (Irish) Inspector-General of Customs and shows more penetration into the real nature of what was happening than do the other two. Putnam Weale's *Indiscreet Letters from Peking* (1906) is the best known of the siege books and the most entertainingly written, but probably the least reliable.

Peter Fleming in *The Siege at Peking* (1959) has produced a vividly written account of the episode, based mainly on the eye-witness accounts of Europeans, on official publications, and the private papers of Sir Claude MacDonald, but it contrives to give the impression that China is of interest only in providing a sombre background of barbarism to the shining exploits of a Christian (if not necessarily civilized) West.

PAGE 255

1 This is made possible by Chester Tan's study, but the new collections provide a mass of additional material for expanding and elaborating the picture.

PAGE 256

1 The fiction evolved: it was never precisely formulated.

PAGE 259

1 W. L. Langer, *The Diplomacy of Imperialism*, II, p. 699, citing *Die Grosse Politik*, XVI, nos. 4598 ff.

PAGE 260

1 Jung-lu's position was dubious. In order to justify his conduct to the allied Powers, the famous 'Diary of His Excellency Ching Shan' is alleged to have been forged and placed where it was likely to fall into the hand of the foreign diplomats. See Appendix A.
2 The monument was removed in 1917 when China joined the Allies against Germany.

PAGE 261

1 Though it is fair to add that the Powers over the next few years remitted their shares of the indemnity one by one, or applied them to purposes advantageous to China.

PAGE 262

1 Langer, II, p. 704.

PAGE 264

1 *BSOAS*, XIII, 2 (1960).
2 *China in Convulsion*, I, 44.
3 *Ibid.* p. 63.
4 Arthur H. Smith, *Chinese Characteristics* (New York, 1894), p. 330.

PAGE 266

1 E. J. Hobsbawm, *Primitive Rebels* (Manchester, 1959), p. v, and *passim*.

PAGE 267

1 *Ibid.* p. 57.

PAGE 268

1 *The Siege at Peking* (1959), p. 48.

PAGE 269

1 *Ibid.* pp. 46–7.

PAGE 271

1 *Chinese Social and Political Science Review*, X (1926), 956.

PAGE 273

1 In a review of Duyvendak's translation of the diary in *The Chinese Social and Political Science Review*, X (1926), 'Reginald Irving' (pseudonym of (Sir) R. F. Johnston) says 'strange as it may seem, many readers who should have known better—the late Sir John Jordan among them—stoutly maintained that it [the diary] existed only in English and emanated from the brain of one of the authors of *China Under the Empress Dowager*...so far as I am aware he [Sir John Jordan] never admitted that his critical faculty had been at fault...I found it quite impossible to shake his conviction that the Diary was a brilliant fabrication'.

PAGE 275

1 See Bibliography under Wang Wên-shao.

PAGE 276

1 A. Hummel, *Eminent Chinese of the Ch'ing Period*, p. 409.
2 Hope Danby in *DNB* (1941–50).

PAGE 277

1 In any case he could have got a Chinese to help him, which he probably did.

2 The authenticity of Wang Wên-shao's 'journal' or 'letter' is itself questionable. See Chester Tan, *The Boxer Catastrophe*, p. 118, n. 9.

PAGE 278

1 Although there is no mention of Ching-shan's diary, there is a record of a not entirely dissimilar case in which letters (herein preserved) were discovered in the house of a prominent Boxer, Wenjui, in the Tartar City, incriminating one Ch'ang Ming (Satow to Prince Ch'ing, 228 (1900) of 8/12/00).
2 Chester Tan, *op. cit.* p. 135.

PAGE 279

1 Notably in *IHT*, I, 57.
2 It was written before the appearance of Duyvendak's article in *T'oung Pao*.

PAGE 283

1 1409 V.P.

PAGE 284

1 P.R.O. G.D. 33/10/4, China, misc., various.
2 Ch'êng Ming-chou, in *Chung Kuo Chin Tai Shih Lun Ts'ung* (Taipeh, 1956), considers that the diary is a forgery, probably intended to 'whitewash' Jung-lu. He points out that it contains a number of Japanese terms and a reference to the Boer War (which could not have been within Ching-shan's knowledge) and remarks that whereas Ching-shan was known to be a calligrapher of the Su Tung-p'o school, the handwriting of the diary shows no sign of this.

PAGE 285

1 The following should, when it is published, provide a very useful tool for researchers: Leslie R. Marchant, *A Guide to the Archives and Records of Protestant Christian Missions from the British Isles to China, 1795–1914*.
2 Dr Sewell S. MacFarlane arrived in China in 1888; Mr William Hopkyn Rees arrived in Peking in 1883 (Norman Goodall, *A History of the London Missionary Society 1895–1945* (1954), pp. 161, 168).

PAGE 290

1 31 December 1899, the day Brooks is stated by all sources to have been murdered, was a *Sunday*. If the Rev. Mathews is not mistaken, he received news of Brooks's *wounding* the previous day, Saturday, 30 December 1899.
2 P'ingyin is about 50 miles south-west of Chinan. Brooks was travelling by wheelbarrow.

BIBLIOGRAPHY

*Chinese authors are listed under their surnames, which may be the first or
second component of their name, but is always a monosyllable.*

I. MANUSCRIPT SOURCES

Public Record Office, F.O. 17 (*China*). Besides the correspondence between
the Foreign Office and the British Minister in Peking, there are separate
files of the papers of the Chinese Secretary of the legation and of
correspondence between the legation and consuls and vice-consuls.

British Museum (Department of Oriental Printed Books and MS.). MS. of
Ching-shan's diary, and letter from Sir E. Backhouse (see appendix A)
(in same box).

Salisbury Papers (Christ Church, Oxford). Briefly mentioned in the text.
They contain valuable material for the study of the diplomatic history
of the period.

Records of the London Missionary Society and the Society for the Propagation of the Gospel (see appendix B).

II. OFFICIAL PUBLICATIONS

Parliamentary Papers, Accounts and Papers.

Parliamentary Debates (*Hansard*).

Foreign Relations of the United States (Washington, D.C.).

Further Correspondence Respecting the Affairs of China, printed for the use of
the Foreign Office. (A set is in the Seeley Historical Library, Cambridge.)

The archives of the Quai d'Orsay, Paris, relating to China are open for
inspection up to 1897 only.

III. CHINESE SOURCES

Chao Wei-hsi, *Hsi Hsüeh Shu Mu Ta Wên* (*Bibliography of Western
Studies*) (Kweiyang, 1901).

Ch'êng Ming-chou, 'Ching-shan's Diary', *Yenching Hsüeh Po* (1940).

—— *Chung Kuo Chin Tai Shih Lun Ts'ung* (Taipeh, 1956).

Chiang K'ai, 'P'ingyüan Ch'üan Fei Chi Shih' ('A Record of the Boxers of
P'ingyüan'), *IHT*, I, 353–62.

Chiao Tê-shêng (ed.). *Ch'üan Fei Chi Lüeh* (*A Brief Record of the Boxers*)
(Muramatsu, p. 240 n.).

Chien Po-tsan, and five others (ed.). *I Ho T'uan Tzŭ Liao Ts'ung K'an*
(*Source Materials of the Boxer War*), 4 vols. (Shanghai, 1951).

Chih Tung Chiao Fei Tien Ts'un (*Telegrams Concerning the Suppression of the Boxers*), 4 vols. (1906).

Ch'in Ting P'ing Ting Chiao Fei Chi Lüeh (*Chronological Account, with Imperial Sanction, of the Pacification of the Religious Rebels*) (1817).

Chou Chên-fu. *Yen Fu Ssŭ Hsiang Shu P'ing* (*A Critical Study of Yen Fu's Thoughts*) (Chungking, 1940).

Ch'un Chiu (*Spring and Autumn Annals*).

Fan Wên-lan. *Chung Kuo Chin Tai Shih* (*History of Modern China*) (Peking, 1958).

Fêng Shên Yên I (*The Enfeoffment of the Gods*) (novel).

Hsi Yü Chi (*Pilgrimage to the West*) (novel) (trans. by Arthur Waley, q.v.).

Hsia Hsieh (fl. 1862). *Chung Hsi Chi Shih* (*China's Intercourse with Europe*). See under E. H. Parker, below.

I Ching (*Book of Changes*).

I Ho T'uan Tang An Shih Liao (*Source Materials in Despatches Relating to the Boxers*), 2 vols. (Peking, 1959).

Jên Tsung Jui Huang Ti Shêng Hsün (*Edicts of the Chia Ch'ing Emperor*).

Kêng Tzŭ Chi Shih (*Records of 1900*), compiled by Institute of Historical Research (Peking, 1959).

Lao Nai-hsüan. 'I Ho Ch'üan Chiao Mên Yüan Liu K'ao' ('The Historical Origins of the Boxers'), *IHT*, IV, 433–9.

—— 'Ch'üan An Tsa Ts'un' ('Miscellaneous Boxer Cases'), *IHT*, IV, 449–74.

—— 'Kêng Tzŭ Fêng Ching I Ho T'uan Hui Lu' ('A Collection of Public Notices Banning the Boxers'), *IHT*, IV, 475–90.

Li Chi (*Book of Rites*).

Li Ch'un. *T'ai P'ing T'ien Kuo Chih Tu Ch'u T'an* (*Introduction to the Taiping Administrative System*) (Peking, 1956).

Liu Yen. 'Ming Mo Ch'êng Shih Ching Chi Fa Chan Hsia Ti Ch'u Ch'i Shih Min Yün Tung' ('Urban Movements during the late Ming'), *Li-shih Yen-chiu*, 1955.

Lo Erh-kang. *T'ai P'ing T'ien Kuo Ko Ming Chan Chêng Shih* (*A history of the Revolutionary War of the Taipings*) (1949).

P'êng Kung An (*Prefect P'êng's Cases*) (novel).

Prémare, Joseph Henri de. *Notitia Linguae Sinicae* (Malacca, 1831).

Richard, Timothy. *Shih Shih Hsin Lun* (*Tracts for the Times*) (1898).

—— *T'ai Hsi Hsin Shih Lan Yao* (translation of *The Nineteenth Century*, by Robert Mackenzie, q.v.) (1894).

San Kuo Chih Yen I (*Romance of the Three Kingdoms*) (novel).

Sawara, and other Japanese. 'Ch'üan Luan Chi Wên' ('Recollections of the Boxer Crisis'), *IHT*, I, 170–300.

Shang Yüeh. *Chung Kuo Li Shih Kang Yao* (*An Outline of Chinese History*) (Peking, 1954).

Shih Kung An (*Prefect Shih's Cases*) (novel).

Shui Hu (*Water Margin*) (novel). See under Pearl Buck, below.

Su Tung-p'o (1036–1101). *Works*, part II, ch. 10.

Sun Tsu-min. 'Chung Kuo Nung Min Chan Chêng Ho Tsung Chiao Ti Kuan Hsi' ('Chinese Peasant Wars and Religion'), *Li-shih Yen-chiu*, 1956.

Tai I. 'Chung Kuo Chin Tai Shih Ti Fên Ch'i Wên T'i' ('(Marxist–Leninist) Periodization of Modern Chinese History'), *Li-shih Yen-chiu*, 1956, pp. 1–22.

T'ai P'ing T'ien Kuo Yi Shu (*Art of the Taipings*). Preface by Lo Erh-kang (Kiangsi, 1960).

T'ang Chih-chün. *Wu Hsü Pien Fa Shih Lun* (*Studies in the Reform Movement of 1898*), 2 vols. (Shanghai, 1955).

T'ang Pao, Ching Pao, Ti Ch'ao, Ti Pao, etc. (*Peking Gazette*).

T'ien Ch'ao T'ien Mou Chih Tu (*Land System of the Taipings*).

'Tsa Lu' ('Miscellaneous Boxer Placards and Incantations'), *IHT*, IV, 145–52.

Ts'ao Hsüeh-chin (1715–63), and Kao O (fl. 1791). *Hung Lou Mêng* (*Dream of the Red Chamber*) (novel).

Wang Jên-ch'ên. 'Tui Chung Kuo Chin Tai Shih Fên Ch'i Wên T'i Ti Shang Chüeh' ('(Marxist–Leninist) Periodization of Chinese History'), *Li-chih Yen-chiu*, 1956.

Wang Tsu-yüan. *Nei Kung T'u Shuo* (*Internal Therapeutic Exercises with Diagrams*) (Peking, 1955).

Wang Wên-shao. 'Wang Wên Shao Chia Shu' ('Family Letters of Wang Wên-shao') (1900) in Tso Shun-shêng (ed.), *Chung Kuo Chin Pai Nien Shih Tzǔ Liao Hsü Pien* (see Chester Tan, p. 261).

Wei Yüan. *Shêng Wu Chi* (*Descriptions of the Military Operations*) (1842).

—— *Hai Kuo T'u Chih* (*World Geography*).

Wu Ching-tzǔ. *Ju Lin Wai Shih* (*The Scholars*) (novel).

Wu Han. 'Ming Chiao Yü Ta Ming Ti Kuo' ('Ming Religion and the Ming Empire'), in *Tu Shih Cha Chi* (Peking, 1956).

Yün Yü-ting. *Ch'ung Ling Ch'uan Hsin Lu* (*A Veritable Account of the Crisis of the Kuang Hsü Reign*) (Shanghai, 1911).

IV. OTHER SOURCES

(Place of publication London unless otherwise stated.)

Amiot, J. M. (ed.). *Mémoires Concernant les Chinois*, 'Note du Cong-fu des Bonzes Tao-sse' (Paris, 1779).

Bard, Emile. *The Chinese at Home* (translation and adaptation of *Les Chinois chez eux*, Paris, 1900) (n.d.).

Beresford, Lord Charles. *The Break-up of China* (1899).

Bland, J. O. P. and E. Backhouse. *China under the Empress Dowager* (1910).

Bourne, F. S. A. Article in *China Review* (1879–80) on the 'Eight-legs' essay.

Broomhall, Marshall. *Martyred Missionaries of the China Inland Mission* (1901).

Buck, Pearl. *All Men are Brothers* (translation of *Shui Hu*, q.v.), 2 vols. (1957).

Cameron, M. E. 'The Public Career of Chang Chih-tung', *Pacific Historical Rev.* (September, 1938).

Cammann, Schuyler. 'The Making of the Dragon Robes', *T'oung Pao*, XL (1950–1).

Cary-Elwes, Columba, O.S.B. *Christ and the Cross* (1957).

Chang Chung-li. *The Chinese Gentry* (Seattle, 1955).

Ch'ên, Jerome. 'The Nature and Characteristics of the Boxer Movement—A Morphological Study', *BSOAS*, XXIII, 2 (1960).

—— *Yüan Shih-k'ai, 1859–1916: Brutus Assumes the Purple* (1961).

Chiang Siang-tseh. *The Nien Rebellion* (Seattle, 1954).

Chih P'an (monk). *Fo Tsu T'ung Chi (Records of Buddhism)* (China, 1343).

Chirol, Sir Valentine. *Fifty Years in a Changing World* (1927).

Chu T'ung-tsu. 'Chinese Class Structure and its Ideology', in John K. Fairbank (ed.), *Chinese Thought and Institutions* (Chicago, 1957).

Clements, Paul H. *The Boxer Rebellion; a Political and Diplomatic Review* (New York, 1915).

Cohen, Paul A. 'The Anti-Christian Tradition in China', *JAS*, XX, 2 (February 1961).

Comber, L. *Secret Societies in Malaya* (Locust Valley, New York, 1959).

Cordier, Henri. *Histoire Générale de la Chine*, 4 vols. (Paris, 1920).

Couling, S. *The Encyclopaedia Sinica* (1917).

Creel, H. G. 'What is Taoism?', *JAOS*, 76 (1956).

Danby, Hope, biography of Sir Edmund Backhouse in *Dictionary of National Biography* (1941–50).

Darwin, Charles. *The Origin of Species* (1859).

Davis, Sir J. F. *The Chinese* (1840).

De Groot, J. J. M. *Sectarianism and Religious Persecution in China* (Amsterdam, 1903).

Douglas, Robert K. *Society in China* (1894).

—— 'The Far East', *Cambridge Modern History*, XII, ch. 17 (1910).

Dudgeon, John, M.D. 'Kung-fu, or Medical Gymnastics', *Journal of the Peking Oriental Society* (1895).

Dunstheimer, G. G. H. 'Religion et Magie dans le mouvement des Boxeurs d'après les textes Chinois', *T'oung Pao*, XLVII (1961).

Duyvendak, J. J. L. Translation of Ching-shan's diary, *Acta Orientalia*, III (1924).

—— 'Ching-shan's Diary: a Mystification', *T'oung Pao*, XXIII (1937).

Eichhorn, W. 'Zur Vorgeschichte des Aufstandes von Wang Hsia-po und Li Shun in Szuechuan (993–995)', *Zeitschrift der Deutschen Morgan-ländischen Gesellschaft* (Wiesbaden, 1955).

Escarra, Jean. *Le Droit Chinois* (Peking, 1936).

Fairbank, John K. 'China's Response to the West: Problems and Suggestions', *Cahiers d'Histoire Mondiale*, III–2 (Paris, 1956).

—— (ed.). *Chinese Thought and Institutions* (Chicago, 1957).

Fairbank, John K. *The United States and China* (Harvard, 1948).
—— 'The Manchu–Chinese Dyarchy in the 1840's and '50's', *FEQ*, XII, 3 (May 1953).
—— and Ssŭ-yü Têng. *China's Response to the West, a Documentary Survey, 1839–1923* (Harvard, 1954).
—— and Ssŭ-yü Têng. *Ch'ing Administration: Three Studies* (Harvard, 1960).
Fei Hsiao-tung. *China's Gentry, Essays in Rural–Urban Relations* (Chicago, 1953).
Feuerwerker, Albert. *China's Early Industrialization: Shêng Hsüan-huai (1844–1916) and Mandarin Enterprise* (Harvard, 1959).
Fitzgerald, C. P. *Revolution in China* (1952).
Fleming, Peter. *The Siege at Peking* (1959).
Freeman-Mitford, A. B. *The Attaché at Peking* (1865).
Fried, Morton H. 'Community Studies in China', *FEQ*, XIV, 1 (November 1954).
Fung Yu-lan. *A History of Chinese Philosophy*, 2 vols. (Princeton, 1953).
Fursenko, A. A. *Bor'ba za razdel Kitaja i Amerikanskaja doktrina otkrytych dverej, 1895–1900* (Moscow, 1956).
Giles, H. A. *China and the Chinese* (1902).
—— 'The Home of Jiu Jitsu', *Adversaria Sinica* (Shanghai, 1914).
Goodall, Norman. *A History of the London Missionary Society, 1895–1945* (1954).
Goodrich, L. Carrington. *A Short History of the Chinese People* (New York, 1959).
Greenberg, Michael. *British Trade and the Opening of China, 1800–42* (Cambridge, 1951).
Grosse Politik, Die, vol. XVI. Documents on Far Eastern Affairs (Berlin) (see Langer, below, vol. II).
Hart, Sir Robert. *These from the Land of Sinim* (1901).
Hertslet, Sir Edward. *Treaties between Great Britain and China, etc.*, 2 vols. (1908).
Hinsley, F. H. 'International Rivalry', and 'British Foreign Policy and Colonial Questions', *Cambridge History of the British Empire*, III (1959), chs. 8, 13.
Ho, Alfred Kuo-liang. 'The Grand Council in the Ch'ing Dynasty', *FEQ*, XI, 2 (February 1952).
Ho Kan-chih. *A History of the Modern Chinese Revolution* (Peking, 1960).
Ho Ping-ti. *Studies in the Population of China, 1368–1953* (Harvard, 1959).
Ho Ping-yü and Joseph Needham. 'Elixir Poisoning in Medieval China', *Janus*, XLVIII, 4 (1958).
Hobsbawm, E. J. *Primitive Rebels* (Manchester, 1959).
Holcombe, Chester. *The Real Chinaman*, 2 vols. (New York, 1895).
Hsia Nai, 'The Land Tax in the Yangtze Provinces before and after the Taiping Rebellion', in E-tu Zen Sun and John de Francis (translators), *Chinese Social History: Translations of Selected Studies* (Washington, D.C., 1956).

Hsiao Kung-ch'üan. 'Rural Control in Nineteenth-century China', *FEQ*, XII, 2 (February 1953).
—— *Rural China: Imperial Control in the Nineteenth Century* (Seattle, 1961).
Hsüeh Chün-tu. 'Sun Yat-sen, Yang Chü-yün, and the Early Revolutionary Movement in China', *JAS*, XIX, 3 (May 1960).
Hu Ch'ang-tu. 'The Yellow River Administration in the Ch'ing Dynasty', *FEQ*, XIV, 4 (August 1955).
Hu Shêng. *Imperialism and Chinese Politics* (Peking, 1956).
Hummel, Arthur (ed.). *Eminent Chinese of the Ch'ing Period*, 2 vols. (Washington, D.C., 1943–4).
—— Review of Fei Hsiao-tung, *China's Gentry* (q.v.), in *FEQ*, XIII, 3 (May 1954).
Huxley, T. H. *Man's Place in Nature* (1863).
Ichiko, Chûjô. 'Giwaken no seikaku' (cited by Muramatsu, q.v.).
Isoré, P. Remy, S.J. Diary in *Chine et Ceylan* (Jesuit Magazine) (Abbeville, 1899), I.
Jacobs, Norman. *The Origin of Modern Capitalism and Eastern Asia* (Hong Kong, 1958).
Johnston, Sir Reginald. Review of Duyvendak's translation of Ching-shan's Diary, *The Chinese Social and Political Science Review*, X (1926).
Joseph, Philip. *Foreign Diplomacy in China, 1894–1900* (1928).
Kracke, E. A., Jnr. 'Family versus Merit in Chinese Civil Service Examinations', *HJAS* (1947).
Langer, William L. *The Diplomacy of Imperialism, 1890–1902*, 2 vols. (New York, 1935).
Latourette, K. S. *A History of Christian Missions in China* (1929).
—— *A History of Modern China* (1954).
—— *The Chinese: Their History and Culture* (New York, 1946).
Le Fevour, E. T. Western Enterprise in China, 1842–1895. (Unpublished Ph.D. dissertation, Cambridge University, 1961. Based on Jardine Matheson Papers.)
Legge, James. *The Chinese Classics* (Hong Kong, 1861–72).
Leong, Y. K. and L. K. Tao. *Village and Town Life in China* (1915).
Levenson, J. R. *Liang Ch'i-ch'ao and the Mind of Modern China* (Harvard, 1953).
Levy, Howard S. 'Yellow Turban Religion and Rebellion at the end of the Han', *JAOS*, 76 (1955).
Lewisohn, William. 'Some Critical Notes on the so-called "Diary of His Excellency Ching Shan"', *Monumenta Serica* (Peking, 1936).
—— Second article on same subject, *Monumenta Serica* (1940).
Li Chien-nung. *The Political History of China, 1840–1928*, trans. by Ssŭ-yü Têng and J. Ingalls (Princeton, 1956).
Liang Ch'i-ch'ao. *Intellectual Trends in the Ch'ing Period (Ch'ing Tai Hsüeh Shu Kai Lun)* (1920), trans. by Immanuel C. Hsü (Harvard, 1959).

Lo Hui-min. 'The Battle of the Concessions, 1895–1900' (Ph.D. dissertation, 1956–7, Cambridge University (unpublished)).

Lu Hsün. *A Brief History of Chinese Fiction* (Peking, 1959).

Lyell, Sir Charles. *Principles of Geology* (1830–3).

Lynch, George. *The War of Civilisations* (1901).

Macgowan, Rev. J. *Sidelights on Chinese Life* (1907).

Mackenzie, Robert. *The Nineteenth Century, a History* (1880) (trans. by Timothy Richards, see above).

Mao Tse-tung. *Selected Works*, 4 vols. (Peking, 1955).

Marchant, Leslie R. *A Guide to the Archives and Record of Protestant Christian Missions from the British Isles to China, 1795–1914* (in preparation).

Marsh, Robert M. 'Bureaucratic Constraints on Nepotism in the Ch'ing Period', *JAS*, XIX, 2 (1960).

Maspero, Henri. *Les Religions Chinoises* (Paris, 1950).

—— *Mélanges Posthumes* (Paris, 1950).

Mayer, J. P. *Alexis de Tocqueville: a Biographical Study in Political Science* (New York, 1960).

Mayers, W. F. *The Chinese Government: A Manual of Chinese Titles*, 3rd ed. (Shanghai, 1897).

—— *Treaties between the Empire of China and Foreign Powers* (Shanghai, 1902).

Meadows, Thomas Taylor. *The Chinese and Their Rebellions* (1856).

Michael, Franz. 'Military Organization and Power Structure of China during the Taiping Rebellion', *Pacific Historical Rev.* no. 4 (November, 1949).

Milne, Rev. William (trans.). *The Sacred Edict* (Malacca, 1817).

Morley, John. *Life of Gladstone*, 3 vols. (1903).

Morse, H. B. *International Relations of the Chinese Empire*, 3 vols. (1910).

Muramatsu, Yuzi. 'The Boxers in 1898–1899', *Annals of the Hitotsubashi Academy* (Tokyo, April 1953).

Needham, Joseph. *Science and Civilisation in China*, 7 vols. (1954–).

—— 'The Past in China's Present', *Centennial Rev.* IV, 2, 3 (U.S.A., 1960).

Parker, E. H. *China's Intercourse with Europe* (Shanghai, 1890) (see under Hsia Hsieh, above).

—— *China: Her History, Diplomacy and Commerce* (1901).

—— Unpublished official memorandum to Lord Knutsford (8 February 1899).

Pelliot, P. 'La Secte du Lotus Blanc et la Secte du Nuage Blanc', *BEFEO*, III (1903).

Powell, Ralph L. *The Rise of Chinese Military Power, 1895–1912* (Princeton, 1955).

Pulleyblank, E. G. *The Background of the Rebellion of An Lu-shan* (1955).

—— Review of *Oriental Despotism* by K. Wittfogel (q.v.), *Journal of the Economic and Social History of the Orient*, I (Leiden, 1958).

Purcell, Victor. *Problems of Chinese Education* (1936).

Roy, M. N. *Revolution and Counter-revolution in China* (Calcutta, 1948).
Sansom, Sir G. B. *The Western World and Japan* (1950).
—— Article, 'Japan', *Chambers's Encyclopaedia*, VIII (1950).
Schlegel, Gustav. *Thian Ti Hwui; the Hung League or Heaven–Earth League* (Batavia, 1866).
Schwantes, Robert S. 'Christianity *versus* Science, a Conflict of Ideas in Meiji Japan', *FEQ*, XII, 2 (February 1953).
Sheeks, R. B. 'A re-examination of the I Ho Ch'üan and its Role in the Boxer Movement', *Papers on China* (Harvard, 1947).
Shih, Vincent Y. C. 'Some Chinese Rebel Ideologies', *T'oung Pao*, XLIV (1956).
Smith, Arthur H. *China in Convulsion*, 2 vols. (New York, 1901).
—— *Chinese Characteristics* (New York, 1894).
—— *Village Life in China* (New York, 1899).
Soothill, William E. *Timothy Richard of China* (1924).
Statement of Protestant Missionary Societies. *China's Millions* (China Inland Mission, 1900).
Staunton, Sir G. T. *Ta Tsing Leu Lee (Laws of the Ch'ing Dynasty)* (1810).
Steiger, G. Nye. *China and the Occident* (New Haven, 1927).
Stoecker, Helmuth. *Deutschland und China im 19. Jahrhundert* (Berlin, 1958).
Tan, Chester C. *The Boxer Catastrophe* (New York, 1955).
Têng, S. T. *The Nien Army and their Guerilla Warfare, 1851–1868* (Paris, 1960).
Têng Ssŭ-yü and J. K. Fairbank. *China's Response to the West* (Harvard, 1954).
Thompson, Laurence G. *Ta T'ung Shu: The One World Philosophy of K'ang Yu-wei* (1958).
Tikhvinsky, Sergei L. *Dvizhenie za reformy v Kitae v Kontse XIX veka i Kan IU-vei (The Movement for Reform in China at the end of the Nineteenth Century and K'ang Yu-wei)* (Moscow, 1959).
—— 'Two Different Points of View concerning the Purposes of Reform in China at the End of the Nineteenth Century' (in Russian), *Bulletin of the XXVth International Congress of Orientalists* (Moscow, 1960).
Tsien, Tsuen-hsuin. 'Western Impact on China through Translation', *FEQ*, XIII, 3 (May 1954).
Varg, Paul A. *Missionaries, Chinese, and Diplomats: the American Protestant Missionary Movement in China, 1890–1952* (Princeton, 1952).
Variétés Sinologiques, no. 39, *Recherches sur les Superstitions en Chine*, II, 6, *The Chinese Pantheon* (Shanghai, 1896).
Wade, Sir T. F. 'The Army of the Chinese Empire', *Chinese Repository*, XX (1851).
Waley, Arthur. *Monkey*, translation of *Hsi Yu Chi* (q.v.) (1942).
—— Review of Chang Chung-li, *The Chinese Gentry*, in *RASJ*, parts 1, 2 (1956).
—— *The Opium War through Chinese Eyes* (1958).

Wang Gungwu. 'Chinese Reformists and Revolutionaries in the Straits Settlements, 1901–1911'. (Academic exercise, unpublished.)

Weale, Putnam (Lenox Simpson). *Indiscreet Letters from Peking* (1906).

Wên Ch'ing (Lim Boon-keng) (ed. by Rev. G. M. Reith, M.A.). *The Chinese Crisis from Within* (1901).

Wieger, L. *Textes Historiques*, 3 vols. (Hsienhsien, 1923).

Williams, S. Wells. *The Middle Kingdom*, revised ed., 2 vols. (1883).

Williamson, Alexander. 'Report of Committee on Textbooks', *Chinese Recorder*, 9 (1878).

Wilson, Andrew. *The 'Ever-Victorious Army'* (1868).

Wittfogel, Karl A. *Oriental Despotism: a Comparative Study of Total Power* (New Haven, 1957).

Wright, Mary C. *The Last Stand of Chinese Conservatism: The T'ung Chih Restoration, 1861–74* (Stanford, California, 1957).

—— 'What's in a Reign Name?', *JAS*, XVIII, 1 (November 1958).

Wynne, M. L. *Triad and Tabut* (Singapore, 1941).

Yung Wing (Jung Hung). *My Life in China and America* (New York, 1909).

Zi, Etienne, 'Pratique des Examens Littéraires', *Variétés Sinologiques*, 5 (Shanghai, 1896).

—— 'Pratique des Examens Militaires', *Variétés Sinologiques*, 9 (Shanghai, 1896).

INDEX

335